Honoré Lannuier CABINETMAKER FROM PARIS

Honoré Lannuier

CABINETMAKER FROM PARIS

The Life and Work of a French *Ébéniste* in Federal New York

PETER M. KENNY

FRANCES F. BRETTER *and* ULRICH LEBEN

Photography by Bruce White

THE METROPOLITAN MUSEUM OF ART, NEW YORK

Distributed by Harry N. Abrams, Inc., New York

This volume is published in conjunction with the exhibition
"Honoré Lannuier, Parisian Cabinetmaker in Federal New York," held at
The Metropolitan Museum of Art, New York, March 17–June 14, 1998.

The exhibition is made possible in part by the Maxwell H. Gluck Foundation,
The Horace W. Goldsmith Foundation, and Mr. and Mrs. Peter G. Terian.

This publication is made possible in part by The William Cullen Bryant Fellows.

Published by The Metropolitan Museum of Art, New York

John P. O'Neill, Editor in Chief
Ellen Shultz, Editor
Malcolm Grear Designers, Inc., Designer
Katherine van Kessel, Production Manager
Robert Weisberg, Computer Specialist

Jacket/cover: Charles-Honoré Lannuier. French bedstead (detail). See frontispiece, and plates 41,
54, and cat. no. 5
Half-title: Charles-Honoré Lannuier's engraved No. 3 label. See plate 13
Frontispiece: Charles-Honoré Lannuier. French bedstead (detail). See jacket/cover, plates 41, 54,
and cat. no. 5

Printed in Singapore

Library of Congress Cataloging-in-Publication Data
Kenny, Peter M.
    Honoré Lannuier, cabinetmaker from Paris: the life and work of a French ébéniste
    in federal New York / by Peter M. Kenny, Frances F. Bretter, and Ulrich Leben.
        p.   cm.
    Catalog of an exhibition held at The Metropolitan Museum of Art, Mar. 17, 1998–
    June 14, 1998.
    Includes bibliographical references and index.
    ISBN 0-87099-835-8 (hc). —ISBN 0-87099-836-6 (pbk.: alk. paper). —
    ISBN 0-8109-6517-8 (Abrams)
    1. Lannuier, Charle Honoré, 1779–1819—Exhibitions. 2. Furniture—New York
    (State)—New York—History—19th century—Exhibitions. I. Lannuier, Charles
    Honoré, 1779–1819. II. Bretter, Frances F. III. Leben, Ulrich. IV. Metropolitan
    Museum of Art (New York, N.Y.) v. Title
NK2439.L24A4   1998
749.213—dc21   97-39012
                    CIP

Contents

★ ★ ★ ★ ★ ★ ★ ★

Foreword

The Metropolitan Museum of Art, from its formation in 1870, has maintained a lively concern for the display and study of the decorative arts. A guiding principle of the founding Trustees was enumerated in an early document issued by the Museum: "The Officers of the Museum desire especially to begin at an early day the formation of a collection of industrial art, of objects of utility to which decorative art has been applied, ornamental metalwork, carving in wood, ivory, and stone, painted glass, glass vessels, pottery, enamel, and all other materials." Its superb collection of the decorative arts of many cultures demonstrates the enthusiasm with which the Museum has followed this original tenet.

The Museum's specific focus on American decorative arts, with an emphasis on New York furniture, goes back as far as 1909 and the Hudson-Fulton Celebration, during which Dutch paintings and furniture of the seventeenth century were displayed along with American painting and decorative arts dating from 1625 to 1825. Seventeen items of furniture attributed to Duncan Phyfe were featured in that exhibition. In 1922, the Museum pursued this particular subject when it mounted "Furniture Masterpieces of Duncan Phyfe," the first monographic exhibition devoted to a cabinetmaker ever presented by an American museum. In 1924, the American Wing opened, and contained many fine objects of New York workmanship. A decade later, the important "Loan Exhibition of New York State Furniture" was organized by the Wing's curator, Joseph Downs. Included were four labeled works by Charles-Honoré Lannuier, three of which are also in the Metropolitan's 1998 exhibition. Established as a separate curatorial department in 1934, the American Wing continued thereafter to collect and display New York furniture, as well as the decorative arts of other regions of the nation. From 1964 to 1981, the late Berry B. Tracy was a member of the staff, and for some years curator of the American Wing (later given its present name, the Department of American Decorative Arts). Tracy was a renowned expert on New York furniture of the early nineteenth century, and he assembled a large and extremely valuable archive devoted to New York cabinetmakers active between 1790 and 1825. This body of information has provided an essential contextual background for Peter M. Kenny's work on Lannuier, and it is our hope that this archival material will be published at some future date in the form of a dictionary of New York cabinetmakers of the Federal era.

In recent years, our keen interest in New York furniture has prevailed with two exhibitions: "American Kasten: The Dutch-Style Cupboards of New York and New Jersey, 1650–1800," of 1992, and "Herter Brothers, Furniture and Interiors for a Gilded Age," co-organized with the Museum of Fine Arts, Houston, in 1995.

Three-quarters of a century after our 1922 Duncan Phyfe exhibition, "Honoré Lannuier, Parisian Cabinetmaker in Federal New York" has been brought forth, reaffirming The

Metropolitan Museum of Art's long-term commitment to the furniture of its city and state. The corpus of accepted work by Lannuier has grown, since 1922, to over one hundred and twenty examples. During those years, this Museum, Winterthur, and The White House have moved into the forefront of institutions that own stamped, labeled, and firmly attributed works by Lannuier. The most recent Lannuier acquisitions by the Metropolitan Museum are the exquisite pair of signed and dated card tables from the Van Rensselaer family, the splendid gift of Mrs. Justine Van Rensselaer Milliken, a direct descendant of their original owner, and a superb and extremely rare side chair from the set once owned by the Baltimore merchant James Bosley.

We offer our warmest thanks to the lenders, both public and private, without whose generosity this exhibition could not have been organized. Deep appreciation and thanks go to the Maxwell H. Gluck Foundation; The Horace W. Goldsmith Foundation; Mr. and Mrs. Peter G. Terian; and to the American Furniture & Decorative Arts Department, Christie's, New York, for providing the funding that made this exhibition possible. We also are extremely indebted to The William Cullen Bryant Fellows for their major support of this publication.

John K. Howat
The Lawrence A. Fleischman Chairman
of the Departments of American Art
The Metropolitan Museum of Art

★　　★　　★　　★　　★　　★　　★　　★

Preface

Practically from the moment I was entrusted with curatorial responsibility for the Federal furniture collection at the Metropolitan Museum, in the spring of 1992, my colleague and the senior curator of American Decorative Arts, Morrison H. Heckscher, made it known to me that a book and exhibition on the work of the French émigré cabinetmaker Charles-Honoré Lannuier (1779–1819) virtually was preordained for the American Wing. In my colleague's words, Lannuier was a "natural." Who else was there among major American cabinetmakers with so many documented works of such high aesthetic merit? There was an air of inevitability about the whole enterprise, so I took up the Lannuier cause and began a quest to track down and examine as many stamped and labeled examples of his furniture as possible, and to locate documents in government and family archives that would add contextual richness and historical perspective to a study of one of the great cabinetmakers of the early nineteenth century. I will not pretend for a moment that anything close to the comprehensive monographic treatment of Lannuier to which this book aspires could have been accomplished without the dogged research efforts and intellectual curiosity of my coauthors, Frances F. Bretter and Ulrich Leben, nor that it could have happened without the firm foundation of Lannuier scholarship laid down by several preceding generations of curators and scholars. This entire project stands on their broad shoulders.

There is poetic justice in the fact that the first person to recognize the existence of Lannuier was Ernest F. Hagen (1830–1913), an immigrant cabinetmaker himself, who came to America with his family from Hamburg, Germany, in 1844, and soon after was apprenticed by his father to a New York cabinetmaking firm. Hagen enjoyed a long career in this city as a cabinetmaker, restorer, and antiques dealer, and he also displayed the strong interest of an antiquarian in his predecessors in the New York cabinetmaking trade, particularly Duncan Phyfe, whose furniture he championed, and consequently helped to create the original market for, in the early part of this century. Between 1892 and 1906, Hagen compiled a scrapbook that he filled with labels lifted from old furniture and with biographical notes about early New York cabinetmakers, culled from the city directories. This scrapbook, now preserved in The Museum of the City of New York, contains the first known references to Lannuier—a jumbled transcription of the text of the latter's elegant engraved cheval-glass label (see plate 13), accompanied by Lannuier's name and business address as they appeared in the city directories in 1805, 1810, and 1816: "Lannuier, Henry, cabinetmaker, 60 Broad." After Hagen's death in 1913, his son and successor, Frederick E. Hagen (1868–1948), became the acknowledged authority on Phyfe and other cabinetmakers of the New York school, as well as the keeper of his father's scrapbook. In 1922, he apparently released the nuggets of biographical information it contained about Lannuier to the editor of the magazine *Antiques*, Homer Eaton Keyes, who published them that November in a short article entitled, "Still Shrilling on Phyfe." The article was intended as a cautionary note against the casual attributions to New York's great master, which Keyes felt were bound to proliferate as a result both of the exhibition then on view at the Metropolitan Museum, "Furniture Masterpieces of Duncan Phyfe," and of its eponymous catalogue by curator Charles Over Cornelius. Cautioning his readers "to bear in mind that Phyfe was neither the only furniture maker, nor the only excellent furniture maker in the New York of his day," Keyes illustrated his point with some chairs acquired by a Miss Edith Rand of New York as the probable work of Phyfe, but which, subsequently, were attributed to Lannuier, by Hagen, whom Keyes roundly praised as a "careful student of furniture design and workmanship [who] knows the traditions and methods of the old New York craftsmen." Now, with the benefit of hindsight, it seems obvious that Lannuier could not have made the chairs, which are either English, or, if American, most likely of Philadelphia origin.

Ironically, it was in this very exhibition that the first documented example of Lannuier furniture—a superbly proportioned trictrac table (see plate 11)—made its public debut, not as the work of the French-born master, but attributed to his chief competitor in the realm of fine furniture, Duncan Phyfe. Cornelius apparently was unaware that the table bore both the label and stamp of Lannuier on one of its drawers. The usually "careful" Hagen seems to have missed the Lannuier marks as well (or else he failed to report them to Cornelius), for inscribed on the back of one of the aprons is the note, "E F Hagen 213 East 26 st./New York/June 15, 1922," strong circumstantial evidence that the table's owner at the time, Mrs. Harry Horton Benkard, had had it prepared at Hagen's shop for the Phyfe exhibition. It was not until a dozen years later, according to Thomas Hamilton Ormsbee in the June 27, 1935, issue of the *American Collector*, that an "eagle eye" spotted the Lannuier stamp on the edge of the drawer.

Lannuier's furniture emerged from the shadow of Phyfe's for the first time in 1929, when his magnificent labeled satinwood-and-mahogany pier table (see plate 17) was included in the Girl Scouts Loan Exhibition held at the American Art Galleries in New York. The owner of the table was the collector and sometime dealer Louis Guerineau Myers, the principal organizer of this important early exhibition of American art and author of the show's remarkably complete catalogue. In his entry about the table, Myers was intent on explaining Lannuier's furniture on its own terms, and he noted in particular that it was "built to a much larger scale than an American contemporary's work would have been," and that "the brass borders and the form of the feet are reminiscent of Lannuier's French training." Although this was just the first example in a long list of documented Lannuier furniture that eventually would come to light, the distinctive French character of Lannuier's work already was being cast into sharp relief.

The decade of the 1930s ushered in a modest but steady stream of exciting new Lannuier discoveries, as well as the emergence of the first scholar to take an interest in his work, the aforementioned Thomas Hamilton Ormsbee. Although Ormsbee promised a monograph about Lannuier that he never, in fact, delivered, he did write two important summary articles on the cabinetmaker's life and work, which appeared in 1933 in consecutive issues of the magazine *Antiques*. In the records of the Surrogate Court in New York, Ormsbee located Honoré Lannuier's 1819 will and the inventory of his estate, from which he derived Lannuier's place of birth in Chantilly, France, as well as the names of his parents and of some of his siblings. As far as the furniture is concerned, in New York's city archives Ormsbee unearthed the record of payment to Lannuier for the twenty-four armchairs (see plate 62) he made for the Common Council Chamber in the new City Hall in 1812, although Ormsbee failed to identify any of them among the numerous articles of old furniture that survived in that historic building. Ormsbee also illustrated several works never seen before, including a pair of simple but elegant card tables with canted corners owned by the dealer Charles Woolsey Lyon (see plate 25) and an intriguing bedstead (see fig. 47) and a pier table in the French "antique taste" (see cat. no. 97) from the collection of the dealers Ginsburg and Levy. In addition, he alluded to a labeled sideboard in a private collection, which, according to its owner, was the finest example of New York cabinetmaking he had ever encountered. This could well be the superb sideboard acquired by the Metropolitan Museum in 1972, which, to date, is the only one by Lannuier known to exist (see plate 23).

Following closely on the heels of Ormsbee's seminal articles was the 1934 "Loan Exhibition of New York State Furniture" at the Metropolitan Museum, organized by the legendary curator Joseph Downs, who included in this show the first recognized examples of Lannuier's crowning artistic achievement—a pair of gilded and bronzed card tables with figural supports (see plate 74) from his signature series, made in the last five years of his life. Downs brought together other works by Lannuier, as well, for this exhibition, reprising the satinwood-and-mahogany pier table from the 1929 Girl Scouts Loan Exhibition, which by now was owned by Henry Francis du Pont, and premiering two additional new discoveries— an austerely handsome labeled card table with inlaid brass ornaments (see plate 22) and an attributed high-post bedstead (see cat. no. 10), which also belonged to du Pont. Through the 1940s, Downs kept up his scholarly interest in Lannuier. He published the attributed figural pier table—now in the Brooklyn Museum of Art's collection (see fig. 91)—in the catalogue to the 1943 exhibition "The Greek Revival in the United States," also held at the Metropolitan Museum, and in a contemporaneous article in the magazine *Antiques* he illustrated for the first time the spectacular bedstead with crown (see plate 49) Lannuier made for the wealthy New York merchant Isaac Bell. Downs's unflagging interest in Lannuier finally culminated in 1946 in the Metropolitan Museum's first acquisition of a Lannuier work—a perfectly proportioned card table of pure French design (see plate 94). Since that time, the Museum's holdings of Lannuier furniture have grown sevenfold.

During the 1950s, the locus of Lannuier research shifted southward to Winterthur— Henry Francis du Pont's Delaware home-turned-museum—and its newly created graduate studies program in Early American culture, which helped to spawn a new generation of curators and scholars beginning with the first graduating class in 1954. Among them was Lorraine Waxman, who devoted her 1958 master's thesis to Lannuier and the French influ-ence on American decorative arts in the early nineteenth century. In her thesis, Waxman elaborated on Ormsbee's earlier research in New York; conducted significant inquiries in France, which led to the important discovery of the connection between Honoré Lannuier and his considerably older brother, Nicolas—a Parisian *ébéniste* active in the 1780s and 1790s; and compiled a catalogue of Honoré's known work, which by now had grown to over forty examples. Waxman's excellent thesis, as well as several articles about the cabinetmaker that she published in the late 1950s and early 1960s, became the "final word" on Lannuier. These earned her a reputation that took her all the way to the Kennedy White House in February 1961, and the appointment as its first curator on the recommendation of Henry Francis du Pont, who served as chairman of the newly formed Fine Arts Committee. Waxman was strategically placed, as her interest in French decorative arts and their influence in America dovetailed perfectly with that of the First Lady. In fact, it was during this time that Jacqueline Kennedy acquired a School of Lannuier gilded figural card table for her private collection (the table was included in the wildly successful auction of her estate at Sotheby's, New York, in 1996). While Waxman served as curator, The White House acquired its first two docu-mented examples of Lannuier furniture—a small but exquisite gueridon (see plate 10) and one of the rare early pier tables in the "antique taste" (see plate 28). Before she resigned her post in August 1962, Waxman published an article in *Antiques* entitled, "Lannuier in the President's House," which helped to further polish Lannuier's reputation while also investing his furniture with a new degree of power and prestige. Featured in the article were the exquisite gueridon, a labeled card table on loan from Winterthur (see plate 31), as well as five additional pieces attributed to Lannuier, which now, unfortunately, would not withstand serious scrutiny. Included among these works were Mrs. Kennedy's gilded figural card table, and a sofa table with similar figural supports that had been sold to The White House by the firm of Ginsburg and Levy. The sofa table still is recorded in the official guide to The White House as the probable work of Lannuier, but it should be considered more accurately as having been made under his influence by an accomplished contemporary.

Lannuier's White House connections remained firm in the 1970s and early 1980s through the combined efforts of the restoration architect Edward Vason Jones and the former curator of the American Wing at the Metropolitan Museum, Berry B. Tracy. Jones, a connoisseur of Phyfe and Lannuier furniture, was hired by curator Clement E. Conger as a consultant when The White House underwent redecoration during the Nixon Administration. In this capacity, Jones lent The White House two important Lannuier pieces from his personal collection—an early pier table with term figures (see plate 79), and a labeled card table with inlaid brass ornaments (see cat. no. 58) that subsequently was purchased by The White House from Jones's heirs. In 1973 and 1974, Tracy sold to The White House a card table attributed to Lannuier, which is nearly identical to the labeled one placed on loan by Jones, and a delicate labeled stand with green and black marble inset into the top (see plate 68). After he left the Metropolitan Museum in 1981 to pursue a career in historic restoration and as a private dealer in American furniture, Tracy also sold to The White House a richly ornamented rosewood pier table with white marble columns (see cat. no. 98), bringing to seven the total number of examples of Lannuier furniture in the President's residence.

In his seventeen years as a curator in the American Wing, Tracy earned a reputation as the most discriminating connoisseur of Phyfe and Lannuier furniture. He was responsible, in 1966 and 1968, for the Metropolitan Museum's first acquisitions of gilded figural furniture by Lannuier (see plates 43 and 38, respectively), as well as the previously mentioned labeled sideboard, donated in 1972. For all his knowledge of furniture of the New York school Tracy, unfortunately, wrote only one article about the gilded figural card table by Lannuier acquired in 1966, and nothing on Phyfe. It was always on his mind, however, to publish a history of New York Federal furniture, and to this end he dispatched researchers to the New-York Historical Society Library to survey its collection of New York City directories and newspapers for information on New York cabinetmakers and practitioners of related trades active between 1790 and 1825. When Tracy left the Museum, the results of this research—a typescript of New York cabinetmakers and allied craftsmen compiled by Margaret Van Cott under his direction, and all of the back-up sources—went with him. After Tracy's death, this material came back to the Museum, where it is now housed in the American Wing as the Berry B. Tracy Archives, and we are especially grateful to Ronald S. Kane for the instrumental role he played in its return. The Tracy Archives have been invaluable in enabling me to write about Lannuier's life and work in the overall context of the New York cabinetmaking trade in the early nineteenth century—a wonderfully complex story that has never been explored before. In Tracy's honor, and as a valuable reference tool, it is our sincere hope in the American Wing eventually to publish the manuscript compiled under his direction by Van Cott as a dictionary of New York cabinetmakers and allied craftsmen of the Federal period.

The present book is a synthesis of Ormsbee's, Downs's, Waxman's, and Tracy's past research and publications, with the present authors' new discoveries and fresh approach to

Lannuier's life and work. When I began the project, I saw an opportunity as well as a need for further investigation into Lannuier's life in France, and, specifically, into the Parisian milieu of *ébénisterie* from which he hailed. Ulrich Leben took up this challenge, retracing Waxman's steps and also opening up rich new areas of inquiry that have led to some remarkable discoveries about Honoré's brother Nicolas and the important place that he occupied in the cabinetmaking trade in Paris. It has long been known that Honoré Lannuier made furniture for America's mercantile elite, but precious little documentation was ever found to prove who first owned this furniture. By patiently and astutely delving through the family papers of individuals long assumed to have been owners of Lannuier furniture, Frances F. Bretter managed, in a few instances, to find the rarest of the rare—original invoices signed and dated by Lannuier for purchased furniture. In her chapter on Lannuier's clientele, she explores patterns of ownership, which confirm our suspicions that Lannuier not only catered to the carriage trade but that the people to whom he sold his French-style specialties were, at the same time, also patrons of Phyfe.

Ultimately, this is a book about a great artist and his furniture, which exhibits the highest degree of quality in every detail of its design, materials, workmanship, and construction. Yet, this publication is in no way the final word on Honoré Lannuier. Because he was so painstaking in marking his work, more Lannuier furniture is certain to come to light in the future, which cannot help but alter our perceptions of him and of his oeuvre. This is the pattern that always has been followed since Hagen first discovered Lannuier in the 1890s, and slowly but steadily his furniture masterpieces have surfaced, to our great edification and delight.

I salute my fellow authors for their excellent work and for the many hours of pleasure they have provided me in this wonderfully exciting endeavor—especially Frances F. Bretter, whose assistance was absolutely indispensable. To my wife, Mary Ellen, and my children, Claire and Ian, who have endured my obsession with furniture and with the past patiently and with understanding, I dedicate this book.

Peter M. Kenny

★　　★　　★　　★　　★　　★　　★　　★

Acknowledgments

Honoré Lannuier, Cabinetmaker from Paris: The Life and Work of a French Ébéniste *in Federal New York* and the exhibition that it accompanies have been realized only through the diverse talents and dedicated efforts of numerous individuals with whom we have had the pleasure of working over the course of our planning and research. We owe our first debts of gratitude to the Director of The Metropolitan Museum of Art, Philippe de Montebello, who, from the outset, has lent his encouragement and support to the project, and, in the American Wing, to John K. Howat, The Lawrence A. Fleischman Chairman of the Departments of American Art, for providing the opportunity to organize the exhibition and publish the catalogue, and Morrison H. Heckscher, Curator of American Decorative Arts, for his steadfast support, sage advice, and excellent sense of humor. We also acknowledge our profound debt to Stuart P. Feld for all he has done to help the project succeed; from its inception, he was always available for consultation and to share with us his prodigious knowledge of the subject of New York classical furniture. Not a week passed, it seems, without a phone call or photocopies from Stuart, excitedly apprising us of one of his new discoveries or insights.

At the Metropolitan Museum, numerous individuals worked to make this book and exhibition happen. In the Office of the Director, we are indebted to Mahrukh Tarapor, Martha Deese, and Sian Wetherill; in the Office of the Vice President for Development and Membership, Emily Kernan Rafferty, Lynne Morel Winter, and Terri A. Constant; in the Office of the Registrar, Herbert M. Moskowitz, Aileen K. Chuk, Anna Riehl, Willa M. Cox, William Hickman, and James Sheehan; in the Department of Objects Conservation, Antoine M. P. M. Wilmering, Marinus Manuels, Pascale Patris, Nancy C. Britton, Mechthild Baumeister, Hermes Knauer, Mark T. Wypyski, Rudolph W. Colban, and John Canonico; in the Department of Paintings Conservation, Christopher McGlinchey; in the Design Department, for exhibition design, Michael C. Batista, and for graphic design, Constance M. Norkin; and, in the Photograph Studio, Bruce Schwarz. Assistance was also graciously provided by William Rieder, Wolfram Koeppe, Thomas Campbell, and Clare Vincent, of the Department of European Sculpture and Decorative Arts, and by Elliot Bostwick Davis and Heather Lemonedes of the Department of Drawings and Prints.

We are particularly grateful to our colleagues in the American Wing: curators Amelia Peck, Alice Cooney Frelinghuysen, Catherine Hoover Voorsanger, Frances Gruber Safford, Kevin J. Avery, and Carrie Rebora; administrative assistants Emely Bramson, Ellin Rosenzweig, Katherine Wood, and Julie Eldridge Edwards; research assistants Medill Higgins Harvey and Julie Mirabito; departmental technicians Don E. Templeton, Gary Burnett, and Sean

Farrell. We offer special thanks to the volunteers and interns who helped in key ways: Matthew Floge, Elizabeth J. De Rosa, Leslie Symington, and Cynthia Schaffner.

We acknowledge the enthusiasm and cooperation of our colleagues at numerous museums, historical societies, libraries, and archives, for providing access to their collections and assistance with research, as well as facilitating loans. In France, we wish to thank especially Daniel Alcouffe, curator in charge, Département des Objets d'Art, Musée du Louvre; Christian Baulez, chief curator, Musée National des Châteaux de Versailles et de Trianon; Bertrand Rondot, curator, Musée des Arts Décoratifs; the curators at the Archives Départementales de l'Oise, Beauvais; and Marie-Cécile Comère, director of Documentation Drouot, Paris. Staff at the three main repositories of Lannuier's work in this country, the Albany Institute of History & Art, the H. F. du Pont Winterthur Museum, and The White House, have greeted this project with enthusiasm and wholehearted support, offering unparalleled entree to their collections and helpful advice and ideas throughout. We are particularly indebted to Christine M. Miles, Tammis K. Groft, Mary Alice Mackay, Norman Rice, and Diane Shewchuk of the Albany Institute; Dwight P. Lanmon, Brock Jobe, Wendy A. Cooper, Michael S. Podmaniczky, Greg Landrey, Mark Anderson, Susan Newton, George Fistrovich, Richard McKinstry, Neville Thompson, and Burt Denker at the Winterthur Museum; and Betty C. Monkman at The White House. We also wish to thank the following individuals and their institutions: The Art Institute of Chicago: Judith A. Barter and Seth Thayer; The Bartow-Pell Mansion: Nancy Coe Wixom, Mary Means Huber, Barbara M. Hammond, and, for their financial support in preparing the Bartow-Pell bedstead for exhibition, The Robert Goelet Foundation, The Historic House Trust of New York City, the Bequest of Miss Elizabeth A. Hull, and the Bartow-Pell Landmark Fund; The Brooklyn Museum of Art: Kevin Stayton, Barry Harwood, and Kenneth Moser; Clermont State Historic Site and the New York State Bureau of Historic Sites: Bruce E. Naramore, Robert Engel, David Bayne, and Ron Ducharme; Columbia County Historical Society: Sharon S. Palmer and Helen M. McLallen; The Detroit Institute of Arts: Nancy Rivard Shaw; Georgia Historical Society Library: Eileen A. Ielmini; High Museum of Art: Donald C. Peirce; Historic Charleston Foundation: Robert A. Leath; Historic Deerfield: Philip Zea and Donald Friary; Historic Natchez Foundation: Mimi Miller; The Huntington Library: Amy Meyers; Jefferson County Historical Society: Elise D. Chan; The Liberty Hall Foundation: John Kean and Kate Gordon; Los Angeles County Museum of Art: Leslie Greene Bowman; Maryland Historical Society: Gregory R. Weidman and Nancy Davis; Museum of Fine Arts, Boston: Gerald W. R. Ward; Museum of Fine Arts, Houston: Michael K. Brown; Museum of the City of New York: Deborah D. Waters; The Newark Museum: Ulysses G. Dietz; New York City Art Commission: Deborah Bershad; The New-York Historical Society: Mary Beth Betts; New York Municipal Archives: Kenneth Cobb; The New York Public Library, Manuscripts and Rare Books Division: Angelita Sierra; New York State Museum: John Scherer; Rhode Island School of Design: Thomas S. Michie and Jane Stokes; The Roswell P. Flower Memorial Library: Ann Schwartz and Jeanne Brennan; Saint Peter's Church, New York: Patricia Ruggiero; Telfair Museum of Art and the Owens-Thomas House: Olivia E. Alison; U.S. Department of State, Diplomatic Reception Rooms: Gail Serfati and former curator Harry H. Schnabel, Jr.

There are many individuals who are also worthy of mention and deserving of our thanks. In particular, we would like to acknowledge the contribution of Mark Minor, independent conservator, for his superb work throughout the course of the project and for the valuable insights he provided concerning Lannuier's working methods. Other conservators who generously contributed their professional skills and knowledge in this area, with great enthusiasm, include: Olaf Unsoeld, Peter Fodera, Kenneth Needleman, Giovanni Bucchi,

Robert Mussey, John Driggers, Christine Thomson, Robert Fileti, and Miguel Sacco. Additionally, we owe a debt of gratitude to: Mary Ann Appicella, Gavin Ashworth, Jeanette J. Balling, Fenton L. B. Brown, Margaret B. Caldwell and Carlo Florentino, John Conboy, Ronald and Barbara De Silva, David Dunton, Joel Einhorn, Dean Failey, Sue Feld, Susan Filosa, David Fuerst, Mr. and Mrs. Holcombe T. Green, Lynn Harvey, John Hays, Charles Hillburn, Anne Sue Hirschorn, Ronald S. Kane, Leigh Keno, Leslie Keno, Bruno de La Villarmois, Allison Ledes, Deanne Levison, Bernard Levy, Dean Levy, Frank Levy, Kathleen Luhrs, Richard and Gloria Manney, Justine Milliken, Mary Nevius, John Nye, Sadie O'Dea, Dr. and Mrs. John Paul, Lorraine Waxman Pearce, Albert Sack, Harold Sack, Dr. Thomas J. Schaeper, Thomas Gordon Smith, George Subkoff, Page Talbott, Peter and Juliana Terian, Jack Warner, Walter Wheeler, Dave and Reba Williams, Douglas and Priscilla Williams, Martha Willoughby, and Elise Wright.

We express our deepest appreciation to members of the Editorial Department at the Metropolitan Museum for the realization of this book: John P. O'Neill, Editor in Chief; Barbara Burn, Executive Editor; Katherine van Kessel, Production Manager; and to Penny Jones, for editorial assistance with the bibliography.

Our final and most appreciative words of thanks go to Bruce White for his fine and sensitive photography, which fills these pages, and also for being so professional and thoroughly pleasant to work with; and to Ellen Shultz, our editor, who was unfailingly respectful of our individual ideas, and responsible for whatever clarity, grace, and style this volume has. Lastly, we owe a debt of gratitude to our families and friends for their indispensable support and encouragement.

Peter M. Kenny
Frances F. Bretter
Ulrich Leben

★　　★　　★　　★　　★　　★　　★　　★

Lenders to the Exhibition

References are to catalogue numbers unless otherwise noted.

Albany Institute of History & Art, New York: 5, 70–71, 113; plate 51; figs. 63, 67

Bartow-Pell Mansion Museum, Bronx, New York: 1

Boston Athenaeum: fig. 22

Brooklyn Museum of Art, New York: 62

City of New York, City Hall: 11–12

Clermont State Historic Site, Germantown, New York: 125

Mrs. W. Scott Cluett, through Historic Deerfield, Inc., Deerfield, Massachusetts: 99

Mr. and Mrs. Stuart P. Feld: 102, 104, 115

Hirschl & Adler Galleries, Inc., New York: plate 44

John Kean: 90

Bernard & S. Dean Levy, Inc., New York: 61

Richard and Gloria Manney: 4

Maryland Historical Society, Baltimore: 34, 36, 42

Musée des Arts Décoratifs, Paris: plate 1

Museum of the City of New York: 120

The New-York Historical Society: 49; fig. 54

Nancy W. Priest: fig. 52

Mr. and Mrs. Peter G. Terian: 84, 105

The Warner Collection of Gulf States Paper Corporation, Tuscaloosa, Alabama: plate 27; figs. 49, 95

Winterthur Museum, Delaware: 55, 88, 91, 119, 123

Private collections (six): 3, 44, 57, 66-67, 92, 95, 121, 124

Honoré Lannuier CABINETMAKER FROM PARIS

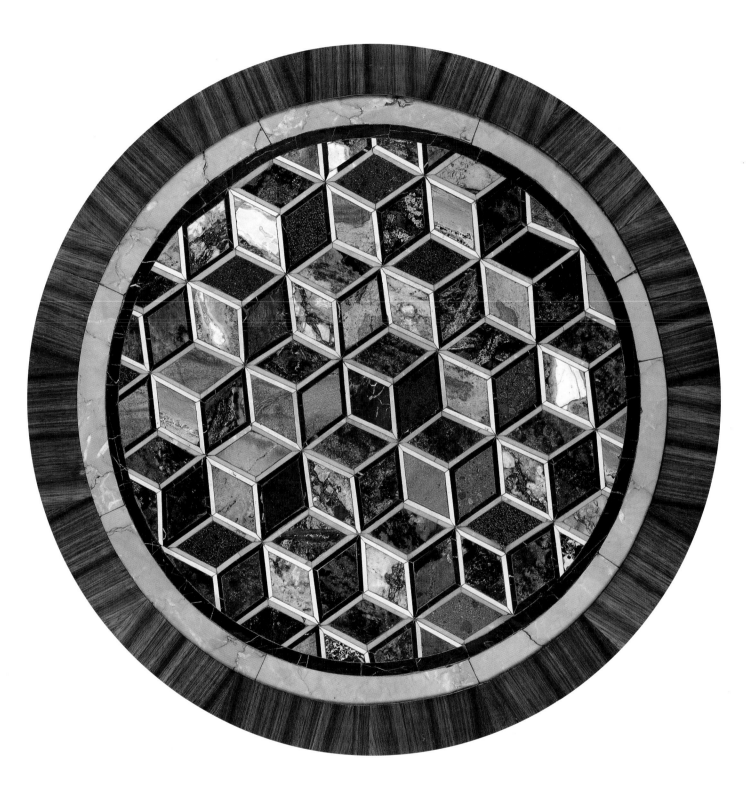

Marble top. Detail of the small center table (gueridon)
by Charles-Honoré Lannuier, plate 10 (cat. no. 116)

☆ ∘ ☆ ∘ ☆ ∘ ☆ ∘ ☆

CHAPTER I   Charles-Honoré Lannuier's Origins in France:
From Chantilly and Paris to New York

W hen Charles-Honoré Lannuier was born in the little town of Chantilly on June 27, 1779, no one could have imagined that this youngest of the ten children of Michel-Cyrille Lannuier, an innkeeper, and his wife, Marie-Geneviève Malice, would become one of the most famous cabinetmakers in early-nineteenth-century America. Since his childhood, Honoré Lannuier had been in direct contact with the art of making fine furniture through his older brother Nicolas-Louis-Cyrille Lannuier and his uncle Jean-Baptiste Cochois, each of whom was an established and quite successful cabinetmaker with a steady clientele in pre-Revolutionary Paris. These family members as well as other craftsmen in their employ might have influenced Honoré Lannuier's vision and subsequent knowledge of cabinetmaking, or *ébénisterie,* as it is called in French.[1]

Young Honoré's experiences were comparable to those of a handful of cabinetmakers whose businesses survived the Revolution in Paris. He belonged to a generation that, as a result of the disastrous social and economic crisis during the Revolution and its aftermath—the wars of the young republic against the rest of Europe—had to be very inventive in addition to being talented. His way of dealing with the situation in France was to leave his homeland for America: As a thoroughly trained craftsman from Europe, he had hopes for a better future there than on the economically troubled, war-torn Continent. What would distinguish Honoré Lannuier from the other skilled furniture makers who arrived in the United States at this time was his determination, from the outset, to promote himself as a Parisian cabinetmaker in New York. From the eighteenth century on, such luxury goods as fine furniture, bronzes, silks, and porcelains from Paris were greatly appreciated by foreign customers for their supreme quality and design and for the prestige they conferred on their owners. Honoré Lannuier also maintained the Parisian tradition of marking his furniture with a stamp, even though, in France, the requirement to stamp furniture with the full name or initials of the maker no longer existed after the abolition of the guilds in 1791 (figs. 1, 2). Nevertheless, a number of cabinetmakers continued this practice, originally initiated as a quality-control measure by the guilds, and the stamp became a kind of trademark or guarantee of the work of a particular craftsman.[2] Sometimes, Honoré labeled his furniture, as his brother Nicolas Lannuier had done in Paris before the Revolution, in imitation of the very fashionable English practice of using trade labels.[3]

Currently, there are enough documented works known in private and public collections to enable one to recognize Honoré Lannuier's personal style of furniture making, the peculiarities of which will be explained in the following chapters. His furniture is striking to us because he had the genius to imbue his designs with a feeling for harmonious proportions, a talent he had learned and developed as an apprentice in France. He never forgot his origins

FIGURE I. *Estampille* of Nicolas Lannuier. Detail of the commode in plate I

FIGURE 2. *Estampille* of Charles-Honoré Lannuier. Detail of the pier table, figure II (cat. no. 89)

in the world of Parisian *ébénisterie*, although he still assimilated easily and quickly the artistic influences he was confronted with in New York. From these two sources of inspiration, he forged his own signature style. Documents as well as the stylistic evidence offered by the furniture that he made in New York prove that not only did he use French elements like gilded ornaments and distinctly French molding profiles but he also employed French craftsmen as cabinetmakers and carvers, who were able to execute his designs with the lavish detail and high quality that distinguished his furniture as being made, at least in part, "in the French style." What makes Lannuier's furniture unique is that technically and stylistically it is neither precisely Parisian nor entirely representative of the Anglo-inspired American vernacular. From his New York workshop, Lannuier's furniture was shipped to clients in such diverse locales as Cuba, Savannah, Baltimore, and Philadelphia, spreading his renown and serving as models for what would become a distinctive Franco-American idiom.

THE ORIGINS OF THE
LANNUIER FAMILY

The Lannuier family originally were from the countryside north of Paris, and are documented as craftsmen in the building trades. The earliest known legal certificate pertaining to the family concerns Honoré's great-grandfather Adrien, who bought two tracts of farmland in 1709. In the contract, he gives his profession as roofer, and the small town in which he resides as Creil, twenty miles north of Paris. He had three sons, Louis-Adrien, Guillaume, and Louis, and a daughter named Françoise.[4]

The youngest son, Louis, at the time was also working as a roofer. The future grandfather of Honoré, he married Marie-Louise Dacheux in 1719, and became the father of three sons, Michel-Cyrille, Louis, and Guillaume. Young Louis was established as a hotelkeeper in Clermont, and Guillaume was a plaster merchant in Creil. Michel-Cyrille (Honoré's father) operated an inn in Creil with his parents, and after his father's death he continued to assist his mother in seeing to its operation.

Honoré's parents, Michel-Cyrille Lannuier and Marie-Geneviève Malice, were married in Creil on October 31, 1757. The Malice family were tenant farmers, and the earliest extant document concerning them, the *acte de mariage* of Charles Malice, a farmer from

Conteuil, and Barbe Durant (Honoré's great-grandparents), dates from 1702. Their son Nicolas Malice, a farmer in Troissy, married Marie-Madeleine Hardiville in 1729.[5] As the surviving rental contracts and land purchase records attest, the Malices tried to increase their property holdings by periodically buying small portions of land or forest. Sometimes they purchased farmland on which there was a house, which they would rent to other tenant farmers to increase the family's income.

The wedding contract between Michel-Cyrille Lannuier and Marie-Geneviève Malice was made in the presence of the groom's widowed mother, Marie-Louise Dacheux Lannuier, and both of the bride's parents, Nicolas and Marie-Madeleine Hardiville Malice.[6] Nicolas Malice declared in the contract that he was a tenant farmer and that the family lived in the village of Saint-Maximin. This same wedding contract informs us that Michel-Cyrille's parents, Louis and Marie-Louise Lannuier, kept the inn at Creil called Le Grand Turc, which they rented from a certain M. Decomble, a former colonel in the service of His Highness the Elector of Bavaria. As recorded in the document, Marie-Louise Dacheux was illiterate, which was not uncommon for a woman at the time, and therefore could not sign the contract herself. The wedding was attended by a number of guests from both sides of the family, among them Michel-Cyrille's brothers Louis and Guillaume, and Charles Panies, a brother-in-law. Also in attendance was a dancing master, Jean Daville, from Senlis, so we can assume that a lively time was had by all.

The groom contributed the sum of one thousand livres in cash, as well as wine and other goods from Le Grand Turc. After the death of his father, Louis, Michel-Cyrille remained actively involved in running the hotel, where he might have been the chef. The bride, Marie-Geneviève, had three sisters, Marie-Madeleine, Marguerite, and Marie-Thérèse Malice. The first, Marie-Madeleine, was married to Charles Panies, and the other two, although they did not attend the wedding, are known from documents. Marguerite Malice, who, in 1770, married the *marchand-ébéniste* Jean-Baptiste Cochois, would later be of great assistance to the Lannuier family when they settled in Paris. Marie-Thérèse married Charles Berot, a Parisian tradesman; after she died, Berot retired, and went to live with his brother-in-law Michel-Cyrille Lannuier in Chantilly.

It is documented that between 1764 and 1781, Marie-Geneviève gave birth to at least ten children, of whom seven are known to have survived early childhood. The five youngest were born in Chantilly, which would indicate that the family moved there about 1770. One son would become a successful cabinetmaker and furniture merchant in pre-Revolutionary Paris; another, a priest; and the remaining sons caterers or confectioners, except for Honoré, the youngest of the Lannuier children, who would gain fame as New York's foremost French cabinetmaker.[7]

THE LANNUIERS' MOVE
TO CHANTILLY After having lived for a time in Creil, the Lannuier family moved, sometime between 1767 and 1770, to Chantilly, where they first rented and later acquired one of the best inns in town. Known locally as Le Grand Cerf, it was located opposite the impressive Baroque parish church of Notre-Dame.[8] The reason for the move is still a matter of speculation. The Lannuiers must have hoped that life would be easier operating an inn in a town like Chantilly. One indication of its intensified urban development was the establishment of the permanent office of a notary public in Chantilly in 1778. At the time the city was graced by the presence of the prince de Condé, a cousin of the king, who maintained a château there, which he was continuously embellishing. Notarized documents in the archives at Beauvais record the prince's ongoing acquisition of property from smaller landowners to enlarge

FIGURE 3. Building in Chantilly,
France, which once housed Le Grand
Cerf, the Lannuier family's inn

his estate, create landscaped gardens, and build lavish architectural monuments at the western edge of the town. The prince, who was known for his love of art and architecture, landscape gardening, as well as nature, also had a passion for horses, and he built extensive stables and a riding ring in the center of Chantilly. Today, these are the most impressive of the buildings that remain from the prince's ambitious projects, as the castle itself was mostly demolished during the Revolution.

Chantilly, surrounded by verdant forests, acquired a reputation among foreigners, many of whom visited the bucolic town during the hunting season. It is not surprising that Michel-Cyrille established himself in such a place, which seemed to ensure him plenty of clients for his new business. Various documents suggest that the Lannuier family was introduced to, and enjoyed the protection of, the Condé family. Nicolas Lannuier is known to have sold several pieces of furniture to the prince de Condé, as well as to Louis-Stanislas-Xavier, Duc d'Anjou and Comte de Provence, a brother of King Louis XVI, between 1785 and 1789.[9]

Prospects for the Lannuier family were badly shaken when Honoré's mother, Marie-Geneviève, died on May 15, 1781. While the exact cause of her death is not clear from the archival material, as she gave birth to a child nearly every year, it is supposed that she died in childbirth, as was common at the time.[10] Now a widower, Michel-Cyrille nevertheless persevered, and in 1782 bought Le Grand Cerf from its owners, Louise-Françoise Toudouze, widow of Jacques-Christophe Langlois, a dancing teacher in Paris, and Jacques Toudouze, the prince de Condé's first lieutenant of the hunt. Why Michel-Cyrille later was beset by serious financial problems remains unclear, but perhaps he brought on his troubles himself by continuing to acquire land and overestimating his ability to pay off his loans. Considering the fact that he was pursued so intensively by his creditors despite the relatively modest amount of his debts, one can only assume that it was out of resentment by the citizens of Chantilly, who feared the newcomer would compete with them for privileged economic status. This, in spite of the fact that Lannuier's father apparently was a friend of the local lawyer, Patin, whose name appears as a witness alongside that of the city's schoolmaster on numerous documents signed at the notary's office between 1780 and 1788; ultimately, Patin could not save Michel-Cyrille from being driven toward bankruptcy by his creditors. In an attempt to repair his family's financial situation and, especially, to protect his children's interests and to see that they received their mother's inheritance, he arranged for his deceased wife's estate to be inventoried, eight years after her death, on July 11, 1789.[11] At the time,

Michel-Cyrille lived with his five youngest children; his brother-in-law Charles Berot, who was a retired marshal; and a servant, Marie-Anne Leblond.

Today, Le Grand Cerf remains *in situ* and only little changed (fig. 3). The building has a large door, a first and a second floor with an attic above, stables in the back, a fountain, and a baking oven in the courtyard. The inventory of 1789 began with the stables, which were described in detail; they housed just one old horse valued at only 100 livres. The building was oriented toward the south on the street side and, at the back, bordered on the estate of the prince de Condé; on another side it adjoined the tennis court, or *jeu de paume*.[12]

The inventory of the restaurant's kitchen lists several cabinets filled with copper, brass, and iron cooking utensils. On the ground floor were two large rooms with fireplaces, one of which had wallpaper painted with landscapes and pictures in carved and gilded frames of personalities from antiquity. The restaurant at Le Grand Cerf must have been an important and active part of the inn, to judge from the sideboards and buffets listed as containing fourteen dozen plates as well as twelve soup tureens, probably made of earthenware imported from England, which was very popular in France at this time. The considerable quantity of silver flatware, which gives some indication of the amenities the inn provided, consisted of twenty-four spoons and twenty-eight forks, one soup spoon, one serving spoon, and twelve small silver spoons, all of which bore Paris hallmarks; the entire lot was estimated at 996 livres. The lodging house had eighteen numbered guest rooms, decently appointed with solid-wood furniture and occasionally decorated with paintings. Room number 8 was occupied by Charles Berot, who outfitted it with better-quality furnishings of his own that were excluded from the inventory, as was a small walnut writing table with turned legs, which belonged to "le Sieur Lannuier ébéniste à Paris." Room number 16 served as a bedroom for Marie-Anne Leblond, the family's servant. The complete contents of the house and its annexes had an estimated value of 13,159 livres.

Sorting through the possessions of the Lannuiers took several months and was resolved when Michel-Cyrille gave up all his property to his creditors, asking only "to be allowed to keep his bed, which was the one in the small bedroom whose entrance was through one of the large rooms on the first floor, with a window on the court, and his clothing, linen," and some other personal belongings. The request was granted.[13]

With the bankruptcy proceedings finalized, Michel-Cyrille Lannuier had to start a new life on his own. The Lannuiers had lost everything. By now there were only three children living with him, and they all moved to Paris to receive the support of their relatives. One would presume that not long after the move, when Honoré was about twelve, Michel-Cyrille apprenticed him to his older brother Nicolas-Louis-Cyrille, the Parisian *ébéniste*.

There are no documents to indicate the career that Michel-Cyrille Lannuier followed after the move from Chantilly to Paris. It is known that he lived near his eldest sons, Étienne-Magloire, the priest, and Nicolas, the *ébéniste*, in the rue des Vieilles-Tuileries in the parish of Saint-Sulpice, on the Left Bank of the Seine, the preferred area of the city for people from Chantilly. However, Michel-Cyrille also gave his address as the rue du Petit Lion on various deeds that he signed in 1791 (fig. 4). There exist several notarized documents concerning the sale of a house and some parcels of land in the community of Willy, part of his children's inheritance from their mother, in which he interceded on their behalf; Nicolas-Louis-Cyrille and Étienne-Magloire had declined their part of the inheritance of the house in Willy in favor of their younger brothers Victor-Stanislas, Jean-Stanislas, and Charles-Honoré.[14]

During the late 1790s, Michel-Cyrille remarried. With his new wife, Marie-Victoire Liefquais, he had a daughter, Françoise-Sophie, about 1797, because she was twenty-six years old when she, in turn, married François-Félix Lacroix on June 23, 1823, in the church of Saint-Sulpice.[15]

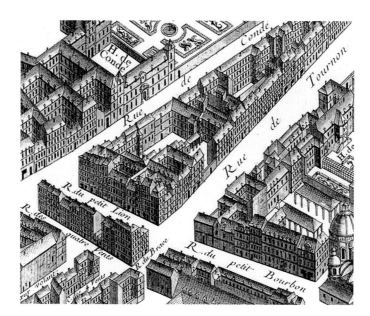

FIGURE 4. Rue du Petit Lion, Paris, the location of Nicolas Lannuier's shop from 1789 to 1791. Detail of the Plan de Turgot, 1739. Bibliothèque Nationale de France, Paris

Charles-Honoré Lannuier

As previously mentioned, Charles-Honoré was born June 27, 1779, the tenth child of Michel-Cyrille Lannuier and of Marie-Geneviève Malice, who died in 1781, just one month before his second birthday. It seems logical that his childhood must have been marked by the loss of his mother at a tender age and by the fact that he therefore was raised by nursemaids, friends, and members of the family. In addition, his father's bankruptcy and the termination of the family's seemingly comfortable situation in Chantilly must have been a tremendous blow to the children. In the summer of 1793, the fourteen-year-old Honoré and his seventeen-year-old brother Jean-Stanislas attained their majority by a legal act, although they had not yet reached the necessary age of twenty-five.[16] Before this date, Honoré did not sign any documents himself. Honoré probably already was apprenticed to his brother Nicolas. It is interesting to note that all those who served as the witnesses to this legal declaration approved of the two boys' "behavior . . . since the death of their mother."[17] Their father was not named as guardian of the boys' possessions—their inheritance from their mother; instead, the task was taken over solely by Nicolas.

The loss of Le Grand Cerf, the outbreak of the Revolution in Paris, and the difficult years that followed, marked by the abolition of the monarchy, the terror of the guillotine, and the rapid and chaotic succession of new governments, were undoubtedly key reasons in the decision of the two youngest Lannuier children, Stanislas and Honoré, to leave France. Emigration to America was one way of avoiding the revolutionary turmoil and was chosen by countless noblemen and tradesmen alike. An elder brother, Maximilien-Michel-Cyrille-Auguste Lannuier, was fortunate to have escaped the country before the Revolution, and, by the time Honoré and Stanislas arrived in New York, he was well established there, having married, raised a family, and started a successful confectionery business on Broadway.

During the sixteen-plus years he spent in New York, Honoré never lost contact with his family back in France, as proven by the mention in his will of his half sister, Françoise-Sophie, and various nieces and nephews in Europe. He also remained in touch with the latest fashion trends and economic news from Paris through the merchants and business contacts there, who provided him with French clocks and fancy goods, which he imported and sold at his warehouse, along with furniture of his own manufacture. It may seem surprising that, although Honoré lived in the United States for so long, he never became a naturalized citizen. His choice to not fully assimilate may have been a conscious one, however. He cast himself as New York's resident French *ébéniste*, and this was one of the keys to his success. He also seems to have conducted other aspects of his life in New York in similar fashion. His wife, Therese Baptiste, for instance, although born in New York, was of French descent. While records show that he knew English, Lannuier nonetheless chose, in 1819, to write his will in French, apparently the language he was still most comfortable using. His cousin Jean-Charles Cochois, who lived and worked in New York for a time, eventually went back to France, and Honoré, too, may have planned at some point on returning home. In this, he differs from some other European craftsmen, who left their countries to settle elsewhere and find work. These included especially the cabinetmakers of German origin who relocated to Paris, such as François Oeben, Jean-Henri Riesener, Martin Carlin, Bernard Molitor, and Gaspard Schneider, all of whom integrated completely into their new country by adopting the language, marrying French women, and later even becoming French citizens. Lannuier's emigration, like that of a number of French citizens who had come to the United States, stemmed from the aforementioned unstable political situation in France, which made many Frenchmen wait for better days to come in their country of exile. Some returned only after 1814, and the restoration of the Bourbon monarchy. One such émigrée was Louise-Alexandrine-Eugénie Hulot, the wife of the exiled French general Jean-Victor-Marie Moreau, who had helped Honoré Lannuier financially in 1811. Lannuier's contact with Mme Moreau is another indication of the close relationship he maintained with his countrymen even in matters pertaining to business.[18]

Maximilien-Michel-Cyrille-Auguste Lannuier

Born about 1766, probably at the family's home in Creil, Auguste was the first of three Lannuier brothers to move to New York, arriving there sometime between 1789 and 1791. In the inventory taken in 1789 at Chantilly, it was noted that Auguste was twenty-three years old and lived with his father. The idea to emigrate must have occurred soon after, because a legal document related to the sale of a house inherited from his mother, dated November 23, 1791, records that he is a "marchand traiteur . . . à New York, Province du Canada, en l'Amérique Septentrionale" (a merchant caterer in New York, in the Province of Canada, in North America).[19] Auguste may have worked at Le Grand Cerf, and therefore found it necessary to move on after the forced insolvency of his father. The outbreak of the Revolution in Paris also may have discouraged him from embarking on a career as a confectioner in France. The extent of Auguste's or any other family member's relationship with counter-revolutionaries is unknown, but this, too, could have precipitated his departure. Precisely when Auguste Lannuier arrived in New York City is unclear. He seems to have been instrumental in the establishment of a French lodge of freemasons in the city in 1797, and by 1799 was listed in the city directory as a confectioner at 100 Broadway. His activity in his trade is documented in a number of New York advertisements. He, too, must have remained in contact with his family in France, and it is possible that he later encouraged his younger brothers Stanislas and Honoré to come to America to try to build a better future for themselves in New York.[20]

Jean-Stanislas Lannuier

Little is known of the life of Jean-Stanislas Lannuier before his arrival in New York. Born on May 10, 1776, he was three years older than Honoré and shared at a tender age the trauma of their mother's death and the family's bankruptcy in Chantilly. By 1793, he was living in Paris in the rue de l'Égalité, near his brother Nicolas.[21] Sometime between 1789 and the early 1800s, when he made his way to New York, he probably served an apprenticeship with a confectioner in Paris. There is a good chance that Stanislas and Honoré, soul mates in many ways, left Paris together, although the exact date of their emigration is still uncertain. After his arrival in New York, Stanislas is known to have worked at his brother Auguste's confectionery shop, for it is from this address, in 1805, that he advertised "for sale, independent of his Sugar-Work, a beautiful assortment of ornaments [including] the Equestrian Statue of the Great King Frederick."[22]

Sadly, Stanislas was stricken with yellow fever in the fall of 1805, and died at the age of twenty-nine. The record of his death was tersely reported in the New York press on October 31, 1805, in a list of those who died between September 1 and October 25 from "malignant fever." In the notice, Stanislas's address was given as 60 Broad Street, the same as Honoré's. Stanislas's sudden, tragic demise, which probably occurred right in Honoré's home, must have been shocking and terrible to witness, as death from yellow fever is among the most horrible a person can suffer.[23]

Étienne-Magloire Lannuier

Born about 1765, also probably in Creil, Étienne-Magloire was one of the older of the Lannuier children, and was blessed with a relatively peaceful early childhood spent with both his parents. As a young man, he was given the opportunity to enter a seminary and study to become a curate. He did not sign the wedding contract of his brother Nicolas, the *ébéniste*, in 1784, because at the time he was still a minor. In two different documents from the early 1790s, he was designated as the curate of the church of Saint-Augustin, in Paris, in the Place des Victoires, and as the "priest and keeper of the archives of the Parish [of] Saint-Germain-l'Auxerrois,"[24] and was then living in the rue du Petit Lion. By 1793, he was head of the diocese of the city of Tours, on the Loire River, where he had also taken up residence. Étienne-Magloire's plight during the Revolution, when religion was abolished and priests were persecuted, remains uncertain. No documents from later than the summer of 1793 are known to include his name.[25]

Stanislas-Victor-Auguste Lannuier

Another son, who was Honoré's senior by many years, was Stanislas-Victor-Auguste Lannuier. Born about 1767, he is documented as a confectioner in Paris. Legal records indicate that he rented a large shop with an apartment above, in Paris, in January 1794 for 1,500 livres a year,[26] and just two months later he married Marie-Rose Goguet.[27] The young couple may not have remained long in Paris for, by the end of 1794, they had transferred all their rights from the legacy Stanislas-Victor had received from his mother to his brother Nicolas, and put the shop and apartment up for rent.[28] They may have left Paris as early as this time for Ghent, Belgium, the city that Honoré mentions in his will of 1819 as his brother Stanislas-Victor's place of residence.[29] It was Stanislas-Victor who may have been responsible for training Jean-Stanislas to be a confectioner, either in Paris or in Ghent.

Nicolas-Louis-Cyrille Lannuier

The facts about Nicolas Lannuier's personal life and his business are of the utmost importance in the unfolding story of the Lannuiers since he played such a major role in helping the family to reorganize and settle in Paris after they had lost everything in Chantilly.

Nicolas Lannuier's precise birth date is unknown, but he was born probably about 1766/67. He most likely was trained in his craft by his uncle Jean-Baptiste Cochois, a well-established Parisian cabinetmaker. Nicolas was made a master in the Paris guild of *menuisiers-ébénistes* on July 23, 1783,[30] and, as is often the case with tradesmen during the ancien régime, he waited to marry until he had attained this status. He celebrated his wedding to Charlotte-

Sophie Parent, the daughter of Marie-Françoise-Opportune Pignard and Robert Parent, a tenant farmer at Mortefontaine, on August 20, 1784, with a large and splendid party. Neither the bride nor the groom, it is interesting to note, had reached the age of majority, which, in ancien-régime France, was twenty-five.[31] The list of witnesses to the wedding and the twenty-three other signatures that appear on the contract reveal the social mixture that could exist even in the highly restrictive, hierarchical society of the ancien régime. One not only finds the names of numerous relatives of the bride and groom, among them several farmers and a tradesman, but also the names of a number of government officials and professional men who might have helped Nicolas on his way to becoming a well-known and fashionable cabinetmaker and furniture dealer in Paris. Included in this group of influential people were Maître Antoine-Charles Beaupoint de Saint-Aulaire, vicar general of Soissons, abbot at the Royal Abbey of Coulombs, and almoner to the queen; Jacques-Augustin Landon, armor-bearer to the duc de Chartres; Guillaume Bouffetin, a barrister serving in parliament; Pierre de la Ferte, the secretary to a Paris police lieutenant; and a family friend, Marie-Charles-Nicolas Lanier, a former official at the Château de Chantilly, whose name appears in several later documents.[32]

By the time of his wedding, Nicolas Lannuier already seems to have been well established in his cabinetmaking business in the rue Saint-Thomas-du-Louvre, in the parish of Saint-Germain-l'Auxerrois (fig. 5), and as was customary in French wedding contracts, he listed the extent of his estate. This declaration provides precious information for modern researchers because it chronicles the wealth of an individual at a given moment in time. Nicolas Lannuier declared the cash value of his estate as 2,760 livres, but his stock of furniture was far more impressive at a total value of 18,638 livres, although he had outstanding debts of 5,487 livres. The furniture that he declared was for his own use was worth 3,135 livres. In addition, he noted that he had paid the high fee of 1,304 livres in order to be received into the Paris guild of "marchands, tapissiers et ébénistes." Out of his total assets he owed 12,840 livres to his father, the amount Michel-Cyrille Lannuier had advanced his son to help him establish himself as a cabinetmaker. His father gave Nicolas a wedding gift of 5,300 livres, which left him with a debt of 7,540 livres that he agreed to repay in two parts: the first 3,000 livres "one day before or after his wedding" and the second, in the amount of 4,540 livres, in several subsequent installments.[33]

The declaration also indicated that Nicolas owed money to several merchants and workmen, whose names, sadly, are not listed in the document. However, the total value of his possessions, 28,566 livres, was a considerable sum for a young cabinetmaker just starting

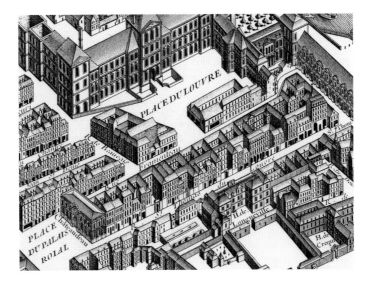

FIGURE 5. Rue Saint-Thomas-du-Louvre, Paris, where Nicolas Lannuier established his first shop in 1784. Detail of the Plan de Turgot, 1739. Bibliothèque Nationale de France, Paris

PLATE I. Nicolas Lannuier. Commode.
About 1790. Mahogany, mahogany veneer,
and oak, 35½ x 54 x 24⅜ in. Musée des
Arts Décoratifs, Paris

FIGURE 6. Commode. 1780–90. Bears the
trade label of Nicolas Lannuier, but possibly
made by Charles Topino. Whereabouts
unknown

out on his own, and illustrates that, from the beginning, he had a talent for the furniture business. The bride's dowry was valued at 8,000 livres, and consisted of money inherited from her father as well as furniture and linen worth 2,000 livres.

PARIS CORPORATIONS AND THE FURNITURE TRADE

Before the Revolution, the production and sale of fine furniture were controlled by a restrictive system of corporation or guild rules. This system, which had survived since medieval times, greatly limited the free expansion of production and markets, although it did ensure consumers that they were getting a high level of quality that was guaranteed by the strict regulations of the corporation. These regulations were upheld by control officers, who visited a cabinetmaker's workshop, examined the furniture, applied the quality-control mark, or stamp, JME—*Jurande des Menuisiers-Ébénistes*—and collected a special tax on every item that met with their approval.

A master cabinetmaker who was a member of the corporation, as was the case with Nicolas Lannuier, could also purchase furniture at a discount on the outskirts of Paris, as, for example, in the Faubourg Saint-Antoine, where foreign craftsmen were protected by royal privilege, which allowed them to make and sell furniture despite the fact that they were not members of the guild.[34] Nicolas Lannuier is known to have purchased furniture in the Faubourg Saint-Antoine. Typically, he would have made a selection and then had the items sent to his shop in the area of the city where fine cabinetwork and upholstered furniture traditionally were sold. He may have changed or added a gilded mount and then applied his stamp or a label, before putting the piece on display. In his wedding contract, Nicolas identified himself as a *marchand-tapissier-ébéniste* (a dealer in upholstered furniture), which suggests that he ran a full-service shop that could provide all that was necessary to furnish an interior space, from mirrors, to seating furniture, to veneered cabinetwork.

Furniture from Nicolas Lannuier's workshop is characterized by its fine mahogany veneers (plate 1), and, while several examples have marquetry panels, this technique does not figure prominently in his work (fig. 6). Some of his furniture has fine brass inlays and moldings

FIGURE 7. Nicolas Lannuier. Architect's table. 1790–1800. Whereabouts unknown

FIGURE 8. Nicolas Lannuier. *Bureau à cylindre* (cylinder desk). 1785–90. Whereabouts unknown

that enclose the surfaces within a narrow frame—a fashion that caught on just before the Revolution and reached its height in the early years of the new century (figs. 7, 8).

Nicolas Lannuier, it seems, was more a businessman than a craftsman. The furniture that he bought cheaply in the Faubourg Saint-Antoine he sold at a considerable mark-up to an exclusive clientele in the city—a fairly common practice among the *marchands-merciers* of Paris, who dealt in fine furniture and accessories and often made high profits retailing such objects. By the second half of the eighteenth century, more and more cabinetmakers came to realize that they were not able to earn serious money solely by producing furniture, and could only prosper by selling the work of others in addition to furniture of their own manufacture. As a result, an increasing number of them, including Nicolas, functioned as furniture dealers as well as makers. Nicolas, in all likelihood, was also associated with an upholsterer, who was able to work from his designs. Several Parisian newspaper advertisements indicate that Nicolas Lannuier was actively engaged in promoting his own business.[35] His use of a trade label in the 1780s for advertising purposes was not very common at the time in France, and shows that Nicolas was in the forefront of a trend that would become far more pronounced after the Revolution. It is from Nicolas that Honoré must have learned the art of self-promotion.

Two important clients, whose names best illustrate Nicolas Lannuier's prominent position in the furniture trade and his commercial success, were the prince de Condé, cousin to Louis XVI, and the king's younger brother, the comte de Provence. Unfortunately, neither of the documents that mention the commissions Nicolas Lannuier received from these two royal personages is detailed.[36] It is known that between 1786 and 1788 Nicolas Lannuier sent furniture worth 5,000 livres from Paris to Chantilly for the prince and other members of his family.[37] Precisely why the prince de Condé chose to patronize Nicolas Lannuier is unknown, but many former residents of Chantilly, who had moved to Paris, formed a kind of colony around the prince's *hôtel* in the rue de Condé, in the parish of Saint-Sulpice (see fig. 4), and the prince and other members of his entourage may have exercised a certain economic and social solidarity with them.

Practically nothing is known of the commission from the comte de Provence, who had gained a reputation for his lavish way of life and had acquired many luxurious furnishings before the Revolution. The day after the fall of the Bastille, he emigrated from France and began a journey in exile that took him through Europe to Russia and, eventually, to England, where he lived at Hartwell House in Buckinghamshire until after the abdication of Napoleon Bonaparte in 1814, whereupon he returned to France to become King Louis XVIII.

Whether Nicolas Lannuier's cabinetmaking shop continued to be successful throughout the Revolution and its aftermath is uncertain, but according to an 1801 document, he and his wife applied for a loan to allow him to continue in business.[38] Nicolas-Louis-Cyrille Lannuier is last documented as a cabinetmaker in a Paris commercial directory in 1804.[39] As he is not mentioned in Honoré's will, but his daughter is, one can suppose that Nicolas already had died by 1819. No further details about his business and his personal life after 1804 are known.

NICOLAS LANNUIER'S COLLABORATION WITH OTHER PARISIAN CABINETMAKERS

Although one would expect the style of Nicolas Lannuier's furniture to be mixed since he sold furniture made by a variety of craftsmen, his surviving work reveals a unity of design characterized by Late Neoclassical forms, sober outlines, choice veneers, and lavish gilded-brass ornaments and mounts. The choice of craftsmen with whom he worked therefore seems to have been determined by stylistic as well as economic concerns. Nicolas Lannuier's cooperation with other workshops is extremely well documented. During the economic crisis

PLATE 2. Stamped by Nicolas Lannuier and Ferdinand Bury. *Tricoteuse*. About 1795–1800. Mahogany, 29½ x 23½ x 16¼ in. Michael Werner Gallery, New York

PLATE 3. Louis-Léopold Boilly. *Les Deux Soeurs* (*Les Deux Amies*). Oil on canvas, 18 x 14⅞ in. Private collection. The *tricoteuse* depicted in this 1790s Paris interior is similar to the example stamped by Lannuier and Bury shown in plate 2.

following the Revolution the market for luxury goods collapsed, with the result that numerous Parisian cabinetmakers became insolvent. Their shop records and declarations of bankruptcy are in the city archives in Paris. Family connections appear to have played a role as well, as evidenced by his collaboration with his younger cousin Jean-Charles Cochois, who recorded in his daybook in 1804 that Nicolas bought furniture at his shop.[40] Nicolas Lannuier's collaboration with other Parisian craftsmen can be documented in two other instances as well. In one case we have the ideal combination of proof: Not only is Nicolas listed as a client in the cabinetmaker Charles Topino's declaration of insolvency in December 1789, but, in addition, there is a surviving console table that bears the stamps of both masters (fig. 10).[41]

In the other instance, we find the stamp of Lannuier along with that of Ferdinand Bury, a German-born cabinetmaker, on a lady's worktable, or *tricoteuse*, probably made by Bury for retail sale at Nicolas's shop (plates 2, 3).[42] Knowing that Nicolas Lannuier sold the work of different craftsmen, it is interesting to consider examples that bear only his stamp, but which are idiosyncratic enough to be attributable to another master. Ferdinand Bury's furniture is particularly curious from this point of view, and more than one piece with the stamp of Lannuier just as likely was made by Bury, since these are identical in design and conception, as well as in the use of veneers and gilded-brass mounts, to documented Bury examples.[43]

Jean-Charles Cochois

Nicolas and Honoré Lannuier were the nephews of the *ébéniste-tabletier* (cabinetmaker and inlay worker) Jean-Baptiste Cochois, who had married their mother's sister Marguerite Malice in 1770.[44] Both Jean-Baptiste and his wife died very young, which resulted in the drafting of two very detailed inventories to determine their legacy. Michel-Cyrille Lannuier, their brother-in-law, was present when both inventories were made in Paris, underscoring the close family ties between the Cochois and the Lannuiers. It is very likely that Jean-Baptiste Cochois, in fact, may have been the master who taught Nicolas Lannuier the art of the cabinetmaking trade. The Cochois had two sons: Jean-Charles, who was born in 1776, and Jean-Nicolas, who must have been born about August 1780, since his age was recorded as only three months in the inventory taken when his mother died tragically late that year. The first inventory gives a very detailed picture of the young craftsman, so bitterly shaken by the sudden loss of his wife.[45] Cochois chose his brother-in-law Michel-Cyrille Lannuier as his witness and Antoine Héricourt and Roger van der Cruse Lacroix as his appraisers. The last two, famous *ébénistes* of their day, were excellent choices to appraise their fellow cabinet-maker's estate. Cochois had a retail shop in the rue Saint-Honoré, along with a storeroom and workshop in the back in which there were two benches, tools, cabinet woods, and veneers. The diverse array of furniture in the shop was dominated by fashionable chiffoniers, small upright secretaries, satinwood and rosewood commodes, oval tables, and cylinder, or rolltop, desks. The diversity of forms among the more than 120 items recorded in the inventory, as well as the variety of woods he had on hand, provide an image of a very dynamic establishment with a large clientele. It is intriguing to imagine Nicolas Lannuier in this environment, and to consider that he may have modeled himself after his uncle once he was on his own.

With the two little boys in his charge, Jean-Baptiste Cochois was fortunate to marry again in 1784. His new wife was Michelle-Jeanne Bertrand, the oldest daughter of Lames Bertrand, a paper manufacturer, and they had a daughter named Agathe-Charlotte.[46]

At the time of Jean-Baptiste Cochois's death in 1789, the family had moved from the rue Saint-Honoré to the rue Croix-des-Petits-Champs, a favorite location for cabinetmakers and furniture dealers. Although today few stamped pieces by Jean-Baptiste Cochois are known, the inventory taken at the time of his death nonetheless offers a sense of the richness and variety of his work. The appraisals of Cochois's workshop and retail store were made by the cabinetmaker and furniture dealer Jean-Baptiste Tuart II, who was the guardian of Jean-Charles Cochois, and the sculptor Denis-Marie Chénu, guardian of Jean-Charles's half sister, Agathe-Charlotte. As in the previous inventory, a large assortment of various types of refined rosewood, marquetry, and mahogany furniture is recorded, such as upright secretaries, commodes, corner cabinets, and cylinder desks. In addition, there were also boxes for toiletries, reading stands, and a case for silver, all of which indicate his speciality as a *tabletier* (a maker of small, fancy objects in marquetry or intarsia). Also recorded in the inventory but rarely found in a cabinetmaker's workshop were two mahogany bedsteads. The comparatively modest amount of family silver documented in both inventories was estimated in 1789 at forty-seven livres and five sols and consisted of two beakers and some flatware.[47] Jean-Baptiste, nevertheless, must have liked fine objects, since it is known from an advertisement in a Parisian newspaper in 1783 that he offered a reward to the person who returned to him an "oval-shaped Egyptian gemstone"—probably a scarab, which he had lost in the street near his home.[48]

Jean-Baptiste's son Jean-Nicolas died as a child in 1789, but another son, Jean-Charles, followed in his father's footsteps and established himself as a cabinetmaker in Paris, where it is known that he made chairs and other seating furniture.[49] He kept a shop at no. 182, rue des Tournelles, his address for the balance of his career, until he declared insolvency on January 13, 1804.[50]

According to his daybook, on November 1, 1802, Jean-Charles Cochois sold his cousin Nicolas Lannuier 486 francs worth of furniture, including an upright secretary (or *secrétaire à*

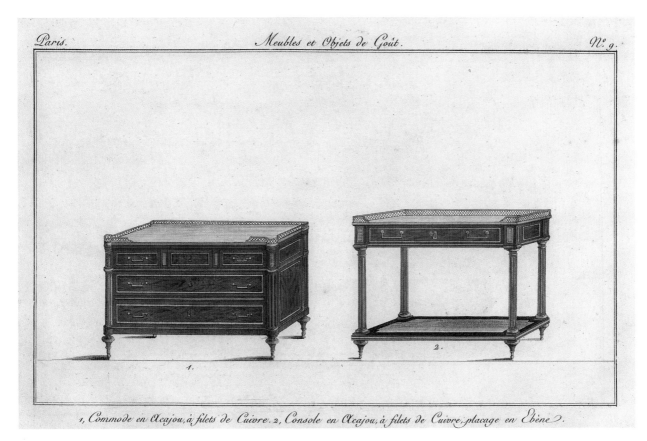

1, Commode en Acajou, à filets de Cuivre. 2, Console en Acajou, à filets de Cuivre, placage en Ebène.

PLATE 4. Pierre de La Mésangère. Designs for a commode and console in the "modern taste"
(Plate 9 from *Collection de Meubles et Objets de Goût*). 1802. Colored engraving, 7³/₈ x 12¹/₄ in.
The Metropolitan Museum of Art, New York. Harris Brisbane Dick Fund, 1930

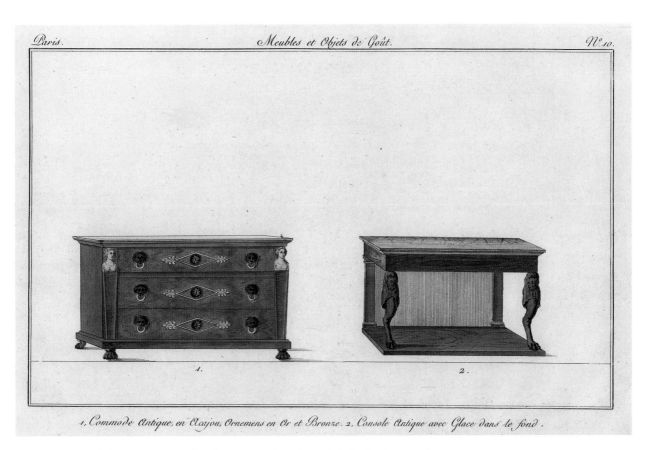

1, Commode Antique, en Acajou, Ornemens en Or et Bronze. 2, Console Antique avec Glace dans le fond.

PLATE 5. Pierre de La Mésangère. Designs for a commode and console in the "antique taste"
(Plate 10 from *Collection de Meubles et Objets de Goût*). 1802. Colored engraving, 7³/₄ x 12¹/₄ in.
The Metropolitan Museum of Art, New York. Harris Brisbane Dick Fund, 1930

abattant) and a commode for 300 francs, both described as in the modern taste and ornamented with gilded-brass mounts; two gaming tables for quadrille; two pedestals, or socles; and a small dressing glass.[51] The *secrétaire* and commode, in *le goût moderne*, were in a style that today is called Directoire—Late Louis XVI forms, veneered in mahogany, with fluted columns at the corners, and ornamented with polished brass inlays and mounts. In 1802, *le goût moderne* was a complementary style to *le goût antique*, which, during the Consulat period (1799–1804), represented the more contemporary form of furniture based on classical architectural models. Bernard Molitor, a cabinetmaker working during the same period in Paris, informed his clients, on his trade label, that he made and sold "every kind of cabinetmaker's work in the antique as well as in the modern taste."[52] Plates 9 and 10 of Pierre de La Mésangère's *Collection de Meubles et Objets de Goût* give a precise visual depiction of these two style trends as they coexisted during the first years of the nineteenth century (plates 4, 5).

Unfortunately, to date not a single piece of furniture bearing the stamp of Nicolas Lannuier and his cousin Jean-Charles Cochois has been discovered.

The language of Jean-Charles's January 1804 declaration of insolvency makes it clear that his workshop was a very active one. Apparently, he was forced out of business when a number of his clients, including furniture upholsterers and retailers like his cousin Nicolas, neglected to pay him. The bitterness this situation engendered in him is made evident when Jean-Charles declares at the end of the list of his debts, "that it was by no means his own misconduct that led him to seek legal redress" and "that he was maintaining his faith not only in his work, but, even more so, in the prospect of a future inheritance that would surely be greater than the amount of his debts."[53]

Knowing the size of his father's estate in 1789 and the Cochois family's relatively comfortable situation at the dawn of the Revolution, it is easy to understand Jean-Charles's resentment over his bankruptcy. This resentment, in combination with his confidence in his abilities and his optimistic attitude about his future could be the key factors in his decision to leave Paris for New York. His presence in the city sometime between 1804 and 1808 is documented by a bedstead that bears both the Cochois mark and that of his first cousin Honoré Lannuier (see plate 14), as well as by a passport he obtained from the French Consulate in New York for his return trip back to France on September 24, 1808. It is not known whether he ever returned to New York.[54] A cabinetmaker named Cochois is listed in Parisian business directories between 1816 and 1853, but since only the surname is given, we cannot be certain that the man referred to is Jean-Charles Cochois.[55]

Ferdinand Bury

As previously noted, Ferdinand Bury (1740–1795) was one of the Parisian cabinetmakers known to have made furniture retailed by Nicolas Lannuier. Currently, one documented example exists that bears the stamp of both craftsmen (plate 2). In addition, an authentic but altered writing table adorned with rich ormolu mounts and porcelain plaques also is known—it is in the Post Collection at the Hillwood Museum in Washington, D.C.—and while it was stamped by Nicolas Lannuier, it actually may have been made by Bury. This attribution is made possible by a jardinière, of identical design and similar measurements, in the Musée des Arts Décoratifs, Paris.[56] Other examples that may have been made by Bury but that bear the Lannuier stamp are recognizable by the presence of certain types of ormolu mounts favored by both *ébénistes* (compare plate 6 and fig. 8 to fig. 9).

Ferdinand Bury became a master in the Paris guild of *ébénistes* and *menuisiers* in 1774. He was of German origin and employed German workers, and although he was entitled to work in other precincts of the city, he never left the Faubourg Saint-Antoine, where he kept a workshop in the rue de Charonne. A victim of the recession that immediately followed the

PLATE 6. Stamped by Nicolas Lannuier, but possibly made by Ferdinand Bury. *Secrétaire à cylindre* (lady's cylinder desk). 1785–90. Mahogany and satinwood veneer, 47¼ x 30¼ x 17¾ in. Private collection, Northern Ireland

FIGURE 9. Ferdinand Bury. *Bureau à cylindre* (cylinder desk). 1785–90. Whereabouts unknown

FIGURE 10. Stamped by Nicolas Lannuier and Charles Topino. Console table. 1785–90. Whereabouts unknown

FIGURE 11. Charles-Honoré Lannuier. Pier table. 1805–10 (cat. no. 89)

outbreak of the Revolution, Bury was bankrupt by October 1789.[57] His declaration of insolvency indicates that he had business dealings with the cabinetmakers Dupras, Coniard, Houff, and Haut, to all of whom he owed money. He bought his cabinet woods from the merchants Melchior and Bernard Poulhié, to whom he owed 2,712 livres, and his bronze mounts from Ravriot and Septre, to whom he owed the startling sum of 12,605 livres. Bury must have been quite a hot-tempered fellow, as a Parisian police document states that he and three of his workmen started a fight with the wife of the wine dealer Moutenot, beating her with a bellows and her husband with their fists, after drinking liberal quantities of wine in the courtyard of their building.[58]

Ferdinand Bury specialized in working for a number of important Parisian cabinetmakers, in addition to Nicolas Lannuier, who bought furniture from him to sell at their exclusive retail shops. Bury's stamp also appears on furniture alongside that of Jean-Henri Riesener, who is known to have purchased works by the best of his colleagues, such as Adam Weisweiler and Bernard Molitor.[59] Bury's stamp is also found on furniture together with those of Jean-Baptiste Tuart II, Daniel Deloose, and even the celebrated Martin Carlin. Tuart, a cabinetmaker, functioned more as a furniture dealer, and therefore his stamp appears on a number of examples made and stamped by others. Tuart was the brother-in-law of Jean-Baptiste Cochois, whose sister, Marie-Anne-Gabrielle Cochois, he had married just a few days before becoming a master in the Paris guild of cabinetmakers.

Charles Topino

Charles Topino achieved the rank of master cabinetmaker in 1773. His workshop was also in the Faubourg Saint-Antoine, where he specialized in small and delicate, light furniture, such as occasional tables and bonheurs du jour, as these were especially favored for use in the private apartments of members of high society. Topino's furniture typically contains marquetry depicting garlands, bouquets of flowers, vases, or chinoiserie on a tulipwood ground. He worked for such *marchands-ébénistes* as Jean-Baptiste Tuart II, Louis Moreau, the brothers Antoine and Nicolas Héricourt, and Roger van der Cruse Lacroix. Nicolas Lannuier is not mentioned in Topino's daybooks, but the name Lannuié [*sic*] does appear in his declaration of insolvency in the fall of 1789. A console table that bears the stamps of both Nicolas Lannuier and Charles Topino is known (fig. 10), and a commode with Nicolas Lannuier's label but with marquetry in the style of Topino was sold earlier in this century, which may indicate that it was made by Charles Topino for Nicolas Lannuier (fig. 6).[60] The Nicolas Lannuier-Charles Topino console table is indicative of the type of Parisian furniture that informed the early designs of Honoré Lannuier in New York (fig. 11).

MATERIALS OF THE FRENCH *ÉBÉNISTE*: CABINET WOODS, METALWORK, MARBLE, CARVING, AND GILDING ON HONORÉ LANNUIER'S NEW YORK WORK

Most of the known furniture by Honoré Lannuier is made of the finest quality mahogany (plate 9), satinwood (plate 7), and rosewood veneers (see plate 42). In Paris, Honoré and his brother Nicolas worked most often in mahogany, although other exotic veneers also were appreciated in the late eighteenth century. Excessive taxes made the prices of all imported woods high in Paris, and a craftsman had to be both careful and pragmatic in his choice of wood in order to balance aesthetics and cost and to keep a work in an affordable range.[61] Upon his arrival in New York, Honoré Lannuier had access to high-quality exotic hardwoods in unlimited quantities—a situation that allowed him to use these precious materials on a scale he hardly could have imagined in his homeland. He had the veneers sawn and

PLATE 7. Charles-Honoré Lannuier. Occasional table. 1803–5 (cat. no. 119)

used them in characteristically French ways that differ markedly from the manner in which such sheets of veneer were cut and employed in Great Britain and on the Continent. Honoré seized upon this newfound abundance of materials, and made the most of the opportunity.

Very little marquetry furniture is known by Honoré Lannuier, although, in a few instances, dark inlaid borders frame the surfaces of a piece and inlaid paterae are used at the tops of legs (see plate 18). During the period between 1790 and 1810, marquetry seems to have fallen out of favor in France, and it was only in the 1820s that it again was used on fine furniture. Instead, the decoration on Honoré's furniture consists of fine metal inlays and borders, which were stamped out of brass and wood at the same time, in order to match them perfectly, in a manner similar to the marquetry technique made famous by André-Charles Boulle at the beginning of the eighteenth century. The only difference was that the patterns were geometrical and very fine, and required skilled patternmakers to devise stamping machines expressly for this purpose. The technique seems to have been invented in Paris, and the earliest pieces on which it appears date from the late 1780s (plate 8).[62] By the early 1800s, there were craftsmen in Paris who specialized in this type of inlaid ornament for fine furniture. From an advertisement in New York in 1816, we learn of Honoré Lannuier's association with a French family by the name of Frichot, who were specialists in the fabrication of stamped metal and wood borders for use on furniture and picture frames. In a commentary on his prize-winning work, which was shown at one of the early industrial exhibitions after the Revolution, Citizen Frichot himself is quoted explaining how he applied the methods of a certain M. Jouvet, whom he succeeded in this business.[63]

As in France, Honoré Lannuier used marble tops for his console tables as well as on a few known case pieces. He seems to have had a preference for very white Carrara marbles

PLATE 8. Bernard Molitor. Commode. 1787–91. Mahogany veneer and oak, 35⁷⁄₈ x 53³⁄₄ x 24³⁄₄ in. Private collection

PLATE 9.   Charles-Honoré Lannuier. French bureau. 1805–12 (cat. no. 44)

PLATE 10. Charles-Honoré Lannuier. Small center table (gueridon).
About 1810 (cat. no. 116)

(plate 9), which were shipped at a high cost from Italy to the United States, and with which he was familiar from his experience in Paris, where the same taste for Italian white marble tabletops prevailed in the late eighteenth century. The style of gilding—on a reddish bole ground—of the surfaces of the winged caryatids on Honoré Lannuier's tables is also typically encountered on French works from this period. (Lannuier's sophisticated carving, gilding, and bronzing techniques are discussed at length later on.)

Elaborate gilt-bronze ornaments and mounts are one of the characteristics of the finest late-eighteenth-century French furniture, and Nicolas Lannuier is known to have used the very best examples on his work. Their availability, of course, was no problem for him, since, in Paris, ornamental metalwork could be obtained in a wide range of designs and prices. From the time he arrived in New York, Honoré was able to provide customers with French mounts and cabinet hardware (plate 10). According to his first New York advertisement, we know that he brought his initial stock with him from France, but as time wore on, and French-style ornaments began to be copied in England and in Germany, he also may have used English copies of French models, which were cheaper and also were imported into New York, especially after the War of 1812. However, these ornaments produced outside of France for the mass market rarely attained the quality of the French originals.

Honoré Lannuier may have been the first cabinetmaker in the United States to have used Parisian cast-brass ornaments on his furniture—sumptuous additions, which, to his American clients, conveyed the impression of extreme luxury and refinement. The trade in these ornaments from France might have persisted during the Napoleonic Wars, through the intervention of agents and factors, although it probably became more intense in the period after the wars, when commerce with France was reopened, and French industries built up and supported by Napoleon were seeking new markets. By this time, however, they encountered direct competition from the cabinet brass founders in Birmingham, England.

Honoré Lannuier had been superbly trained as a cabinetmaker in Paris by the time he came to this country, and, therefore, the character and quality of his work—which, in many ways, remained distinctly French—should come as no surprise. Nonetheless, however, some of his ambitious projects must have suffered (especially early on) from his inability to find New York craftsmen with enough skill to realize them. It is only logical that the craftsmen

Honoré employed did not always share his high standards and aesthetic approach. Yet, at his best, as in several of his exquisitely executed carved-and-gilded table forms, Lannuier shows himself to have been both a designer of considerable talent and a great artist, with a personal style all his own. Honoré Lannuier's genius as a craftsman and a businessman is that he was able to adapt his French background to the requirements of his American clientele, who desired furniture and furnishings that would bestow the same prestige on their homes as would the genuine articles, imported directly from France.

At the time Honoré Lannuier left Paris for New York, very elegant mahogany furniture that maintained the forms of the Late Louis XVI period was still fashionable in France. In the formal conception of case furniture, there was also little change, and decoration with brass inlays and lavishly gilded bronze ornaments and mounts was at its height, although a tough republican would have much preferred the harshness and shine of inlaid polished brass to the richness and warm glow of cast gilt-bronze ornaments.

Honoré Lannuier's formative development in Paris spans the early years of the Revolution up to the Consulat period (1799–1804). Some of the most elaborate and refined Parisian furniture ever realized dates from post-Revolutionary France, nowadays often referred to as the Directoire period (1795–99), after the ruling government formed in the wake of the Terror that lasted until an unknown young general from Corsica named Napoleon Bonaparte was made First Consul. This is the furniture that Honoré Lannuier might have seen during a stroll along the boulevards of Paris. In addition to the public sales of furniture confiscated from the aristocracy, new furniture was being produced and sold to foreign princes as well as to a French clientele whose newfound wealth kept them busy building and lavishly furnishing their homes, as they tried to imitate the comforts and luxury enjoyed by the privileged society of the ancien régime.

From a stylistic point of view, one observes an attempt by craftsmen to reduce supporting elements to a minimum, in order to create furniture with a light and delicate appearance. In fact, one wonders how some of these tables and chairs from the post-Revolutionary era could possibly support a loaded tea tray or a grown man, let alone survive for two hundred years. Even case furniture often had turned or saber legs, which seem barely to sustain its weight. The surfaces were veneered with sheets of the rarest, most expensive, specimen mahogany, and the refinement of the gilding and finishing of the bronze ornaments and mounts accounted for their jewel-like quality. By the end of the eighteenth century, the traditional rules for cabinetmaking had been set aside in Paris, and everything was sanctioned. As a result, craftsmen pushed their designs to the limits. Craftsmanship was brilliant, and modern techniques such as hidden metal supports and connectors allowed for the creation of the most refined furniture.

By 1800, during the Consulat period, a revolution took place in both seating- and case-furniture forms, and their fragile appearance gave way to very massive architectural conceptions. Commodes in *le goût antique* became heavy and monumental in scale, with high pedestal bases and broad friezes. The cases rested on carved lion's-paw feet in imitation of elements found on bronze furniture excavated at archaeological sites. Seating furniture also was heavy and solid, and was based on antique models, and the motifs used for gilt-bronze ornaments reflected a more archaeological approach as well, with the quality of the chiseling and gilding improved still further.[64]

These were the contemporary furniture styles that Honoré Lannuier brought with him to New York as his stylistic legacy. Even though he kept in contact with his homeland and received journals and engravings of furniture designs in the later Empire style, while working in New York he seems to have clung to the basic precepts of his training. These remembrances of his French education became the ideal that he remained attached to, and that led him to continue to make furniture in the Late Directoire and Consulat styles into the 1810s, whereas by then trends in Paris had changed completely. His allegiance to the forms of the late eighteenth century, combined with the new influence of New York furniture styles, together characterize the early work of Honoré Lannuier. By the mid- to late 1810s, he, too, discovered the elaborate monumental gilded furniture of the French Empire, but he modulated the style somewhat, based on English Regency designs as well as on his earlier French design sensibilities, for he had become as subject to European influence—specifically, from England and France—as were native New York craftsmen. Honoré Lannuier's furniture—which he himself designated as being in the French style—is definitely not Parisian, but, instead, his own original American expression. His experiences are typical in many ways of those of all who lived before the age of the ocean liners and who undertook the risks of a hard and dangerous journey, guided by the prospect of a better future in America. They often brought with them nothing but their cultural legacies and their skills, with which to build a new life. What makes Honoré Lannuier unique is that, to date, he is the only individual in the very specialized field of fine cabinetmaking in the early nineteenth century whose life and work are so splendidly documented, and, together, trace so clearly the transference of French cultural influence and taste to the young American nation.

Ulrich Leben

NOTES

1
An *ébéniste* was a French cabinetmaker who specialized in veneered furniture, as opposed to carved furniture in solid wood—especially chairs, beds, and tables—which was the province of the *menuisier,* or joiner. The term *ébéniste* comes from *ébène,* the French word for ebony, an exotic wood that was so rare and expensive that it was used only as a veneer in early-seventeenth-century France. The distinction between *ébénistes* and *menuisiers* persisted through the eighteenth century until the Revolution.

2
The use of a stamp was an old guild regulation intended to control and regulate the methods of fabrication and thus to protect a cabinetmaker's clients. The practice, which dated to the seventeenth century, was renewed in 1743 and in 1751. In 1791, the guilds were abolished and stamping was no longer an obligation for the cabinetmaker. At this point, its significance changed from that of a control mark of the guild to a mark guaranteeing that the work was by a particular qualified craftsman. See also Augarde, 1985; Pradère, 1989, p. 435.

3
The text of Nicolas's label, which appears on a commode known from two sales earlier in this century, reads: "LANNUIER, M^d Tapissier-Miroitier, Ebéniste de S. A. S. Monseigneur le Prince de Condé, rue St-Thomas du Louvre, n° 12 à Paris." The commode was in the sale held at the Hôtel Drouot, Paris, on February 13 and 14, 1941, of the collection of a certain M. Dubois Chefdebien.

4
Françoise Lannuier married Nicolas Daguin on January 24, 1737. If not otherwise indicated, all information concerning the Lannuier and Malice families is given according to the listing of the family papers in the 1789 inventory, now in the Archives Départementales de l'Oise, Beauvais, 2E 24/13, for July 11–31, 1789.

5
Archives Départementales de l'Oise, Beauvais, 2E 24/13, for July 11–31, 1789.

6
Archives Départementales de l'Oise, Beauvais, 2E 32/856, for October 31, 1757. The exact date of the death of Louis Lannuier, Michel-Cyrille's father, is not known, but his mother, Marie-Louise Dacheux, died in 1778.

7
Waxman, 1958, pp. 219–20, and further research by the present author have succeeded in identifying the ten children of Michel-Cyrille Lannuier and Marie-Geneviève Malice Lannuier, in order of their birth dates, as Marie-Geneviève-Émilie, born about 1764, died in May 1788; Étienne-Magloire, born about 1765, vicar in Tours in 1792, died, possibly under the Terror, during the French Revolution; Maximilien-Michel-Cyrille-Auguste, born about 1766, caterer and confectioner, emigrated to New York between 1789 and 1790, died in New York in 1811; Nicolas-Louis-Cyrille, born about 1766/67, *ébéniste* in Paris from 1783 to at least 1804; Stanislas-Victor-Auguste, born about 1767, documented in Honoré's will in 1819 as living in Ghent, Belgium; Thérèse-Julie, born January 8, 1771, later whereabouts unknown; Angélique-Justine, born August 29, 1772, later whereabouts unknown; François-Casimir, born April 26, 1775, later whereabouts unknown; Jean-Stanislas, born May 10, 1776, confectioner, died in New York in 1805; Charles-Honoré, born June 27, 1779, cabinetmaker in New York, died 1819.

8
The exact date of the move from Creil to Chantilly is still unknown. The birth date of the first Lannuier child born in Chantilly, Thérèse-Julie, which is documented in the Chantilly city archives, indicates that

the family was there at least by January 1771. The baroness d'Oberkirch visited Chantilly during her journey with the Russians Paul and Maria Feodorovna to Western Europe and France in 1784, and provided a good description of the city in her memoirs. See d'Oberkirch, 1970.

9
Archives de Condé, Château de Chantilly, and Archives Nationales de Paris, 60 AP 1.

10
For example, the wife of Bernard Molitor, a famous Parisian cabinetmaker in the same period, died in childbirth at the age of forty in 1796, leaving a husband and a seven-year-old daughter; see Leben, 1992.

11
The very detailed description of the interiors of Le Grand Cerf comes from the inventory taken after the death of Marie-Geneviève Malice Lannuier in 1789. Archives Départementales de l'Oise, Beauvais, 2E 24/13, for July 11–31, 1789.

12
According to an eyewitness account by an inhabitant of Chantilly in April 1996, the hotel's name, Le Grand Cerf, was not removed from the building until a restoration campaign in recent years.

13
Archives Départementales de l'Oise, Beauvais, 2E 24/13, for October 5, 1789, and March 24, 1790. The value of the old-fashioned bed described as "une couchette paillasse à bas pilliers de bois de chêne à roulettes" was estimated at 170 livres: "Ledit Sieur Lannuier requiert ses créanciers de lui accorder son lit qui est celui étant dans la petite chambre à coucher ayant entrée par une salle au rez-de-chaussée et vue par une croisée sur la cour . . . et les vêtements et linges d'un usage indispensable qui contiennent ensemble six chemises, un habit de drap, une redingote, une culotte de serge de Rome . . . deux gilets en toile le tout aussi compris dans l'inventaire les créanciers ont accepté."

14
Archives Départementales de l'Oise, Beauvais, 2E 24/16, Contributions et Quittances, for January 3, 1790; May 12, 15, and 20, 1792; and May 2, 1793; Archives Nationales de Paris, D 10 U 1/26, for June 10, 1791. The Archives Départementales de l'Oise, Beauvais, 2E 24/15, for October 6, 1791, November 7, 1791, and February 9, 1792, record the sale of the house and land in the village of Willy to "Sieur Thibault-Éléonore Léfer and Geneviève Gautier," who resided in Paris, in the rue Saint-Antoine, in the parish of Saint-Paul.

15
The Register of marriages, Archives Nationales de Paris, Régistre des mariages: 1795–1825, records that Françoise-Sophie Lannuier, the twenty-six-year-old daughter of Michel-Cyrille Lannuier and Marie-Victoire Liefquais, of 16, rue Guisarde, married François-Félix Lacroix, the twenty-seven-year-old son of Nicolas-Félix Lacroix and Rose Taussier. Charles-Honoré Lannuier's will, October 13, 1819, Liber 55, p. 367, Wills, Surrogate's Court, New York, also mentions his half sister Sophie. Michel-Cyrille Lannuier had died by 1814, according to the acte de mariage between Charles-Honoré and Therese Baptiste, dated October 12, 1814, Centre des Archives Diplomatiques de Nantes.

16
Archives Nationales de Paris, D 11 U 1-3, for August 23, 1793, Émancipation des Mineurs Lannuier.

17
Ibid.

18
Mortgage, July 7, 1811, Liber 22, p. 175. Register of Mortgages, City Register's Office, Surrogate's Court, New York. For more on the Moreaus see Samoyault and Samoyault-Verlet, 1992. I wish to thank Peter M. Kenny and Frances F. Bretter for this information.

19
Archives Départementales de l'Oise, Beauvais, 2E 24/015, for November 23, 1791.

20
See Waxman, 1958, pp. 67–68.

21
The Polish name Stanislas was popular in eighteenth-century France—the former Polish king Stanislas was the father-in-law of Louis XV—and it remains so, to this day. See Cabourdin, 1980.

22
See the New-York Gazette of January 7, 1805; the advertisement probably refers to King Frederick II of Prussia, who died in Potsdam in 1786.

23
See the American Citizen of October 31, 1805. Ironically, a John Phyfe of 80 Wall Street, who may have been a relative of New York's other great master, Duncan Phyfe, also was listed among the dead. No one was spared in the yellow fever epidemics that swept through lower Manhattan in the late summer and early fall.

24
Archives Nationales de Paris, D 10 U 1/26, for June 10, 1791; Archives Départementales de l'Oise, Beauvais, 2E 24/15.

25
Archives Nationales de Paris, D 11 U 1/3, for August 23, 1793. It is possible that Étienne-Magloire was a victim of the Revolution.

26
Archives Nationales de Paris, Minutier Central, Étude XCI-1307, for January 28, 1794.

27
Archives Nationales de Paris, Minutier Central, Étude XCI-1308, for March 7, 1794.

28
Archives Nationales de Paris, Minutier Central, Étude XCI-1320, for October 16, 1794, and XCI-1333, for December 7, 1794.

29
See note 15, above: Will of Charles-Honoré Lannuier, New York, October 13, 1819.

30
See Salverte, 1962, p. 188.

31
Archives Nationales de Paris, Minutier Central, Étude XXVI-724, for August 20, 1784.

32
In June 1791, Lanier witnessed the signing of the act that allowed Michel-Cyrille Lannuier to sell the house in Willy. Lanier also had left Chantilly, and worked as an attorney in Paris, in the rue Montorgueil. Archives Nationales de Paris, D 10 U 1/26, for June 10, 1791.

33
Nicolas Lannuier reimbursed his father for the total amount of 7,540 livres in three separate payments: 3,000 livres on September 11, 1784; 2,540 livres on April 15, 1787; and 2,000 livres on August 22, 1788. Not until April 5, 1789, probably when his father's financial problems were being resolved, was a receipt for the three payments signed, in the presence of a notary. Archives Départementales de l'Oise, Beauvais, 2E 24/13.

34
A number of foreign craftsmen are known to have worked in neighborhoods like these, and only occasionally did they become guild members.

35
The advertisements are interesting because they illustrate the wide range of furniture forms at Nicolas Lannuier's shop. They include an organ case, a writing desk and filing cabinet with a bronze clock on top, an architect's table, and two cylinder desks, all of which were made of mahogany and mahogany and ebony veneers, and decorated with gilded-bronze mounts. Advertisements appeared in Affiches, Annonces, Avis divers, March 13, 1783, pp. 1163–64, for a "Joli buffet d'orgues en bois d'acajou propre pour un ameublement" and a "Beau bureau de six pieds, avec deux armoires serre-papiers et pendule garnie de deux figures de bronze le tout orné de bronzes dorés d'or moulu, représentant les attributs de la Marine, chez le Sieur Lannuier, Marchand de meubles, rue Saint-Thomas-du-Louvre"; on Wednesday, April 28, 1784, no. 119 bis, Supplément de la feuille, for a "Belle table mécanique de bois d'acajou et d'ébène formant [un] secrétaire qui monte et descend à volonté orné de bronzes dorés d'or moulu, avec flambeaux et garde-vue, chez le Sieur Lannuyer [sic], Ébéniste, rue Saint-Thomas-du-Louvre"; and on Thursday, March 22, 1787, no. 81 bis, Supplément de la feuille, for "Deux beaux Secrétaires à cylindre de 4 pieds 1/2 en bois d'acajou moucheté, ornés de bronzes dorés, avec dessus de marbre blanc et maroquin vert, chez le Sieur Lannuyer [sic], Ébéniste, rue Saint-Thomas-du-Louvre."

36
See note 9, above. The prince de Condé and his family left Chantilly and emigrated from France on July 17, 1789. With his cousin the comte d'Artois, the prince became one of the most active opponents of the Revolution. During his exile in Germany he raised the so-called armée des princes to fight along with his European allies against the French republic. See Diesbach, 1984.

37
The inventory made at the time of Michel-Cyrille Lannuier's bankruptcy in 1789 mentions "a small walnut table with turned legs" that belonged to "Mr. Lannuier cabinetmaker in Paris," who, apparently, had originally sent it to a certain C. Seveau, a nephew of the prince de Condé. M. Seveau rejected it for one reason or another.

38
Archives Nationales de Paris, Minutier Central, Étude XCI-1375, for February 3, 1801.

39
See Salverte, 1962, p. 188.

40
These daybooks were kept when a master declared insolvency. Archives Nationales de Paris, D 11 U 3, Carton 24, Do 1622–1623, for January 13, 1804.

41
In Charles Topino's declaration of insolvency dated December 21, 1789, Lannuier (spelled Lannuyer) is listed with an open account in the amount of 100 livres for furniture sold to him. At a time when phonetic

spelling was usual, the incorrect spelling of names was so common that it is often difficult to discern a craftsman's identity in contemporary documents. Archives Nationales de Paris, D 4 B 6, Carton 108, Do 7648, for December 21, 1789. A photograph of the console table stamped by Lannuier and Topino is in the furniture documentation files of the Musée du Louvre. For another console table in the same Late Louis XVI style, by Nicolas Lannuier, see Nicolay, 1956, ill. p. 271. On Topino's work see Salverte, 1962; de Bellaigue, 1974, vol. 2, p. 880.

42
Two similar worktables stamped only F. Bury are documented: A *petite table travailleuse* was sold at the Palais Galliéra, Paris, February 7, 1976, and a *table tricoteuse* was sold in Paris on November 1, 1988. On the work of Bury see Salverte, 1962; Kjellberg, 1989.

43
Stamped Nicolas Lannuier furniture with oval-shaped mounts typical of Bury's documented work includes several cylinder desks sold at the Palais Galliéra, Paris, June 10, 1971, and at Christie's, London, June 23, 1994. Examples by Bury were sold in Versailles, May 25, 1986, and at the Hôtel Drouot, Paris, December 8, 1987.

44
Archives Nationales de Paris, Minutier Central, Étude LXI-529, for December 18, 1770.

45
Archives Nationales de Paris, Y 14 108, for September 30, 1780 (the inventory taken after the death of Marguerite Malice). On Cochois's work see Ledoux-Lebard, 1984.

46
Archives Nationales de Paris, Minutier Central, Étude LXXI-58, for December 8, 1784.

47
Archives Nationales de Paris, Minutier Central, Étude LXXVII-400, for October 3, 1780, and XXXI-254, for September 15, 1789.

48
The advertisement appeared in *Affiches, Annonces, Avis divers,* April 6, 1783, p. 833: "Le 2 avril, environ à 4 heures du soir on a perdu, depuis le passage de S.-Germain-l'Auxerrois jusqu'au Pont Neuf un caillou d'Égypte, ovale, d'environ 2 pouces et demie de long. Récompense honnête à qui le rapportera au Sieur Cochois, Ébéniste, rue Saint-Honoré, No. 609."

49
See Nicolay, 1976, p. 497.

50
Archives Nationales de Paris, D 11 U 3, Carton 24, Do 1622–1623.

51
Nicolas Lannuier is named in a document concerning Cochois's bankruptcy. Archives Nationales de Paris, D 5 B 6 4530 No. 1622-1623. Even though his name, once again, is spelled incorrectly, it is undoubtedly his purchases in 1803 that are listed in Cochois's daybook as follows:

Du 10 brumaire vendu à Mr. L'annuyée [*sic*], Ébéniste,
—un Secrétaire et une Comode [*sic*] moderne, garnis pour le prix de 300 francs
—Deux Piedesteau [*sic*] ordinaire 72 francs
—deux Tables de jeux de cadrille [*sic*] 96 francs
—un Petit miroir de toilette 18 francs

Total: 486 francs

Sur lesquels j'ai reçu comptant 48 francs. Reste du 438 francs.

52
For an illustration of the label see Leben, 1992, p. 11.

53
The original text reads, "Que ce n'est nullement l'inconduite qui le met dans le cas d'avoir recours à la justice . . . que ce n'est pas seulement sur son travail qu'il fonde son espoir, mais bien encore sur un avenir certain d'hérédité qui ne peut surpasser que de beaucoup le montant de ses dettes." See Archives Nationales de Paris, D 5 B 6 4530 No. 1622-1623, document dated 22 *nivôse* XII (January 13, 1804).

54
Centre des Archives Diplomatiques de Nantes.

55
See Ledoux-Lebard, 1984, p. 130.

56
The writing desk owned by Marjorie Merriweather Post, in the Hillwood Museum, Washington, D.C., appears to have been transformed from a plant stand or *table jardinière* in the late nineteenth or early twentieth century, when marquetry and bronze mounts were added in order to make it more attractive for a potential client. The comparable table in the Musée des Arts Décoratifs, Paris, of mahogany and mahogany veneer, with inlaid brass, in the modern taste, approximates how the Hillwood example might have looked before these alterations were made.

57
Archives Nationales de Paris, D 4 B 6 107–7606, for October 20, 1789.

58
Archives Nationales de Paris, Y 14 115, for April 17, 1785.

59
A commode bearing the stamps of F. Bury and J.-H. Riesener is in the Musée du Louvre, Inv. OA 6495. Other double-stamped examples include: a *secrétaire* marked F. Bury and D. Deloose, sold at Ader, Picard, Tajan, in Paris, April 2, 1971; a commode marked F. Bury and J.-B. Tuart, sold at the Hôtel Drouot, Paris, September 30, 1988; a chiffonier marked F. Bury and J.-B. Tuart, sold at the Hôtel George V, Paris, November 7, 1991; and a commode marked F. Bury and M. Carlin, sold at Pardridge, London, 1983.

60
See note 3, above.

61
Until the 1820s in France, veneers were cut by hand, with a saw, between 2 and 4 millimeters thick, which caused considerable loss of material. Thinner, machine-cut veneers, from 1 to 2 millimeters thick, came increasingly into use in the French furniture trade after 1820. Parisian cabinetmakers liked their veneers custom sawn in radial and tangential cuts that produce the greatest optical effects from the grain. Radially and tangentially cut veneers, especially those from the post-Revolutionary, Consulat, and Empire periods, are quite distinctive, and very different from the veneers found on English or German furniture.

62
The German weekly newspaper *Zeitung für die elegante Welt* informed its public in the June 7, 1803, edition under the heading, "Furniture Decoration with inlaid strips," about the technique for creating these decorative borders, as well as providing information about all the different materials in which they could be made: "In Paris hat man zur Verzierung der Möbel eine Art von Leistenwerk erfunden, das einen vortrefflichen Effekt macht. Es besteht aus zwei glatt gewalzten polierten Metallstreifen von zwei oder mehreren Zollen in der Breite, in welche ein geschmackvolles Muster ausgepreßt und mit allerhand seltenen Holz, Elfenbein, Perlmuttern etc. ausgelegt wird. Man hat die Leisten von Bronzen, Messing und Silber; aber die von poliertem Messing mit einem ausgepreßten, mit schwarzem Ebenholz ausgelegten Muster machen die brillanteste Wirkung" ("In Paris they have invented a style of decoration for furniture, which

has a beautiful effect. It consists of two flattened strips of polished metal two or more inches wide, in which there are stamped tasteful designs, which are filled with rare woods, ivory, mother of pearl etc. One finds these strips in bronze, brass, and silver; but those made from polished brass with inlays of black ebony are the most brilliant in effect [author's translation]"). "Ameublement–Möbelverzierung durch Leistenwerk," 1803.

63
As recorded in the catalogue of the French Industrial Exhibition of 1806: "Citoyen Frichot, rue des Jardins-Saint-Paul, no. 3 a présenté une collection de bordures et de cadres ornés en marqueterie de cuivre, d'acier et d'or, fabriquée suivant les procédés de M. Jouvet, dont M. Frichot est le successeur" ("Citizen Frichot, rue des Jardins-Saint-Paul, no. 3 has presented a collection of decorative borders and frames decorated with marquetry work in copper, steel and gold, made according to the invention of M. Jouvet, to whom M. Frichot is the successor" [author's translation]). *Exposition des produits,* 1806. Brayer, 1805, documents M. Jouvet, of "Rotonde du Temple, No. 26," as a manufacturer of marquetry in metal on wood, stating that he received a "médaille d'encouragement" in the year 9 [1800] for models of chairs, which were judged to be perfect in the choice and disposition of their ornaments. The jury awarded Frichot a silver medal. This type of decoration, which apparently was used in France as early as the 1780s by such cabinetmakers as Bernard Molitor, Adam Weisweiler, and others, became very fashionable in England and the United States, and was later more easily and cheaply produced by means of a stenciling technique. (See also Chapter Four: Materials and Workmanship.)

64
Contemporary journals commented quite critically about the new forms of seating furniture in *le goût antique.* For example, the *Journal des dames* of 1805 noted: "On a admiré la forme des meubles antiques . . . et l'on s'est empressé de les imiter . . . pour l'usage de petites femmes qui, grâce à la mode, meurtrissent leurs membres délicats sur leurs formes anguleuses, et peuvent à peine les remuer au besoin" ("We admired the lines of antique furniture . . . and we hastened to imitate [it] . . . for the enjoyment of the ladies, who, as slaves to fashion, bruise their delicate limbs on its angular forms, and could scarcely move it if they had to").

PLATE 11. Charles-Honoré Lannuier. Gaming table (trictrac table), with its writing surface removed. 1805–10 (cat. no. 120)

CHAPTER 2   Lannuier's Life and Work in New York, 1803–19

Honoré Lannuier is a naturally sympathetic figure, whose life inspires both empathy and admiration. Born to a decent, hard-working family that knew their share of difficulties in post-Revolutionary France, Lannuier made his way to New York, where, seemingly, he lived out the immigrant success story, only to die young at the height of his creative powers. In many ways, however, Lannuier remains an enigma, having left neither personal papers nor shop records to provide the basis for a more subtly nuanced telling of his life story in New York. All that has come down to us from his sixteen years in this city are the record of his marriage and the birth of his children, half a dozen newspaper advertisements, a handful of invoices, his will and inventory, some personal and real-estate tax data, and a few other tantalizing documents. Luckily, what survives in abundance is his stamped and labeled furniture—that large and splendidly documented body of work, which speaks so eloquently and directly of Lannuier's talent and artistic sensibilities. In the end, this is a remarkable legacy, and one like no other in the history of pre-industrial American furniture.

LANNUIER'S
ARRIVAL, AND THE
ESTABLISHMENT OF A
MANUFACTORY AND
WAREHOUSE AT
60 BROAD STREET

In the absence of diaries, letters, or other documents of a personal nature, one can only speculate on why Honoré Lannuier chose to emigrate to New York in the spring of 1803. The recent collapse of the Treaty of Amiens and the resumption of hostilities between France and its arch-enemy, Britain, may have been among the motivating factors. During the French Revolutionary wars (1792–1802), while Honoré was passing from adolescence to manhood and receiving his training as an *ébéniste,* France raised its first national conscript army. With the collapse of peace, Lannuier, single and twenty-three years old at the dawn of a new martial age, may have seen the handwriting on the wall. It was also about this time that General Jean-Victor-Marie Moreau, a hero of the French Revolutionary wars, was implicated in a plot to depose Napoleon Bonaparte and, along with his nettlesome wife, was exiled to America. Later, in New York, Mme Moreau provided Lannuier with a substantial loan. Perhaps the Moreaus were patrons and protectors of the Lannuiers in Paris, and may have counseled Honoré to leave, knowing First Consul Bonaparte's imperial designs and the desolate life in store for so many young Frenchmen.

Economic betterment would, of course, be the other logical explanation for why Honoré chose to leave France. Business conditions and opportunities in New York could have been relayed to him by his older brother Auguste, who had emigrated here in the 1790s and established a confectionery shop at 100 Broadway in one of the city's most fashionable neighborhoods. In 1807, the British traveler John Lambert described Broadway in the area of Auguste's confectionery as one of the finest avenues in the city, "lined with large commodious shops of every description, well stocked with European and India goods, and exhibiting as splendid and varied a show in their windows as can be met with in London."[1] Auguste's apparent success in New York may have had a magnetic effect on Honoré, who envisioned a brighter future there than in Paris, where competition was fierce, wages low, and the prospects uncertain for a young *ébéniste* who wished to set up on his own.

A fascinating notice, signed simply "A Citizen," which was published in the New York press in February 1803 but probably was intended originally for a French audience, explains perfectly the situation in Paris just a few months before Honoré's departure. If that notice had appeared in Paris before New York, one might have expected that Lannuier would have read it himself. Under the heading, "On the trade of France with the United States . . . Cabinet Ware," it continues, in part: "Paris should be the principal . . . exporting place . . . of this article from France, where [there] are such vast numbers of the most ingenious artists in this branch. At present, nearly the whole of their cabinetwork is manufactured by the Americans themselves, for two reasons, because they get the wood for it with more facility and at a cheaper rate than we do; and because their furniture differs much in form from ours, and is framed and finished in a manner peculiar to the use of Americans, or suited to their houses. Our first step, therefore, must be to procure models or patterns of every article of this nature suitable to the American taste. . . . In pursuing this method, it is probable that our goods of this sort will not only sell to advantage at first, but that in a short time it will in a great measure take [the] place of the same manufacture in the United States, on account of the vast difference in the price of Journeymen's labor in the two countries. But notwithstanding these observations, it would be adviseable to send now and then some pieces made to suit our own taste."[2] Thus, a glutted labor market in Paris, and cheap and plentiful mahogany and a wide-open market in America may have been contributing factors in Honoré's decision to leave France. Another intriguing coincidence is the disappearance of Honoré's brother Nicolas from the Parisian cabinetmaking scene after 1804. Did he get into financial trouble like many of his contemporaries who had worked during the ancien régime, only to be forced into bankruptcy by the increased competition and new ways of doing business after the Revolution? Did he become ill? Or was there some other reason why he disbanded his shop, leaving Honoré with little choice but to seek employment with another master, or to try to establish himself on his own? Unfortunately, too many unanswered questions remain regarding both Nicolas Lannuier and his Paris shop, and Honoré's motivations and his attitude toward abandoning France. Whatever Honoré's reasons, New York represented a break with a past marked by dislocation and stress brought on by his family's financial misfortunes, as well as a place in which to make a fresh start for a young man who, from a tender age, knew the high cost of failure. These early experiences left their mark on Honoré; throughout his New York career, he seems to have been a cautious businessman, who carefully gauged his market and never let his reach exceed his grasp. This determined, conservative approach, combined with his superb French training and astute and consistent marketing techniques, allowed Lannuier to establish a solid niche for himself in the burgeoning New York cabinetmaking trade in the early nineteenth century.

One of Honoré's great joys upon his arrival in New York must have been his reunion with Auguste and his young family, although it may have been his first meeting with his nephews, John and Augustus, and his brother's wife, Elizabeth Baptiste. Little did Honoré know that, in two-years' time, he would marry her sister Therese. Auguste, twelve years older than Honoré, probably took a great interest in his talented younger brother's welfare, and undoubtedly introduced him to the people he would need to cultivate in order to succeed in New York. In France, as we have seen, the Lannuiers were adept at attracting the right clientele to both their hospitality and cabinetmaking concerns. This family tradition was continued in New York by Auguste, who, as previously mentioned, operated a luxury food business in the finest retail district, catering to the elite while keeping his finger on the pulse of the city. In his shopwindows he occasionally exhibited sculptures of spun sugar of his own creation as well as other displays that were of interest to the local citizenry. In February 1800, for example, Auguste—like other Freemasons, officially in mourning for George Washington a full year after his death—was inspired to fashion a "Monument in Sugar to the memory of the late illustrious, General Washington." He placed his creation on view in his shopwindow, where, according to a newspaper advertisement, it would "scarcely fail to excite the admiration of the curious."[3] As Auguste was a businessman in addition to being an artist, the monument was, of course, also for sale. In 1803, he again promoted one of his window displays, this time advertising that "A Transparancy [*sic*] of the Design that the Corporation have accepted for the New City Hall, painted by Messrs Margin [*sic*] & Macoube [*sic*] may be seen at the store of Aug. Lannuier, Confectioner."[4] This ad emphasizes the centrality of Auguste's shop in the lives of New Yorkers, for the new City Hall was among the most important and ambitious building projects to be undertaken in the young Republic, and one about which the public obviously was both curious and justifiably proud. This connection with City Hall also foreshadows Honoré's later association with the project, for, in 1812, upon the building's completion, he was commissioned to make the armchairs used by the city aldermen in the Common Council Chamber (see plate 62, and fig. 82).

Auguste appears to have earned a solid living in New York, although tax records reveal that he was far from wealthy. He bought and sold properties in Manhattan on several occasions and also may have operated a coffeehouse in the saloon of the Park Theatre (see fig. 56).[5] As evidence of his sense of responsibility toward his siblings, Auguste took another younger brother, Stanislas—who, possibly, came to New York with Honoré—into his confectionery business, but this lasted for only a brief period as Stanislas was to die suddenly, and tragically, of yellow fever in 1805. Auguste's brotherly concern may have seemed more like meddling to Stanislas, however, since he left Auguste a mere shilling in his hastily executed will, bequeathing the entire remainder of his estate to Honoré. Although no proof exists, it is entirely conceivable that Auguste provided Honoré with some financial help in establishing his fledgling cabinetmaking enterprise.[6]

The first official mention of Honoré Lannuier in New York is recorded on June 3, 1803, in the account books of James Ruthven, a turner, who noted Honoré's purchase of sixteen table legs at a shilling apiece.[7] Buying furniture parts from a turner may have been a fairly standard New York practice in the trade, but it is just as likely that Lannuier's purchase may have been necessitated by the lack of a proper shop and a full complement of machinery at this early date. It is exciting as well as tempting to hypothesize that the legs made by Ruthven are the tapered and reeded ones found on some of the earliest of Lannuier's surviving tables (plates 11, 12), and that this "jobber" of parts thus may have been responsible for the cross-pollination of the vernacular New York reeded style of the early 1800s with the up-to-date Parisian furniture designs of the Consulat period (1799–1804). Lannuier's inaugural newspaper advertisement a month and a half later, on July 15, 1803, indicates that he was still without his own business address and that he continued to rely on his older brother, but what is remarkable is how Lannuier heralds his arrival, succinctly outlining the essentials of his professional background, his special product line, and his hopes and ambitions for success in New York: "HONORÉ LANNUIER, Cabinet Maker, just arrived from France, and who has worked at his trade with the most celebrated Cabinet Makers of Europe, takes the liberty of informing the public, that he makes all kinds of Furniture, Beds, Chairs, & c. in the newest and latest French fashion; and that he has brought for that purpose gilt

PLATE 12. Charles-Honoré
Lannuier. Pier table. 1803–10
(cat. no. 88)

and brass frames, borders of ornaments, and handsome safe locks, as well as new patterns. He also repairs all kinds of old furniture. He wishes to settle himself in this city, and only wants a little encouragement. Those who choose to favor him with their custom, may apply to Mr. Augustine Lannuier, Confectioner and Distiller, No 100 Broadway. N.B. A good smart Young Man is wanted as an Apprentice."[8]

Not until the publication of *Longworth's American Almanack, New-York Register, Directory* in 1804–5 do we find Lannuier at the 60 Broad Street address that he would occupy throughout his career in New York. City directories generally were published in June or July, and remained in print until June or July of the following year. Thus, information for the 1804–5 directory would have been solicited in the latter part of 1803 and the early months of 1804. Since we know that at the time of his inaugural ad on July 15, 1803, Lannuier was still operating from his brother's confectionery shop, it had to be after this date and before about April 1804 that he settled in at his new address.[9]

Number 60, Broad Street, was in the first ward of old New York (fig. 13). The physical appearance of the house and lot is unknown, but a street view from 1797 (fig. 14) provides an accurate visual account of what this mixed commercial and residential neighborhood

FIGURE 14. John Joseph Holland. *A View of Broad Street, Wall Street, and the City Hall, New York City.* 1797. Watercolor, 12³⁄₈ x 17⁷⁄₁₆ in. (overall). The New York Public Library, I.N. Phelps Stokes Collection. Miriam and Ira D. Wallach Division of Art, Prints and Photographs

FIGURE 13. Peter Maverick, after Joseph François Mangin and Casimir T. Goerck. *Plan of the City of New-York* (detail). Drawn 1799, issued 1803. Engraving. The New-York Historical Society

looked like not long before Lannuier moved there. Broad Street was among the earliest and historically most interesting thoroughfares in New York. In the Dutch period it was actually an inlet or a canal, subject to the ebb and flow of the tides that reached almost as far as the old City Hall, which is visible at the center of the street view. (Old City Hall was transformed into Federal Hall during New York's brief tenure as the capital of the United States.) After the canal was filled in, it became a wide, commodious street, in sharp contrast to others in the older parts of the city, such as Pearl and Water Streets, which were described in the period as "low and too narrow, not admitting, in some places, of walks on the sides for foot passengers."[10] At first, Lannuier leased the property, which had an assessed value of $4,000, from Henry Brooks, a tanner, who is listed in the 1802 tax records as its occupant or owner.[11] In all likelihood, Lannuier signed a long-term lease, since he undoubtedly intended to make improvements and adapt the property for his own particular use. The terms of the lease may have expired in the fall of 1810, since, that October, Honoré purchased the property outright from Brooks and his wife for $5,900. The deed of conveyance describes it as located on the west side of Broad Street, with a street frontage of 24½ feet, including half of an alley or gangway four feet wide and seventy feet long shared with the adjacent property. The lot was irregularly shaped and extraordinarily deep, measuring 14 rods 6 feet along its southerly border.[12] In 1802, Brooks had been taxed for a house and a stable that stood on the site. By 1807, the first year in which Lannuier's name can be found in the tax rolls, the buildings on the lot were designated as a "house and back house," the latter probably the stable that had been remodeled into a manufactory.[13] The deep lot provided Lannuier with ample space for racks on which to store lumber, and the gangway, access for moving supplies and finished goods into and out of the premises. After Lannuier's death, George Deloynes, a mahogany merchant, set up a retail lumberyard in 1820 in the back, which suggests that Lannuier's backyard was larger than average. Lannuier seems to have dabbled in the lumber trade himself, advertising "some beautiful Caraccas [*sic*] Wood by the log, or a greater quantity" for sale to cabinetmakers in 1806.[14] With its sizable yard and the existing structure

FIGURE 15. Unknown American artist. *The Shop and Warehouse of Duncan Phyfe, 168–172 Fulton Street, New York City.* 1816–20. Watercolor and gouache on paper, 16⅝ x 19⅝ in. The Metropolitan Museum of Art, New York. Rogers Fund, 1922

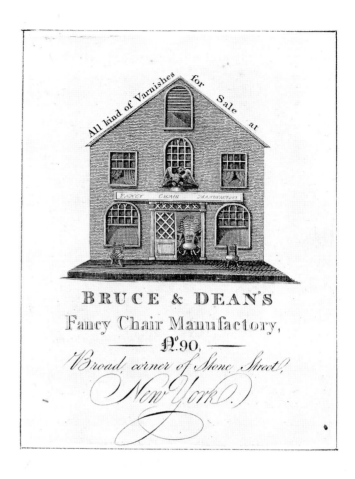

FIGURE 16. Trade label of the chairmaking firm of Bruce and Dean, 90 Broad Street, New York. 1818–20. Engraving. The Metropolitan Museum of Art, New York. The Edward W. C. Arnold Collection of New York Prints, Maps, and Pictures, Bequest of Edward W. C. Arnold, 1954

in the back, 60 Broad must have seemed to Lannuier like an ideal property to develop into his furniture manufactory and showroom. It was also where he and his family lived, probably on the second floor—and perhaps on the third, if it was a substantial house like the two-and-a-half-story buildings indicated in the 1797 view (fig. 14). Lannuier's combination warehouse and home contrasts markedly with that of Duncan Phyfe, who lived on Partition Street (later renamed Fulton Street): first, in the handsome brick structure situated on the right in the informative watercolor, now in the Metropolitan Museum, of Phyfe's furniture warehouse, workshop, and showrooms (fig. 15), and later in a house across the street, separate and distinct from his place of business.[15]

The ground floor of the house that fronted on Broad Street, with its striking and seductive façade, undoubtedly was fitted out in the most elegant manner, with an attractive trade sign and large shopwindows similar to those at the fancy-chair warehouse of Bruce and Dean just down the street at Number 90 Broad (fig. 16). It is hard to imagine that Lannuier stinted in projecting a fashionable image, given his fine design sense and the obvious pride he took in once having worked in Paris, the epicenter of fine shops and luxury goods. Nor could he afford to shrink from the competition provided by Duncan Phyfe, whose establishment has already been described. An impression of Lannuier's furniture warehouse and manufactory, undoubtedly more compact but no less refined, unfortunately can reside only in the imaginations of those who know his beautiful furniture.

On May 8, 1805, Honoré Lannuier, twenty-five years old and apparently confident enough in his abilities to support a family, took as his bride Therese Baptiste, the eighteen-year-old sister of his brother Auguste's wife, Elizabeth. Their marriage may be a measure of how closely knit and insular the Lannuiers of New York were, as well as of the continuing influence of Auguste on Honoré.

Therese, like Honoré, was French, although she is documented as having been born in New York. Little is known of her parents, Jean Baptiste and Suzanne Piquet, except that by 1814 both were deceased. The father may have been in the marine building trades, as two men by the name of John Baptiste, one a caulker and the other a boatbuilder, are listed in the 1801 city directory.[16] In addition to Elizabeth, Therese had at least two other sisters, Jaine and Susan, and a brother, Francis, whose names appear in Honoré's and Therese's wills.[17] Susan's married name was Molle, an uncommon French surname in New York City, which strongly suggests a link through marriage to either Mark or Deker Molle, two cabinetmakers who are known to have worked in New York between 1807 and 1812. The name of the former appears in the city directory from 1809 to 1812, where he is described as a "French cabinetmaker" on Broad, Murray, and Chamber Streets, respectively, and it is included among those listed as debtors in the inventory of Lannuier's estate, which indicates that there was a business link between the two men.[18]

Information about the birth of Therese and her marriage to Honoré in New York is derived from an important document recently discovered in France at the Centre des Archives Diplomatiques in Nantes. This document, an "acte de mariage" dated August 12, 1814, provides not only the names and birth dates of three of the four Lannuier children but also the first evidence that Honoré was still a French citizen eleven years after he came to New York (see Appendix 7). Honoré and Therese apparently were ignorant of French civil law when they married in 1805. In order to comply with what was required—which was that the ceremony be performed by a representative of the French state instead of by the Roman Catholic priest or justice of the peace who officiated at their first wedding—they renewed their vows in an *acte de mariage* nine years and three children later, before officials of the Consulat Général of France in New York.[19] Later proof that Lannuier retained his French citizenship occurs in an 1816 jury list in which he is referred to as an alien. No evidence has been found that he changed his mind and became a United States citizen before his death three years later.[20] The fact that Lannuier was either ignorant of or lax about his legal obligations as a French citizen may indicate that he was not particularly fastidious about government rules and regulations. If so, he also may have been unaware of—or procrastinated over—how to fulfill the United States requirements for naturalization, as was a Scottish contemporary of his in New York, the merchant John Johnston, who bitterly lamented his failure to meet the qualifications prior to the Alien and Sedition Act, which forced him into exile in the Hudson Valley for an extended period during the War of 1812.[21] Just as likely, however, is that Lannuier never for a moment considered renouncing his French citizenship. A case in point is a list of aliens who were naturalized in New York, which was compiled between 1802 and 1814 and records only two Frenchmen out of one hundred and fourteen foreigners.[22] In his *Travels*, the duc de La Rochefoucauld-Liancourt wrote about the feelings of a certain M. Devatines, who was among the first wave of French émigrés to escape to the wilderness of northern New York state in the aftermath of the French Revolution: "He is about thirty years old, sprightly, obliging, always merry, inured to labor and never troublesome with complaints of his fate. But he is prejudiced against the Americans, on account of their unfair dealings in the course of business, as he says, and especially, because they are extremely dull and melancholy. All his ideas are fixed on France, and on the moment when peace shall allow him to return into a country, which he prefers to

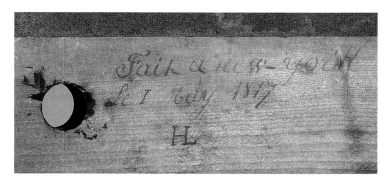

FIGURE 18 a–b. Details of the inscriptions on the front-to-back brace inside the apron (above), and on the head of the gilded figure (right), on Lannuier's card table, plate 53 (cat. no. 72)

FIGURE 17. Detail of the inscription on the inside of the bottom board of Lannuier's specimen marble table, plate 16 (cat. no. 117)

PLATE 13. Charles-Honoré Lannuier's engraved No. 3 label on the card table, plate 25 (cat. no. 55)

any other. Dry bread in France he would not exchange for property and wealth in any part of the globe. This frame of mind is common to all Frenchmen."[23] Perhaps Lannuier, used to the sophistication that accompanied trade in luxury goods in Paris, shared some of these same sentiments.

French doubtlessly was the daily language in the Lannuier household and probably in Honoré's workshop as well, as evidenced by French inscriptions in his own hand on two tables made thirteen years apart (figs. 17, 18). Two of his three known labels are bilingual, however, and all of his surviving invoices are written in English, so we know that he was capable of communicating in the language of his adopted city, although how comfortable he was with English as opposed to French is another question. Egregious errors in his beautifully engraved cheval-glass label (plate 13) suggest that his command of English was limited; in translating a French phrase into English, he (or perhaps a French engraver) resorted to phonetic spelling: "Kips is Whare house" ("Keeps his Warehouse"). Many an American tourist in France who has made a similar mistake can sympathize with this error, and can attest to the vast difference between basic communication and actually engaging in conversation with a native French speaker. Lannuier could have had a similar experience in New York, although polishing his English may not have been a high priority, since he could converse in French with his family and probably with a majority of the workmen in his shop. Many of Lannuier's sophisticated clients, regardless of their backgrounds, would also have had some facility in French. So, from the point of view of customer relations and marketing, Lannuier's perpetuation of the French language would have been a plus for a man who promoted himself as New York's resident French *ébéniste*. However, this practice may not have served him as well in other aspects of his life, such as assimilating into the artisan class in New York, or participating in New York's non-French-speaking society outside of the realm of work. Lannuier, unlike Duncan Phyfe, for instance, never was a member of the General Society of Mechanics and Tradesmen of New York, a mutual aid society of mostly master craftsmen.[24] If, as suspected, Lannuier intentionally or by circumstance was not fully engaged in the life of the city, then a parallel might be drawn here between his personality and character and his documented furniture, which selectively partakes of the local New York vernacular but at the same time stands apart, elegant and well composed, with a distinctive French flair.

By the time that they renewed their marriage vows in 1814, Honoré and Therese had three children: two boys and a girl. The oldest was Moyse Stanislas, born July 28, 1806. In typical French fashion, he would later become known by his middle name, Stanislas, which was chosen by his parents in fond remembrance of his uncle, who, only the year before, had succumbed to yellow fever. The source of Moyse (Moses in English) is less certain, but the boy could have been named after Moyse Seixas *père*, an older man who served as a witness to the *acte de mariage* and who possibly influenced Lannuier's life in some way. In addition to Seixas, the other witnesses to the ceremony were François Caille, Jean Juhel, and Joseph Lopez Dias, the last, a merchant and trusted friend whom Lannuier later appointed as one of the executors of his estate. Seixas, Caille, and Juhel are men about whom little is known except that Caille may be the same person as François Chailleau, Lannuier's only documented apprentice, who began a six-year stint in 1809 at the age of fifteen (see Appendix 6); Seixas may have had business dealings with Lannuier; and Juhel might be the merchant listed in city directories from 1798 to 1817. Lannuier may have prevailed upon them to serve as witnesses at this largely pro forma French civil ceremony.

Young Stanislas grew into manhood in New York, and was first listed in the city directory in 1828 as a grocer at 53 Delancey Street. Without the guiding influence of his father, however, who died when he was thirteen, Stanislas seems to have had a hard time settling into a career. For the next nineteen years his occupations are given in the city directory as

FIGURE 19. Hatch and Smillie, after Charles Burton. *St. Peter's Church, Barclay Street, New York.* 1831. Engraving, 3⁹/₁₆ x 2³/₄ in. The New York Public Library, I. N. Phelps Stokes Collection. Miriam and Ira D. Wallach Division of Art, Prints and Photographs

Drawn by C. Burton.   Engraved by Hatch & Smillie.

hatter, accountant, manufacturer of fishing tackle, and policeman. Stanislas and his wife, Martha, whom he married in 1833, had a son who, sadly, died in 1834, when he was nine months old, and a daughter, who died in 1838, when she was only two. One son and a daughter survived to maturity, however, and are mentioned in the will of their paternal grandmother, Therese. Only the son, Frederick Mortimer Lannuier, is later recorded in New York, where, in 1876 and 1877, he operated an eating establishment at 7 Catherine Street—just about a century after his great-grandfather Michel-Cyrille Lannuier opened his inn, Le Grand Cerf, in Chantilly. Stanislas, like his father, Honoré, died prematurely at the age of forty-one, and was buried at Greenwood Cemetery in Brooklyn, which may indicate that he was living in that borough at the time of his death.[25]

The second oldest child of Honoré and Therese Lannuier was a daughter, Sophie, born on March 7, 1810. (Honoré's older brother Nicolas in Paris also had a daughter named Sophie, who is mentioned in Honoré's will.) By 1830, Sophie was married to Charles Laurence, with whom she had three sons, Charles Henry, Theophilus W., and Joseph L.; their names appear in their grandmother Therese's will. Theophilus was listed in the 1870 city directory as residing in Brooklyn, but his bookselling business was located on Nassau Street in lower Manhattan. Charles Henry, his grandfather's namesake, is the only child or grandchild of Honoré Lannuier known to have engaged in the woodworking trade; he is listed in a city directory of the 1880s as the owner of a planing mill on Cherry Street. Therese's will, written in 1856, specifically notes that by this date Sophie was deceased; although the precise year of her death is unknown, she could not have lived to be older than forty-six. It is curious and possibly more than just coincidence that Honoré and his two oldest children—all of whom had married, become parents, and otherwise seemed to lead productive lives—should not have lived beyond their middle years. Perhaps the family was predisposed genetically to a life-shortening condition or to a particular disease.[26]

The third child mentioned in the *acte de mariage,* another boy, Louis Theophilus, born April 25, 1813, was only sixteen months old at the time his mother and father renewed their vows, and may have not lived to maturity. His sister Sophie may have named her son in his memory.[27]

A fourth Lannuier child, Charles Aurore, was born August 7, 1816, and baptized on October 5, 1816, at Saint Peter's church on Barclay Street, as recorded in the baptismal register.[28] Saint Peter's, built in 1786, was the Lannuiers' parish church and the first Roman Catholic church in the city (fig. 19). Charles Aurore's godparents were Pierre-Aurore Frichot and Jaine Jeard. The former apparently was an important enough friend for Lannuier to have named his youngest child after him, as well as a business associate, which will be discussed shortly, and the latter possibly was Therese's sister Jaine. Charles Aurore probably also died as a child, for, like his brother Louis Theophilus, his name does not appear in any later family documents, nor is he mentioned in his mother's will.

It is a pity that none of the Lannuier children were old enough to have been trained in their father's shop and, consequently, to carry on the Lannuier name among New York cabinetmakers of the next generation. However, Honoré's brother Auguste had had two sons, Jean (birth date unknown) and Auguste, Jr. (baptized October 23, 1801), who, by about the age of fourteen, could have been apprenticed to their uncle. Auguste Lannuier died in 1811 and his wife, Elizabeth, died just three years later, leaving their two adolescent boys orphaned. Both Jean and Auguste are mentioned in their uncle Honoré's will, and, given their tragic situation, it seems likely that their welfare would have been of great concern to him. Auguste became a clothier and is listed as such in the city directory from 1822 to 1828. He dabbled in real estate, and rental fees may have supplemented his income. By 1820, a year after his uncle's death, Jean's activity as a woodworker was noted in the city directory, in which he was listed as a carver at 69 Eldridge Street. If Jean had received specialized training in this aspect of furniture making at his uncle's manufactory in the 1810s, then he would have learned from the best, for no New York carved-and-gilded figural furniture of this period can compare with Lannuier's. As an apprentice carver he could have roughed out

FIGURE 20.   Charles-Honoré Lannuier. Dining table. 1815–19 (cat. no. 122)

the winged-caryatid or swan table supports typical of Lannuier's designs for a recutter, who would later work fine detail into their gessoed surfaces. It is more likely, however, that he would have been assigned such ordinary, repetitive tasks as carving leafage on ogee-shaped balusters like those shown in figure 20.[29]

Another family of French cabinetmakers in New York, the Poillons, might have been responsible for Jean Lannuier's training. John Poillon, the father, was a trusted friend of Auguste Lannuier, who was appointed an executor of the latter's estate in 1811. From 1800 to 1810, the elder Poillon worked on Warren, Nassau, and Pearl Streets, and had two sons, John, Jr., and James, who followed him in the trade in New York until 1826. The fact that the senior John Poillon is no longer listed as a cabinetmaker in the city directory after 1810 lessens somewhat the possibility that Jean Lannuier trained with him, but Jean certainly could have apprenticed with Poillon's sons, who appear on their own in the directory beginning in 1811. In the end, all this speculation seems to matter little, as Jean became a grocer after 1823 and, like his brother, also was involved in real estate. One would assume that Jean and Auguste, Jr., had money to invest once they reached maturity and inherited the legacies left to them by their father and mother.[30]

SHOP ORGANIZATION AND
SCALE OF PRODUCTION

One of the great ironies is that despite all the signed and labeled furniture by Honoré Lannuier that has come down to us, virtually no records survive to document the way he organized his business. In order to establish himself in New York he needed working capital, which initially may have been in the form of a loan from a family member or the modest dowry he received upon his marriage to Therese Baptiste. Later, he generated capital by mortgaging his property at 60 Broad Street. According to surviving records he did this at least twice, first in 1811 and the second time closer to the end of his life, when an outstanding mortgage of $4,000 was recorded in the inventory of his estate. Specific details are available only for the earlier mortgage loan of $2,000, which Lannuier negotiated for a one-year term in 1811 with Mme Moreau, the wife of the famous French Revolutionary War general.[31] The loan was negotiated only eight months after Lannuier purchased the property he had formerly leased at 60 Broad Street, which may indicate that he was about to embark on a program of capital improvements.

In addition to mortgage loans, Lannuier resorted to another fairly typical method of raising capital and took on a partner to lessen the risk. This relationship was discovered in a May 15, 1816, advertisement in the *New-York Gazette & General Advertiser*, which announced the sale of "a general assortment of French Goods among which are one dozen Clocks" by the firm "A. Frichot & Lannuier No. 60 Broad." This is probably the French *ébéniste* Pierre-Aurore Frichot (1785–1867), son of the Parisian metalworker mentioned in Chapter One, who was awarded a silver medal at the French industrial exhibition in 1806 for his die-stamped ornamental borders in copper, steel, and gold.[32] Unfortunately, other than these few fleeting insights into Lannuier's business practices, the historical record remains blank. Certainly, Lannuier employed whatever means it took to keep his business in the black and his stock current and appealing. City tax records and his estate inventory (see Appendix 9) imply that throughout his New York career Lannuier's financial underpinnings and personal wealth remained steady but relatively modest.[33] To the best of his ability, he modeled himself after his brother Nicolas, the "marchand-ébéniste," selling elegant, distinctive, top-quality furniture in the French style, as well as a range of other French luxury goods. Based on the nature of Honoré Lannuier's surviving furniture and the few documented indicators of his financial status over time, it would seem that his business was relatively small in scale, geared almost exclusively toward that segment of the market intrigued and captivated by French fashion and taste. His furniture was expensive, and extant examples suggest that he had little interest in courting the middle or low ends of the market. Quality, stylishness with a French accent, and novelty would appear to have been the watchwords of the Lannuier enterprise.

When Lannuier left the highly refined world of the Parisian cabinetmaking trade and arrived in New York in 1803, he must have experienced a degree of culture shock. In the words of his fellow countryman, the early-nineteenth-century traveler to New York Baron de Beaujour, manufacturing in the United States at this time could "scarcely be considered on a level with the Europeans, unless in some coarse works the most necessary of the wants of life; in all others, and particularly in those that require a great perfection of the hand and a great division of labour, they are extremely backward. . . ."[34] With his background and superb training, Lannuier had an open field ahead of him in which to establish in New York City a first-rate furniture manufactory, based on sophisticated European models. However, there also were some obstacles to face—most notably, a smaller group of talented cabinet-makers, turners, carvers, gilders, and metalworkers to call upon than were available in Paris, as well as the considerably higher wages these journeymen earned in New York. Still, the opportunities here outweighed the drawbacks, and Honoré positioned himself to capture a significant share of the expanding market for luxury household furnishings. He must have had a good marketing sense and a personal style that set him apart as New York's local pur-veyor—and quite possibly resident connoisseur—of French-style furniture and decoration.

By the second decade of the nineteenth century, interest in fashionable furniture and interior decoration had grown to such an extent among wealthier New Yorkers that the painter Samuel F. B. Morse, disdainful of their mindless materialism, wrote to his wife in the spring of 1814: "Man here is weighted down by his purse, not by his mind. . . . A fine painting or a marble statue is very rare in the houses of the rich in this city." He further lamented that "individuals who would not pay fifty pounds for either, expend double that sum to vie with a neighbor in a piece of furniture."[35] By inclination and background, Lannuier was perfectly suited to take advantage of this trend, and it would seem that he became an industry leader of sorts, at least according to Jean Milbert, a French artist and naturalist, whose published travel account, *Itinéraire pittoresque du fleuve Hudson*, recorded his visit to New York City in 1815 as well as later sojourns in upstate New York. Milbert's comments are so specific and sugges-tive of an intimate knowledge of the French cabinetmaking community in New York—of which Lannuier clearly was the dominant figure—that they bear repeating here at length:

> Furnishings for the home . . . are either manufactured by the Americans or imported from France or England. Beds, tables, chairs, chests of drawers, secretaries, etc. are made here, and they are superior in construction and solidity if not in taste and shape. Elegant but fragile pieces of French furniture are occasionally ordered for use as mod-els but, as they are veneered on an inferior quality of white wood, poorly made and glued, and intended merely to please the eye, it is easy to see how, in a damp climate subject to extreme variations in temperature, they can not stand competition with the perfectly fitted American products of heavy mahogany. However, to pay our country its due homage, I shall add that French workmen started this business in America and it is they who are developing it most successfully. They use the best models and books on furniture and interior decoration by Messieurs Percier and Fontaine [figs. 21, 22].[36]

Further evidence of Lannuier's leadership role within the trade, as well as that of his major competitor in the realm of fine furniture, Duncan Phyfe, has been discovered by Marilynn Johnson in the account books of the New York master cabinetmaker John Hewitt, an entre-preneurial type heavily involved in the venture-cargo furniture trade to the American

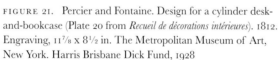

Secrétaire exécuté à Paris pour M.r V.

FIGURE 21. Percier and Fontaine. Design for a cylinder desk-and-bookcase (Plate 20 from *Recueil de décorations intérieures*). 1812. Engraving, 11⁷/₈ x 8½ in. The Metropolitan Museum of Art, New York. Harris Brisbane Dick Fund, 1928

FIGURE 22. New York maker. Cylinder desk-and-bookcase. 1815–20. Rosewood veneer, 98 x 49 x 23 in. Boston Athenaeum. Gift of Mrs. Walter Muir Whitehill, 1982

South. He annotated an entry in his account book in March 1811 with the lengths and proportions of columns used by Phyfe and Lannuier, with the obvious intent at some point of imitating them: "Phyfes Collum [*sic*] 23 [28?] Inches with leafe carv'd 2⁸/₇ wide / Lanaus Collum [*sic*] 2 ft 3 Long 2½ Wide Bottom."[37]

A similar parallel between these two leading craftsmen occurs in estate auction ads in 1815 and 1816, the former offering for sale valuable furniture from the "Mansion House known by the [name of the] Hermitage, 3 miles from this city, on the Bloomingdale Road . . . the mahogany furniture made by Mr. Lannuier," and the latter "a variety of . . . mahogany furniture of genteel description, of Phyfe's best workmanship," being sold for "a family about to leave the country."[38]

In the absence of any of Lannuier's account books or other business records, one of the only ways to make a reasonable estimate of the scale of his enterprise is through comparison with other master cabinetmakers, and by placing him in the overall context of the cabinetmaking trade in New York. Between the time of Lannuier's arrival in 1803 and his premature death sixteen years later, the population of New York City doubled from approximately sixty to one hundred and twenty thousand. Concomitant with this growth was a steady increase in the number of cabinetmakers in the city (table 1). However, yearly totals tell only part of the story. The significant factor is how many of the master cabinetmakers operated their own retail businesses, as opposed to the number of journeymen available to work for them full time, or part time on a piecework basis. Determining this ratio unfortunately is not easy, due to the fact that city directories, with the notable exception of the 1805–6 edition published by Longworth, fail to specify whether cabinetmakers owned their

TABLE 1. Cabinetmakers active in New York, 1803–19, by year

Year	Number
1803	136
1804	142
1805	171
1806	188
1807	177
1808	192
1809	200
1810	271
1811	212
1812	249
1813	229
1814	206
1815	217
1816	269
1817	240
1818	249
1819	304

Source: Transcripts of New York directories and newspapers, Berry B. Tracy Archives, Department of American Decorative Arts, The Metropolitan Museum of Art, New York

retail establishments or worked as journeymen for others. Luckily, the latter included a separate trade directory at the front, which listed sixty-six individual master cabinetmakers, including three partnerships. With a total of somewhere between 171 and 188 cabinetmakers active in the city at this time, a ratio of just under two journeymen for each master cabinetmaker can be established. This pattern appears to hold through 1810, when only ninety-two journeymen are listed officially as members of the New-York Society of Cabinet Makers, a journeymen's trade association. Even as late as 1817, the essential nature of the trade had changed very little, as reflected in the comments of the British traveler Henry Bradshaw Fearon, who stated: "Cabinet-makers shops . . . are generally small concerns, apparently owned by journeymen, commenced on their own account. These shops are perfectly open, and there is seldom any person in attendance. In the centre, a board is suspended with the notice, 'Ring the bell.' I have conversed with several proprietors: they state their business to have been at one time good, but that there is now too much competition."[39]

Of course this does not mean that the work force divided neatly along the lines of the formula worked out above. Some master cabinetmakers who operated retail establishments worked on their own with the aid of an apprentice and occasionally a journeyman, while others may have employed half a dozen journeymen or more during periods of peak demand. Masters could avoid bringing extra journeymen into their shops by engaging other retailers as subcontractors—as was the case with Fenwick Lyell, whose name appears in the separate Longworth's trade list of 1805–6. During this same period, Lyell is documented as having made: "2 Sopha [*sic*] frames" for Duncan Phyfe; a "field bedstead, 2 Sopha [*sic*] frames, 2 Candle and 2 Bason [*sic*] Stands" for William Dove; and "12 Mahogany Chair frames" for the firm of Slover and Taylor.[40] In this small world of interlocking business relationships masters could usually get what they needed when they needed it, without always having to take on extra help. In essence, the entire city became their workshop. Masters generally knew what to expect from one another when, for instance, they subcontracted for a "best" pillar-and-claw Pembroke table with leaf carving on the urn and claws (fig. 23). This may help to explain the strong regional identity and stylistic homogeneity of much of the so-called Phyfe furniture of this period. Use of the master's name as a style appellation must

FIGURE 23. Moses and Stephen Young. Pembroke table. 1810–18. Mahogany and mahogany veneer, 28⅝ x 35⅜ x 24⅜ in. Diplomatic Reception Rooms, U.S. Department of State, Washington, D.C. Funds donated by Mr. and Mrs. J. Bruce Bredin

be tempered, however, by our knowledge that Fenwick Lyell and probably a number of other New York master cabinetmakers subcontracted for Phyfe as well as for each other on a regular basis.

Given the general character of the cabinetmaking trade and the fact that the assessed value of Lannuier's real estate and personal wealth remained relatively modest throughout his lifetime in New York, a safe estimate of the maximum size of his work force would probably be somewhere between seven and ten journeymen and apprentices. Anecdotal evidence culled from New York newspapers of the 1810s reveals the approximate number of workmen that two competing firms of roughly equal financial standing employed in their shops. One of these was the partnership of Moses and Stephen Young, who kept a furniture warehouse and workshop across the street from Lannuier at 79 Broad. In 1817, they advertised to hire "two or three Journeymen, that are competent to make good sideboards, and card, tea and dining tables."[41] (A pillar-and-claw Pembroke table or a "tea" table labeled by these makers is shown in figure 23.) The two Youngs, a couple of apprentices, and three additional journeymen equals a work force of seven. The number of journeymen already in their employ at the time of the advertisement is unknown. A second informative ad that appeared in the *Mercantile Advertiser* in 1816 provides the only known instance when the physical size of a workshop is mentioned explicitly: "To Cabinet Makers. . . . First rate stand for the above business, with a good Stock of every article in the line for sale, with an excellent work shop in the rear, to hold ten benches, and sufficient yard. . . . For further information apply at no. 62 Vesey-Street."[42] The cabinetmaker selling out was Thomas Constantine, a former apprentice and journeyman in John Hewitt's shop, who had commenced business on his own in 1815 at 60 Vesey Street and, the following year, moved next door, to number 62. In 1818, the energetic and ambitious Constantine established a "Cabinet Furniture Store" at 157 Fulton Street, near Duncan Phyfe.[43] (A pier table made about 1817–20, while Constantine was at this address, is shown in figure 24.) Hewitt, despite his entrepreneurial zeal, apparently also ran a relatively modest-sized workshop. In analyzing his account books, Johnson determined that, over a four-year period, sixteen different cabinetmakers made furniture for him, but about two-thirds of these were other masters to whom he subcontracted work.[44] Expanding markets in the 1820s and a drive for gains in productivity and increased

FIGURE 24. Thomas Constantine. Square pier table. 1817–20. Mahogany veneer, 35 x 46 x 19 in. Brooklyn Museum of Art, New York

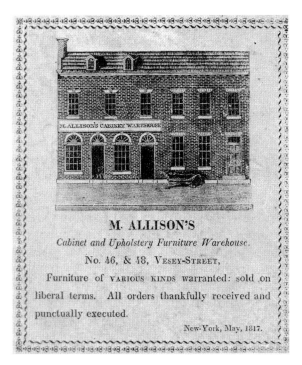

FIGURE 25. Trade label from a French press by Michael Allison of New York. 1817. Whereabouts unknown

FIGURE 26. Michael Allison. Pembroke table. 1817–19. Mahogany and mahogany veneer, 28¾ x 37⅜ x 45¾ in.(open). The Metropolitan Museum of Art, New York. Rogers Fund, 1948

profits would spell the end of the era of small-time journeymen "commenced on their own account." To get a sense of the degree of consolidation that had occurred in the trade within half a dozen years of Lannuier's death one need only compare the Moses and Stephen Young help-wanted ad of 1817 with one placed in August 1825 in the *New-York Gazette & General Advertiser* by the cabinetmaking partnership of Kinnan and Mead, in which they sought at once "TWENTY good Workmen of steady habits."[45]

Using 1817 as a benchmark, it is interesting to compare Lannuier's tax records with those of the masters just mentioned and of a couple of other, well-known cabinetmakers. With an assessed value of $4,000 for his combination home-warehouse-and-manufactory at 60 Broad Street, and $2,000 for his personal estate, the total assessed value of Lannuier's property was $500 less than that of the Youngs' ($5,500 in real estate at 79 Broad Street and $1,000 for their personal estate) but identical to that of Constantine's (all in real estate at 157 Fulton Street). However, in terms of property value and capital investment, the cabinetmaking establishments of Lannuier, the Youngs, and Constantine seem dwarfed in comparison to Duncan Phyfe's, which, in 1817, occupied three adjacent buildings at 168, 170, and 172 Fulton Street, with a combined assessed value of $23,000. Phyfe's residence alone, across the street at 169 Fulton, was appraised for tax purposes at $10,000 and his personal estate at $3,000. Smaller than Phyfe's but still probably over double the size of Lannuier's furniture warehouse was the cabinetmaking establishment of another major figure, Michael Allison. The combined assessed value of his two properties at 46 and 48 Vesey Street equaled $10,000, and the value of his personal estate was assessed at $3,500. If Lannuier, the Youngs, and Constantine employed ten or fewer men, one wonders how many Phyfe or Allison had working for them in 1817. Although without shop records it is impossible to say, the previously published, and often casually restated, figure of up to a hundred men employed simultaneously by Phyfe seems wildly out of line, given the nature of the industry in New York at this time. It would not be surprising, however, if Phyfe had twenty or more men and boys working in his shop by the late teens, or if Allison had a dozen to fifteen.

PLATE 14.   Charles-Honoré Lannuier and Jean-Charles Cochois.
French bedstead. 1805–8 (cat. no. 4)

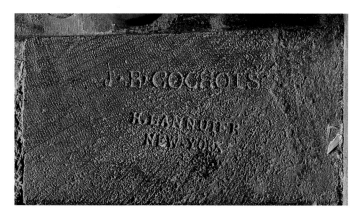

PLATE 15 a–b.   *Estampilles* of Charles-Honoré Lannuier and Jean-Baptiste
Cochois (above), and large French caster (right). Details of the French
bedstead, plate 14 (cat. no. 4). Jean-Baptiste Cochois's son, Jean-Charles,
apparently continued to use the stamp well after his father's death in 1789.

Something of the appearance and scale of the businesses run by these two major entrepreneurs can be discerned from views of their establishments dating approximately to 1815–20 (figs. 15, 25, and 26).[46]

Documentation of actual employment in Lannuier's furniture manufactory or of some other close working relationship with him exists for just four cabinetmakers, all of whom were French. Chronologically, they include his first cousin Jean-Charles Cochois, François Chailleau, Pierre-Aurore Frichot, and Jean Gruez. Cochois was the son of the Parisian *maître ébéniste* Jean-Baptiste Cochois. Jean-Charles came to New York possibly as early as 1804, the year he declared insolvency in Paris, and apparently stayed until 1808, when a passport list from the French consulate in New York indicates that he returned to France. His association with Lannuier is known through a bedstead (plate 14) that contains typical New York secondary woods—yellow poplar and ash—and bears Honoré's stamp, as well as that of his cousin, on all four corner blocks (plate 15). (Jean-Charles must have used his late father's *estampille*.) Whether Cochois actually worked at Honoré's furniture manufactory or merely was subcontracted by him, in the way that he is documented as having worked for Nicolas Lannuier in Paris, is unknown. Cochois's name never appeared in the city directory, which may mean that he lived with Honoré or Auguste during his time in New York. Two other pieces of furniture that he may have had a part in making or designing are a specimen marble table dated 1804 (plate 16) and a stylistically related mahogany and satinwood pier table (plate 17), both of which have marquetry decoration in the blocks above their carved and reeded legs (plate 18). J.-B. Cochois, Jean-Charles's father, was an *ébéniste-tabletier*, or cabinetmaker-inlayer, in Paris, and inlay work may have been a family specialty that was carried on for generations. *Tabletiers* specialized in marquetry panels on such objects as small inlaid boxes and game boards, so another intriguing possibility is that Jean-Charles participated in the manufacture of an early combination backgammon-card-and-writing table, with its

49

PLATE 17. Charles-Honoré Lannuier. Pier table. 1805–10 (cat. no. 91)

green-and-white marquetry backgammon board, which dates to about 1805–10 (plate 11). François Chailleau, the second worker documented with a French name, was a destitute fifteen-year-old in 1809 when he was assigned to Lannuier for a six-year term by the Commissioners of the Almshouse in New York (see Appendix 6). Chailleau's origins and details of his life are unknown, but he may be the same man as François Caille, who is named as a witness in Lannuier's 1814 *acte de mariage*. Aurore Frichot, an *ébéniste* from Paris and Lannuier's partner, is the third cabinetmaker to be documented in New York, but only in 1816, in the aforementioned baptismal register of Saint Peter's church—where he is listed as the godfather of Honoré's son Charles Aurore, who had been named after him—and in the ad that revealed his partnership with Lannuier. How much sooner he was in New York or how much later he stayed is unknown, but his participation in Lannuier's manufactory was very important and probably had a great deal to do with the quality and ornament of Lannuier's splendid late furniture. Jean Gruez, the fourth documented craftsman, also from Paris, apparently held a position of some importance at the Lannuier manufactory during its last few years, when some of the most spectacular gilded figural table forms (plate 19) were made, as recounted in a newspaper advertisement in November 1819, shortly after Lannuier's death, which reads in part: "Mr. J. Gruez, from Paris . . . has taken the establishment of the late Mr. Lannuier, No. 60 Broad-street, where he continues . . . to make . . . furniture and fancy work, for which said establishment was so well known throughout the United States. J.G. . . . for several years superintended the interior part of Mr. Lannuier's business. . . ."[47] Later, Gruez continued to advertise himself as Lannuier's successor in the New York City directory (see fig. 27). If the ad is accurate, we can interpret it to mean that Lannuier himself, late in his career, but maybe sooner, devoted considerable time to aspects of his business other than directly managing or personally participating in the manufacture of furniture. Such

PLATE 19. Gilded figure. Detail of the Lannuier card table, plate 53 (cat. no. 72)

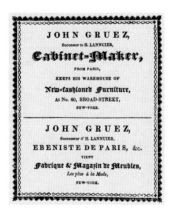

FIGURE 27. Trade label of John Gruez, from Longworth's *Directory*. 1821

developments therefore make it a little surprising to see his handwritten initials and inscriptions in French on a card table made in May 1817 (see plate 53, and fig. 18 a, b) as part of a major commission that he received from William Bayard for wedding furniture for his daughters. However, these inscriptions may represent a gesture by Lannuier to involve himself personally in this important and lucrative commission from one of New York's wealthiest merchants. (Bayard's furniture purchases are discussed in detail in the next chapter.)

The names of others who once may have been employed by Lannuier or had some other kind of business relationship with him can be gleaned from the inventory of his property and his will of 1819 (see Appendix 8, 9). Listed as sworn witnesses, estate executors, appraisers, and those owing him money at the time of his death are five cabinetmakers, four merchants, and two mahogany dealers. The five cabinetmakers include Lannuier's shop foreman, Gruez; the previously mentioned "French cabinetmaker" Mark Molle, a possible Lannuier in-law, who is recorded as owing him about $80; William H. Walsh, who was in partnership with Abraham S. Egerton by 1817, and who owed Lannuier about $100; John Van Boskirk (or Van Boskerck) of Broad Street, who was listed in the city directory beginning in 1817 and who owed Lannuier $7.93; and Thomas H. Powell, who, along with Gruez, witnessed the probating of Lannuier's will by Surrogate Sylvanus Miller on October 22, 1819 (see Appendix 8).[48] Powell was listed in the city directory as a chairmaker from 1805 to 1811, and a cabinetmaker from 1818 to 1820. The debts recorded for three of these five cabinetmakers probably were derived from Lannuier's account books, in which the names and credits and debits of all those with whom he had regular business dealings would have been noted. It is important to remember that the recorded debts of Molle, Walsh, and Van Boskirk were the net results of accounts balanced by Lannuier's estate appraisers that may have dated back over a considerable period of time. Such was the nature of open accounts.

Draperies Jumelles avec Console.

PLATE 20. Pierre de La Mésangère. Design for draperies (Plate 304 from *Collection de Meubles et Objets de Goût*). 1808. Colored engraving, 7³/₄ x 12¹/₄ in. The Metropolitan Museum of Art, New York. Harris Brisbane Dick Fund, 1930

If we were fortunate enough to be privy to these account books, we might then know the precise relationships of these and other craftsmen to Lannuier. The recorded debts probably represent only the tip of the iceberg with regard to financial transactions between Lannuier and other New York cabinetmakers, carvers, gilders, and upholsterers.[49]

Of the four New York merchants mentioned in the inventory, D. A. Smith seems to have had one of the more intriguing relationships with Lannuier. Smith actually is recorded twice, first under the heading "Notes & Drafts due him [Lannuier]," where it is indicated that he owed $1,502.59, and a second time under "Stock in Furniture [etc.]," where "Silks, fringes [etc.], left on hand by D. A. Smith" are valued at $900. The name D. A. Smith does not appear in the city directory, but it seems likely that the Daniel Smith listed first as a grocer at 64 Broad Street in 1812, and from 1813 to 1817 as a merchant at number 62, next door to Lannuier, is our man. By 1818, Smith had died, as only his widow is listed at the 62 Broad address.[50] One can presume from the inventory reference that fabrics and trims were one of Smith's merchandise lines, and that the goods "left on hand" in Lannuier's shop may indicate that these next-door neighbors had worked out some sort of mutually beneficial arrangement that allowed Lannuier to offer clients a selection of fabrics and trims for seating furniture, bed hangings, and window treatments.

Honoré had learned the importance of offering customers a wide range of household furnishings and services from his brother Nicolas in Paris, whose dual role as a cabinetmaker and upholsterer is made clear on his trade label, where he refers to himself as "Tapissier-Miroitier, Ébéniste de S. A. S. Monseigneur le Prince de Condé."[51] The interdependence of upholsterers and cabinetmakers in this period cannot be overemphasized. One relied on the other in the execution of elegant ensembles, such as those depicted in the engraved fashion plates of the period (plate 20). Lannuier's documented furniture is so heavily weighted toward French-style pier tables and bedsteads that it seems he may well have specialized in these forms. A newspaper advertisement from the last year of his life, offering for sale "two sets of French Blue Damask Silk Furniture, with Fringes, etc. for two drawing rooms," also hints at the hand-in-glove relationship he had with one or more New York upholsterers over the course of his career.[52]

Two of the indebted merchants also were dealers in fabrics and decorative materials for the home. One of these was Alfred S. Pell, whose liabilities to the estate totaled $791.43, and the other was a certain E. Malibran, who had two debts outstanding totaling $951. As early as 1807, an advertisement appeared in the New York press that offered "Moreens, Brandy, & Beef . . . for sale by A. S. Pell & Co. 284, Pearl Street," and it is possible that this was the same Pell, who, a year later, under the company name Coffin and Pell, advertised "Furniture Moreens. —Orange, sky blue, straw coloured, crimson and green Heavy Moreens . . ." for sale. Pell moved around quite a bit, but at the time of Lannuier's death in 1819 the directory gave his address as 501 Broadway. Malibran's name first appears in the city directory in 1817, when he is listed as a merchant at 38 South Street; however, the earliest ad that referred to the type of merchandise he sold dates from 1826, when he offered to "Upholsterers & Paper Hangers. A LARGE and splendid assortment of French Paper Hangings, comprising every variety of patterns and quality, and proceeding from the manufactory of P. Simon fils, Boulevard Des Italiens, Paris. . . ."[53]

What do these outstanding debts owed by Smith, Pell, and Malibran, which totaled over $3,200, signify? Perhaps all three men purchased furniture from Lannuier for their personal use or for resale and paid with bank notes that came due at a future date. Another possibility might be that Lannuier was importing large quantities of French goods, some of which he sold at retail in his own establishment and some he wholesaled to other New York retailers. One thing for certain is that Lannuier's business dealings were complex by the late 1810s, and he was engaged in a far wider range of activities than merely supplying cabinetwork.

The fourth merchant whose name appears in the inventory is Joseph Lopez Dias, one of the executors of the Lannuier estate along with Therese and with J. M. J. Labatut, a mahogany dealer, who will be discussed shortly. That Dias was named an executor meant that he and Lannuier were trusted friends. From 1808 to 1826, Dias is listed in the city directory as a merchant situated on Pearl Street, not far from Lannuier's home and business establishment. Ads in New York newspapers attest to the fact that Dias was a broker and a commission merchant, who was involved in overseas trade with France. In September 1808, for instance, Dias announced in the *New-York Gazette:* "For Bordeaux (by special permission) the brig BATAVIAN, Captain Fieltas, will positively sail on the tenth inst. . . ." (Securing "special permission" was essential, since the embargo imposed by the Jefferson Administration in late 1807 on all shipping in and out of American ports was still in effect.) Embargoes, blockades, and even the War of 1812 did not stop the intrepid Dias from sending cargo abroad. In November 1812, he advertised again, this time in the *New-York Evening Post:* "For France, the remarkable fast sailing copper bottomed Baltimore built brig BRUTUS will sail for Bordeaux in about 12 days. . . ." Dias's name appears in conjunction with Lannuier's for the first time in 1814, when he witnessed the *acte de mariage* between Honoré and Therese, which would imply that the two men probably had developed a relationship at an even earlier date. The precise nature of this relationship is uncertain, but it is possible that Dias was a lifeline back to France for Lannuier, carrying correspondence, negotiating with French suppliers, and importing fashionable French luxury goods and furniture ornaments for Lannuier and his one-time partner, Frichot.[54]

The two dealers in mahogany referred to in the inventory were both of French descent. They were George Deloynes, who was chosen by the executors along with the

PLATE 21. Attributed to Charles-Honoré Lannuier. Square pier table. About 1815–19 (cat. no. 102)

cabinetmaker Jean Gruez to expertly appraise the value of Lannuier's stock-in-trade, and J. M. J. Labatut, mentioned above. At this time, Deloynes may have been working for Labatut as Gruez previously had, for Lannuier. Deloynes is not included in the 1819 city directory, but his name does appear in 1820–21 as the proprietor of a mahogany yard at none other than 60 Broad Street![55] Deloynes and Gruez, the estate appraisers, later split up the yard and the furniture warehouse and manufactory at 60 Broad, possibly paying Therese Lannuier an income in exchange for using the facilities. Labatut apparently knew the finer things in life, and he offered them in large quantities to New Yorkers, as his June 12, 1809, advertisement in the *New-York Evening Post* amply attests: "Choice St. Domingo Mahogany and Champagne Wine. . . . About 40,000 feet, choice and very large St. Domingo Mahogany of superior quality, picked out of different cargoes for exportation. 28 hampers of very excellent sparkling Champagne wine. For sale by J. M. J. Labatut no. 10 Frankfort-street."[56] In 1812, Labatut announced in a newspaper ad that he had opened a mahogany yard on Orange Street, where he sold "Mahogany in Logs, Planks, Boards, and Veneers. . . ."[57] He maintained the Orange Street yard throughout Lannuier's lifetime and into the late 1820s. Through Labatut, Lannuier may have had his pick of the choicest veneers and mahogany boards custom sawn in the French manner. When Lannuier began to use rosewood veneers extensively after about 1812, he may have purchased these too from Labatut, as the grain patterns of the veneers he used seem to have more in common with the kingwood favored by French *ébénistes* than with the coarser-grained Brazilian rosewood veneers employed by most of the other New York cabinetmakers, who apparently followed London fashion. (Brazilian rosewood veneers, with their random coarse, dark veins, inlaid with brass, were a favorite of English Regency cabinetmakers.) Labatut also may have supplied

Lannuier with veneers of burl elm, a light-toned wood fashionable in France after 1806, when the continental blockade and a *dictat* by Napoleon forced *ébénistes* to use indigenous timbers. (Mahogany had become so expensive in Paris that it was sold by weight, and the only solution, according to the fashion magazine *Journal des dames*, was to cut veneers thinner than ever.)[58] Lannuier used burl-elm veneers on the superb French bedstead he made for Stephen Van Rensselaer IV in 1817 (see plate 54), as well as on a pier table, of uncertain provenance, with marbleized or bronzed *tôle vernie* front columns (plate 21). Light-colored woods, including burl elm, maple, and sycamore, were utilized increasingly by the top Parisian *ébénistes* during the Late Empire and Early Restauration periods—a fact not lost on the Frenchmen Lannuier or Labatut, or on Lannuier's client Van Rensselaer, who had toured France as a young man in 1813.

MARKETING   Lannuier's marketing techniques are largely unknown, although it seems likely that he would have given this side of his business considerable attention. As a young man, he had become familiar with the exquisite shops selling luxury goods in Paris, and we can be sure that he was sensitized to such issues as merchandise display and shop design through first-hand experience with his brother, the *marchand-ébéniste*. In her book about the luxury-goods merchants of Paris, the *marchands-merciers*, Carolyn Sargentson states that their shops were designed "from the exterior to the innermost rooms . . . to create a memorable context within which the highly designed luxury objects on sale could be viewed and purchased." Sargentson, referring specifically to the *magasins anglais*, explores the idea that the identities of these shops were created by their proprietors as part of a marketing strategy geared to meet and further stimulate the demand for English and English-style goods, whose "simpler forms and distinctive style" grew increasingly popular in France after the Seven Years' War (1756–63) and into the 1780s. By substituting French and French-style goods for English ones, it seems likely that Lannuier was following a similarly single-minded, thematic market-ing approach in New York. His elegant, bilingual trade label provides ample evidence of this (plate 13), for not only did it link a finished piece with its author and provide a mark of distinction for his label-conscious customers but it also operated on a subliminal level—as all successful advertising does—by offering through its style, refinement, and use of the French language, the promise of a shopping experience at 60 Broad Street second only to that available in Paris.[59]

The French aura that surrounded Lannuier's "magasin de meubles" became more and more fixed in the minds of New Yorkers as he developed his client base and used his per-sonal style and flair to set himself apart from others in the trade. The previously alluded to partnership between Lannuier and the Frenchman Frichot seems to have occurred in May 1816. The minutes of the Common Council on April 21, 1817, record that Lannuier rented "the upper Appartments [*sic*] of the Engine House in Beaver Street" for a period of three years at an annual rent of $310.[60] (Beaver Street intersected Broad just four doors south of Lannuier's shop.) This may imply that Lannuier, alone or with Frichot, was experiencing some success and had expanded the French import side of the business to the point that more room was required for stock, or perhaps that Frichot brought workmen with him from France, who were in need of housing.

A curious parallel to the growth of this segment of Lannuier's business after 1816 is the agreement between Duncan Phyfe and the New York merchant George I. Newberry, to display Newberry's imported London merchandise. In a series of advertisements placed between November 1817 and February 1819, Phyfe announced that Newberry's imported

FIGURE 28. Joseph Brauwers. Card table. About 1815. Mahogany and mahogany veneer, 28 x 36 x 18 in. Winterthur Museum, Delaware. Gift of Mr. and Mrs. David Stockwell

goods could be examined at his furniture warehouse on Fulton Street.[61] Following the War of 1812, New York became a dumping ground for English-manufactured products, and there was a great proliferation of notices advertising auctions of goods lately imported from London, Birmingham, and Liverpool. Along with the surge in English merchandise, there was a marked upward turn in the quantity of imported French goods as well, including furniture. Lannuier may have been spurred on by competition from merchants like Lornier and Bailly, located just up the street from him at 42 Broad, who, in December 1815, advertised an array of articles manufactured in Paris, including "an assortment of Ornaments for Architecture, Furniture, Looking Glasses."[62] Two years later, another merchant, Lewis Sollier, advertised that he had opened a store in Maiden Lane that sold French furniture and fancy goods, and where he offered for sale in 1818 a suite of upholstered seating furniture, "the whole in crimson sattin [*sic*], with silk bindings, very superb."[63] This furniture probably was similar in style to the upholstered bergères, chaises, and canapés (see figs. 63, 67) imported from France by William Bayard in 1817 as wedding gifts for his daughters Harriet and Maria, whom he also presented with gilded card tables and pier tables by Lannuier (see plate 51).

By the 1810s, Lannuier also may have met with some competition from other Parisian *ébénistes*, who came to New York after the restoration of the Bourbon monarchy. One such individual was Joseph Brauwers, whose trade label identified him as "ebenist [*sic*] from Paris. . . ." Brauwers's two known card tables are richly ornamented, but they clearly are derivative of the work of Lannuier (fig. 28, and plate 22).[64] Another direct French competitor was a man named Gicquel, whose June 1819 advertisement reads, in part, "J. M. GICQUEL, French cabinetmaker, No. 76 John-street . . . informs the public, that he works in this line of business in the newest and neatest style. He also repairs and varnishes (with French varnish) all kinds of furniture. All orders left for work will be thankfully and punctually attended to, either abroad or at his own shop."[65] Gicquel apparently did not last long on his own, as 1819 is the only year in which his name appears in the city directory. Later, he may have worked as a journeyman, for his advertisement makes clear that he was willing to take his "French" cabinetmaking skills "abroad" to other masters' shops.

Some typical marketing and sales techniques that are documented as having been employed by other New York cabinetmakers also may have been adopted by Lannuier. In Michael Allison's trade label, dated 1817 (fig. 25), for example, an elaborate Grecian sofa is

PLATE 22. Charles-Honoré Lannuier. Card table. 1810–12 (cat. no. 57)

depicted in front of the store, calculated to beckon passersby to take a closer look. That such sidewalk displays were fairly typical in New York is suggested by a note at the end of an 1819 ad by the partners Gillespie and Walker, which read: "N.B. Observe No. 46, and walk in, as they don't wish to exhibit much on the street."[66] Another practice was the speculative manufacture of showpieces—stylish, novel examples of furniture that played an important role in a master cabinetmaker's attempts to win customers. The flip side of such showpieces was that they consumed many hours of labor and lots of expensive materials, so if they failed to strike a customer's fancy they became white elephants of sorts. On June 6, 1814, Charles Christian advertised what originally may have been a showpiece, which he was then pressed to sell at auction: "LIBRARY CASE AT AUCTION - C. Christian will, in order to obtain room in his ware room, sell by auction . . . the elegant library case at present standing there. The case has been made nine months and is as perfect as when sent down from the workshop . . . dimensions eight feet one inch long, ten feet one inch high including the pediment which is loose. There is in the lower part a highly finished secretary drawer. The glass doors are an elegant gothic figure, the baas [sic] supported by carved lion claws, the cornice richly furnished with fluted blocks and carved pine apples [sic]."[67] A desk and bookcase, or library case, now in the Brooklyn Museum of Art, which fits this description in all ways except for its overall height and length, may have been produced in Christian's shop.

Robert Kelly, a former Phyfe employee, was another cabinetmaker who advertised a showpiece. In a February 1814 ad, Kelly "begs leave to inform the public, his pretensions in the line of his business, as a CABINET MAKER" and concludes with a plea to potential customers to "call at his shop No 23 Partition-street and examine a side board modelled after his own taste and which he has just finished with his own hand. . . . N.B. Enquire 5 doors above the well-known cabinet ware-house of Mr. Phyfe, by whom he was employed to make the best side-boards for three years previous to setting up in business for himself where he now is."[68] Due to the novelty of the form and the several permutations it went through over the course of the Federal period, the sideboard probably was often made as a showpiece by New York cabinetmakers during the first two decades of the 1800s. A good example of a new type of sideboard, from about 1812–19, is Lannuier's "French sideboard" (plate 23), whose massive cubic volumes, French-style socle, or "baas [sic] supported by carved lion claws," and "carved pine apples [sic]" (actually, pinecones), based on classical Roman precedents, bear a close resemblance to the description of Christian's 1813 showpiece library case. Just which items in Lannuier's documented oeuvre might be classified as showpieces is a matter of conjecture, but one might guess that some examples of his signature series of gilded figural tables or his more inventive forms of pier tables, such as those with cast-metal caryatid supports (plate 24) or front columns wrapped in tin and painted to imitate bronze or black-and-green marble (plate 21), were displayed in an eye-catching way when they were first introduced.

Besides marketing their furniture locally, many New York cabinetmakers, including Lannuier, sought far-flung markets in the American South and the Caribbean. Lannuier's participation in such coastal trade is known only through the inventory of his estate (see Appendix 9), which lists, under the heading "Property abroad," $2,401.25 worth of furniture "sent to A. S. Bulloch of Savanah [sic]," and $534 worth "dito [sic] to Trinidad de Cuba, consigned to Capt. Roy." Whether the furniture sent to Savannah was consigned to Bulloch with the intention that he and Lannuier share in the profits of its sale, or was for Bulloch's personal use, remains a confusing question linked to a series of possibly related events. Ship manifests for the port of Savannah document the arrival there on October 5, 1819, aboard the brig *Levant* of ten cases of furniture marked "A.S.B.," sent by "Honoré Lannuier" of New York.[69] On October 14, the auction firm of Watts and Joyner offered for sale "at the

PLATE 23.   Charles-Honoré Lannuier. French sideboard. 1812–19 (cat. no. 52)

house of A.S. Bulloch, Esq. Reynolds Square" a large assortment of "ELEGANT FURNI-
TURE," which could have been Lannuier's shipment, or, perhaps, other furniture that Bulloch wished to dispose of before he moved into his recently completed house on Orleans
Square (see fig. 77), designed by the brilliant young British architect William Jay.[70] The Watts
and Joyner ad appeared just two days before Lannuier's death in New York. About a month
earlier, on September 2, 1819, Lannuier issued a last appeal to customers that stated his intention to give up the cabinetmaking business altogether on account of ill health, and offering
for sale "at very reduced prices" his entire stock of furniture.[71] After seeing this ad, one of
Bulloch's New York agents, or perhaps even Jay himself—who is known to have traveled to
New York—may have made a selection and had it sent on to Savannah to see if it would
prove to Bulloch's liking. As Lannuier was ill and possibly even aware of his impending
death, such an arrangement would have been viewed as expedient and as his best chance to
dispose of a fair amount of stock. Only two surviving articles of furniture by Lannuier have
Georgia histories: a mahogany pillar-and-claw dining table (fig. 20) and an ornate rosewood
pier table, with white marble columns (cat. no. 98), but neither of these tables can be traced
back to Bulloch, whose household furnishings all were auctioned in 1822 to satisfy the debts
that led to his bankruptcy.[72] The furniture sent to Bulloch by Lannuier became widely dis-
persed—and thus disassociated from Bulloch at an early date—as a result of either this sale
or of the one held three years before.

Research by Page Talbott for the catalogue that accompanied the exhibition "Classical
Savannah"—specifically, examination of ship manifests for the years 1800 to 1840 in the
National Archives in Washington—only uncovered this one reference to Lannuier having
sent furniture shipments to Savannah. Similarly, for his excellent article on the warehousing
of furniture imported from the North to southern Atlantic ports between 1783 and 1820,

PLATE 25. Charles-Honoré
Lannuier. Card table. 1815–19
(cat. no. 55)

Forsyth M. Alexander made an extensive search of old newspapers for documentation without turning up Lannuier's name in any of the records, even in Savannah and Charleston—
the two ports, he concluded, that were the most receptive to New York master cabinetmakers who wished to market their wares. Thus, it would appear from this that Lannuier
did not participate to any significant extent in marketing large quantities of ready-made
furniture on speculation in the American South. This he left to others, including John
Hewitt, John H. Oldershaw, William Mandeville, and Duncan Phyfe; Phyfe tried his hand at
it for a while through an agent in Savannah named J. W. Morrell. Instead, Lannuier probably relied on custom orders for such customers as the Bosleys in Baltimore and the Wickhams
in Richmond. His dealings in places like Cuba remain an exotic mystery. Given his ties with
Joseph Lopez Dias, the commission merchant, who, undoubtedly, was of Spanish descent,
and to Labatut, the mahogany retailer, the possibility exists that on more than this one occasion Lannuier sent speculative shipments of furniture to the Caribbean or perhaps even to
South America, where French, Spanish, English, and American trade interests were vital in
such commodities as sugar and mahogany, and large markets for manufactured goods were
emerging.[73]

One of the favored methods of selling furniture consigned to ship captains or local
agents in the port cities of the South was by public sale or auction. This same sales technique
was used in New York by master cabinetmakers who wished to dispose of excess stock or to
clear inventory when they were dissolving their businesses or moving to another address.
Lannuier never advertised an auction of his shop goods, although this does not mean that

he refrained from consigning furniture of a less expensive type (plate 25) to one of the several auctioneers in the city who sold mixed lots of new cabinet ware from various makers. The previously mentioned Charles Christian was appointed as an auctioneer for the city and county of New York in April 1803, and a year later, Christian announced the closing of his cabinet-ware room at 79 Broad Street, and the auction of "his valuable stock of Furniture, all of which is his own manufacture. . . ."[74] Christian obviously was concerned about the public's perception of auction sales, and tried to reassure potential buyers with this last clause. However, with Christian the public probably should have been wary, as he seems not to have been a man of high moral character. After he became an auctioneer, similar complaints were filed against him by four different apprentices between June and August 1803. Typical of these was the accusation by James Murray—"that his master has beaten him without cause, has not furnished him sufficient clothing, and, having been appointed auctioneer, pays no attention to his business of cabinet maker and so does not teach his apprentice." The court ruled against Christian in all the complaints and canceled the indentures of the boys.[75] In November 1803, Christian formed a partnership with another auctioneer, named Paxton, and opened a "store for the reception and sale of furniture at auction or on commission." Outlets like these and the furniture that they sold prompted cabinetmaker Michael Allison to include the following advice for potential customers on a trade label dated 1821: "Knowing the deception in work made for Auction, he [Allison] trusts that if people would call and examine for themselves, and compare the work and the price, that that business, so destructive to all good work, a[nd] deceptive to the public, would have an end."[76] Lannuier and his workmen probably were well acquainted with Charles Christian, if not personally then by reputation. Historians know him better as a model of one type of aggressive entrepreneur, who transformed the cabinetmaking industry in New York.

PRICING AND PROFITS   Like so many other aspects of Lannuier's business affairs, his pricing and profits are also difficult to assess. Evidence in the city's tax records over time, the amount of real estate that he owned, and the cash that he had in the bank when he died argue strongly against supposing that he reaped large profits. Given the high-end nature of his cabinetmaking operation, he probably had to reinvest most of the available capital in the business in order to maintain an adequate inventory of materials and stock of ready-made furniture and imported luxury goods.

Profit margins aside, Lannuier's cabinet warehouse seems to have been one of the more expensive in town. Unfortunately, this assessment is based on only one instance in which an item of furniture survives with its original invoice. The invoice, dated June 19, 1817, records that Lannuier charged the wealthy New York merchant William Bayard an astounding $300 for one of his best gilded figural pier tables (see plate 52), and an additional $250 for a pair of card tables (see plate 51) made *en suite*; the furniture was intended as a wedding gift for Bayard's daughter Maria and his son-in-law Duncan Pearsall Campbell (see Appendix 5 for the invoice). With prices like these, it is little wonder that Lannuier's known patrons—many of whom are discussed in the next chapter—came from the uppermost strata of American society.

Comparison of the furniture Lannuier made for Bayard with another suite by Duncan Phyfe for James Brinckerhoff in 1816—some of which also still survives with its original invoice—illustrates just how expensive Lannuier's furniture was. Among Brinckerhoff's purchases recorded on the invoice is a card table (see fig. 71), originally one of a pair; the cost for both tables was $135, or just ten dollars more than Lannuier charged for a single table.[77]

PLATE 26. Gilded figure. Detail
of the card table that Lannuier
made for the Harrison family
(cat. no. 67)

This price differential is staggering when one considers that the tables are essentially of the same swivel-top design and in the same antique style, with broad plinths and gilded-and-bronzed lion's-paw feet. They also have identical gilded-brass ornaments centered on their front aprons. Where they differ is in what caused the substantial variation in price: the additional applied gilded-brass ornaments, die-stamped brass borders, and, most especially, the gilded-and-bronzed sculptural and columnar supports on the Lannuier example. Charles Montgomery, the late historian of American Federal period furniture, devised a formula to approximate the time required to make a piece of early-nineteenth-century furniture by dividing the retail price by three and one-half.[78] Montgomery believed that materials, rent, heat, and other overhead, with profit, increased retail prices an average of three-and-one-half times over the cost of labor, which in this period averaged about a dollar a day for a skilled journeyman. This equation translates to just under thirty-six days of labor to complete one of Lannuier's $125 card tables, and just over nineteen days to make one of Phyfe's less-elaborate examples, which sold for $67.50 apiece. As the two tables are essentially of the same form, they therefore would have required roughly the same amount of time to assemble their component parts, yet it is conceivable that the gilded-and-bronzed sculptural and columnar supports on Lannuier's table took an additional two weeks or more to prepare. Lannuier's gilded figures are extremely sophisticated, and were executed in the best French manner, with extensive recutting in the gesso layer to provide crisp detail, and exquisite mat and burnished gilding (plate 26). With the introduction of this line of figural furniture sometime during or just after the War of 1812, Lannuier's manufactory probably became increasingly expensive to run. The woods, gilded-brass ornaments, and die-stamped brass borders that he used were the best that were available, and his workmen, given the evidence of documented examples, appear to have been encouraged to strive for perfection, regardless of the time involved and the corrosive effect this may have had on profit.

The history of early-nineteenth-century New York furniture design is rich and complex, and Lannuier must take a major share of the credit for its development, along with the illustrious Duncan Phyfe and a handful of lesser-known but influential native-born as well as immigrant craftsmen. So brightly burnished is Phyfe's reputation that his name literally has become a metaphor for all the handsome, compact, reeded mahogany furniture—including scroll-back chairs with crossed banisters and the multifarious pillar-and-claw tables with double and treble elliptic tops and distinctive water-leaf carving—made in the city during this period. Such was the vibrant, Anglo-inspired vernacular that confronted Lannuier as he tried to establish himself in New York. Accommodations had to be made by the newcomer, and thus the intricate melding of Old and New World styles began. For the most part, Lannuier eschewed the soft, elliptical shapes of Sheraton-inspired early-nineteenth-century New York furniture, although on occasion he did choose to graft onto his furniture such typical New York design features as urns and saber legs decorated with water-leaf carving. Despite these additions, however, the tectonic clarity of French post-Revolutionary and Consulat design elements always shines through—a constant reminder of Lannuier's French origins and training (plate 22).

There is no evidence to suggest that Lannuier followed precisely the advice "to procure models or patterns of every article of this nature suitable to the American taste" offered in the 1803 newspaper notice that encouraged the importation of French furniture to America, but it is almost certain that he studied the work of his competitors. A comparison of the construction of the furniture produced in Lannuier's New York shop with that of examples by his brother Nicolas, which were made and sold in Paris (fig. 29), makes clear that Honoré, despite his training, quickly caught on to the peculiarities of cabinetmaking and the economies of workmanship necessary in a place subject to wider fluctuations in temperature and humidity and where labor costs were considerably higher than in his native France. In terms of style, it may not have been Lannuier's intention to effect too many changes, however, since his goal was to promote himself as New York's resident Parisian *ébéniste*. He was also lucky, in that New Yorkers already had been exposed to the French style by the Royalists and aristocrats who emigrated there during the Revolution and the Terror, as well

FIGURE 29 a–b. Nicolas Lannuier. Commode (left), in plate 1, and Charles-Honoré Lannuier. French bureau (right), in plate 9, shown with their marble tops removed

as by the thousands of Frenchmen who escaped the slave uprisings in the West Indies in the early 1790s. During this period, the French architects L'Enfant, Ramée, and Mangin played major roles in the redevelopment of a city that had been ravaged by fire and by the British occupation during the American War of Independence. A new church, Saint Peter's (fig. 19), was built in New York for the growing French and Spanish Roman Catholic population, and even a French-language newspaper, *The French and American Gazette,* was published, with English translations of French news items. Auguste Lannuier was part of this vibrant subculture, and in the vanguard of those attempting to create and satisfy a taste among New Yorkers for refined French luxuries. In so doing, he paved the way for his younger brother, Honoré, and other French-immigrant craftsmen and retail merchants who came to New York in large numbers, especially after the fall of Napoleon.

In light of the fact that French fashion was not immediately or universally accepted by New Yorkers during the Federal period, it is intriguing to imagine the reception Lannuier may have received, and the type of clientele he attracted. The kind of upper-class customers he hoped to gain in New York is suggested by the family represented in a painting by the artist François-Joseph Bourgoin—a French artist from the West Indies, who came to New York via Philadelphia—executed in New York in 1807 (plate 27). The painting may depict the home and family of John Robert and Eliza Livingston, the brother and sister-in-law of Chancellor Robert Livingston, who served as the American minister to France from 1801 to 1804.[79] The room setting is conservatively stylish overall, but not particularly French; in fact, the carpeting and much of the furniture are decidedly English in character, as are the father's tight black breeches. (In fashionable French circles, high-waisted, full-length trousers were *de rigueur.*) The red tôle Argand lamps above the mantel appear to be French, however, and the mother's hairstyle and dress have a certain Gallic flair. On the whole, the setting and its occupants accord nicely with contemporary accounts published by the British traveler John Lambert of the homes and the personal style of wealthy New Yorkers:

Their houses are furnished with every thing that is useful, agreeable, or ornamental; and many of them are fitted up in the tasteful magnificence of modern style. The dress of the gentlemen is plain, elegant, and fashionable, and corresponds in every respect with the English costume. The ladies in general seem more partial to the light, various, and dashing drapery of the Parisian belles, than to the elegant and becoming attire of our London beauties, who improve upon the French fashions. But there are many who prefer the English costume, or at least a medium between that and the French. . . . I . . . believe . . . that there existed a sort of rivalry among the New York beauties . . . methought I could discern a pretty "Democrat" a la mode Francoise [*sic*], and a sweet little Federalist a la mode Angloise [*sic*]. I know not whether my surmises were just; but it is certain that Mrs. Toole and Madame Bouchard, the two rival leaders of fashion . . . have each their partisan admirers: one because she is an Englishwoman, and the other because she is French.[80]

There may be some truth to these observations with regard to furniture fashions as well. It is hard to escape the analogy of Mrs. Toole and Madame Bouchard, for instance, when comparing two contemporary New York marble-topped consoles or pier tables: one, a first-rate example from the Sheraton-derived, pillar-and-claw, "Phyfe" school, and the other, a pure French Consulat form, labeled by Lannuier (fig. 30, and plate 28). Extending this analogy a bit further, Lambert's comments about the preference of some New York ladies for costumes "at least a medium" between English and French tastes would seem applicable to a multipurpose gaming table by Lannuier (plate 11). Lannuier modified the pure French form of this kind of table, known in France as a *table à trictrac*, for local consumption by grafting onto it the ubiquitous New York reeded-and-turned leg identical in design to those used by the cabinetmaker George Woodruff on a Pembroke table of about 1810 (fig. 31).

The style of furniture made by Lannuier during his time in New York seems to fall into two broad phases, each encompassing roughly half of his sixteen-year career. The first phase was dominated by his attempts to establish purely French styles and forms in New

FIGURE 30. New York maker. Pier table. 1810–15. Mahogany and mahogany veneer, 36¾ x 41⅞ x 21 in. Collection Mr. and Mrs. Peter G. Terian

PLATE 28. Charles-Honoré Lannuier. Square pier table. 1805–10 (cat. no. 94)

York, combined with a willingness to make furniture that was "at least a medium" between the Anglo-based local vernacular and pure French taste. The second phase represents the denouement of his career, when French furniture forms had finally caught on and he was able to develop his own distinctive, luxuriously ornamented "American Empire" style.

The Pure French Styles: Furniture à l'anglaise, le goût moderne, *and* le goût antique

The earliest signed and dated work by Lannuier is a rather squat inlaid mahogany table with carved-and-reeded legs and a brass-bound marble top (plate 16), which, traditionally, is reputed to be made of marble specimens collected in Crete by the wife of Commodore Richard Valentine Morris (1768–1815), the leader of a U.S. naval squadron in the Mediterranean in 1802–3. On the concealed side of a board that forms a well under the marble top of this table is the chalk inscription "*fait a new-york/le 26 Decembre/1804*," crowned by Lannuier's conjoined initials (fig. 17). The table also bears his earliest printed label (see fig. 87), which appears on only one other documented table (see plate 7)—a small, exquisitely refined example in satinwood, crossbanded with a dark, exotic hardwood; the ebony stringing on the drawer fronts is identical in pattern to the lightwood holly stringing on the specimen marble table. The slim, attenuated Tuscan columns of the satinwood table are characteristic of the simplicity and restraint of post-Revolutionary French furniture of the 1790s, some of which took as its inspiration the published Neoclassical designs of Hepplewhite and Sheraton; their pattern books, equipped with French translations, were disseminated across the Channel to an appreciative audience of *ébénistes* and designers, who admired English furniture for its workmanship, functionality, and understated elegance. The use of satinwood also had strong English overtones in France, as indicated by this comment in the *Journal des Luxus* in April 1794: "In England, mahogany has been dethroned by a novelty, which charms us by its lemon-yellow colour. Because of its satin brilliance, we commonly called it *bois des iles* or Satin Wood."[81]

Another example of Lannuier's early work with strong English overtones is a pier table of mahogany and satinwood veneers (plate 17) that in scale and ambition presages some of his later monumental carved-and-gilded masterpieces. Its close stylistic affinity with the dated specimen marble table suggests that the two must be nearly contemporary, although the pier table has to be considered as the slightly later example because it bears Lannuier's second printed label (see plate 67), which appears on some furniture that stylistically is much later in date (cat. no. 98). The inverted cup-like device at the top of the turned, tapered legs is found on a number of English tables of similar form from the 1790s, where it is sometimes reeded. Here, however, it is carved in classic New York fashion, with each pendant water leaf made up of a series of gadroons separated by a central vein. The drawer front, with its astragal-ended satinwood panel; the inlaid paterae on the top blocks of the legs; the precise reeded urn on the cross stretchers; and even the English socket casters—which, rather ironically, terminate the unmistakably French-style feet—make this table Lannuier's great homage to English Neoclassical furniture design. These three special examples of furniture *à l'anglaise*—a style that Nicolas Lannuier might have offered to the sophisticated and somewhat daring French clientele of his Paris shop in the 1790s, who were willing to adopt the tastes of their nation's sworn enemy—may represent Honoré's earliest attempts to please a largely Anglo-centric New York market at a time when the Sheraton-based New York "Phyfe style" was still in its formative stages.

Light, elegant furniture in a style referred to today as Directoire, but known in France during the 1790s as *le goût moderne*, together with the more massive, architectural, and archaeologically correct forms of *le goût antique* that succeeded it in the Consulat period, were the models that served as Honoré Lannuier's stylistic legacy in New York. Roughly concurrent with his arrival was the introduction of a new fashion journal in Paris, the *Collection de Meubles et Objets de Goût*, published in serial form by Pierre de La Mésangère beginning in 1802.[82] The advent of this serial publication was especially fortuitous and timely for Lannuier, for whom it functioned as an excellent marketing tool. Filling its pages were attractive colored engravings of all the luxury items that appealed to the newly wealthy French bourgeoisie—dresses and bonnets, handsome coaches, and, most importantly from our perspective, adaptations of the latest creations by the leading *ébénistes* of Paris. In his inaugural advertisement Lannuier maintained that he had brought "new patterns" with him from France, for the purpose of making "all kinds of Furniture, Beds, Chairs, & c. in the newest and latest French fashion."[83] The relationship of several of his earliest and purest French designs to illustrations in La Mésangère's publication makes it clear that the journal was their source. One can imagine the surprise and delight of New Yorkers at having the latest Parisian forms and styles illustrated in La Mésangère available to them either for immediate purchase or by custom order at Lannuier's "Magasin de Meubles les plus à la Mode."

Furniture in *le goût moderne* became popular in France about the time of the Revolution and remained so for over a decade into the Consulat period (1799–1804), as evidenced by some of the reproductions in early editions of La Mésangère's journal (see plate 4). These showed essentially Late Louis XVI-style forms, simplified to suit the prevailing mood of the new French Republic. Furniture in this style has as one of its dominant formal characteristics fluted or reeded legs or columns at the corners, which frequently extend up through the frame to form turrets near the top, although examples with plain tapered legs are also known. Sometimes this furniture was quite plain and relied for its aesthetic appeal solely on fine proportions and beautifully matched mahogany veneers (fig. 32). In its most striking and expensive form, however, it was inlaid and outlined with sheet brass and wood-core brass moldings, which gave it a severe, hard-edged quality reflective of sober Republican attitudes and the firm rejection of the overwrought Louis XVI court style. Lannuier's three early pier tables (plate 12; see also fig. 11 and cat. no. 90), the only known examples by him in this austere brass-bound style, relate closely both to designs illustrated by La Mésangère and to examples made and sold by his brother Nicolas in Paris (see fig. 10). That so little furniture of

FIGURE 32. Bernard Molitor.
Secrétaire à abattant. 1789–98.
Mahogany and mahogany veneer,
54 x 37 x 15 in. Galerie Daxer and
Marshall, Munich

this type by Honoré has come down to us may be explained by the fact that the style was on the decline in France by the early 1800s, and some Americans considered it too risky a choice because it carried with it connotations of the excesses of the French Revolution. Interestingly, James Monroe had no qualms about buying a stylish suite of furniture in *le goût moderne* when he served as minister to France in the mid-1790s. Monroe brought this furniture back to America, where it is still preserved today, at the Monroe Foundation in Fredericksburg, Virginia. Monroe, a confirmed Francophile, purchased French furniture again in 1817, when he was President, for use in the Executive Mansion—a decision that created political problems, however, for some citizens felt that he should have set an example by patronizing the American cabinetmaking industry.[84]

Echoes of *le goût moderne* resonate in early-nineteenth-century New York furniture in the numerous examples with reeded or fluted columns and touches of brass highlighting rich mahogany veneers. A pair of marble-topped pier tables (one of which is illustrated here: plate 29); a large dressing glass, or *psyché* (see fig. 70); a monumental French press, or armoire (fig. 33); and a simple but elegant mahogany bureau (fig. 34) all have design features derived from *le goût moderne*. The French press and the bureau, in particular, display a strong visual kinship to a mahogany *secrétaire à abattant* made in Paris in the 1790s (fig. 32).

In the years leading up to Lannuier's departure from France, furniture was undergoing a significant change as the elegant but rather astringent style of *le goût moderne* gradually was replaced by the more monumental and massive forms of *le goût antique*. The earliest issues of

PLATE 29. New York maker. Pier table. About 1815. Mahogany and mahogany veneer, 34 x 36 x 15½ in. The Metropolitan Museum of Art, New York. Gift of John C. Cattus, 1967

FIGURE 33. New York maker. French press. About 1815. Mahogany and mahogany veneer, 93 x 58 x 26½ in. The Metropolitan Museum of Art, New York. Bequest of Maria Dehon Polk, 1941

FIGURE 34. New York maker. Bureau. About 1810. Mahogany and mahogany veneer, 47¾ x 45½ x 22½ in. Boscobel Restoration, Inc., Garrison-on-Hudson, New York

La Mésangère's *Collection de Meubles* indicate that at least for a time *le goût moderne* and *le goût antique* coexisted (see plates 4, 5, and 97). However, by 1805, when the following critical comments on furniture in the new style appeared in the *Journal des dames*, *le goût moderne* seems to have been in decline: "Furniture that was made only a few years ago, so light and so fragile that we were afraid to touch it, is today so massive and so heavy with smooth surfaces and bronze accessories that we can scarcely move it. When a lady enters a modern salon, it takes two gentlemen to bring her an antique chair."[85] These new foursquare conceptions, based on ancient architectural forms such as altar tables and pedestals, were made in a variety of shapes and sizes that were adapted to meet the functional needs of modern living. Their imposing, monumental character was achieved through the combination of broad planar surfaces of a rich uniform tone with clearly delineated tectonic features arranged logically, according to the classical architectural principles of symmetry and balance. The predominant structural and ornamental features were raised plinths often supported by carved paw feet painted a beautiful sea green in imitation of the patina on excavated bronze, flanking columns and pilasters with cast-brass capitals and bases, and broad friezes with classically derived gilded-brass ornaments distributed across their façades.

Among Lannuier's purest examples in *le goût antique* are five pier tables or consoles (plates 28 and 30; see also plate 79, and cat. nos. 95 and 96), three commodes or French bureaus (see plate 9, and cat. nos. 45 and 46), a bedstead (cat. no. 2), and two nearly identical, exquisitely proportioned card tables that capture in small scale the precise outlines and geometric clarity of the style (plate 31, and cat. no. 53). The pier tables have either tapered term supports, with carved wooden Egyptian- and Grecian-style busts in imitation of the cast-bronze busts found on French examples, or round columns veneered in mahogany with gilded cast-brass capitals and bases. Each of Lannuier's three early pier tables with round columns has rather small ornaments of the same design on its frieze, which suggests that

PLATE 30. Charles-Honoré Lannuier. Square pier table. 1805–10 (cat. no. 92)

73

PLATE 31. Charles-Honoré Lannuier. Card table. 1805–12 (cat. no. 54)

FIGURE 35. New York maker.
Square pier table. About 1810.
Satinwood veneer, 36⅛ x 52⅜ x
20⅛ in. Collection Mr. and Mrs.
Stuart P. Feld

they all were made fairly close in time. Small ornaments like these appear to be an early feature of furniture in *le goût antique* in New York. However, New York furniture made before 1812 in this pure French style is quite rare, and few examples other than those by Lannuier are known. An elegant satinwood pier table by an unknown maker, with white marble columns and small-scale gilded cast-brass ornaments, is among these (fig. 35), and may be the work of another French *ébéniste* in New York, possibly even one of Lannuier's in-laws, the Molles, or his first cousin Jean-Charles Cochois.

Merging Pure French Style with the New York Vernacular

From the start, Lannuier was affected by the native-born craftsmen he encountered in New York and by the furniture that they offered for sale on a daily basis at their warerooms around the city. His brass-inlaid pier table in the modern taste, of 1803–10 (plate 12), utilizes the standard New York reeded leg between the upper frame and the lower shelf, as does his previously mentioned trictrac table (plate 11)—a clear indication that Lannuier was not averse to introducing aspects of the local vernacular into his work. Based on the evidence of his documented furniture, it appears that almost never did Lannuier adopt verbatim the styles of his many talented competitors, the most conspicuous of whom was Duncan Phyfe. There was an attempt by the architect and collector Edward Vason Jones, in an article published in *The American Art Journal* in 1977, to widen the body of known Lannuier work by attributing to him a substantial number of anonymous examples from the Sheraton-based Phyfe school, through some finicky connoisseurship that relied on matching singular features found on documented Lannuier furniture with similar ones that appear on undocumented pieces. The article, although admirable in its intent, greatly oversimplifies the entire matter by ignoring totally the complexities of the New York cabinetmaking trade in the period from 1800 to 1820, when hundreds of talented journeymen worked on their own as well as for others, upholding an accepted standard of workmanship and in a

FIGURE 36. Jacob frères. Fauteuil made for General Jean-Victor-Marie Moreau. About 1800. Mahogany, 35 x 23⅛ x 25¾ in. Musée National du Château de Fontainebleau, France

sanctioned style.[86] Jones's discovery of a labeled Pembroke table by Lannuier (plate 32) that is clearly in the mainstream of New York furniture design of the period 1810–20 makes understandable his attempts to relate to it other unattributed examples in this style. If Lannuier did, indeed, produce much furniture like this, one must question why more labeled examples have not surfaced. Perhaps future discoveries will shed more light on this aspect of Lannuier's work.

Lannuier's skill at marrying new and diverse influences with his French design aesthetic is apparent in a square card table of about 1810–12 (plate 22): Its upper section has the precise, clear-cut outlines of French Consulat forms in *le goût antique*, accentuated by inlaid-brass ornaments scattered like Egyptian hieroglyphics across its frieze-like apron. The four Tuscan columns that support the top are also French in origin and are strikingly similar to those on a fauteuil, now at Fontainebleau, originally made for the Paris home of General Jean-Victor-Marie Moreau about 1800 (fig. 36). The table's overall design, however, with its pillar-and-claw base, is strongly English in character, and its saber-shaped legs, or "claws," are reeded and carved in classic New York Phyfe-school fashion. The diversity of sources apparent in this table makes it uniquely American—and something Lannuier could never have dreamed up had he remained in Paris.

The great masterpiece of Lannuier's amalgamated style is a superbly balanced and proportioned gueridon also of about 1810 (see plate 10) that miraculously incorporates within its compact form the warmth and color of figured mahogany, satinwood, patinated metalwork, and soft-toned Italian marbles. Gueridons are distinctly French table forms,

PLATE 33. Cast metal bust. Detail of the Lannuier gueridon, plate 10 (cat. no. 116)

generally round, with marble tops. In this small gem, one of the first examples of its kind made in America, Lannuier seamlessly melds typical New York serpentine legs of a type sometimes seen on seating forms such as chairs and window benches (see plate 50) into his design, transforming them into term supports with gilded and bronzed cast-metal classical busts (plate 33). In their general outline, these supports presage the shapes of the bodies of the winged figures on a much grander center table, or gueridon (plate 34), and on other table forms made in New York in the latter part of Lannuier's career.

A few other examples of Lannuier's furniture that display motifs often associated with Phyfe are also worth noting. The set of twenty-four armchairs (see plate 62) he made for New York's City Hall in 1812 has a French character because of the square backs and "French elbows" (or arms mortised on the stumps of the front legs), but the chairs also incorporate the ubiquitous Phyfe-school urn-shaped turnings with water-leaf carvings under the handholds. Another circumstance that makes these chairs less purely French is the distinct probability that they were made under the general direction of the architect in charge of the project, John McComb, whose personal library included a copy of Sheraton's pattern book, which depicts an anglicized version of French upholstered chairs.[87] For the most part, Lannuier avoided using the familiar New York motif of the carved urn on his furniture. Nonetheless, its appearance on the City Hall armchairs and his marked inclination to borrow other typical New York features raise the possibility that he made more furniture with carved urns than his documented work suggests. An intriguing pair of swivel-top, pillar-and-claw card tables

PLATE 34. Charles-Honoré Lannuier. Center table (gueridon). 1812–17 (cat. no. 115)

FIGURE 37. New York maker. Card table. 1810–15. Mahogany and mahogany veneer, 30⅛ x 36½ x 18⅛ in. The White House, Washington, D.C.

with carved-urn supports (now at The White House; fig. 37) shares several distinctive features associated with Lannuier's labeled work: the deep cavetto moldings beneath the lower leaf, brass-baguette moldings along the top edges, and veneered candle corners. On the other hand, the square panels at the center of the apron and at the corners seem antithetical to Lannuier's typical emphasis on smooth, frieze-like aprons with clean, veneer-wrapped corners, thus making it difficult to assign this pair of tables to him with confidence.

The documented pillar-and-claw tables that bear Lannuier's printed label always have four pillars on an octagonal block. These pillars can be in the form of plain columns or of double-ogee balusters, with the lower balusters enveloped in water-leaf carvings executed in the conventional New York manner with a central vein flanked by a series of gadroons. Wrapped around the baluster thus (plate 35), this type of carving takes on a more sculptural, naturalistic appearance than it has when it is used for the standard New York urns (fig. 37). During the second decade of the nineteenth century, naturalistically carved ogee balusters largely supplanted urns with water-leaf carvings as supports on pillar-and-claw tables, and the possibility exists—although it is difficult to prove—that Lannuier was the innovator in introducing this motif, just as Phyfe might have been for the carved urn. Balusters and other architectural forms lushly enveloped in acanthus leaves appear regularly on pedestals and candelabra in Percier and Fontaine's *Recueil*, which emphasized the elaborateness of Roman rather than the clarity of Greek designs,[88] and Lannuier consistently displays an inclination toward such ornamentation in his work. The back supports on his figural card tables, for instance, are based on antique candelabra and have Corinthian columns sprouting from naturalistic buds (plate 26), and the water-leaf carving on a unique set of chairs owned by the Baltimore merchant James Bosley (plate 36) wraps and molds itself around the incurvate legs, which emerge at the base like new shoots or tendrils. Close examination of the legs reveals that the leaves are formed from the typical New York-style gadroons (fig. 38). It is interesting to compare these Lannuier chairs with a more typical New York example of the kind often credited to Phyfe (plate 37).

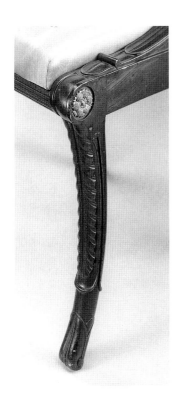

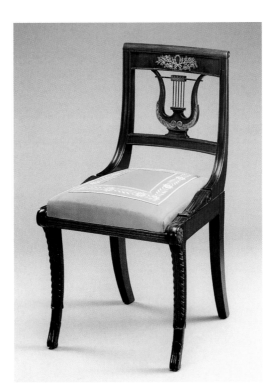

FIGURE 38. Front leg. Detail of the side chair attributed to Lannuier, plate 36 (cat. no. 36)

PLATE 36. Attributed to Charles-Honoré Lannuier. Side chair. 1815–19 (cat. no. 36)

PLATE 37. Possibly by Duncan Phyfe. Side chair. About 1815. Mahogany and mahogany veneer: Height, 32¼ in. The Metropolitan Museum of Art, New York. Gift of the family of Mr. and Mrs. Andrew Varick Stout, in their memory, 1965

Lannuier's Mature Antique Style, and the Triumph of French Forms

American Empire is a designation no longer popular among academics and connoisseurs of American furniture of the Late Federal period, who prefer to call this furniture classical. The term regains some currency when discussing Lannuier's luxuriously ornamented antique-style furniture of the period from 1812 to 1819, however, which clearly was intended to provide customers with the monumental grandeur of French Empire designs. It was during this time that Lannuier gained renown, and he seemed to develop a single-minded sense of purpose both as a designer and a businessman, concentrating his furniture line on a few signature forms that, over time, would cement his reputation as one of America's foremost artistic cabinetmakers. This was also the time when some of the pure French forms he pioneered in the early 1800s finally took hold and captured the imaginations of a generation of Americans for whom French-style dressing glasses, marble-topped pier tables, center tables, bedsteads, bureaus, armoires, and sideboards would become *de rigueur* through the 1830s.

Labeled examples of Lannuier's furniture in his highly decorative style, with only two exceptions,[89] all have his handsome engraved bilingual label (plate 13) that in itself is highly expressive of the trend in French furniture, during the Napoleonic era, toward more massive, richly ornamented architectural conceptions. The dressing glass depicted on the label, of a type known as a *psyché* in France, was described for the first time in 1817 in the New York cabinetmakers' price books, where it was called a "screen dressing glass." Given that it is a distinctly French form, and was chosen by Lannuier as his trademark, one might expect to find a *psyché* among Lannuier's documented work. Such is not the case, however, for all the surviving examples are of unknown authorship, including the one depicted in figure 70.

A pre- and a post-1812 pier table by Lannuier provide an excellent means of comparison to show the changes that occurred over time in *le goût antique* (plates 28, 42). Although essentially of the same rectilinear form, the later example is profusely decorated with larger and more naturalistic gilded cast-brass and composition ornaments, while its white statuary marble columns and massive lion's-paw feet add to its impression of monumentality and antiquity. Another pier table (plate 24) shows Lannuier at his novel and innovative best, demonstrating how he achieved extraordinary results by utilizing uncommon materials. For the front supports of this labeled and stamped pier table that epitomizes the later phase of *le goût antique,* Lannuier used cast white-metal caryatid figures like those found on large French fluid-burning bronze lamps, only he gilded them to mask the inferior metal. Lamps may have been part of his line of imported French metalwork products and fancy goods in the later stages of his career, and thus would have been available to him if he wished to make patterns from them.

Marble-topped pier tables with looking-glass plates at the back comprise over twenty percent of Lannuier's known oeuvre, so we can be certain that they were one of his French specialities. Due to their site-specific dimension requirements, these tables probably were custom ordered most of the time—a suspicion borne out by the variations in size, and especially in width, among those examples by Lannuier that are known. They were meant to stand against the part of the wall between two windows known architecturally as a pier (plate 38), a function that resulted in their being called pier tables instead of consoles in England and America. Either a tall, framed looking-glass plate of the same width as that at the back of the table, or a smaller, carved-and-gilded example would have been attached to the piers above the table. The former treatment best conveyed the intended effect of luminous reflection and limitless space, which is depicted in an 1808 plate in La Mésangère's *Collection de Meubles* (plate 20). In one instance, the purchase of a Lannuier pier table can be placed close in time to the building of a new architect-designed house. Unfortunately, it has not been possible to document the degree of participation and the dynamics among the

PLATE 38. Charles-Honoré Lannuier. Square pier table with canted corners. 1815–19 (cat. no. 112). The table is shown *in situ* in the Richmond Room, The American Wing, The Metropolitan Museum of Art, New York

client, the architect, Lannuier, and the upholsterer, all of whom collaborated to create one of these stylish ensembles.

That French-style pier tables had captured the fancy of New Yorkers by the 1810s is confirmed by the inclusion of the form for the first time in an undated pre-1815 list of additional, revised prices meant to be tipped into the 1810 edition of the New York cabinetmakers' price book in which the type was described in its most basic form, without extras, as a: "Square Pier Table—Three feet long, one foot six inches wide, framing five inches deep; rail veneered; framed with flush stumps or mitre dovetail'd; to stand on [a] framed plinth of hard wood, with two braces across ditto; plain turned columns in front, framed with a pin prepared by the Turner; square pillars at back framed with tenons." All the French design features are accounted for: a square format with no top because marble was intended, the deep veneered rail or frieze, columns at the front, and a raised plinth. Even "rabbiting [*sic*] the back to receive a glass" was cited in the list of extras that followed.[90] Probably because of several unfortunate accidents, the next published edition of the New York price book in 1817 included the following payment arrangement in the preamble: "When glass plates are put in any piece of work, [the master is required] to pay five percent on the value thereof, the workman to take the risk. It shall be optional by the employer to have them put in by the workman or not."[91] Given the risk and expense involved, every master cabinetmaker may not have kept looking-glass plates in stock or handled them regularly. Such may have been the case with a dressing-glass frame priced at $135 that Lannuier made for James Brinckerhoff in June 1816. A search of the family's papers has revealed that one month before, Brinckerhoff had purchased a looking-glass plate for $75 from Charles Del Vecchio.[92] Did Lannuier have one of his workmen install this looking-glass plate or was the installation the responsibility of the client and the looking-glass retailer? The fragile and expensive nature of looking-glass plates, which were imported from England, France, and Germany, was sure to have been a cause of conflict. One can almost hear the journeyman at his bench slyly commenting, "I wouldn't touch that monstrous glass with a ten-foot pole, but for seven percent."

In addition to French-style square pier tables, five additional new French forms became standard items produced in New York between 1810 and the end of Lannuier's life. One of these was the *psyché*, or "screen dressing glass," which already has been discussed. The remaining four furniture forms were designated specifically as "French," and comprise a sideboard, press, and bedstead, all of which appeared for the first time in the June 1810 price book, and a bureau, which appeared for the first time in the pre-1815 revised price list referred to earlier. The several updated and revised versions of the price books, which were issued between 1810 and the end of Lannuier's career, are a sign of the vitality of the cabinetmaking trade in New York and of the pressures this highly competitive environment put on master cabinetmakers to strive for novelty and innovation. The firm establishment of French furniture forms in New York by 1810, as evidenced by their inclusion in the price books, is unprecedented in any other American city, and must be considered to have been a personal triumph for Lannuier.

Very little case furniture by Lannuier survives, but what does fits exactly the descriptions of French forms in the price books. Standard and optional features of his previously discussed commodes in *le goût antique* (see plate 9) are enumerated under the heading "French Bureau" in the pre-1815 list of additional revised prices; some of these include: "three drawers veneered outside . . . making the upper drawer to lap over the legs . . . a plinth three inches wide or under with a molding on the edge . . . preparing and gluing on blocks for pilasters, and breaking the plinth round ditto," and, in the instance of the example with cupboard doors below (cat. no. 46), "when made with flat panel doors below the top drawer . . . extra from drawers."[93] Two other French bureaus with attached dressing

FIGURE 40. Attributed to Bernard Molitor. *Desserte*. 1808–10. Mahogany, 38⅜ x 78¾ x 24 in. Private collection

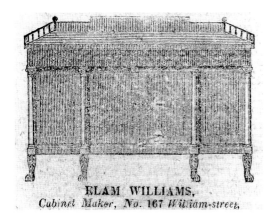

FIGURE 39. Charles-Honoré Lannuier. French bureau with dressing glass. 1815–19 (cat. no. 47)

FIGURE 41. French sideboard. Advertisement in the [New York] *Mercantile Advertiser*, April 17, 1813

glasses, probably made near the end of Lannuier's career (fig. 39, and cat. no. 48), are of a more complicated and less coherent design, due perhaps to the dual function they were meant to serve. During the Empire period, French *ébénistes* and designers experimented with a wide range of table and bureau forms with attached dressing glasses, many of which were suspended between smooth veneered columns with gilded cast-brass capitals and bases of the type Lannuier used on these bureaus on the front of the case. French-style bureaus with attached dressing glasses became increasingly popular in New York during the 1820s, and numerous examples are known. Many of these are decorated extensively with freehand gilding and stenciled designs that imitated the effect of the applied gilded-brass ornaments and die-stamped brass borders popular in the Lannuier era.

Lannuier's only known sideboard (plate 23), in keeping with the later phase of *le goût antique*, is monumental in scale, and has brilliantly figured matched veneers of crotch mahogany. It clearly derives from the *desserte* (fig. 40)—a French furniture form that served the same function as a sideboard. During the Consulat and Empire periods, the *desserte* was characterized by three upper drawers that overlap the case, four veneered columns, and four lower cupboard doors—the very same features used to describe a "French sideboard" in the 1810 New York price book. Totally alien to the French aesthetic, however, and an obvious nod to English sideboard design, is the heavy backboard on Lannuier's example. French sideboards were the most expensive type available in New York in the 1810s and were made

by all the major shops. In his account books, John Hewitt describes a "French Sideboard like Phyfe's" with "2 shelves in [the] center and as many locks as possible."[94] An example of the form is also depicted in an 1813 New York newspaper advertisement (fig. 41), which attests to the growing popularity of the type. A modified version of the French sideboard with its central cupboard section removed was called a pedestal-end sideboard in the 1817 price book. Examples of this type could accommodate a cellarette, which was designed to hold an evening's selection of dinner wines, in the opening created between the pedestal ends (fig. 42). Pedestal-end sideboards and cellarettes were English forms, so, here again, we see New York cabinetmakers in the 1810s borrowing and blending both French and English sources to create novel and exciting new forms. Lannuier may have made sideboards with "cylinder pedestal ends," as suggested by an advertisement for an auction in 1815 that proclaimed that all the mahogany furniture of the "Mansion House, known by [the name of] the Hermitage" was "made by Mr. Lannuier"; included among this furniture was a sideboard that fits this description.[95]

A New York furniture form often improperly called a wardrobe by scholars and collectors alike is referred to in the price books as a "French press." Its design antecedent is a large, two-door clothing cupboard, a type known in France as an armoire and in Germany and the Netherlands as a *Schrank* and a *kast*, respectively. These large, two-door cupboards were known in Europe from the Middle Ages, but by the Early Baroque period, in England, the form had been rejected for domestic use, and was replaced by a version with a cupboard section over a range of drawers. In New York, cabinetmakers differentiated between the two types, calling the first a "French press," and the latter a "wardrobe." This is an important distinction because it reveals the leverage French styles had gained in New York by the second decade of the nineteenth century. The defining characteristic of a French press, as stated in the 1810 price book, was its "two flat panelled doors, with two panels in each," as opposed to the wardrobe, which, in the same edition, was described as being built "in two carcases; three long drawers in the lower part, veneered and cock-beaded; two flat panelled [*sic*] doors, four trays inside."[96] The pre-1815 list of additional revised prices includes

FIGURE 44. Signature of Charles-Honoré Lannuier, inscribed in the base of a plaster bust. Detail of the French press, figure 43 (cat. no. 49)

FIGURE 43. Charles-Honoré Lannuier. French press. 1812–19 (cat. no. 49)

the following options: "Three quarter rounding the front legs. . . . When pieces glued on for paws or turning. . . . Fitting the cornice to ditto (the piece prepared by the Turner), each corner"[97]—features that, as previously discussed, are derived from French furniture in *le goût moderne*. A New York French press with precisely these optional features is shown in figure 33.

Lannuier's three known French presses (fig. 43, and cat. nos. 50, 51) eschew engaged columns, but they are monumental in scale and lavish in their use of the best crotch-mahogany veneers. One of these presses (fig. 43), once owned by the New York hardware merchant Garret Abeel, has a cast-plaster bust on the pediment, which was discovered to have Lannuier's name inscribed in its base (fig. 44). This may represent another instance in which Lannuier made a pattern from imported French metalwork. He may also have had access to some of the patinated and partially gilded cast-bronze busts of ancient Greek and Roman figures of similar scale that frequently were mounted on the posts of French Consulat and Empire bedsteads, as illustrated by La Mésangère (plate 39; see also plate 55). Microscopic analyses of the finish layers on the bust indicate that originally it was patinated to look like antique bronze.[98]

The form of French bedstead initially recorded in the 1810 New York price book was fairly simple in design, but increasingly elaborate versions were described in later revised price lists, as well as in the 1817 price book. These new-model bedsteads, which joined the

1. *Table de Nuit*. 2. *Lit Ordinaire*. 3. *Table à la Tronchin*.

Rue Montmartre, N° 132.

PLATE 39.   Pierre de La Mésangère. Design for a *lit ordinaire* (Plate 3 from *Collection de Meubles et Objets de Goût*). 1802. Colored engraving, 7¾ x 12¼ in. The Metropolitan Museum of Art, New York. Harris Brisbane Dick Fund, 1930

FIGURE 45. Plate 7 from *The New-York Book of Prices for Manufacturing Cabinet and Chair Work.* 1817

existing high- and low-post and field bedsteads that had been listed in the price books since 1796, were the most expensive available, due to the considerable amount of veneering and cabinetwork involved in their paneled ends. These bedsteads were called French because of their equal-height headboards and footboards, which usually scrolled outward. Bedsteads of this type were staples of the cabinetmaker's and upholsterer's art in late-eighteenth-century France, and were usually placed parallel to a wall, occasionally in alcoves or niches. One of the earliest French-style bedsteads to have been imported to America was a Louis XVI example once owned by Colonel James Swan of Boston (fig. 47).[99]

The description of the basic French bedstead in the 1810 price book, exclusive of extras, is of a model "Three feet wide, with scroll ends, one panel in each, to come within five inches of the top of the scroll, all plain, a frame for a sacking bottom."[100] Under the same heading in the pre-1815 list of additional revised prices the following new options appear: "Preparing for carving and fixing eagle's heads on straight turn'd posts on fronts . . . straight posts six feet high, at the back . . . preparing and framing two sweep'd arms of plank, one bed screw in each to receive a canopy . . . canopy to be paid for according to time."[101] Finally, by 1817, the French bedstead had reached its zenith, and two distinct models were listed in the new price book that year: "French Bedstead No. 1," which repeats verbatim the original 1810 model and the later revisions, and a new and wonderfully elaborate version, logically but rather prosaically dubbed, "French Bedstead No. 2."[102] Line drawings of the two different patterns for the scrolled ends on French bedstead "No. 2" are included in a separate plate at the back of the 1817 price book (fig. 45).

Lannuier's extant French bedsteads closely parallel the descriptions in the price books. There is one with eagles' heads on turned front posts (plate 40), and two made originally with "sweep'd arms of plank" to support the canopy (see plate 49, and cat. no. 2). The bedstead marked jointly by Lannuier and his cousin J.-C. Cochois (plate 14) and the one that Lannuier made for Stephen Van Rensselaer IV about 1817 (see plate 54) have scrolled ends so remarkably close to the patterns shown in the 1817 price book that it seems likely that Lannuier was responsible for having the designs included in the publication. The Van Rensselaer French bedstead is simply the richest and most beautiful ever made in America. In 1812–13, as a young man, its original owner is known to have traveled in France, where, not only was he presented at court but he was steeped in the art and culture of the Empire period.[103] The bedstead has such unique, high-quality applied gilded ornaments and mounts compared to most Lannuier furniture (plate 41), and is so close to a published plate in Percier and Fontaine's *Recueil* (fig. 46), that one might even suspect that Stephen Van Rensselaer, armed with a copy of Percier and Fontaine and some very site-specific gilded-brass mounts purchased in Paris, collaborated on the overall design. The dynamics of the relationship between the client and craftsman are almost always lost to history, but this bedstead presents the most intriguing possibilities that an interchange of ideas occurred between the two parties.

Of course, cabinetwork represented only part of what comprised a finished bed. Mattresses, yards and yards of fabric, trims, and specialized hardware and other accoutrements necessary to dress a bedstead in a sumptuous, elegant style were also required. French bedsteads typically had curtains suspended from above, either from an attached canopy or crown or by other ingenious methods that ranged from a simple ring in the ceiling to elaborate gilded-and-bronzed eagles (plate 39; see also plate 55). These additional materials and the upholsterer's charges would have made the cabinetmaker's labor costs seem relatively minor compared to the overall expense of the bedstead. Lannuier prepared his bedsteads for later dressing in certain characteristic ways that are not necessarily obvious to the casual observer. The bottom, on which the hair and the feather mattresses were piled, most often

PLATE 40. Charles-Honoré Lannuier. French bedstead. 1810–15 (cat. no. 3)

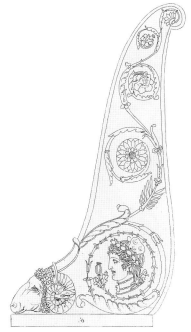

FIGURE 46. Percier and Fontaine. Design for the end of a bedstead (detail of Plate 15 from *Recueil de décorations intérieures*). 1812. Engraving, 11⅞ x 8½ in. The Metropolitan Museum of Art, New York. Harris Brisbane Dick Fund, 1928

consisted of a loose type of frame, which rested on short, stub-like tenons inserted in the rails (plate 14; see also plate 54). Bottoms of this type, which were listed as "extra" in the New York price book entries for bedsteads after 1810, have been observed by this author on beds in France that date to about 1800 or slightly earlier. Another typically French functional feature found on several Lannuier bedsteads is large wooden casters in iron frames (plate 15). Casters this size, which made it easier to move a fully dressed bed away from the wall for cleaning or when the curtains had to be changed, can be seen in the plate in La Mésangère's *Collection de Meubles* that also served as the basis for the curtain treatment on the French bedstead by Lannuier originally owned by Isaac Bell (plate 39; see also plate 49). The earlier, imported Louis XVI bedstead in the Museum of Fine Arts, Boston, also has large casters (fig. 47). In *The Cabinet Dictionary*, there is a description by Sheraton of "Large French casters, for the largest and best beds, the wheel of which is fixed to a bar of iron, which is made with transverse straps at each end, by which the caster is screwed to the underside of the rails of the bed."[104] The use of these French casters is quite rare on American bedsteads before 1820, restricted so far to bedsteads by Lannuier; three of them have such casters. Their presence on a high-post bedstead of supreme quality in the Winterthur Museum (cat. no. 10) therefore adds further weight to Charles Montgomery's attribution of it to Lannuier, although he failed to mention the casters in his entry on the bedstead in Winterthur's catalogue of Federal furniture.

The existence of this bedstead and of two other documented ones by Lannuier (cat. nos. 8, 9) confirms that he also made high-post bedsteads. While the other examples probably were not executed until after 1815, they have equal-height headboards and footboards similar in profile to the Louis XVI bed in the Boston Museum of Fine Arts (fig. 47). A third variety by Lannuier is also known, but, unfortunately, only from the literature (fig. 48); it, too, has headboards and footboards of equal height, but there are unusual terminals on the

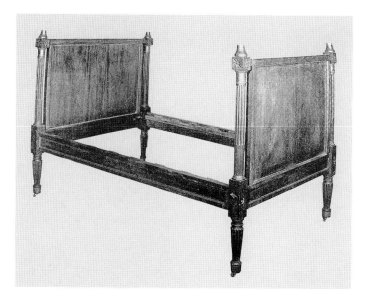

FIGURE 47. Jean-Baptiste-Claude Sené. Bedstead. 1787. Gilded wood, 54¾ x 63¾ in. Acquired in France by Colonel James Swan of Boston. Museum of Fine Arts, Boston. Gift of Miss Elizabeth Howard Bartol

FIGURE 48. Charles-Honoré Lannuier. Bedstead. 1803–12 (cat. no. 6)

tops of the posts that look something like the knob on the end of a baseball bat. At first glance it appears that these may be the stumps of high posts that were cut down, but, since they are identical on two known examples (fig. 48, and cat. no. 7) and would represent a rather improbable-looking transition from a block to a turned post—especially when compared with the known high-post examples—another possibility presents itself: In France, there was a type of bedstead made in the eighteenth century that was known as a *lit à la polonaise*. Such beds also had truncated posts with attached, curved iron rods that rose on an angle toward the center, where they supported a circular dome or canopy. It is possible that catalogue numbers 8 and 9 originally also had curved iron supports and a central dome or canopy. These rods would have been held in place by finials with iron pegs on the ends that were threaded through eyes and then pegged into the tops of the posts. In the appendix to Sheraton's *The Cabinet-Maker and Upholsterer's Drawing Book,* a design for a "French bed" is shown with slightly higher posts, but with the kind of canopy used on a *lit à la polonaise*. One final point worth noting is that, regardless of their form, all the known Lannuier bedsteads—whether French, high post, or even the theoretical *lit à la polonaise*—feature balanced headboards and footboards of equal height, so that Lannuier's customers consistently were given the option of placing their bedsteads either perpendicular to the wall or sideways, in a niche or alcove, in the French manner.[105]

While French forms came to share center stage with established English ones in New York after 1810, English furniture designs continued unabated as sources as well, although by now these, too, were strongly colored by the influence of French Empire style and ornament. In an advertisement of April 1811, the cabinetmaker William Graham begged "leave to inform the Ladies and Gentlemen of New-York that he has received from London some of the newest patterns of Mahogany Chairs, Grecian Sophas [*sic*], Couches, Window

Stools, London patent dining Tables, etc. ever offered to the public in this city, which he is able to manufacture on reasonable terms."[106] Two likely sources of these patterns were George Smith's *Collection of Designs for Household Furniture and Interior Decoration* of 1808, which put into general circulation and popularized anglicized versions of French forms in *le goût antique*, and Rudolph Ackermann's *The Repository of Arts, Literature, Commerce, Manufactures, Fashions, and Politics*, a monthly fashion magazine not unlike La Mésangère's *Collection de Meubles*, which was published in London between 1809 and 1828 and has been called by Mario Praz the "pinchbeck Percier and Fontaine."[107] According to Lorraine Waxman, Ackermann's *Repository* was available in New York in 1819 at the circulating library of A. T. Goodrich and Company at 124 Broadway, and in the April 1816 edition, the following notes accompanied a design for a "French Bed": "The annexed plate is a design lately imported from Paris, and represents one of those pieces of furniture which are consequent on the reciprocal exchanges of British and French taste . . . the framework is made of rose-wood, ornamented with carved foliage, gilt in matt [*sic*] and burnished gold."[108]

English Regency furniture frequently employed exotic Brazilian rosewood veneers—a trend that New York cabinetmakers, including Lannuier, were quick to pick up on, and they began working in rosewood in the early 1810s, although the type Lannuier preferred seems to have more in common with kingwood, a kind of rosewood that had enjoyed wide use in France since the eighteenth century. Typical of London Regency rosewood furniture was the use of inlaid-brass ornaments.

New York newspaper advertisements attest to the popularity of this highly decorative English style in the late teens. On May 4, 1818, the partnership of Gillespie and Walker, "Lately From London," offered for sale "a choice and elegant assortment of CABINET FURNITURE; neat ornamented SIDEBOARDS and PIER TABLES; rosewood CARD TABLES, richly ornamented with high polished brass."[109] A few weeks later, on May 30, cabinetmaker A. M. Haywood thanked "those ladies and gentlemen who have been kind enough to honor him with their commands, and to inform them, and the admirers of handsome furniture in general, that he has on hand . . . [a] grand sideboard, inlaid with high polished ornamental brass-work and rose-wood, [and] card tables to match. . . . All furniture warranted of the best quality and workmanship, and of the newest European fashions."[110] In addition to Lannuier's documented examples in this style (plates 24, 38, 42, and 43; see also plate 73), a variety of related New York rosewood furniture also survives (plates 44, 45, and figs. 49, 54), some of which conceivably could be by Gillespie and Walker, or A. M. Haywood. The beauty of Lannuier's large and splendidly documented legacy of surviving work is that it allows us to affirm with a high degree of certainty that none of these other rosewood examples is by him. This knowledge, however, only raises more questions as to whether other makers were following Lannuier's lead, or whether he was borrowing from them. The very existence of this other extremely ornate furniture reminds us to be careful about casting Lannuier as a monolithic presence in New York, and of the importance of recognizing the contribution of English Regency furniture design to the formulation of a monumental antique style in New York.

This was also the era of sculptural table forms, when classically derived winged monopodes, caryatids, full-bodied griffins, and lyres were used extensively as supports. A separate plate at the back of the 1817 New York price book shows the most popular standards used on pier tables, sofa tables, worktables, and card tables (fig. 50)—the last primed for a variety of decorative treatments between the apron and the plinth by the introduction of the swivel top, which was recorded for the first time in New York in the pre-1815 list of additional revised prices for cabinetwork. Lannuier's two favorite figural supports, a winged caryatid (plates 19, 46) and a swan (see plate 98), are missing from this plate, however—

PLATE 42. Charles-Honoré Lannuier. Square pier table. 1815–19 (cat. no. 99)

FIGURE 49. New York maker. *Secrétaire à abattant.*
1815–20. Rosewood veneer, 60⅛ x 34⅜ x 20 in. The
Warner Collection of Gulf States Paper Corporation,
Tuscaloosa, Alabama

PLATE 43. Attributed to Charles-Honoré Lannuier. Card table. 1815–19 (cat. no. 83)

PLATE 44. New York maker. Square pier table or sideboard. 1815–20. Rosewood veneer, 38⅝ x 66⅛ x 21¾ in. Hirschl & Adler Galleries, Inc., New York

PLATE 45. New York maker. Card table. About 1820. Rosewood veneer, 30 x 36 x 18 in. Private collection

93

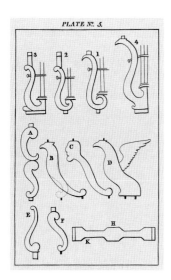

FIGURE 50. Plate 5 from *The New-York Book of Prices for Manufacturing Cabinet and Chair Work*. 1817

which may indicate either that he ran a closed shop, and the carvers and gilders whom he employed executed his figural supports exclusively, or that he was just developing these designs by 1816 or 1817. Lannuier, at least according to his known work, never appears to have used full-bodied griffin supports. Others, however, with limited success, copied his trademark winged caryatids (fig. 51; see also fig. 95). The master or masters of the griffin furniture (figs. 52, 53) have yet to be identified, but certain features on a few of the card tables with griffin supports relate closely to the documented pillar-and-claw card table made by Phyfe for James Brinckerhoff in 1816 (see fig. 71). This raises the distinct possibility that the tables utilizing griffins and winged caryatids were the innovations and shop specialities of New York's two great masters, Phyfe and Lannuier, and represent these two titans going head to head in the highly competitive environment of the late 1810s.

The source of inspiration for monopodes, caryatids, and griffins was the remains of ancient marble sculpture and architectural furniture that had been excavated and collected in Italy since the Renaissance. Avant-garde French designers adapted these Greco-Roman sculptural details to a variety of furniture forms during the late eighteenth century, and, by the early 1800s, popularized versions of furniture with gilded and bronzed antique-style monopodes began to appear with regularity in the pages of La Mésangère (see plate 5, and plates 47, 48). Late-eighteenth-century English architects and designers mined ancient sources as well. Henry Holland, architect to the prince of Wales, sent his chief draftsman

FIGURE 51. New York maker. Card table. 1815–20. Mahogany veneer, 29 x 35⅞ x 18½ in. The Warner Collection of Gulf States Paper Corporation, Tuscaloosa, Alabama

FIGURE 52. New York maker. Card table. 1815–20. Rosewood veneer, 30 x 35⅝ x 18 in. Collection Nancy W. Priest

FIGURE 53. New York maker. Card table. 1815–20. Rosewood veneer, 32½ x 36 x 18⅛ in. Yale University Art Gallery, New Haven, Connecticut. The Mabel Brady Garvan Collection

FIGURE 54. New York maker. Pier table. 1815–20. Rosewood veneer, 36¾ x 25¼ x 15 in. The New-York Historical Society. Gift of the Beekman Family Association

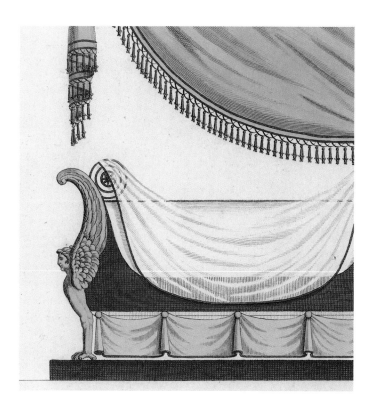

PLATE 47. Pierre de La Mésangère. Design for a *lit à la flèche* (detail of Plate 224 from *Collection de Meubles et Objets de Goût*). 1806. Colored engraving, 7³⁄₄ x 12¹⁄₄ in. The Metropolitan Museum of Art, New York. Harris Brisbane Dick Fund, 1930

FIGURE 55. Martin-Guillaume Biennais. Coffeepot. Early 19th century. Gilded silver: Height, 13¹⁄₈ in. The Metropolitan Museum of Art, New York. Rogers Fund, 1934

Charles Heathcote Tatham to Italy for three years in 1794 to make sketches from original sources, and in 1799 Tatham's drawings were published in *Etchings of Ancient Ornamental Architecture*. In 1807, Thomas Hope published *Household Furniture and Interior Decoration*, a design book filled with classical masks, monopodes, and human and mythological sculptural figures. After Hope, popularization of archaeologically correct antique forms and ornament in England fell to George Smith and Rudolph Ackermann. Both the French and English versions of *le goût antique* made their influence felt in New York, and, ironically, it may have been English developments that were responsible, in part, for inspiring Lannuier to create some of his most memorable "French Empire"-style furniture in the later phase of his career.

Lannuier always viewed the innovations of the English Regency style with a French sensibility. His winged caryatids are clearly French in character and have a stylized classical beauty similar to that seen in French Consulat and Empire metalwork (plate 19, and fig. 55), which, as already noted, was of interest to Lannuier. If English Regency designers were enamored of inlaid-brass ornaments, after the French style, then Lannuier would outdo them in New York by incorporating on his furniture die-stamped brass and wood borders exactly like those used in post-Revolutionary France. These were the types of borders that Thomas Hope praised so highly in *Household Furniture and Interior Decoration*, and for which the father of Aurore Frichot, Lannuier's partner in 1816, was awarded a prize at the Paris Industrial Exposition in 1806.

All of Lannuier's labeled figural furniture, with one exception, bears the latest of his engraved trade labels, and the canted corners on the majority of this work suggest a date of manufacture that ranges somewhere between 1812 and 1819,[III] although it is this writer's opinion that most of this furniture was not made until 1815 or later. In place of canted corners Lannuier frequently chose to employ hollow ones on his card tables (see plates 53, 73)—a form seen on French Louis XVI and post-Revolutionary consoles and commodes, and thus yet another "souvenir" of his French training. Lannuier's hollow corners may have been his contrary response to the rounded corners (plate 45; see also fig. 95) that, while extremely popular in Regency England and exploited extensively by New York cabinetmakers in the late 1810s and early 1820s, he apparently completely rejected.

3.   2.   1.

1, Table à Manger. 2, Table de Nuit. 3, Table de Jeu.

PLATE 48. Pierre de La Mésangère. Design for a *table à manger* (Plate 19 from *Collection de Meubles et Objets de Goût*). 1802. The Metropolitan Museum of Art, New York. Harris Brisbane Dick Fund, 1930

Honoré Lannuier knew his days were numbered in the late summer of 1819 when he placed the following advertisement in the *New-York Gazette & General Advertiser* on September 2: "The Subscriber, grateful for the liberal patronage he has met with in his line of business, from the ladies and gentlemen of this city, during 17 years past that he has been established here, is encouraged with the hope that in this his last appeal, the marked favors he has hitherto been honored with will be continued to him . . . on account of ill health, he finds himself under the necessity of declining business altogether; for which reason he offers for sale, at very reduced prices, his entire STOCK of CABINET FURNITURE."[112] Just over six weeks later he was dead. Three different newspapers carried the same notice on Monday, October 18, 1819, of the death, "On Saturday evening, after a lingering illness, [of] Mr. Charles Honore [*sic*] Lannuier, aged 40," and a fourth announced his death and invited his "friends and acquaintances and the Cabinet-makers in general . . . to attend his funeral from his late residence No. 60 Broad Street."[113] Lannuier was of sound mind and judgment at the time that he died, and left a will written in French that has provided us with many of the limited facts we have about his life. Signed and dated October 13, 1819, just three days before his death, the will is of the simplest kind, investing his wife, Therese, with the full rights to all his real estate and personal property (see Appendix 8).

Therese continued to raise the surviving Lannuier children on her own, and did not remarry until 1832. None of the sons, as previously mentioned, followed in his father's footsteps and became a cabinetmaker, but, as Therese did feel a sense of continuity about the business, she rented the manufactory and warehouse in the early 1820s to Jean Gruez, and the yard to the mahogany merchant George Deloynes. J. M. J. Labatut, Therese Lannuier, and her husband's close friend Joseph Lopez Dias all served as executors of the estate. With the agreement of Labatut and Dias, several months after Lannuier's death, Therese authorized Jean Gruez "to dispose of the remainder of the stock of the manufactory—consisting of Gilt Ornaments, Mahogany Boards and Veniers [*sic*], on the most reasonable terms."[114] Over a year later, in May 1821, the remaining stock of furniture was put up for auction by order of the executors of the estate. In their advertisement, the auctioneers Franklin and Minturn announced a "peremptory sale of a very superb and fashionable assortment of the best made mahogany furniture, consisting of bed-steads, side-boards, dining, card, pier, breakfast, and tea tables, sofas, bureaus, chairs, ladies dressing and work tables, with a great variety of fancy articles, etc. etc."[115]

Lannuier died just as the American economy was feeling the effects of its first economic crisis, the Panic of 1819. He had felt the acute pressure of competition at the close of his career, and it must have been a tremendous struggle for him near the end to persevere, get his financial affairs in order, and prepare his wife and young children for his impending death. The inventory of his estate records a balance of $17,749.58 in his favor—an entirely respectable sum for a craftsman in a time of rampant business failures. (There was only $174.62 cash in the bank, however, which explains Therese's need to sell off the contents of the shop.) Yet, sums of money, regardless of the amount, can provide little measure of the courage, determination, and genius of this French immigrant artist, or of the priceless legacy of the furniture that he has left us.

Peter M. Kenny

1

See Lambert, 1813, p. 56.

2

The notice, which appeared in the *Morning Chronicle* of February 24, 1803, is quoted in Gottesman, 1965, pp. 159–60.

3

The ad, which ran in the *Mercantile Advertiser* of February 24, 1800, is quoted in Gottesman, 1965, pp. 387–88.

4

As quoted in Stokes, 1915–28, vol. 5, chronology p. 1397. The names should be Mangin and McComb, the architects of record of the new City Hall.

5

In an advertisement in *L'Oracle and Daily Advertiser* on September 1, 1808, Auguste Lannuier offered for sale "the Furniture of the Saloon in the Theater, known by the name of Hamiltons Coffee house. . . ."

6

For Auguste Lannuier's real-estate transactions and Stanislas's death and last will and testament see Waxman, 1958, pp. 69–71.

7

For a reference to the transaction between Lannuier and Ruthven see Brown, 1978, p. 11. James Ruthven's account books for 1792 to 1804 are in the collection of the New-York Historical Society.

8

Lannuier's ad appeared in the *New-York Evening Post* of July 15, 1803, as quoted in Gottesman, 1965, p. 148.

9

See Waxman, 1958, pp. 71–72.

10

See Stokes, 1915–28, vol. 5, chronology p. 1315.

11

See the Assessed Valuation of Real Estate, First Ward, New York, 60 Broad Street, 1802. New York Municipal Archives.

12

See the deed of conveyance from Henry and Ann Brooks to Charles-Honoré Lannuier, October 31, 1810, Liber 91, p. 470. Register of Deeds, City Register's Office, Surrogate's Court, New York. See Waxman, 1958, p. 72.

13

See the Assessed Valuation of Real Estate, First Ward, 60 Broad Street, 1807. New York Municipal Archives. (Records for 1803 to 1806 are missing from the city archives.) The combined assessed value of the "H. and back H." on the property was $4,000, and Lannuier's personal estate had an assessed value of $500.

14

The ad appeared in *The People's Friend & Daily Advertiser,* October 16, 1806. Caraccas [*sic*] wood is listed in table IV of the 1810 New York cabinetmakers' price book as a material for banding or filling up shaped panels.

15

For information on Phyfe's various properties see McClelland, 1939.

16

See Longworth's *Directory,* 1801.

17

Will of Charles-Honoré Lannuier, October 13, 1819, Liber 55, p. 367. Wills, Surrogate's Court, New York. See Waxman, 1958, pp. 98–99.

18

See Longworth's *Directory,* 1807–12.

19

See the *acte de mariage* between Charles-Honoré Lannuier and Therese Baptiste, August 12, 1814. Centre des Archives Diplomatiques de Nantes.

20

Jury book for 1816. Microfilm, Library, New-York Historical Society; typescript, Berry B. Tracy Archives, Department of American Decorative Arts, The Metropolitan Museum of Art, New York.

21

See de Forest, 1909, pp. 77–79. In a letter written May 1, 1813, to then Secretary of State James Monroe, John Johnston asks to be allowed to return to the city and his business, and explains that, "It was my intention from the time of my first arrival in the U[nited]. States to become a citizen but not being sufficiently acquainted with the Law on that subject, it was not until I applied for citizenship in May 1809 that I was apprized of a previous declaration of intentions being necessary, which declaration I then made in the manner required by Law."

22

See Wolfe, 1963, pp. 211–17.

23

Cited in Clarke, 1941, pp. 36–39.

24

See Brown, 1978, p. 2.

25

See Waxman, 1958, pp. 75–76, 100.

26

According to the *acte de mariage,* 1814; see Waxman, 1958, pp. 74–75, 99.

27

According to the *acte de mariage,* 1814; see Waxman, 1958, p. 99.

28

Baptismal register, Saint Peter's church, Barclay Street, New York. I would like to thank Ms. Patricia Ruggiero at Saint Peter's for allowing me to examine the register. Waxman read the name in the ledger as Charles-A<u>nso</u>re, but it is more plausibly Charles-A<u>uro</u>re. The Jaine Jeard listed in the register may be Therese's sister Jaine; by 1819, she was remarried to Robert Year, whose name is recorded in Lannuier's will, which was drawn up that same year.

29

Jean and Auguste are both mentioned in their uncle Honoré's will (Baptismal register, Saint Peter's church, New York). The boys' lives and careers are discussed in Waxman, 1958, p. 70.

30

Will of Auguste Lannuier, August 6, 1811, Liber 49, p. 370. Wills, Surrogate's Court, New York.

31

Mortgage, negotiated between Charles-Honoré and Therese Lannuier and Mme Jean-Victor-Marie Moreau, July 27, 1811, Liber 22, p. 175. Register of Mortgages, City Register's Office, Surrogate's Court, New York.

32

See Chapter One, note 63.

33

See the Assessed Valuation of Real Estate, First Ward, 60 Broad Street, 1807–10, 1812, 1813, and 1815–19. New York Municipal Archives. First Ward assessment records are missing for 1811 and 1814. The assessed values of Lannuier's property over these years remained steady at $4,000 (real estate) and $500 (personal estate). The highest assessments were made in 1815, when his real estate was valued at $5,000 and his personal estate at $2,500. By the time of his death, his real estate was again assessed at $4,000 and his personal estate at $2,000.

34

See Beaujour, 1814, p. 92.

35

As cited in Fowble, 1974, p. 121.

36

See Milbert, 1968, p. xxiv.

37

See Johnson, 1968, p. 199. John Hewitt's account book, now in the New Jersey Historical Society, Newark, covers the periods from 1800 to 1803 and 1810 to 1813. A microfilm copy is in the Joseph Downs Collection of Manuscripts and Printed Ephemera, M491 (hereafter, the Downs Collection), Library, Winterthur Museum, Delaware. Johnson slightly mistranscribed the entry to read "leafe hand carv'd" instead of "with leafe carv'd," and "Lanuas Collum" instead of "Lanaus Collum."

38
See the *New-York Evening Post* of January 6, 1815, and the *New-York Gazette & General Advertiser* of March 21, 1816.

39
See Fearon, 1818, p. 24.

40
Fenwick Lyell account book, 1800–1811 (original in the Monmouth County Historical Association, Freehold, N. J.); a microfilm copy, M-2436.3, is in the Downs Collection, Library, Winterthur Museum, Delaware.

41
The ad, which appeared in the *New-York Gazette & General Advertiser* of March 20, 1817, does not name Moses and Stephen Young, but it invites journeymen to apply at 79 Broad Street, their address from 1810 to 1818.

42
According to the city directory, in 1816 Thomas Constantine was the occupant of 62 Vesey Street, the address given in the ad in the *Mercantile Advertiser* of June 15, 1816.

43
Constantine advertised in the *New-York Evening Post*, September 1, 1818.

44
See Johnson, 1968, pp. 199–200.

45
Kinnan and Mead's ad appeared on August 19, 1825.

46
See Brown, 1978, p. 51, n. 12, who cites the original source of the estimate of one hundred cabinetmakers in Phyfe's shop as Marshall, 1915.

47
See the *New-York Evening Post* of November 8, 1819.

48
John Van Boskirk remained on Broad Street throughout his career: from 1817 to 1819, at no. 59; 1819 to 1820, at no. 51; 1820 to 1823, at no. 51½ and 53; 1823 to 1824, at no. 60; and from 1824 to 1826, at no. 58. An announcement of the newly formed partnership of William H. Walsh and Abraham S. Egerton appeared in the *New-York Gazette & General Advertiser* of April 24, 1817. Before this, Walsh's address was listed as 44 Stone Street from 1806 to 1808, and 6 New Street from 1810 to 1816.

49
Despite the roughly one thousand cabinetmakers who worked in New York during Lannuier's lifetime, only four account books survive from 1800 to 1820. The previously noted ones belonged to Fenwick Lyell and to John Hewitt, a third book was kept by the cabinetmaker David

Loring (now in the possession of one of his descendants), and a fourth (now in the New-York Historical Society) belonged to the cabinetmaker Elisha Blossom, Jr., and covers the period from 1811 to 1813. David Loring came to New York from Fairhaven, Massachusetts, about 1800, and worked in the city until his shop was devastated by fire in 1814. He then moved to Cincinnati, Ohio, where he worked from 1815 to 1817. (For more on Loring and his account book see Sikes, 1976, pp. 147–49.) Lannuier's name was recorded in Hewitt's account book, and a transaction with Lannuier also appears in Loring's, for which see Sikes, 1976, p. 47. I would like to thank Jane Sikes Hageman for information on the Loring account book, which, along with the Elisha Blossom, Jr., day-book, is the subject of a forthcoming article by Peter M. Kenny.

50
See Longworth's *Directory*, 1813–18. Daniel Smith's address is also listed in the city tax-assessment records as 62 Broad Street, next door to Lannuier, from 1813 to 1815, when his personal estate had an assessed value of $10,000. From 1816 to 1819, Mrs. Smith is listed at the address. Assessed Valuation of Real Estate, First Ward, 62 Broad Street, 1813–19. New York Municipal Archives.

51
See Chapter One, note 3.

52
See the *New-York Gazette & General Advertiser*, September 2, 1819.

53
Pell's ads appeared in *The Public Advertiser* of December 8, 1807, and April 19, 1808, and Malibran's in the *New-York Gazette & General Advertiser* of January 23, 1826. Malibran's role as an import merchant rather than a shopkeeper is made clear by his reference at the end of the ad to the fact that these goods were offered "for sale by an agent of the manufacturer, at reduced prices. Apply at the counting house of E. Malibran, 31 South-street."

54
For Dias's advertisements in the *New-York Gazette* and the *New-York Evening Post* see Waxman, 1958, pp. 79–80.

55
See Longworth's *Directory*, 1820–21.

56
See Waxman, 1958, pp. 77–78.

57
See the *New-York Morning Post* of May 9, 1812.

58
See Leben, 1992, pp. 82, 90.

59
See Sargentson, 1996, pp. 113–14.

60
See *Minutes of the Common Council*, vol. 9, 1917, p. 11.

61
See Brown, 1978, p. 22.

62
See the *New-York Gazette & General Advertiser* of December 7, 1815.

63
See the *New-York Evening Post* of June 11, 1818.

64
A cellarette by Brauwers with this same label is illustrated in the Christie's, New York, sales catalogue of January 22, 1994, pp. 102, 103.

65
See the *New-York Evening Post* of June 9, 1819.

66
See the *New-York Daily Advertiser* of April 5, 1819.

67
See the *Mercantile Advertiser* of June 6, 1814. Earlier in his career, Christian advertised a showpiece sideboard in the *Republican Watch Tower* of October 16, 1802. It was described as, "An elegant Side Board, with pedestals, vase, knife cases, plated scrools [sic] and candle branches . . . this specimen of Cabinet Furniture . . . [is] well calculated for a spacious dining room."

68
See the *New-York Evening Post* of February 19, 1814.

69
For the Lannuier shipment to Bulloch on the brig *Levant* see the Inward Coastwise Manifests, Port of Savannah, October 5, 1819. Record Group 36, Box 13. National Archives, Washington, D.C. As cited by Talbott, 1995, p. 84.

70
For the sale of Bulloch's furniture in 1819 see Chapter Three, note 89.

71
See the *New-York Gazette & General Advertiser* of September 2, 1819.

72
For the sale of Bulloch's furniture in 1822 see Chapter Three, Southern Clients.

73
I would like to thank Page Talbott for offering to keep a lookout for Lannuier references during her research. See also Alexander, 1989, p. 36. For the relationship between Phyfe and Morrell see Brown, 1978, p. 27. Illustrative of the marketing of furniture in South America is a notebook (now in the Downs Collection, M-6, Library, Winterthur Museum,

Delaware), kept between 1798 and 1809 by an unidentified American who discusses what kind of American furniture will sell in Rio de Janeiro.

74
See the *American Citizen* of May 3, 1804.

75
See Scott, 1988, pp. 53, 57.

76
Allison updated his trade labels about every two years, beginning in 1817 and continuing until 1825. This warning to customers appeared for the first time in 1821, but it was repeated in 1823, 1825, and 1831. For an 1825 label see Scherer, 1984, p. 56.

77
See Sloane, 1987.

78
See Montgomery, 1966, pp. 23, 26.

79
See Weber, 1994, p. 8.

80
See Lambert, 1813, p. 90.

81
See Leben, 1992, p. 89.

82
Pierre de La Mésangère's *Collection de Meubles et Objets de Goût*—hereafter referred to as La Mésangère, 1802–35—comprising 755 colored engravings, was published serially, a few at a time, in Paris, from 1802 to 1835. The most complete collection of these engravings is in the Department of Drawings and Prints at The Metropolitan Museum of Art, New York; for the most comprehensive study of them and of how they relate to American furniture see Woodside, 1986.

83
See the *New-York Evening Post* of July 15, 1803.

84
See Brown, 1978, pp. 65–67. Michael Brown cites an editorial in the *New-York Evening Post* of November 13, 1817, in which the author felt "regret and mortification" that the Monroe Administration would purchase a suite of French furniture for the Executive Mansion when fine furniture could be procured from American craftsmen, and he mentions specifically the work of Duncan Phyfe. For Monroe's furniture in *le goût moderne* see Otto, 1961, p. 373; for Monroe's White House furniture see Conger and Monkman, 1976.

85
See Leben, 1992, p. 132.

86
See E. Jones, 1977, pp. 5–14.

87
See the John McComb, Jr., Papers, Library, The New-York Historical

Society. McComb's list includes a copy of *The Cabinet-Maker & Upholsterer's Drawing-Book* by Thomas Sheraton. In the third revised edition of 1802, Sheraton illustrates "A Plan & Section of a Drawing Room" (plate LXI), with armchairs having square backs identical to those of Lannuier's City Hall armchairs.

88
See David Watkin, in Hope, 1971, p. viii.

89
Lannuier's round, center table with four gilded figures (cat. no. 115) bears the remnants of a printed No. 2 label inside the rail, and one of his columnar rosewood pier tables with white marble columns (cat. no. 98) has a complete printed No. 2 label inside the back rail.

90
The undated list, which survives without a title page, is in the Library at the Museum of Fine Arts, Houston, where it is tipped into the 1810 price book. Both are enclosed within a brown leather binding. The cabinetmaker's name, Daniel Turnier, is impressed into the front cover in gold letters and it also appears, along with the date 1816, on the frontispiece. Comparison of this price list and *Additional Prices,* 1815, proves that the undated one is earlier and therefore was issued sometime between the time of publication of the 1810 price book and the list of July 1815. A copy of the 1815 list of additional prices is also in the Library at the Museum of Fine Arts, Houston. I would like to thank Michael K. Brown for bringing these lists to my attention and for making them available to me for study.

91
See *The New-York Book of Prices,* 1817, p. 5.

92
Invoice from Charles Del Vecchio to James Brinckerhoff, May 23, 1816. Robert Troup Papers, Box 3, Folder 4, Manuscripts & Archives Section, Rare Books and Manuscripts Division, The New York Public Library.

93
See the pre-1815 list of *Additional Revised Prices,* n.d., p. 1, a copy of which is in the Library at the Museum of Fine Arts, Houston.

94
See Johnson, 1968, p. 196.

95
See the *New-York Evening Post* of January 6, 1815. See also Chapter Three, note 2.

96
See *The New-York Revised Prices,* 1810, p. 13.

97
See the pre-1815 list of *Additional Revised Prices,* n.d., p. 2. See note 93, above.

98
Samples of the finish on the bust were taken by Mark Minor and analyzed by Marinus Manuels in 1997, Department of Objects Conservation, The Metropolitan Museum of Art, New York.

99
For more on Swan, a Scottish-born American patriot from Boston and a real-estate speculator—who, in exchange for furniture and luxury goods, bartered food staples and other essential raw materials necessary for the French to sustain their war effort against the English—see Watson, 1976, pp. 286–90.

100
See *The New-York Revised Prices,* 1810, p. 55.

101
See the pre-1815 list of *Additional Revised Prices,* n.d., p. 6. See note 93, above.

102
See *The New-York Book of Prices,* 1817, pp. 96, 97.

103
Letter from Stephen Van Rensselaer IV to Stephen Van Rensselaer III, Paris, August 24, 1813. Stephen Van Rensselaer Papers, Library, The New-York Historical Society.

104
See Sheraton, 1970, vol. 1, p. 139.

105
For a description and illustration of the *lit à la polonaise* form see Verlet, 1991, p. 67, fig. 51. For French eighteenth-century engravings of the form, with and without bed hangings, see Pallot, 1995. For an illustration of the Sheraton bed see *Pictorial Dictionary,* 1989, p. 18. A bedstead with similarly truncated posts, which never have been altered, is owned by Joe Kindig III, of York, Pennsylvania. When it was examined, it was discovered to have brass ferrules around the tops of the posts, and holes in the ends, into which the iron

pegs of its original finials are inserted. The original tester is missing. A bedstead described in a New York auction ad by G. A. & T. Bibby on January 11, 1808, as "an elegant dome bedstead with matrasses [*sic*], feather bed, dimity curtains, etc.," could be a reference to a *lit à la polonaise,* which, typically, has a small, circular dome-like canopy; see Waxman, 1958, p. 47.

106
See the *New-York Gazette & General Advertiser* of April 19, 1811.

107
As cited in Morley, 1993, p. 393.

108
See Ackermann, 1816, vol. 2, p. 244, as cited in Waxman, 1958, pp. 52, 53.

109
See the *New-York Daily Advertiser* of May 4, 1818.

110
See the *New-York Evening Post* of May 30, 1818.

111
Canted corners are listed in the 1811 edition of *The London Cabinet-Makers' Union Book of Prices,* on p. 146, and they appear for the first time in the undated, pre-1815 list of *Additional Revised Prices* (see note 93, above). This would seem to indicate that canted corners did not firmly take hold on New York furniture until the 1810s, after which the style became something of a mania, turning up on everything from bureaus to sideboards, card tables, pier tables, and worktables in the 1817 New York book of prices. A labeled Duncan Phyfe worktable with canted corners, now at the Winterthur Museum, Delaware (see Montgomery, 1966, pp. 409–10), can be dated between 1811 and 1816 based on the address given on the label.

112
See the *New-York Gazette & General Advertiser* of September 2, 1819.

113
See the *New-York Spectator,* the *Commercial Advertiser,* and the *New-York Columbian,* all of October 18, 1819. For the invitation to the funeral see the *New-York Gazette & General Advertiser* of October 18, 1819.

114
See the *Mercantile Advertiser* of January 7, 1820.

115
See the *Commercial Advertiser* of May 2, 1821.

PLATE 49.   Charles-Honoré Lannuier. French bedstead with crown.
1812–19 (cat. no. 1)

CHAPTER 3   Lannuier's Clients in America:

A Taste for French Style

The study of Charles-Honoré Lannuier's furniture has uncovered a number of his clients, which, in turn, has led to more information about him and the historical and social background of the time in which he worked. This process—locating the family papers of his clients and searching through contemporary newspaper notices and New York City archives—not only has provided descriptions of Lannuier works no longer extant but at times the actual prices he charged for them. These sources have also revealed which furnishings were in the houses of particular clients and, in some instances, what the houses themselves were like.

Of the 125 documented or firmly attributed examples of Lannuier's furniture that presently are known, about twenty original owners can be identified. Not surprisingly, most of his clients were merchants. Preserved among the papers of two such New Yorkers, William Bayard and James Brinckerhoff, are invoices that disclose that they patronized a number of craftsmen, but that Lannuier was their cabinetmaker of choice for French-style furniture. Not only do records show this to be a common practice but even where no personal papers exist, the pattern can still be discerned when a client's furniture is partly known to us. The New York merchant Isaac Bell purchased an elegant French bedstead, replete with crown (plate 49), and a pair of card tables in *le goût antique* (see plate 22) from Lannuier, and, possibly from Duncan Phyfe, a set of mahogany chairs in the most up-to-date English Regency style (plate 50). Similarly, the New Yorker Thomas Cornell Pearsall owned a columnar pier table in the Consulat taste that bears Lannuier's label (see plate 28), as well as a large suite of mahogany and cane seating furniture probably by Duncan Phyfe, including a dozen side chairs, a pair of armchairs, and a sofa, all with "Grecian cross legs" (these are now in The Metropolitan Museum of Art). The group represents an English Regency interpretation of the antique style, as does a pair of pillar-and-claw card tables—each of which has a cluster of four carved pillars—attributed to Phyfe, which Pearsall had installed at Belmont, his mansion on 57th Street and the East River.[1]

In New York in the early decades of the nineteenth century, one had a choice of English or French-style goods. Lannuier established himself as the premier cabinetmaker of "French" furniture for those able to buy works of the highest quality. This point is underscored by an 1815 auction notice that advertised "elegant french mahogany bedsteads" and mahogany chairs, "The Mahogany furniture made by Mr. Lannuier and in good preservation."[2] These items were among the furniture to be sold at the Hermitage—the mansion north of the city on the Bloomingdale Road—by a family departing for Europe, and may have belonged to John Leake Norton, who was then the mansion's owner.

A labeled card table (see plate 35), closer in design to the vernacular New York style influenced by the English Regency, shows that Lannuier made furniture other than that in

PLATE 50. Possibly by Duncan Phyfe.
Side chair. 1810–15. Mahogany:
Height, 32¾ in. Private collection

the French taste. The inscription "Hosack" beneath the top of this table identifies a Lannuier customer from the professional classes. David Hosack, who was probably the table's original owner, was a professor of medicine and botany at Columbia College, and the founder, in 1801, of the Elgin Gardens—a twenty-acre public botanical garden located between what today are Fifth and Sixth Avenues, from Forty-seventh to Fifty-first Street. The table's restrained style perhaps was influenced by this client, who was at the center of New York's expanding intellectual and cultural life.

In the discussion of Lannuier's patrons that follows, two New Yorkers—William Bayard, a client and link to the Van Rensselaer-Campbell furniture, and James Brinckerhoff—will be considered first, because of their numerous surviving personal papers. Next, Lannuier's known French clientele in the United States will be explored, preceding a section on the small number of southern merchants who owned his furniture, and, lastly, Lannuier's public commission for armchairs for New York's new City Hall, as well as a large looking glass thought to have been made for a Hudson River steamboat, will be examined.

THE BAYARD-VAN
RENSSELAER-CAMPBELL
COMMISSIONS

The earliest-known Lannuier invoice, dated February 23, 1805, was issued to William Bayard, a pivotal figure in the study of Lannuier's patrons. Lannuier charged Bayard thirty dollars for a mahogany bedstead. The invoice gives no further description of the piece, but on it Lannuier proudly proclaims he is a French cabinetmaker—"Dʳ [*sic*] to h. Lannuier french Cabinet Maker Broad St No 60" (see Appendix 1)[3]—the distinction he wished to impress upon the New York market. This bed is not known today, and one can only surmise

FIGURE 56. John Searle. *Interior of the Park Theatre*. 1822. Watercolor, 38 x 23 in. The New-York Historical Society. The heirs of Mrs. Harriet Elizabeth Bayard Van Rensselaer, 1875

FIGURE 57. Invoice from the Manufacture de Porcelaine de Nast. 1803. Bayard-Campbell-Pearsall Papers, The New York Public Library

its design. Based on the early date of the invoice and the relatively low price, it may have been like Lannuier's two known *lits à la polonaise*—a French term for a bed with a headboard and footboard of equal height, and with short posts from which issue curved iron rods that support a dome fully finished on all sides. The two Lannuier beds in this Late Louis XVI or Directoire style have high, paneled ends flanked by columns with stopped fluting and with vase-shaped terminals, which were meant to hold the iron rods (see fig. 48, and cat. nos. 6, 7). In 1933, when both beds were illustrated in *Antiques*, the rods and testers were missing. The price that Lannuier charged Bayard may have been for the bedstead alone, and the tester could have been supplied by an upholstery shop. Upholsterers often worked with cabinetmakers in the execution of a design, and either type of shop could have provided the tester and subcontracted the ironwork.[4] The mattresses and the fabrication of the bed curtains, however, were the domain of the upholsterer.

William Bayard (1761–1826) exemplified the entrepreneurial New York merchants, who achieved prominence in the decades following the Revolutionary War. His Loyalist father had sailed to England in 1783, taking his family but leaving William behind in New York to reclaim the family's extensive landholdings that had been confiscated by the new government. William Bayard's attempts were to prove unsuccessful, but that same year he married Elizabeth Cornell (1763–1854). In 1786, with his wife's brother-in-law Herman LeRoy, he founded LeRoy and Bayard, and after James McEvers, a cousin, joined the firm, it was renamed LeRoy, Bayard & McEvers.[5] It proved to be an astute and canny partnership. Trading with Europe and the East and West Indies, LeRoy, Bayard & McEvers capitalized on the wars in Europe and on Europe's need for American and foreign products by providing transportation on their ships. At a time when New York City was growing rapidly in population as well as commercially, their business expanded and prospered. In the years following the War of 1812, the firm commanded an important position in New York commerce, and Bayard became one of the city's wealthiest citizens.

A watercolor of 1822 of the interior of the Park Theatre (fig. 56), executed by the artist John Searle for William Bayard, depicts Bayard in profile standing in the first tier of boxes near the stage, in front of a doorway. Bayard's older son, William, Jr., also shown in profile, is seated at the front of the box and his son-in-law Duncan Pearsall Campbell is standing in the rear, to the left of a column. The occasion is the staging of the farce "Monsieur Tonson" by the English dramatist William T. Moncrieffe, with the actors Charles Mathews and Miss Johnson, which was presented three times at the Park Theatre in November 1822.[6] Bayard probably commissioned the watercolor as a kind of memento, for seated in the audience are his friends and social acquaintances (eighty-four are identified on a key later made to accompany the drawing), many of them among New York's most notable citizens.

In addition to ordering a bed from a French cabinetmaker in New York, Bayard ordered French-made goods from Paris. An invoice with an elaborately engraved billhead, from the Paris porcelain manufacturer Nast, dated in the Revolutionary calendar 15 *pluviôse an* 11 (1803), shows that Bayard purchased directly from the firm a porcelain service ornamented with blue cornflowers and bordered with a gold fillet (fig. 57).[7] The service included oval dishes in three sizes, *pots à jus* (covered gravy or custard cups), ice-cream bowls with covers, and several *guéridons*, or stands. At this time, several of Bayard's seven children were studying French at home with French tutors, and, in 1806–7, William, Jr., was attending school in Paris.[8] Apparently, Bayard wished to expose his children to the French language and culture, and to surround them with the French objects he acquired for his home.

His firm's success led Bayard to move from his residence on Greenwich Street in 1806 to a new, grander town house at 6 State Street, facing the Battery and New York Harbor— an area that, with lower Broadway, then formed the city's most fashionable quarter. The panoramic views from the houses on State Street, which overlooked the green lawns and shade trees of the Battery, prompted the educator Timothy Dwight (1752–1817) to remark that "the western shore of the Hudson; the village on Paulus Hook . . . ; the islands in the bay, particularly Governors Island; . . . the handsome town of Brooklyn, rising on a beautiful eminence directly opposite . . . ; together with the Hudson, the East River, and the bay; form a combination of objects alternately beautiful and magnificent. A great part of this fine scenery is visible from the houses in State Street at the south end of the city" (fig. 58).[9]

Bayard purchased 6 State Street from the merchant Moses Rogers for $20,000. It was the larger, eastern portion of the Georgian-style red-brick mansion built by James Watson in 1792, which Rogers had acquired in 1805 and then divided.[10] Moses Rogers retained for himself the westerly part of the house, and, on the adjoining lot to the west, he built a three-story colonnaded addition that curved to follow the bend in State Street. Miraculously, Moses Rogers's house at 7 State Street still stands in lower Manhattan—a Federal brick edifice dwarfed by glass-and-steel skyscrapers on three sides (fig. 59).

Bayard at once set about remodeling his residence in the latest modern classical taste, and built a fine stable and coach house at the rear of the property, which faced Pearl Street. He chose the master carpenter John E. West to execute the design and supervise the building and the mason Thomas Taylor to carry out the stonework.[11] West, in 1803, had been appointed a master carpenter for the new City Hall, and along with John McComb, Jr., its supervising architect, was listed as one of sixteen master builders and architects in Longworth's 1805–6 city directory. The addition that Moses Rogers built onto 7 State Street, which, based on its architectural plan and the excellence of the design rather than on any documented evidence, is usually attributed to McComb, could just as likely be the work

FIGURE 58. Isidore-Laurent Deroy, after Jacques-Gérard Milbert. *View of New-York Taken from Weehawk* (Plate 1 from *Itinéraire Pittoresque du Fleuve Hudson . . .*). Drawn 1816–23, issued 1828–29. Lithograph, 9⅞ x 12¾ in. The Metropolitan Museum of Art, New York. The Edward W. C. Arnold Collection of New York Prints, Maps, and Pictures, Bequest of Edward W. C. Arnold, 1954

of West, the builder of record who altered the Watson house for Bayard. It would have been practical for Bayard to hire Rogers's builder to ensure that the two buildings shared a cohesive design. At the rear of the Bayard house, a curved, three-story garden façade created rooms with elliptical ends, and related the building architecturally to Rogers's addition.[12] An illustration in Valentine's *Manual* of 1859 (fig. 60) shows Bayard's and Rogers's homes as they appeared before they were altered in the late 1850s for use as boardinghouses for the many Irish and German immigrants who arrived at Castle Garden in the Battery. William Bayard's residence is on the right, a three-story brick town house over a high basement, twenty-six-feet wide, with a three-bay façade, the windows embellished with splayed lintels and double keystones. The Flemish-bond brickwork was probably painted red, which was customary in New York, and the mortar in between picked out in white. Architectural details, including the pilasters, lintels, basement story, and alternating rectangular and oval panels between the second and third floors, were of brownstone—painted to simulate marble. Moses Rogers's house, with its curved colonnade, is seen to the left of Bayard's.

The floor plan of the renovation followed a basic New York town-house design that John McComb, Jr., has been largely credited for developing in the late 1790s. Entering the Bayard house through the fan-lit front doorway one encountered a vestibule with a corridor at the back that led to the second-floor stairway. To the right of the corridor were a large parlor and a dining room, one behind the other. Additional stairways gave access to the kitchen and service areas in the basement. The second story contained either a drawing room and a master bedroom, or two bedrooms, and several additional bedrooms were on the third story.[13]

The interiors of Bayard's home were richly appointed and elegant. Probably through his master carpenter, West, he employed the Dublin-born and London-trained carver and gilder John Dixey to execute the interior ornament of his new house. Dixey, later elected a

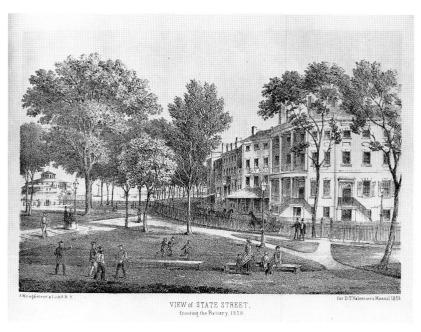

FIGURE 59. Number 7, State Street, New York. 1997

FIGURE 60. A. Weingärtner. *State Street, New York*. Lithograph (from D. T. Valentine, *Manual of the Corporation of the City of New-York for 1859*). The Metropolitan Museum of Art, New York. Bequest of Charles Allen Munn, 1924

vice-president of the Pennsylvania Academy of the Fine Arts, was the sculptor of the statue of *Justice*, which stood atop the dome of New York's City Hall. He also executed architectural carvings for a number of public and private buildings in the nearly two decades he maintained a studio in New York City.[14] Dixey's invoices provide a picture of the architectural richness of the interiors of the Bayard house. On October 6, 1806, he charged £8 "To carving 20 patterns for Cornices," £20 "To Carving two large Ionic capitals with leaves for the neck of the Columns," and £10 "To two do [large Ionic capitals with leaves] for pillasters [*sic*]" and a month later he charged £40 for "Carving four rich Composition Capitals for pillasters [*sic*]" and £8 for "two rich trusses for Stairs."[15] Dixey did not supply all the interior architectural embellishments; in 1806, Albert Westerfield was paid $19 for ceiling ornaments.[16]

In addition to the richly carved ornaments in the Bayard interiors, four marble mantelpieces were ordered from Italy in the spring of 1807 for the parlors and more formal rooms. Purchased through his firm's agents in Leghorn (Livorno), one was a "handsome and ornamented" example that cost over three times more than any of the others.[17] When Bayard's daughter Maria traveled to England in 1814, she noted in her diary that the mantelpieces in the drawing rooms at Corsham Court near Bath, which she visited to view the paintings collection, "were of white marble, two Figures supporting them, very much in the manner of ours tho' much larger and more elegant."[18]

When furnishing his new house, Bayard did not seek out Lannuier, from whom he had acquired the bedstead in 1805. Instead, he chose Duncan Phyfe, who was fast becoming a household name in New York for fine furniture. Another Lannuier client, the merchant James Brinckerhoff, purchased a "French" bed from him too, and obtained his seating furniture from Phyfe. This may have reflected a certain conservatism on their part—French taste seemed appropriate, even desirable, for decorations and selected pieces, but for most furnishings the greater restraint of the Anglo-Regency style, as interpreted by Phyfe and other New York craftsmen, was a safer and more popular choice. This ever-present English influence was remarked upon by a foreign visitor about 1818: "English tastes are prevalent in the interior of the homes, their furnishings and furniture."[19]

The order that Bayard placed with Phyfe in November 1807 was large and, but for three items, the furniture clearly was intended for the parlor and dining room. The surviving invoice includes, among other items: one set of twenty-eight mahogany chairs ($12.50 each), another set of fourteen chairs ($15 each), three sofas ($65 each), two pairs of card tables ($75 and $80 the pair), two tea tables ($30 and $35), a sideboard ($125), and a set of dining tables ($160). Several scroll-back side chairs and a matching pair of armchairs with double, crossed banisters in the backs, which descended in William Bayard's family to his granddaughter Maria Louisa Campbell and are now in the Phyfe Room at the Winterthur Museum, are thought to be from one of the sets of chairs listed on Phyfe's bill.[20] In a remarkable coincidence, the interior woodwork and the chimneypiece in this installation come from the first-floor parlor of Bayard's next-door neighbor, Moses Rogers (fig. 61). A pier table, the work of a New York cabinetmaker of the first rank—possibly Lannuier or Phyfe—and made for Rogers's State Street house, is now in the American Wing at The Metropolitan Museum of Art (see plate 29).

In addition to Phyfe, Bayard turned to other cabinetmakers as well. From Jacob Brouwer he had purchased earlier, in 1806, a sideboard with pedestal ends (£36), and, in January 1807, a "Secatary [sic]" (£16), which, judging from its cost, was probably quite plain. He also bought twelve fancy chairs painted white and gold from William Palmer for $39. The Lannuier bed acquired in 1805 still must have satisfied the Bayards, for it is notable that there is no bed listed on the Phyfe invoice, although there are several other items of bedroom furniture, including a wardrobe ($100), dressing table ($65), and basin stand ($9). Additional beds purchased for his new home were all field bedsteads to be used in secondary bedrooms, and, again, these came from other makers: one from Jacob Brouwer and four from William Mandeville in 1811, each costing between £5 and £6. An exception is a high-post bedstead Bayard ordered from Mandeville for £9.12.0 on May 14, 1811, along with two "gilt balls" for £2.16.0, possibly intended as ornamentation for the bed. To go with the bedsteads, he obtained from the cabinetmaker John Ball two circular and two square basin stands ($9 each and $4 each, respectively) and from J. & J. Vecchio a shaving glass at $1.25 and a more elegant looking glass for $24. From Joseph Meeks, Jr., whose shop was located on Broad Street across from Lannuier's, he bought a bureau, in 1812, for $17.00.[21]

As fascinating and voluminous as Bayard's correspondence and accounts are, they fail to convey the true elegance of the interiors of his house, which, newly decorated, was just the type of dwelling the British traveler John Lambert commented on in 1807 when discussing the life-style of the city's principal merchants: "[They] associate together in a style of elegance and splendour little inferior to Europeans. Their houses are furnished with every thing that is useful, agreeable, or ornamental; and many of them are fitted up in the tasteful magnificence of modern style."[22] A tantalizing hint of the richness of Bayard's townhouse interiors is the description of a pair of elegant London-made window curtains sent to him on approval for purchase by a Boston acquaintance departing for Europe. The curtains were described in an original London memo as being of "Blue Striped tabaret & drapery of plain Orange Do lined with orange calico counterlined with wadding made to turn over a black & gold tierce[?] with carved & guilt pine apples [sic], the curtains to throw over antique Bronze & guilt [sic] Patra's the whole bound with new pattern french lace, the draperies ornamented with Parisian fringe."[23] Except for dimity, a woven white-striped cotton that was purchased to drape the field beds, and some patterned chintz, there is no other mention of furnishing fabrics in the Bayard papers.[24] The patterned chintz, fifty-eight yards of it, could have been used for the Lannuier bed bought two years earlier, or it may have been made into covers for the Phyfe chairs, which were not ordered until eleven months later.

Bayard actually placed two orders with Duncan Phyfe on November 21, 1807. The first and larger one, already discussed, was for furnishings for his State Street residence, and the second—for fourteen mahogany chairs, one sofa, a pair of card tables, and a tea table, totaling $345—very likely was intended for his oldest daughter, Susan (1785–1814), who, on December 10, 1807, quite literally married the boy next door, Benjamin Woolsey Rogers (1775–1859). The furniture would have graced the parlor of their home at 3 State Street, only a few doors from their parents' residences. Bayard twice more returned to Phyfe, perhaps to augment his set of chairs with four additional ones at $12.50 each and a worktable for $32 in 1809; the following year, he purchased a writing table for $35.00.[25]

In 1817, with a renewed enthusiasm for things French possibly sparked by the Francophile inclinations of his daughters and future sons-in-law, William Bayard purchased elaborate gilded furniture in the French Late Empire style as interpreted by Lannuier. Two of his three surviving daughters were married in 1817: Harriet (1799–1875), Bayard's youngest child, on January 2, to Stephen Van Rensselaer IV (1789–1868) of Albany, and Maria (1789–1875), on June 16, to Duncan Pearsall Campbell (1781–1861), the former husband of another Bayard daughter, Catherine, who had died in 1813. In celebration of these marriages, and, no doubt, of his own good fortune as well, Bayard presented each daughter with a dowry that included furniture made in the French taste by Lannuier and a suite of seating furniture from Paris.

Before her marriage, in the fall and winter of 1814–15, Maria traveled to England and France in the company of her brother Robert and her brother-in-law Benjamin Woolsey Rogers, recording the trip in lively detail in her diary. For a twenty-five-year old lady at that time, and in her position, she displayed an uncommon interest in British manufactures, doubtless acquired from her businessman father. At Bristol, where they stopped after London and Bath, she visited the glass-house manufactory, and was "much disappointed to hear that

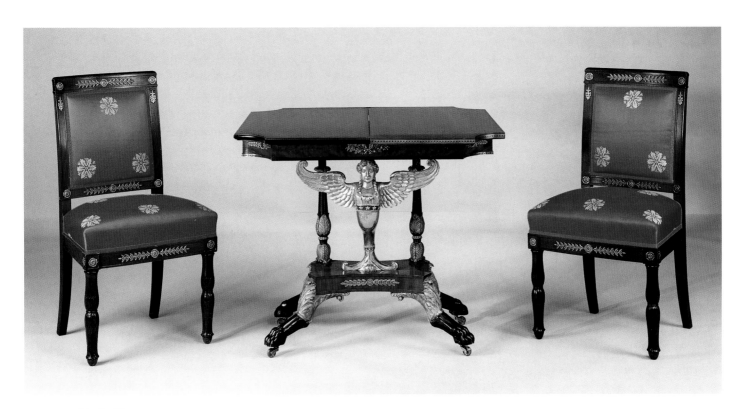

they were not blowing but merely cutting the glass, that since the American War they found three times a week made more than they had sale for,"[26] and after they visited a brass foundry in Birmingham, she noted in some detail the method of casting and lacquering furniture ornaments (see Chapter Four).

The following March, the small party took the packet to France. Entering Paris just before dark, Maria was transported by its beauty and noted, "It is impossible to imagine any thing more elegant." She described their parlor at the Hôtel d'Artois, where they occupied a suite of five apartments, as having "Blue and Yellow silk furniture, 3 Looking Glasses, 2 Marble Pier Tables, Elegant Clock & etc. [In] My bedroom is a canopy bed with blue silk furniture."[27] She, too, was prey to the current French fashions, inquiring the day after her arrival "for the Fashionable Milliner. . . . I am too much English to appear in the streets as they laugh at them. The ladies here dress elegantly except their Bonnets which are of an immense height. . . . I took the addresses Mr. Archer [Bayard's agent in Le Havre] was so good as to give me . . . for Dresses Hats & c & and the next day I was completely equipped."[28]

In Paris, Maria took in the latest styles, and her diary is replete with images of the fading Empire. Visiting Notre-Dame, she touched the gold laurel crown worn by the emperor Napoleon, and the Empress Marie-Louise's "crimson velvet and gold" coronation cushions. The three travelers were present when Napoleon returned to Paris, briefly triumphant, for his fleeting hundred-day rule. On March 20, Maria breathlessly recorded that "the king [Louis XVIII] has gone, and the Louvre and Palace [are] shut. A great number of Buonparte's [*sic*] friends are already arrived, his advance guard has already appeared, without any bloodshed Buonparte [*sic*] arrived at 10 at night." The Louvre, Maria noted, was rehung with paintings of Napoleon's military victories, at Versailles "the rooms in the Grand Trianon are filled with exploits of Buoneparte [*sic*]," and in one there was a beautiful Sèvres pitcher painted with his likeness. Twice she saw the emperor—reviewing his troops, and at chapel with his brothers and Marshal Bertrand.[29] Later that spring, Maria returned to New York a devoted Francophile, bringing back a taste for gilded furniture in the Late Empire and Early Restoration styles.

PLATE 52. Charles-Honoré
Lannuier. Square pier table with
canted corners. 1817 (cat. no. 113)

Following their wedding in 1817, Maria and Duncan Campbell resided at 51 Broadway,
a three-story Georgian-style brick house that Campbell inherited with other real estate from
his grandfather Thomas Pearsall.[30] Among their new furnishings were a mahogany pier
table, a pair of card tables—both richly ornamented, gilded, and bronzed—and a worktable, purchased from Lannuier's shop and in the most up-to-date French taste that was
available in New York. All four pieces of furniture are recorded in an invoice of June 19,
1817, from Lannuier to William Bayard, with instructions for delivery to "P. D. Campell [*sic*]
Broad Way" (see Appendix 5).[31] Also on the invoice is a charge for the repair of the gilded
figure and ornament on a pier table, which, from the description, suggests that it was either
French or possibly another of Lannuier's figural tables.

Four gilded-and-bronzed figural card tables, identical but for the addition of two extra
gilded-brass ornaments on one pair, have come down in the Van Rensselaer family: One
pair, each with a cheval-glass label, is now in the collection of the Albany Institute of History
& Art (plate 51), and the other pair is in The Metropolitan Museum of Art (plate 53). Although
it is not possible to determine with absolute certainty which pair of tables belonged to
Maria Bayard Campbell and which to her sister Harriet Bayard Van Rensselaer, a letter to
the Albany Institute from the donor's wife, Mrs. Stephen Van Rensselaer Crosby, states that
the Empire furniture owned by her husband came from the Campbells and not the Van
Rensselaers.[32] Since the donor's gift included French and American furniture, it is unclear
whether the reference was to the French pieces or to both. If one accepts the broader interpretation, then the pair of card tables and the labeled pier table in Albany (plate 52)—both
Crosby gifts—are the card tables and pier table that Lannuier made for Maria Campbell.

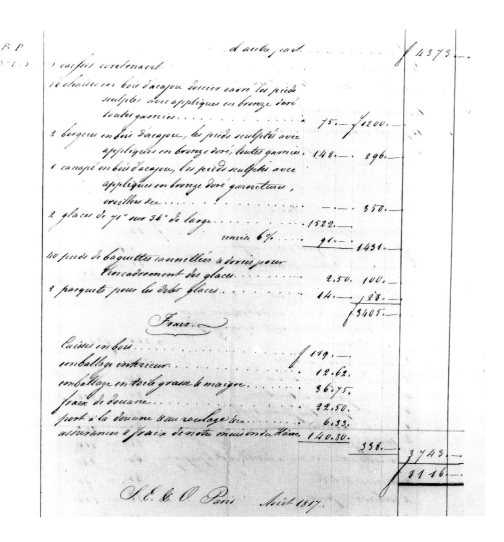

A worktable with the same provenance, now at Winterthur (see plate 70), is probably the one noted on the invoice, and it, too, most likely belonged to the Campbells.

With the exception of the furniture Lannuier produced for James Bosley, he is not known to have made seating furniture for domestic interiors. It was perhaps for this very reason—as well as to gratify his newly married children's taste for French furnishings—that Bayard ordered a suite of seating furniture and a set of porcelain from Paris, through his Le Havre agents, in August 1817. The invoice to Bayard, in French, is uncommonly descriptive: sixteen chairs in mahogany, with square backs, carved legs, and gilded-brass mounts;

FIGURE 64. Probably Italian. Chimneypiece. About 1816. Marble, 49 x 71 ¹/₂ x 12 ³/₄ in. Museum of Art, Rhode Island School of Design, Providence. Gift of the Viscountess Rothermere, 1982

two upholstered armchairs and one sofa in mahogany, with carved legs and gilded-brass mounts; two mirror plates, 71 by 34 inches; and forty feet of fluted and gilded molding for framing the mirrors and two backboards for them (fig. 62).[33] This suite must have been intended for Maria, for, with only one exception, invoices for Harriet's furniture were not found among Bayard's papers. Part of the suite—eight side chairs (plate 51), an upholstered armchair, and a sofa (fig. 63)—also was given by Stephen Van Rensselaer Crosby to the Albany Institute, and, as its design matches the description on the invoice, is certainly the Empire furniture mentioned in Mrs. Crosby's letter.

The French porcelain service, which was ordered through the same agents, was extensive and costly. The most elaborate pieces were the eight dozen dessert plates painted with landscapes of flowers and animals encircled by a demi-mat gold border. At a cost of Fr 300 per plate, they were the most expensive items on the invoice; the next most costly objects were two vase-shaped ice-cream coolers at Fr 200 each. The other forms, which were ordered in sets of four, included round and oval footed stands, fruit stands on raised feet, fruit baskets, and strawberry bowls; two pairs of each were indicated, which suggests that Bayard intended to split the service between his two daughters.[34]

If, by 1817, Duncan and Maria Campbell's three-story Georgian brick town house appeared a bit old-fashioned on the exterior,[35] the interiors, in the latest French taste, were decidedly not so. The Lannuier pier table, with its gilded swan supports and elaborate gilded-brass ornaments, probably stood in the front parlor on the pier between the two windows that looked out onto Broadway; the six-foot-tall gilded French pier glass above the pier table, its width nearly the same as that of the looking-glass plate at the back of the table, helped to create a seamless illusion of extended space. Fashionable French taste, as reported in Pierre de La Mésangère's *Collection de Meubles et Objets de Goût* (see plate 20), dictated that swagged drapery fabric, suspended on poles, be carried across the tops of the windows and the pier in a continuous design, with sheer muslin or silk curtains hung vertically at the sides of the windows. A related reference in the Bayard papers of November 1819 indicates that the upholsterer William W. Galatian charged William Bayard for "putting up 2 Silk window Curtains & pier Drapery / [and] putting [up] 1 Sett [*sic*] Damask Drawing Room Curtains."[36] Earlier, Bayard had bought Brussels carpeting with borders in several patterns—"Bronze & Scarlet" and "the Large light figure as was supposed to be used by Mrs. Campbell"—for the young couple.[37] Bayard also purchased French scenic wallpapers from a New York purveyor in 1818: two sets each of "Italian Scenery" and border and "India

Landscape" and border, and two "Sets Hangings" (usually a drapery-panel design).[38] These, too, perhaps were meant for the homes of his newly married daughters. Probably also in the Campbells' front parlor were the Lannuier card tables, which most often would have been displayed symmetrically against a wall; they would be brought out into the room for social occasions, their tops swiveled and their leaves unfolded for lively card games that included the popular whist and loo. The French canapé, pair of bergères, and chaises completed the parlor suite. Together, this furniture—some from Paris and some made in New York—represented the zenith of fashionable French taste in America in the early nineteenth century.

In 1816 and 1817, Bayard ordered through his firm's agents in Leghorn two sets of marble chimneypieces that may have been for his Campbell and Van Rensselaer daughters' homes. For the first order of four chimneypieces, the agent advised Bayard that "we have very handsome Sculpture in alabaster of figures and roses for ornements [*sic*] for Chimney Pieces if you [would] like to have any."[39] Three months later, apologizing for the fact that the chimneypieces were unfinished, the agent wrote, "The workmen of Carrara are engaged . . . for the United States to furnish the Marble Work of the capitol in Washington, besides which the English Travellers have engaged many workmen to make . . . ornaments like chimney pieces, monuments etc."[40] When, after further delays, the mantels were shipped in February 1817—a year after the order was placed—the anxious agent noted: "I hope by the particular attention paid in the choice of the Marble & the accuracy the artist has made in his work you will be satisfied. I have to observe . . . that one of them has been worked according to the genius of the Artist & [he] hopes it will meet your tastes."[41] Bayard may not have been pleased; the mantel may have been too elaborate or too costly, for the agent wrote in May 1817 that he had received Bayard's "fresh order for 6 Chimney Pieces, Two of them Elegant & Four less so for Bedrooms. I shall strictly confine myself to your instructions & limits hereon."[42] A chimneypiece formerly in the Van Rensselaer Manor House in Albany, with female caryatid figures balancing tasseled Turkish-style cushions on their heads and supporting an elaborately carved classical frieze with a rosette at each end (fig. 64), is like the mantel described in the Bayard correspondence, but may or may not be the same one.[43] A number of chimneypieces in this style are known, and, in fact, a similar pair was ordered from abroad by James Monroe in 1817 for The White House and installed in the State Dining Room.

Harriet Bayard's marriage to Stephen Van Rensselaer IV in 1817 united two old New York families. The success of William Bayard's firm in the flush of postwar prosperity—by 1817, it had become the most important commercial house in New York—had long made up for the loss of Bayard-family lands. The Van Rensselaers continued to reside on and derive their livelihood from their manorial Hudson Valley estates near Albany, which had been granted under Dutch rule. At the time of her wedding, Harriet, not yet eighteen years old, was considered a beauty. She must have been beguiling, for two years earlier her brother Robert, writing to the family from Paris, reminded Harriet that "she must wait [to marry] till her brother's return! I hear her beaus are numerous and that she is without exception the greatest belle in New York."[44]

Like many upper-class young men of the period, to broaden his education, Stephen Van Rensselaer traveled abroad in 1812–13, visiting some of the principal sites of antiquity. A letter to his father in the summer of 1813 describes his visits to England and Paris and provides a long-winded explanation of his expenses as a prelude to asking for a large sum of money. After a leisurely tour of France and Switzerland, he crossed into Italy, where "we were plundered by a band of Ruffians who took all my cloaths [*sic*], watch, & money. . . . At Florence I purchased a few lamps and all the most celebrated Statues in Alabaster & at Rome engravings of the pictures of Raphael." Having returned to Paris, he explains that "on my arrival . . . I was presented at Court which was a very great expense. I was obliged

FIGURE 65. James Eights. *Entrance of the Canal into the Hudson at Albany.* 1823. Watercolor, 3 ¹⁄₈ x 6 in. (image). Albany Institute of History & Art, New York. Gift of James Eights, 1836

to purchase a dress of velvet, sword, & hat." The spendthrift son then writes that he has taken lodgings in the environs of Paris—less costly than a city hotel—to save money, but reminds his father nonetheless that "There is a Certain form to keep up when one goes to Court & in society."[45] Stephen was presented to both the empress Marie-Louise and the former empress Joséphine. He observed the newest styles at the French court, and, like his sister-in-law Maria Campbell, returned with firsthand knowledge of the latest in French Empire furniture and interior decoration.

In preparation for his son's marriage to Harriet Bayard, Stephen Van Rensselaer III began building a town house for his namesake in 1816 on North Market Street in Albany, adjacent to the entrance to the grounds of his own manor house. Completed about 1818, the three-story, four-bay-wide structure is attributed to the talented regional architect Philip Hooker (1766–1836), whose Regency-style masterpiece, Hyde Hall, still stands at the north end of Otsego Lake, near Cooperstown, New York. The plain façade of the Albany house featured a raised porch with decorative wrought-iron railings and a semi-circular fan-lighted doorway with a balustrade that extended across the front at the roof line. A watercolor of 1823 by the Albany artist James Eights, celebrating the opening of the Erie Canal (fig. 65), shows a view of the back façade of the house, which faced the Hudson River. A curved wall on the right half of the rear elevation discloses a drawing room with an elliptical end wall located at the rear of the building—a feature not often found on Albany houses at this date. The three oval windows on the side elevation probably indicate the position of an interior staircase.[46]

When Harriet and Stephen Van Rensselaer moved into their newly built town house shortly after their wedding, it—like the Campbells' New York town house—was fashionably furnished in the latest French taste. In Albany, the state capitol, Harriet was hostess to the political and social elite. In a letter to their father, detained in Albany on business early in 1819, Harriet's brother William Bayard, Jr., noted that a few more days "will only afford you the prolonged society of the Albanionized young patroness who we are told lives a gay life and a happy one, entertaining our Sovereigns & administering to their bodily comforts while they (alas are not always) working for the good of our political constitution."[47]

What little is known of the classical-style interiors of Harriet's new home can in part be gleaned from an estimate by the builder John Boardman for finishing work on the doors and columns of the principal story.[48] Doorcases and windows were framed with pilasters and some featured Grecian-style double architraves; an arch, finished on both sides, graced the

FIGURE 66. Encoignure. 1840 (altered from a square pier table with canted corners, of 1817, by Charles-Honoré Lannuier) (cat. no. 114)

PLATE 53. Charles-Honoré Lannuier. Card table. 1817 (cat. no. 72)

FIGURE 67. French maker. Bergère (armchair). 1817. Mahogany, 38½ x 25 x 20 in. Albany Institute of History & Art, New York. Gift of Mrs. Justine Van Rensselaer Hooper, 1951

hallway. Possibly installed in the more important rooms were the Italian marble chimney-pieces purchased through Bayard's Leghorn agents, with the most elaborate perhaps located in the parlor with the elliptical end wall.

No invoices have been found for Harriet's furniture,[49] but the existence of a second suite of Lannuier tables and French seating furniture with a Van Rensselaer provenance suggests that William Bayard presented both daughters with matching sets of furniture. A pair of encoignures, or corner tables, with gilded swan supports (fig. 66), given to the Albany Institute by Harriet's and Stephen's great-granddaughter Justine Van Rensselaer Barber (Mrs. Roger Hooper), and a pair of card tables (plate 53) at the Metropolitan Museum, donated in 1996 by Justine Van Rensselaer Hooper Milliken, Mrs. Hooper's daughter, likely belonged to Harriet and Stephen Van Rensselaer. Long thought to have been "en suite" with the pier table, the corner tables were instead altered from a pier table—an exact match to the Campbell one—that was literally cut in half (see cat. no. 114) at some point to suit the taste of the Van Rensselaers or to fit a specialized location in the house.

A second partial suite of French seating furniture at the Albany Institute, which includes a canapé and a pair of bergères (fig. 67) with the same provenance as the cut-down pier table/encoignures, also must have belonged to Harriet and Stephen Van Rensselaer. The two suites are nearly identical in form and may be by the same French maker. They differ mainly in ornamental details: The legs on the first—or Campbell—set (fig. 63) are carved, and terminate in a four-lobed petal design, while those on the Van Rensselaer set end in turned rings; the foliate gilded-brass ornaments of the first set are in a laurel-leaf pattern and those on the second set in an oak-leaf pattern; the design of the rosettes and of other mounts, as well as their placement, also vary; and the arms of the Campbell canapé and bergère are carved with a leaf pattern, whereas the arms of the corresponding furniture from the Van Rensselaer set are reeded as well as carved with a leaf design. No side chairs from the Van Rensselaer set are at the Albany Institute, but correspondence indicates that other side chairs were in the possession of family members in 1938.[50] The Van Rensselaer French

PLATE 54. Charles-Honoré Lannuier. French bedstead. 1817–19 (cat. no. 5)

suite also includes a matching pair of armless settees with oak-leaf-patterned bronze mounts and ring-turned feet—a furniture form not listed on the surviving French invoice.

Perhaps because she had not received a French pier glass, William Bayard apparently also purchased a pier mirror for Harriet from Isaac Platt in 1818, along with a packing box in which to ship it to Albany.[51] Platt advertised in several New York City newspapers that he sold "large sized Looking Glass Plates, suitable for Piers and Chimneys . . . framed to any pattern or to fit any particular place" at his looking-glass store on Broadway.[52] A year earlier, Bayard noted that he had received two boxes of china for "Mr. Van Ranselaer [sic],"[53] which either may have been a part of the Paris porcelain service ordered in August 1817 or of a very large cargo of wares and commodities, which included furniture, astral lamps, looking glasses, china, and glass, that was shipped from France in July 1816.[54] Bayard made additional purchases from Lannuier, as attested by two promissory notes dated May 29, 1818, each for $505.25, although one perhaps is a duplicate of the other.[55] That the notes are "on account of my bill rendered" and "Value Received" argues that they are in payment for furniture, which, in the absence of a surviving invoice, cannot now be identified or otherwise matched to the notes. William Bayard returned as a client to Duncan Phyfe yet again, as indicated by his personal check to Phyfe in 1819 for $1,305.77,[56] but it is unclear for whom this furniture was intended. Of Bayard's other living children, a daughter, Eliza Justine, married Joseph Blackwell in 1811; his older son, William, married in 1812; and his younger son, Robert, in 1820. It may be that this furniture was for the home of one of them—or

even for Bayard's own—but it is quite possible, too, that he purchased more furniture for Maria or Harriet, perhaps for a dining room or bedroom.

No invoice is known to survive for the French bedstead (plate 54) that Lannuier made for Harriet and Stephen Van Rensselaer. The most elaborate extant example of the form from Lannuier's shop, it is enriched with burl-elm, rosewood, and mahogany veneers, gilded-brass ornaments of winged griffins, rams' heads, and winged female goddesses flanking a classical head with sprays of flowers, and die-stamped brass-and-wood borders. Since this bedstead is very much like the ones that Stephen may have seen at the French court, it is reasonable to suggest that it was executed to his special order—and that it could have been a Van Rensselaer wedding gift to the young couple.

Following the death of his father, Stephen Van Rensselaer III, in 1839, Stephen and Harriet moved into the Manor House, which had been built in 1765 in the Georgian style and modified in 1818 and 1819 by the Albany architect Philip Hooker. Two single-story wings were added at the ends of the house, as well as a piazza on the garden front.[57] In the early 1840s, the house was extensively remodeled for its new occupants by the architect Richard Upjohn. A photograph of the drawing room (fig. 68), taken sometime after Harriet Van Rensselaer's death in 1875 and before the house was dismantled and partially rebuilt in Williamstown, Massachusetts, in 1893, shows some of the Van Rensselaer furniture acquired at the time of Harriet and Stephen's wedding. To the left of the fireplace is one of the Lannuier card tables, an encoignure is partially visible at the left side of the photograph, and placed in front of the fireplace and against the walls are the pair of French bergères and eight side chairs with oak-leaf-patterned ornaments and legs terminating in ring turnings— further documentation that this Lannuier and French furniture did, indeed, belong to Harriet and Stephen Van Rensselaer.

James Brinckerhoff (1791–1846), a merchant in partnership with his brother Abraham in a dry-goods firm on Pearl Street, followed a pattern similar to Bayard, patronizing both Phyfe and Lannuier. On the occasion of his marriage in January 1815 to Charlotte Troup (d. 1873), a daughter of the jurist and land investor Robert Troup, Brinckerhoff purchased a quantity of mahogany furniture from Duncan Phyfe for their Pine Street home. Brinckerhoff's purchases are documented in a bill of sale from Phyfe for $2,125.50, which itemizes furniture made and delivered between September 1815 and July 1816. Included on the invoice are parlor, dining-room, and bedroom furniture, some of which still survives in the possession of Brinckerhoff's descendants.[58] Brinckerhoff placed an order with Lannuier in June 1816 for what appears to have been a special French-style bedroom suite, which included a mahogany bedstead ($95), a pedestal ($35), and a large and expensive mahogany dressing-glass frame ($135), and, two months later, he ordered a mahogany crib ($42) (see Appendix 3, 4).[59] None of this furniture is known to survive, but the invoices are among the Brinckerhoff papers. Another invoice, dated June 22, 1816, and probably related to the Lannuier bedstead, reveals the decorative scheme for the drapery. The upholsterer Peter Turcot billed Brinckerhoff for "a Large Eagle & dart" ($25), "making 2 Fancy Bed curtains" ($16), and "20 yds fringe" ($25) (fig. 69).[60] Typical of the classically inspired window- and bed-curtain treatments in the early nineteenth century was a large carved-and-gilded eagle with outstretched wings, which would have been affixed to the ceiling or to a wall above the bed; its talons would grasp a dart or arrow of bronzed-and-gilded metal or wood, from which the "Fancy" bed curtains would be hung.[61] An engraving from La Mésangère illustrates a bed draped with curtains that are suspended from an eagle gripping a ring (plate 55). In its general form, the Lannuier bedstead may have looked something like this, with the headboard and footboard of equal height, set parallel to the wall. This was the form and the typical placement in a room of what was referred to as a "French bedstead" in the 1817 New York cabinet-makers' price books.

The Lannuier pedestal and dressing-glass frame also were to be used as bedroom furnishings. The pedestal may have been a veneered mahogany column with a marble-inset top and an enclosed cupboard below for necessities—a *table de nuit*, as described in the French fashion plates of the period. In May 1816, Brinckerhoff purchased from Charles Del

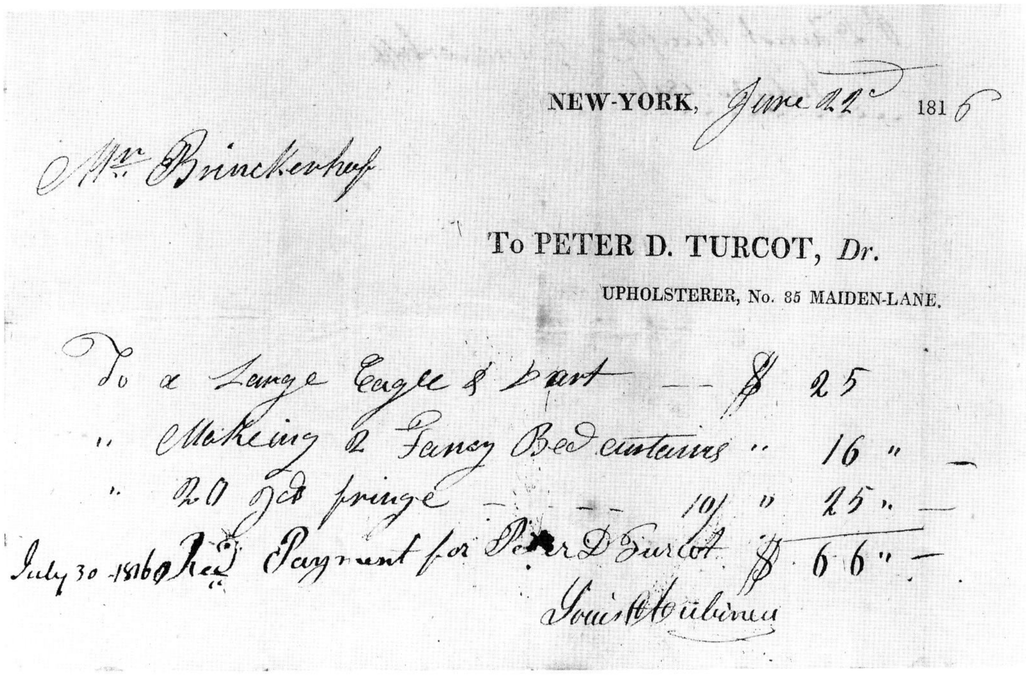

FIGURE 69. Invoice from Peter D. Turcot to James Brinckerhoff, June 22, 1816. Robert Troup Papers, The New York Public Library

Lavoir.   Lit à la Romaine.   Chiffonnier.

PLATE 55. Pierre de La Mésangère. Design for a *lit à la romaine* (Plate 26 from *Collection de Meubles et Objets de Goût*). 1802. Colored engraving, 7 ¾ x 12 ¼ in. The Metropolitan Museum of Art, New York. Harris Brisbane Dick Fund, 1930

FIGURE 70. New York maker. *Psyché* (cheval glass). Mahogany, 75 x 44⁷⁄₈ x 27³⁄₄ in. The Metropolitan Museum of Art, New York. Gift of Ginsburg & Levy, Inc., in memory of John Ginsburg and Isaac Levy, 1969

FIGURE 71. Duncan Phyfe. Card table. 1816. Mahogany, 30 x 36 x 18 in. Private collection

Vecchio's looking-glass and print store a costly "pair [of] New Fashion Framed Chimny [*sic*] Glasses" for $475 and a looking-glass plate for $75.00.[62] The latter may have been intended for the mahogany dressing-glass frame. The high price of the frame, $135, suggests that it was a large dressing glass of the type that originated in France and was known as a *psyché*. One of these *psychés* appears on Lannuier's engraved trade label (see plate 13), and an unsigned example with the same pitched pediment as the *psyché* depicted on the label is in the collection of the Metropolitan Museum (fig. 70).

Phyfe sold Brinckerhoff a French-style "canapee" bedstead in May 1816, for which he charged $200. The bedstead, which survives, has Egyptian term figures for front posts, but the canopy and its supporting arms are missing. The high cost of the bedstead reflects the additional charges for the canopy and arms and possibly for fabrics and trim as well. Although bedding and furnishing fabrics are not noted on Phyfe's bill, his invoice to Brinckerhoff attests to the presence of an upholsterer in his shop, for it specifies charges for making covers for two easy chairs and for covering a footstool.[63] The lack of a second upholsterer's invoice for bed hangings supports this view.

Brinckerhoff's sedulous record keeping and preservation of tradesmen's invoices were in preparation for an appraisal that was made December 6, 1816, prior to purchasing an insurance policy on his household furnishings.[64] The amount of the appraisal totaled $6,610 and was based on the actual cost of purchases. The value assigned to his mahogany furniture was $2,857, of which $2,100 was spent with Phyfe, $307 with Lannuier, and $450 with Joseph Wilson for a pianoforte.[65] Looking glasses were listed separately and appraised at $565. Brussels, ingrain, and Venetian carpeting was valued at $948, following mahogany furniture as the second most costly item, and window and bed curtains and fixtures were third at $855.

In addition to the drapery the upholsterer Peter Turcot may have made for the Lannuier bed, he also fabricated five pairs of fully lined and trimmed window curtains for the Brinckerhoffs' town house. (Turcot's name suggests that he, too, was French, or of French descent.) In 1807, he advertised for sale a secondhand Paris-made bed with elegantly trimmed curtains. Styling himself an "upholsterer and tent maker" in an ad of 1811, Turcot offered for sale elegant trimmings from France, including fringes, gimps, tassels, and cords in such bold color combinations as green and orange, purple and orange, black and orange, black and yellow, and crimson and orange.[66] He made and hung the curtains in a style *le plus à la mode*, including as ornamental fixtures four swans ($60), two bronzed-and-gilded bows ($12), twelve curtain pins, and 150 yards of silk ribbon. The bronzed-and-gilded bows, the eagle-and-dart motif—an imperial Roman emblem—and the swans were all popular elements of French Empire style.

Charlotte Troup Brinckerhoff and the two Bayard daughters, Maria Campbell and Harriet Van Rensselaer, were married within a span of two years, and acquired furniture contemporaneously for their new households. As a Phyfe card table (fig. 71)—originally one of a pair—purchased by the Brinckerhoffs, and two pairs of Lannuier card tables made for the Campbells and Van Rensselaers (plates 51, 53) survive, it is informative to compare the tables as potential choices available to customers in New York in 1816–17. Both sets of card tables have swivel tops veneered in richly figured mahogany that form a square when open; both share identical gilded-brass ornaments at the center of the apron; and both have octagonal plinths with elliptical, hollow sides from which issue four carved-and-gilded hocked animal legs. The Phyfe card table, however, has a decidedly English flavor. The canted-corner top supported by four columns with reeded drums and bulbous-shaped turnings is in the English Regency style as Phyfe chose to interpret it. It is a table designed for the prosperous upper middle class—a bit conservative and of restrained elegance, although the bronzed-and-gilded lion's-paw feet and brass ornament are a timid bow to extravagant French taste. At $135 for the two, or $67.50 for each table, the price was a little more than half that of the Lannuier pair, which cost $125 each. The die-stamped brass-and-wood borders in two patterns along the edges of the apron and the top, the additional gilded-brass mounts, the carved-and-gilded winged female figure, and the *vert antique*-and-gilded rear columns added substantially to the cost of Lannuier tables. These card tables, among the richest interpretation of the French Late Empire style available from a New York cabinetmaker, were meant to suit the tastes of the wealthiest clients and were priced accordingly. Simply put, Phyfe was not the equal of the French-trained Lannuier when it came to French style.

FRENCH CLIENTS IN THE UNITED STATES

Napoleon's pardon of most émigrés in 1802 spawned a welcomed repatriation to France for many Frenchmen who had sought a haven in the United States from the excesses of their Revolution. There were those, however, who, for varying reasons, chose to remain. Some elected to stay to oversee their American investments, while others, mainly inveterate Royalists, were joined by a wave of more recent arrivals seeking political asylum from Napoleon's new government. Some of these Frenchmen—James Leray de Chaumont, General Jean-Victor-Marie Moreau, and later Joseph Bonaparte, who resided in America only for a time—are believed to have been clients of Lannuier.

Of the three men, Lannuier's most important French patron was James Leray de Chaumont (1760–1840)—or Jacques-Donatien Leray de Chaumont, as he was known in his

FIGURE 72. Unknown French artist. *James Leray de Chaumont at the Château de Chaumont-sur-Loire*. About 1800. Private collection, France

native France (fig. 72). The scion of a wealthy and titled family of merchants whose fortune derived largely from trade with the French West Indies, Leray first came to America from France in 1785 to represent his father and other French citizens with claims against the United States government that stemmed from loans to the fledgling Republic during the Revolution. Leray's father, Jacques-Donatien Leray de Chaumont (1725–1803), was Benjamin Franklin's landlord for the eight-and-a-half years Franklin served as America's first minister to France. Beginning in 1777, Franklin resided at Chaumont *père*'s suburban Paris estate at Passy, the magnificent Hôtel Valentinois, first in the garden pavilion, and, from 1779, in a wing of the mansion itself.

For most of this time, Franklin and the Chaumont family enjoyed a warm and affectionate relationship. For the Salon of 1779, Chaumont *père* commissioned Joseph-Siffred Duplessis to paint the notable portrait of Franklin during his years in France, known as the "Fur Collar" portrait, now in the Metropolitan Museum. At the family's château, Chaumont-sur-Loire, Chaumont *père* employed the Italian sculptor Jean-Baptiste Nini, from 1772 until his death in 1786, to produce terra-cotta portrait medallions in bas-relief of famous persons, including almost a dozen versions of his well-known portrait busts of Franklin. In 1770, Chaumont had erected a large, circular workshop to house a pottery and glass manufactory on the grounds of the château—a massive, turreted stone structure, dating to the late fifteenth and the early sixteenth century, which he had purchased in 1750 along with its surrounding two-thousand-acre estate, including four villages. The medallions were mass produced and sold throughout Europe, with the profits split evenly between Nini and Chaumont. A shrewd entrepreneur and ambitious businessman of substantial wealth, Chaumont was willing to take enormous risks. He was the leading supplier in France of goods and munitions for the American Revolution. His financial collapse, brought about principally by speculation in American paper currency received as payment for American debt incurred during the Revolution, began after Congress steeply depreciated paper dollars in 1780.[67]

James Leray de Chaumont, who learned English from Franklin, John Adams, and others in the circle of American diplomats that resided at various times at the family's Passy estate, spent the five years from 1785 to 1790 in the United States urging Congress to compensate his financially failing father for unpaid debts and depreciated currency. It was during this time, in 1788, that he became an American citizen, and the following year he married the wealthy Grace Coxe, the daughter of Charles Davenport Coxe of Sidney (now Franklin Township), New Jersey. Leray's citizenship conferred on him the right to purchase real estate in North America and, over the course of the next twenty years, he invested large sums in vast tracts of land in northern and central New York and northern Pennsylvania. At one point, James Leray's New York holdings encompassed nearly six hundred thousand acres, the larger part of the four northern counties today called Jefferson, Lewis, Saint Lawrence, and Franklin.

After unsuccessfully petitioning the American Congress, Leray returned to France in 1790, where, for the next twelve years, he worked to restructure his father's collapsing financial empire (the Passy estate had to be sold in 1791) and to defend his father and the Château de Chaumont-sur-Loire from being seized by Revolutionary tribunals. In 1793, he invested in a French syndicate that purchased two hundred thousand acres of wilderness in northern New York from the New York land speculator William Constable, who was in Paris eagerly promoting his land sales. The land, inaccessible and only partly surveyed, lay along the Black River on the western side of the Adirondack Mountains, bordered by the north shore of Lake Ontario where it joins the Saint Lawrence River. Named Castorland by the French syndicate, after *castor*, the French word for beaver—in which the area abounded—the tract idealistically was conceived as a colony for émigrés escaping the Reign of Terror. It was never a success. Its European directors were blind to the reality of establishing a wilderness settlement, and James Leray, later the colony's director and main creditor, would acquire the unsold land in 1814, adding it to his already considerable holdings in northern New York.

Together with Gouverneur Morris, a family friend from Morris's days as President Washington's Minister to France (1792–94), Leray owned other lands, also purchased from Constable, directly north of Castorland, in the Antwerp Company syndicate. In spite of a wooden leg, Morris was confident in his ability as a sailor and guide, and in 1803 the two men spent an adventurous September camping and exploring Leray's lands. Caught in bad weather on the Saint Lawrence, they navigated in darkness to a sheltered cove where, Morris recorded, they pitched their tent: "mattresses laid on . . . straw, and a large fire before us. . . . How delicious . . . to enjoy Repose in Shelter from the Storm." At dawn, "a heavy squall . . . blows the fire into our Tent, menacing us with a sudden conflagration . . . the tent is blown down and a heavy shower drenches us completely."[68] Leray returned to France in 1804. In 1806, he sent an agent to America charged with the task of building a fine house for him north of the Black River, near present-day Watertown, New York. It was constructed at least in part by 1808, when Leray arrived with his wife and children. He began an ambitious building program: The small village of Leraysville was laid out a short distance to the north, and formal gardens, ponds, water courses, and roads were planned. Leray remained for two years, until 1810, when he departed for France with his family, leaving his older son, Vincent, in charge of developing the property. Leray's American wife, Grace Coxe, died in 1812, and he did not revisit his northern New York home until 1816, accompanied by his newly married daughter Theresa, and her husband, Hippolyte, Marquis de Gouvello de Kériaval.

At this time, the widowed Leray resolved to make his home in northern New York. Shortly after his arrival, Leray or his son Vincent is thought to have purchased a quantity of

PLATE 56. Charles-Honoré Lannuier. Square pier table with canted corners. 1815–19 (cat. no. 105)

PLATE 57. Charles-Honoré
Lannuier. Square pier table with
canted corners. 1815–19 (cat. no. 106)

gilded furniture from Lannuier in the antique or Late Empire style of the period, among which were two pairs of pier tables that are presently known (plates 56, 57). The near-perfect proportions, elaborate gilded-brass ornaments, highly figured veneers, marble tops, looking-glass plates, and gilded winged figures on the smaller, but richer, pair of these tables make them among the finest produced by Lannuier's shop. A French columnar pier table of about 1800, with term figures, although known only from a photograph, is also said to have once been part of the furnishings of the Leray mansion. Surviving, in addition, is a small group of French furniture of the same date—including a marble-topped bureau, a *secrétaire à abattant*, and some French metalwork—which, by tradition, is said to have belonged to James Leray and which descended in the family of Jules-René Payen (1800–1862), who purchased the mansion in the 1840s from Leray's estate.[69]

In the late 1810s or early 1820s, the French naturalist Jacques-Gérard Milbert (1767–1840), on a trip to northern New York gathering natural-history specimens for the restored Bourbon monarch Louis XVIII, visited Leray and described his home as located:

In the remote wilderness [where] he has succeeded in creating an estate, which, for luxury, beauty, and comforts of every kind, could be compared with the most famous châteaux and parks in France . . . to give an idea of its former, and probably present, luxury, it contained a large drawing room, billiard and music rooms, a library, and two separate wings with guest rooms for visitors and friends. From the drawing room the windows overlooked a vast and magnificent vegetable garden, planted in French fashion. . . . In another direction lay a fine pond filled with a multitude of trout. Beyond that the ancient forest formed an immense park, with avenues, winding paths, clearings, and dense, picturesque thickets.[70]

FIGURE 73. Hippolyte, Marquis de Gouvello. *James Leray's Mansion.* About 1816. Chalk. Private collection, France

A sketch of the mansion by Leray's son-in-law Hippolyte de Gouvello, from a notebook dated 1815 but executed in 1816 shortly after the family's arrival, shows an elevated main section with a two-story portico framed by a balustrade on three sides (fig. 73). There appears to be only one wing; the second, perhaps, had not yet been erected. A building to the left in the drawing may have housed servants. Upended tree stumps in the foreground leave no doubt as to the wilderness-like setting and reveal that the site and the house were still under construction and the gardens barely begun. The mansion, thought to have been a frame dwelling, was damaged by fire about 1822. Milbert acknowledges this when he writes of the building's "former luxury," and notes that it was "entirely rebuilt and arranged with even more elegance then before."[71] (This later house of stuccoed limestone is the Le Ray Mansion, which, today, is part of the United States Army base at Fort Drum.) Scholars have long debated whether the present structure, distinguished architecturally by two linked octagonal parlors on the garden façade of the central block, is substantially the earlier house, renovated after the fire, or an entirely new construction.[72]

James Leray also built a house for his son Vincent about 1815 on the Saint Lawrence River at Cape Vincent. This simpler two-story stone building, with elliptical windows and doorway on the ground floor, still stands, and some of the furniture Leray purchased from Lannuier may have been intended for this house. Vincent Le Ray (1790–1875)—Vincent always used what he considered the more aristocratic spelling of the family name, but his father did only occasionally[73]—married Cornelia Juhel (d. about 1823), the daughter of John Juhel, a French émigré, and Cornelia Livingston Juhel, of New York City, in 1821, and they lived both in this house and in the Leray mansion.

James Leray transported the French manorial style to the area, and stories abound of his seigneurial manner, liveried servants, and opulent hospitality. He continued to promote the sale of parcels of his New York land to émigrés and settlers and to develop the North Country, constructing sawmills, encouraging agriculture, and donating land for the building of several churches. Napoleonic exiles arrived in northern New York state following the fall of the First Empire, and Leray enjoyed a short period of prosperity derived from sales to them and from rents. In 1816, he sold twenty-six thousand acres to Joseph Bonaparte, who erected three houses in the area and a hunting lodge nearby at Natural Bridge, where, beginning in 1818, he resided during the summer months, for four years, during his American

FIGURE 74. Percier and Fontaine. *Lit exécuté à Paris pour Mme M.* 1801 (Plate 19 from *Recueil de décorations intérieures*, 1812). Engraving, 11⅞ x 8½ in. The Metropolitan Museum of Art, New York. Harris Brisbane Dick Fund, 1928

sojourn. Besides Joseph Bonaparte, who was a frequent visitor, De Witt Clinton and President Monroe also were guests. The opening of the Erie Canal in 1825 ruined land speculation in northern New York. In debt, with his investment a failure, Leray returned to France permanently in 1836. Milbert was prescient when he predicted in his account, "The population is sparse and scattered, and it will probably never increase to any extent on account of the long, cold winters."[74]

An important French general, Jean-Victor-Marie Moreau (1763–1813), the celebrated commander of the French Army of the Rhine, had business dealings with Lannuier and may have bought furniture from him. Moreau was banished from France by Napoleon for supposed anti-government sympathies provoked by his ambitious wife and the Royalist circles in which she moved, and they arrived in Philadelphia in August 1805. He and Mme Moreau resided on an estate in Morrisville, Pennsylvania, and from 1806 until 1813, when they returned to Europe, they also maintained a residence in New York; from 1809, they lived at 119 Pearl Street.

Four months after his marriage to Louise-Alexandrine-Eugénie Hulot, in March 1801, General Moreau purchased an *hôtel* in the rue d'Anjou in Paris. For the next fourteen months the noted architects Percier and Fontaine undertook the renovations and decorations of the building, Fontaine at one point declaring it one of their most important commissions.[75] Three watercolors of designs for the grand salon, three sketches for Mme Moreau's bedroom, and a study for her painting studio, all drafted in the architects' studio, are known. Several engravings of Mme Moreau's furniture appear in the architects' highly influential *Recueil de décorations intérieures*: One plate, number 19, shows her bed (fig. 74) and another, number 60, her boudoir; an engraving of a worktable and a night table in the

FIGURE 75. French maker. Console. About 1800. Mahogany, 36½ x 60⅝ x 19⅜ in. Musée National du Château de Fontainebleau, France

Recueil—plate 23—is also thought to represent the Moreaus' furniture. The bed, now at Fontainebleau, was executed in 1802 by Jacob frères, *ébénistes*, who made much of the furniture for the house. The design is a more elaborate version of Lannuier's French-style beds, except perhaps for the very ornate one he made for Stephen Van Rensselaer IV in 1817.

In 1802–3, Mme Moreau's *hôtel* briefly was the setting for lavish balls and concerts. She herself was an accomplished musician and virtuoso pianist, and her entertainments and those of Mme Récamier are among the events most often celebrated in contemporary accounts. Unwisely, she surrounded herself with a circle of friends whose dislike of the government was well known. Moreau was arrested in February 1804, and Napoleon, pretending to exercise leniency, commuted the general's jail sentence to exile. The following July, the First Consul ordered the purchase of the Moreaus' Paris *hôtel*, with its furnishings, and their château at Grosbois, both at a handsome price, and he had the furniture deposited at the royal château of Fontainebleau.[76]

Moreau must have emulated his home in Paris in outfitting his New York town house, which became noted for the luxury and elegance of its furnishings. It is unfortunate that no furniture owned by the Moreaus in this country has been identified, but a most intriguing link, alluded to earlier, between Mme Moreau and Lannuier exists: In 1811, she lent Lannuier $2,000 for which she held a mortgage on his Broad Street property as collateral. From this evidence, it is not unreasonable to suggest that, while living in New York, Mme Moreau patronized Lannuier, the foremost French cabinetmaker in the city, whom she had encouraged in business, as she had patronized Percier and Fontaine and their favorite cabinetmaker, Jacob, in Paris. The Moreaus' American furniture probably was related stylistically to the simpler furniture in their Paris town house. The straightforward rectilinear form of a French console with term figures, in the antique style, from their Paris *hôtel* (fig. 75), is comparable to two pier tables of about 1805–10 by Lannuier (see plate 30, and plate 79). This is the kind of furniture that the Moreaus probably chose for their American homes, although they must have owned French-made furniture as well. Mme Moreau was the acknowledged leader of French society in America. However, a French wag in New York, who once

PLATE 58. Attributed to Charles-Honoré Lannuier. Card table. 1810–15 (cat. no. 59)

"asserted . . . that nothing was more lovely in the world than the Moreau elegances," later avowed that these were "only crabgrass beside that luxury" found in the New York home of an unidentified lord.[77]

The Moreaus returned to Europe in 1813, and not long after the general was mortally wounded in the Battle of Dresden, in which he had been acting as an adviser to Napoleon's enemy Czar Alexander. On March 15, 1814, the Moreaus' American possessions were sold at auction from their town house at 119 Pearl Street. The furnishings included "large Pier Looking Glasses, several large Chandeliers, Pier Tables, Mahogany Dinning [sic], Tea and Card Tables, Mahogany Sophas [sic] and Chairs, Gilt Chairs with fancy Satin Cushions, . . . Mahogany Bed Steads . . . several handsome sets of Window Curtains, a Grand Piano forte . . . various sets of elegant French China."[78] The gilded chairs were probably French, but a number of the mahogany items very likely may have been purchased from Lannuier.

Of the émigrés who came to America in the early decades of the nineteenth century, Joseph Bonaparte (1768–1844), the elder brother of Napoleon, was the most famous. The ex-king of Naples and Spain arrived in 1815, following the collapse of the First Empire and Napoleon's final exile to the island of Saint Helena. During his own nineteen-year exile— Joseph lived in the United States until 1839, with a five-year hiatus, from 1832 to 1837, in England—he was almost a celebrity, leading the life of an affable but grand country gentleman at Point Breeze, his eighteen-hundred-acre Bordentown, New Jersey, estate on the Delaware River. The comte de Survilliers, as Joseph Bonaparte was called here, brought the rich style of the faded French Empire with him to America, where he entertained numerous distinguished visitors in his lavishly appointed residence. The original version of

Jacques-Louis David's portrait of the emperor, *Napoleon Crossing the Alps*, painted for the Spanish Bourbon king, hung in the large drawing room along with Baron Gérard's full-length portraits of Joseph as king and his wife, Julie, as queen of Spain, portrayed with their two daughters.[79] Joseph's art collection contained paintings by Rubens, Poussin, Rembrandt, and Canaletto, as well as marble busts of family members by Bartolini; richly ornamented Empire furniture brought from France graced the interiors; and extensive gardens were laid out with statuary in the Italian manner.[80] Like Leray's mansion, Bonaparte's, too, burned in 1820, but much of the furniture and art was saved, and the house was rebuilt and refurnished in even grander form.

A pair of surviving card tables attributed to Lannuier (plate 58) has a traditional history of having been purchased at the June 1847 sale of Bonaparte's household furnishings.[81] Stylistically, the tables appear to be a few years earlier in date than 1815, when Joseph arrived in America, although Lannuier may have continued in his earlier mode at the same time that he began to produce his signature gilded figural furniture. These card tables are almost identical in form to a labeled pair (see plate 22) made for Isaac Bell, presumably about the time of his marriage in 1810. Of course, the tables could have been acquired by Bonaparte secondhand. They are remarkably distinctive in design and are related stylistically to the furniture made by Jacob for General Moreau in France. Unfortunately, there is no evidence to indicate that General Moreau owned these tables, or that they came from the 1814 Moreau estate auction in New York. The catalogue of the 1847 Bonaparte sale lists "Two mahogany Lyre front card tables" in the library—the only instance in which card tables are mentioned in the auction catalogue. Although each table has a small inlaid brass lyre at the center of its apron, the lyre is not featured as prominently as on other New York examples, like the one shown in plate 80.

SOUTHERN CLIENTS   A small number of prosperous southern merchants are known to have owned Lannuier furniture, which they may have purchased on visits to New York or through a factor. There is slight evidence that Lannuier participated in the venture-cargo furniture trade from New York to southern ports and the Caribbean, and that, just prior to his death, he made a modest shipment to Cuba and a larger one to A. S. Bulloch in Savannah. Noteworthy among his southern patrons was the Baltimore merchant and real-estate developer James Bosley (1779–1843), who, at the time of his marriage to Elizabeth Noël (1797–1851) in 1822, either owned a suite of Lannuier furniture or purchased it secondhand shortly thereafter for his newly acquired Fayette Street town house. The suite, which includes the only extant seating furniture by Lannuier aside from that for a publicly commissioned set of chairs for New York's City Hall, contained at least two armchairs, ten side chairs, two small backless settees or ottomans, a pair of card tables, and perhaps some other items as well (plates 59, 60; see plate 36, and fig. 108). The inventory of Bosley's estate, of 1844, lists a yellow damask upholstered sofa, a dozen mahogany chairs with yellow damask covers, a sofa covered in red fabric, a pair of ottomans, and a pier table with a marble top and a looking-glass plate beneath, all in the front parlor. At the time of the inventory, a pair of mahogany card tables stood in the upstairs front room, along with twelve additional mahogany chairs with damask seats.[82] In the portrait of Mrs. Bosley painted in the year following her marriage by the miniaturist Anna Claypoole Peale (1791–1878), she is shown seated on a red-upholstered Empire sofa with a gilded rail and scroll end (fig. 76). The sofa, likely of New York or Baltimore manufacture, is perhaps the red sofa recorded in the inventory, as it is not seen in Anna Peale's portraits of other Baltimoreans. Bosley, who is known to have patronized the leading local

PLATE 59. Attributed to Charles-Honoré Lannuier. Armchair. 1815–19 (cat. no. 34)

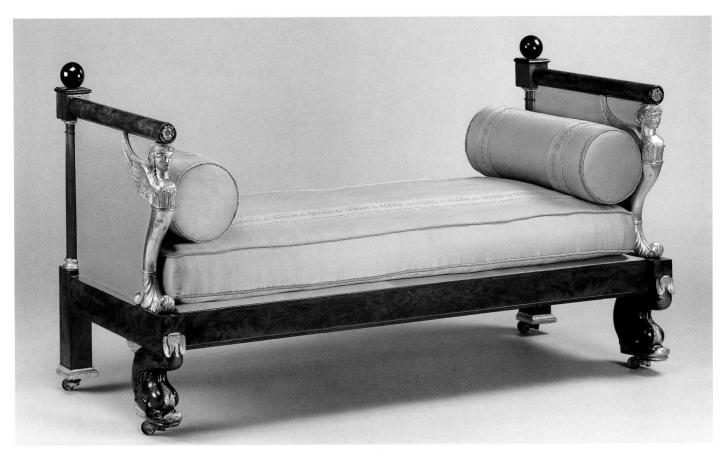

PLATE 60. Attributed to Charles-Honoré Lannuier. Bench or ottoman. 1815–19 (cat. no. 42)

FIGURE 76. Anna Claypoole Peale. *Mrs. James Bosley.* 1823. Watercolor on ivory, 3⅛ x 2⅝ in. Maryland Historical Society, Baltimore. Bequest of J. B. Noel Wyatt

cabinetmakers, also owned a mahogany-and-satinwood wardrobe, a pair of window seats, and a worktable, all of which are attributed to William Camp (1733–1822). Camp's furniture manufactory was the largest in Baltimore in the early nineteenth century.[83]

In 1820, Baltimore, with a population of 62,738, was the third largest American city, and its protracted decline in the 1820s and 1830s lay ahead. In keeping with the emerging city's postwar climate of prosperity, the Bosleys' town house, befitting that of a successful merchant, was furnished in the latest antique style based on French sources (plate 61): Gilded-caryatid figures, inspired by antiquity, supported card-table tops and served as arm supports on ottomans and armchairs; klismos chairs, their form derived from ancient Greek art, had splats that resembled Greek lyres. The pair of ottomans, set against the wall or possibly in alcoves, with loose cushions piled up in the back, combined comfort and romantic exoticism; as their name implies, they derived—according to Ackermann in *The Repository of Arts*—from "those Eastern nations . . . whose love of ease has taught them to devise ample means for its enjoyment."[84]

Before his death in 1819, Lannuier shipped a large quantity of furniture to Archibald Stobo Bulloch (about 1775–1859), a commission agent, factor, and Collector of Customs for the Port of Savannah from 1810 to 1822. Bulloch was a patron of the young English Regency architect William Jay (1792–1837), whose imaginative talents transformed provincial Savannah. In the four brief years he spent there, from the last days of 1817 until 1822, he erected four mansions and three public buildings in the Regency style. At this moment in Lannuier's career, remarkable architecture was the setting for his remarkable furniture—although, unfortunately, none of the items can be identified today.

The house Jay designed on Orleans Square for Bulloch and his wife, Sarah Glen (d. 1837), was a two-story stucco mansion over a raised basement (fig. 77). Completed by 1819

PLATE 61. Auguste Garneray. *Salon de musique à Malmaison.* 1812. Watercolor. (The suite of furniture with gilded winged-caryatid arm supports shown in the painting was designed by Jacob frères in 1800.) Musée National du Château de Malmaison, France

(it was torn down in 1916), its entrance façade was distinguished by a semi-circular portico of six Corinthian columns, which supported an entablature with a conical roof. On the first story, unusual tripartite recessed windows with Ionic mullions were further enlivened with lead-and-glass roundels, probably executed in tinted glass (barely visible in figure 77 behind the Ionic capitals). The novelty of Jay's architectural genius was revealed in the front entrance hall, where six Corinthian columns encircled and supported a spiral staircase with a mahogany handrail (fig. 78). To each side of the central hall were two twenty-foot-wide rooms, each rich in classical detail: A double drawing room, to the right, was divided by a Corinthian columnar screen and by an Ionic columnar screen placed before the entrance-façade window; situated to the left of the hall was a front drawing room or a dining room, behind which was a circular room with a domed ceiling (fig. 79). An elaborate design consisting of a central ring with a Greek meander motif was incised in the plasterwork dome from which radiating lines formed equal segments that met a large meander-patterned circle above an anthemion cornice. Egyptian masks were placed at intervals on the cornice molding.[85] The analysis of paint pigments from three principal rooms in Jay's surviving Savannah houses shows original finishes that include a mat yellow-green entry hall with green door surrounds, marbleized socles, and Corinthian columns with gilded capitals; a Pompeiian-red dining room; and a grain-painted octagonal room.[86] Bold colors and trompe-l'oeil effects may have been used in the Bulloch house as well.

William Jay is known to have visited New York in November 1818, in the company of William Scarbrough, a prominent Savannah merchant and the owner of a Jay mansion.[87] Jay may have chosen furniture for Archibald Bulloch or other Savannah clients on this trip, or Bulloch himself may have traveled to New York, for ten cases of furniture marked "A.S.B.," and consigned by Honoré Lannuier of New York to "A. S. Bullock [*sic*]," arrived in Savannah on the brig *Levant* on October 5, 1819.[88] Later that month, Bulloch presumably sold his outmoded parlor, dining-room, and bedroom furnishings to make room for the new Lannuier furniture.[89] The inventory of Lannuier's estate compiled shortly after his death

FIGURES 77, 78, and 79. Archibald Bulloch House, Savannah. Exterior (upper left), 1896; main stair hall (upper right), about 1907; and interior of the domed ceiling (lower left), about 1916. Georgia Historical Society, Savannah

(see Appendix 9) discloses that furniture costing $2,401.25 was shipped to "A. S. Bullock [*sic*]" of Savannah. However, the Bullochs' enjoyment of their new home was all too brief: Beginning in 1819, a series of disasters befell Savannah commencing with the first of several epidemics; the great fire of 1820 destroyed a large area of the city including Jay's nearly finished Customs House; and a recession precipitated a steep decline in cotton prices, a principal source of Savannah's wealth. By 1822, three of Jay's clients, among them Archibald Bulloch, were forced to put up their new Regency mansions for sale. As Bulloch also had to sell his Lannuier furniture, it cannot be identified today. Examples by Lannuier may have made up a large part of the sheriff's sale of Bulloch furniture in 1822, which comprised: "2 mahogany couches, 2 do. ottomans, 2 do. sofa tables, 2 do. card do., 12 do. chairs, 2 do. screens, 2 do. foot benches, 1 gilt toilet table, 1 gilt frame looking glass . . . 1 set mahogany tables, 1 do. sideboard with marble tops [*sic*], 1 do. celeret [*sic*], 1 gilt chimney clock . . . 1 British oak table, 12 British oak chairs . . . 2 mahogany bedsteads with curtains complete of chintz, 2 bedsteads with conveniences . . . 2 mahogany liquor cases, 1 large looking glass frame . . . 2 mahogany stands . . . 1 large mahogany bason [*sic*] stand, with apparatus complete."[90]

The one known Lannuier item with a Savannah history is a mahogany dining table of 1815–19; now at Winterthur (see fig. 20), it bears Lannuier's stamp and traditionally is believed to have been owned by John MacPherson Berrien of Savannah.

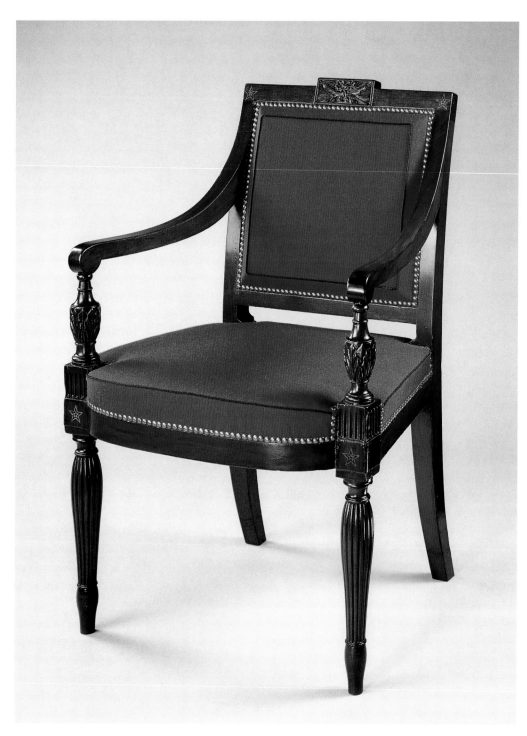

PLATE 62. Charles-Honoré Lannuier. Armchair. 1812 (cat. no. 11)

FIGURE 80. Joseph François Mangin and John McComb, Jr. Design for City Hall,
New York: Front Elevation. 1802. Black ink, with gray and black wash, on paper,
24¼ x 38⅛ in. The New-York Historical Society. John McComb Collection

PUBLIC COMMISSIONS

In 1812, Lannuier was awarded his sole known public commission: to provide armchairs (plate 62) for the Common Council Chamber of New York's new City Hall, the first City Hall interior to be furnished. The year before, when its exterior nearly was complete, a committee of three members, Alderman (then the name for a city councilman) Nicholas Fish and Assistants Peter Hawes and Augustine H. Lawrence, had been authorized "to procure suitable furniture" for the chamber.[91] Construction on the new (and present) City Hall, which began in May 1803, lasted nine years and cost $498,634.00.[92] Following the designs of the architects Joseph François Mangin (about 1771–1813 ?), an émigré of French or West Indian ancestry about whom little is known, and John McComb, Jr., appointed architect in charge of construction, the marble-and-stone structure, an admixture of French and English Neoclassical styles, was built on a monumental scale then unknown among New York public buildings (fig. 80). The new City Hall was the most important edifice in New York and was lavishly praised in travelers' journals and guidebooks. One writer called it "the handsomest structure in the United States; perhaps, of its size, in the world."[93]

The Common Council Chamber, situated at the southwest corner of the second story, and now called the room of the Committee of the Whole, is architecturally distinguished by a plaster-domed ceiling. A pencil sketch by McComb (fig. 81) shows that the architect considered latticed, coffered, and fluted motifs for the ceiling, as well as various ornaments, whose delicate forms derive from the Neoclassicism of the previous century. The architect decided on a fluted design enriched with foliated swags and scrolls for the dome of the council chamber, which rests on a circle of Corinthian columns. A decorative wrought-iron grill created a separate area from which the public could view the council's proceedings. In June 1812, the furnishings committee for the chamber was "requested to proceed . . . with all possible dispatch" to ready the room so that council members could assemble there for the Independence Day celebrations planned at City Hall.[94] The following month, Nicholas

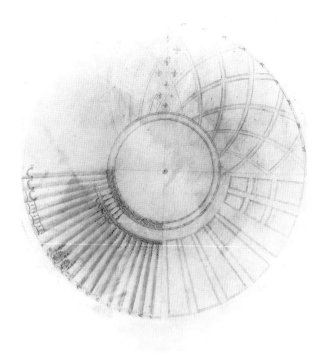

FIGURE 81. John McComb, Jr. Design for the domed ceiling, Common Council Chamber, City Hall, New York. 1804. Graphite and ink, 25 13/16 x 17 3/4 in. The New-York Historical Society. John McComb Collection

FIGURE 82. Charles Burton. *Council Chamber, City Hall, New York.* About 1831. Sepia, 2 3/4 x 3 1/2 in. The New-York Historical Society. Bequest of Stephen Whitney Phoenix, 1881

Fish, the committee chairman, authorized payment of Lannuier's April 25 invoice for $409 for, among other items, twenty-four mahogany armchairs, for which he charged $14 each (see Appendix 2).[95]

The earliest known depiction of the Common Council Chamber is that drawn by the artist Charles Burton about 1831 (fig. 82). The drawing shows the Lannuier armchairs set before desks arranged in tiers in horseshoe fashion around the mayor's chair, which is raised on a platform. The upholstered-back armchairs derive from Louis XVI-style forms, but, as interpreted by Lannuier, are an amalgam of French and English designs. Each chair features a raised tablet of crossed flags and a bowknot at the center of the crest rail, arm supports carved with a water-leaf pattern, and four inlaid brass stars at the corners of the crest rail and the tops of the front legs. There may have been a narrow border of die-stamped brass inlay as well at the top of each front leg in the recessed area below the star, which is now empty. The upholsterer Henry Andrew, who maintained a shop at several addresses on Maiden Lane from 1809 to 1825, billed the city $2,002.30 to upholster the furniture for the room. Andrew's invoice, now missing, must have included charges for the fabrics and upholstery of the Lannuier chairs and of the mayor's chair, a high-backed sofa that, according to a period commentary, was moved to City Hall from Federal Hall, where it had been used by President Washington when he addressed the first Congress.[96] Andrew's bill probably also included the fabrication of window draperies. The cabinetmaker William Mandeville provided tables and desks for the chamber at a cost to the city of $519.34, and John Crigier charged $300 for "gilding cornices Stars Canopy." Crigier's occupation is given as upholsterer in the city directories, where his name is spelled Crygier. He probably was responsible for the carving and gilding of the room's six window cornices and of the domed canopy above the mayor's chair, which is ornamented with stars not shown in Burton's drawing. Additionally, Donald Malcolm supplied carpeting for $418.50 and M. Gelston two hearth rugs for the two fireplaces at $55.00.[97] Full-length portraits by John Trumbull, of Washington,

PLATE 63. John Wesley Jarvis. *De Witt Clinton*. About 1816. Oil on canvas, 48 1/4 x 36 3/8 in. National Portrait Gallery, Washington, D.C. Transfer from the National Gallery of Art, Gift of Andrew Mellon, 1942

Hamilton, and governors George Clinton and John Jay, augmented the room's decoration. Contemporary descriptions of the furnishings unfortunately are terse; one records, "The Common Council Chamber is a splendid apartment, and is decorated with busts and portraits of eminent men."[98]

A portrait of De Witt Clinton (1769–1828) (plate 63), the appointed Mayor of New York for most of 1803 to 1815, painted by John Wesley Jarvis (1780–1840) in February 1816, depicts Clinton before he began his governorship of New York the following year. He stands to the left of a column and window in front of the "Washington" chair, shown upholstered in crimson fabric with twisted black cord and trimmed with brass nails, on what appears to be the dais at the front of the Common Council Chamber. If the setting for this portrait is correctly identified, the Lannuier chairs probably would have been similarly upholstered in the same red fabric.

Today, twenty-four armchairs of this type remain at City Hall,[99] all but two of them thought to have been made in Lannuier's shop. Differences in dimensions divide them into two groups: sixteen chairs have backs eighteen inches wide and a narrower seat depth than the remaining eight chairs, which are nineteen inches wide at the back. Two of the group of eight armchairs have a different brass inlay pattern—a six-pointed star-within-a-star, unlike the five-pointed-star motif on all the other chairs—and their baluster arm supports are heavier and lack a ring on the neck. These last two chairs probably are copies after the Lannuier originals, made in an unidentified New York cabinet shop at a somewhat later date.

As the city grew in size, the number of wards (each represented in the Common Council by an alderman and an assistant) increased from ten in 1808 to twelve in 1826, fourteen in 1828, and fifteen in 1832. Chairs must have been supplied for additional council members.

FIGURE 83. Charles Burton. *Governor's Room, City Hall, New York.* 1831. Sepia, 2¾ x 3½ in. The New-York Historical Society. Gift of Mrs. Ralph Smillie, 1968

FIGURE 84. Charles Christian. Armchair. 1814. Mahogany, 36 x 23½ x 21¾ in. Private collection

Then, too, a much-esteemed alderman may have been presented with an armchair from the council chamber, or with a copy made especially for him, as a token of gratitude for his service to city government. In 1831, the Common Council considered fitting up the southeast room on the second floor as supplementary space for its chamber, and $1,300 was allocated "for procuring Furniture and drapery to correspond with that of the present Council Chamber."[100] Additional chairs that replicate the Lannuier armchairs may have been made at this time.

In the past, further confusion about the City Hall armchairs resulted from an armchair depicted in a second Charles Burton drawing of 1831 of the Governor's Room at City Hall (fig. 83), which was furnished in 1814, two years after the Common Council Chamber. The New York cabinetmaker Charles Christian provided furniture for this room and his invoice included among other items twenty-four mahogany chairs with upholstered backs and seats.[101] Whether they were side chairs or armchairs is not specified on the bill. Nineteen side chairs by Christian and most of the Christian furniture are in the Governor's Room today, and much of it is shown in the Burton drawing. The armchair illustrated has been presumed to be one of the Lannuier chairs moved into the Governor's Room in the sixteen intervening years between the decoration of the room and the drawing's execution, although this would contradict city records, which indicate that the Lannuier chairs were first placed in the room in 1847.[102]

A pair of armchairs (fig. 84) that match the Christian side chairs recently has become known, and one of them very likely is the chair illustrated in the Burton drawing of the Governor's Room.[103] Their similarity to the Lannuier armchairs is striking, although the Christian armchairs lack brass inlays, have carved fasces terminating in eagles' heads on the crest-rail tablets, and front legs with ring and flattened-baluster turnings at their tops identical to those on the nineteen side chairs by Christian currently in the Governor's

Room. A third armchair with a veneered tablet and uncarved arm supports and legs, now in the Museum of the City of New York, probably can be attributed to Charles Christian, and is a plain version of the pair of armchairs by him. The chair has a City Hall provenance, and may be from the group of furniture Christian made for the mayor's office in 1814 and 1815.[104]

The marked similarity of form displayed by the Lannuier and the Christian chairs suggests that the architect John McComb might have been responsible for their design. The chairs are based on plates in Sheraton's *The Cabinet-Maker & Upholsterer's Drawing Book*, a copy of which is listed in an 1808 inventory of books on architecture in McComb's library.[105] McComb might have selected the particular emblems of government for the carved tablets on the two sets of chairs as well, for crossed flags and fasces with eagles' heads and laurel wreaths are not otherwise known on New York furniture. Among the architect's few surviving drawings for City Hall, there are, however, no sketches for furniture.

If Lannuier received further public commissions, no record of them has been found. A looking glass (plate 64) that can be attributed to him—now at Clermont, the Livingston-family estate—has a traditional history of having hung in the Hudson River steamboat *Clermont*, from which it passed to the Red Hook Hotel in Red Hook, New York. The *North River Steamboat*, designed by the inventor, engineer, and artist Robert Fulton (1765–1815), and later given its popular name, the *Clermont*, was the first commercially successful steamship. Built by the North River Steamship Company, a partnership of Robert R. Livingston (1746–1813) and Robert Fulton, it made its first passenger trip in 1807, navigating the 160 miles from New York to Albany in thirty-six hours. Its short, seven-foot-deep hold probably precluded the Lannuier looking glass from being used on this boat.

As the novel mode of steam transportation quickly became popular, Fulton designed more commodious and more powerful steam packets; to meet the demands of expanding river travel, they shortened to eighteen hours the travel time between New York and Albany. The largest of these and the last designed by Fulton before his death, the *Chancellor Livingston*, was built in 1816 and cost over $120,000 (fig. 85). At 157-feet long and 33-feet 6-inches

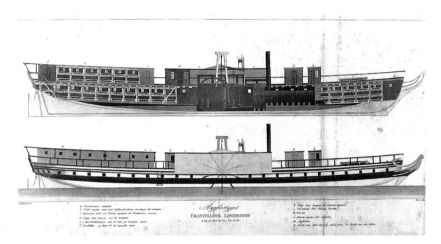

wide, and with a 10-foot-deep hold, it is more likely that the Lannuier mirror was on this steamboat, considered the "handsomest" of the day and able to sail at fifteen miles an hour with wind and tide, although its usual speed was about ten miles an hour.[106] In early November 1818, the Swedish visitor Baron Klinckowström journeyed to Albany on the *Chancellor Livingston* and commented: "The interior of the boat is of extraordinary elegance, almost luxurious. The wooden paneling is done in mahogany. . . . The tables, too, are of mahogany. . . . In the women's lounge there are red satin drapes with attractive fringing. . . . The salon has three mirrors which make a handsome effect."[107] The principal cabin, or salon, was fifty-four feet long and seven feet in height, above the floorboards—of sufficient height for this type of looking glass—had two parallel rows of dining tables that could accommodate more than one hundred people, and, additionally, held thirty-eight beds. In all, the *Chancellor Livingston* contained 135 berths, including 24 beds in the ladies' cabin located on deck above the main compartment (fig. 86).[108] Covered walkways on deck permitted passengers to view the majestic Hudson River scenery of vertical cliffs and dense forests even in inclement weather.

The *Chancellor Livingston* was sold in 1826 for $14,950, after nine years of service on the Hudson.[109] The furnishings may have been disposed of at this time or later, as the steamboat continued to ply other routes until it was dismantled in 1834. It was then that the Lannuier mirror probably was moved to the Red Hook Hotel, from whence it subsequently was brought to Clermont.

Frances F. Bretter

NOTES

1
See Cooper, 1993, p. 162.

2
S. Paxton & Co., "Valuable Furniture At Auction," *New-York Evening Post* of January 6, 1815. The sale also included "an elegant side board bow back with cylinder pedestal ends," dining tables with ends, and a breakfast table, tea table, and card tables, but their woods were not identified.

3
Invoice from Lannuier to Bayard, February 23, 1805. Bayard-Campbell-Pearsall Papers, Box 7, Manuscripts & Archives Section, Rare Books and Manuscripts Division, The New York Public Library. (Hereafter, this is cited as BCP Papers, NYPL.)

4
In January 1819, the Washington, D.C., upholsterer C. Alexander billed The White House $12 for making and installing drapery for a window and a crown bed, and charged $1.27 for iron work for the crown. A month later, the cabinetmaker Benjamin M. Belt supplied Mrs. Monroe with "2 Crowns for bedsteads" at $22 each and "two urns for bedsteads" at $5 each. House of Representatives Report 79, 18th Congress, 2nd Session, 1824–25, pp. 177–79. I am grateful to Wendy A. Cooper at the Winterthur Museum and Betty Monkman at The White House for sharing this information.

5
The firm, again called LeRoy, Bayard & Co., failed a few months after Bayard's death in 1826. At that time, Bayard's sole partners were his two sons, William, Jr., and Robert.

6
See Stokes, 1918, vol. 3, pp. 576–77, pl. 91.

7
Invoice from Manufacture de Porcelaine de Nast to Bayard, *15 pluviôse an 11* (1803). BCP Papers, Box 24, NYPL.

8
Letter from M. Hottinger to Bayard, Paris, May 16, 1806; letter from M. Thurot to Bayard, Paris, September 27, 1806. BCP Papers, Box 2, NYPL.

9
See Dwight, 1969, vol. 3, pp. 335–36.

10
See the deed of conveyance from Rogers to Bayard, for $20,000, for "a part of the Watson house," February 28, 1806, recorded January 28, 1829, Liber 246, p. 75. The sale also included a lot on Pearl Street, which Moses Rogers purchased from James Hunt in 1805 for $2,250: Deed of

conveyance from Hunt to Rogers, 18 Pearl Street, June 13, 1805, recorded January 17, 1806, Liber 71, p. 399. Deed of conveyance from Watson to Rogers, 6 State Street, for $36,000, May 4, 1805, recorded January 17, 1806, Liber 71, p. 397. This sale included an additional thirty feet on State Street to the west of the dwelling house. Register of Deeds, City Register's Office, Surrogate's Court, New York. For the Watson houses see Stokes, 1926, vol. 5, p. 1286 (at February 10, 1792).

11
Invoices from West to Bayard, April 1, 19, June 2, July 26, August 30, 1806; invoice from Blake & Scott, stonecutters, to Thomas Taylor, for Bayard, January 10, 1807. BCP Papers, Box 8, NYPL.

12
Invoice of Blake & Scott to Thomas Taylor, for Bayard, January 10, 1807. BCP Papers, Box 8, NYPL. Among the building materials billed on the invoice but delivered on July 16, 1806, were quantities of circular stone: three thick circular sills and lintels, nine circular sills, nine circular arches, twenty-six feet of circular water table, ten feet of circular ashlar, and four circular steps. That these could not have been used on the State Street façade is apparent. Other stone materials—six arches and sills—may have been for the carriage house and stable.

13
See Stillman, 1956, pp. 37–38, 40.

14
See Dunlap, 1834, vol. 1, pp. 329–30; Craven, 1968, pp. 57–58.

15
Invoice from Dixey to Bayard, October 6–November 14, 1806. BCP Papers, Box 8, NYPL.

16
Invoice from Westerfield to Bayard, December 2, 1806. BCP Papers, Box 8, NYPL.

17
Letter from Grant, Webb & Co., to Bayard, Leghorn, March 3, 1807. BCP Papers, Box 2, NYPL. The chimneypieces cost 85 sequins, 25 sequins, and 20 sequins each for the two simplest. A sequin is noted in the letter to have been about $2.10. Invoice for the shipment of twelve cases of marble chimneypieces, from Grant, Webb & Co. to Bayard, June 22, 1807. BCP Papers, Box 8, NYPL. Seven cases were shipped to New York on the American brig *Eliza* and five cases were shipped to Philadelphia on the schooner *Mary & Elisa*.

18
Maria Bayard, "Diary," 1814–15, n.p. BCP Papers, NYPL.

19
See Klin[c]kowström, 1952, p. 128.

20
Invoice from Phyfe to Bayard, November 21, 1807 (the Downs Collection, Library, Winterthur Museum), as quoted in Montgomery, 1966, p. 118. Maria Louisa Campbell died in 1911 and her nephew Howard Townsend was the donor of the Bayard-Campbell-Pearsall papers to The New York Public Library. The Phyfe invoice to Bayard is illustrated in McClelland, 1939, pl. 243. Hornor, 1930, p. 38, illustrates a side chair with a single cross banister and a pillar-and-claw card table with four colonnettes owned by Bayard descendants that may be the items listed on the invoice.

21
Invoice for the sideboard, secretary, and a field bedstead, among other items, from Brouwer to Bayard, November 22, 1806. BCP Papers, Box 8, NYPL. The invoice total is given in pounds (£58.10.0) and dollars ($146.25), which makes it possible to calculate that the sideboard cost about $90, the secretary about $40. A sideboard with pedestal ends, which descended in William Bayard's family, illustrated in Hornor, 1930, p. 40, and attributed by Hornor to Phyfe, was more probably made by Brouwer. Invoice for the twelve chairs, from Palmer to Bayard, December 8, 1807. BCP Papers, Box 8, NYPL. Invoice for a high-post bedstead, "gilt balls," and four field bedsteads, from Mandeville to Bayard, May 14, 1811; McClelland, 1939, p. 259, cites a large high-post bed owned by a Bayard descendant that may be this example. Invoice for the four basin stands, from Ball to Bayard, June 25, 1811. Invoice for a shaving glass and a looking glass, from [Del] Vecchio to Bayard, June 27, 1811. Invoice for the bureau, from Meeks to Bayard, October 1812. BCP Papers, Box 9, NYPL.

22
See Lambert, 1813, vol. 2, pp. 90–91.

23
Letter from S. G. Perkins to Bayard, Boston, February 18, 1806. BCP Papers, Box 2, NYPL. The London memo, undated, accompanies the letter, and lists the price of the pair of curtains at £36 each. Perkins writes, "As our rooms generally have more than two windows, and as your rooms have but two in general, I thought it advisable to make you the offer of them." With duty, his cost was $365.11, but he offered to sell them for $300. Bayard declined to purchase the curtains. Letter from Perkins to Bayard, Boston, February 10, 1807. BCP Papers, Box 2, NYPL.

24
Invoice from J. Cummings & Co. to Bayard, December 5, 1806. BCP Papers, Box 8, NYPL.

25
Invoices from Phyfe to Bayard, November 21, 1807, March 13, 1809–May 13, 1810. BCP Papers, Box 8, NYPL.

26
Maria Bayard, "Diary," 1814–15, n.p. BCP Papers, NYPL.

27
Ibid., March 8, 1815.

28
Ibid., March 9 and 10, 1815.

29
Ibid., March 12, 20, 29, May 14, 1815.

30
Transfer of an insurance policy from Wynant Van Zandt, Jr., to Pearsall, February 21, 1804. BCP Papers, Box 20, NYPL. The policy is for $5,000 worth of insurance on the Broadway house, described as three stories high, of brick, with a tile roof, a 26-foot 3-inch front, and 58 feet 6 inches deep. Letter from Van Zandt to Pearsall, January 28, 1804, in which he offers to sell his house for £10,000: "I can with confidence assert it is not exceeded in this city . . . the lot runs from street to street, this nearly 200 feet in length and the house is capable of accommodating a large genteel family." BCP Papers, Box 21, NYPL.

31
Invoice from Lannuier to Bayard, June 19, 1817. BCP Papers, Box 24, NYPL.

32
Letter to John Davis Hatch, Director of the Albany Institute of History & Art, from Henrietta Crosby, February 18, 1947 (Archives, Albany Institute of History & Art). Following the death of Maria Campbell's last surviving child, Maria Louisa Campbell, in 1911, there was a private sale of her estate the next year to family members, which could explain Stephen Van Rensselaer Crosby's acquisition of Campbell furniture. See Montgomery, 1966, p. 118.

33
Invoice for furniture from S. E. & O., Paris, to Bayard, August 1817. BCP Papers, Box 10, NYPL. The invoice for the porcelain is on the reverse side.

34
Ibid.

35
The house, at 51 Broadway, is illustrated in Jones, Newman, and Ewbank, 1848.

36
Invoice from Galatian to Bayard, September 18, 1819, for work done on several dates. BCP Papers, Box 11, NYPL.

37
Undated invoice from Secor & Hatheway to Bayard or Mrs. Campbell, for two patterns of Brussels carpet body and three border patterns. Invoice from William Wanam to Bayard, May 2, 1817, for "making Maria's carpets" and for installing carpeting and floor cloth. Invoice from W. W. & T. L. Chester to Duncan Campbell, October 22 and December 15, 1817 (paid by Bayard), for Brussels carpeting. BCP Papers, Box 24, NYPL.

38
Invoice from Mills, Minton & Co., to Bayard, June 25, 1818. BCP Papers, Box 11, NYPL.

39
Letter from J. Webb, Leghorn, to Bayard, February 10, 1816. BCP Papers, Box 24, NYPL. One mantel was to cost £40 or £50, the other three about £20 each.

40
Letter from J. Webb, Leghorn, to Bayard, May 1, 1816. BCP Papers, Box 3, NYPL.

41
Letter from J. Webb, Leghorn, to Bayard, February 22, 1817. BCP Papers, Box 3, NYPL. The total cost for the mantels is recorded as $573.

42
Letter from J. Webb, Leghorn, to Bayard, May 21, 1817. BCP Papers, Box 3, NYPL. The letter continues, "I hope they meet the wishes of your Son (& prove ornaments to his new House) on whose marriage allow me to offer my congratulations." Robert Bayard, who met Webb while traveling in Italy in the spring and summer of 1816, was not married until 1820; William, his older brother, had married in 1812. This may be a misunderstanding on the part of the writer; the mantels were more likely meant for a Bayard daughter.

43
Monkhouse, 1983, p. 20, assigns the Stephen Van Rensselaer IV provenance based upon photographs in the archives of the Society for the Preservation of New England Antiquities, Boston, of interiors of Edgemere (later Four Winds), the Newport, Rhode Island, summer residence of the Thayer family, from whence the mantel came to the Rhode Island School of Design. Cornelia Paterson Van Rensselaer (1823–1897), a daughter of Harriet and Stephen IV, married Nathaniel Thayer (1808–1883) in 1846, and she or a descendant could have moved

the mantel to Newport when the interiors of the Thayer house were remodeled by Ogden Codman in 1895. Photographs taken after the renovation, one of which shows this mantel, carry inscriptions that the woodwork and the mantel came from the Van Rensselaer Manor House in Albany. (I am grateful to Jane Stokes at RISD, who brought this to my attention.) A photograph of a drawing room in the Manor House (fig. 68), made before the building was dismantled in 1893, shows a cornice and doorway that appear in two Edgemere photographs. It is not possible to trace the mantel to the town house designed about 1817 by Philip Hooker for Harriet and Stephen Van Rensselaer, but if it had been in that house, it may have been removed about 1838, when the Van Rensselaers settled in the Manor House, and then installed as part of Richard Upjohn's renovations in the 1840s—or else the mantel may have been imported originally for the Manor House by Stephen III at the time of the 1818–19 remodeling and additions by Hooker. A mantel similar to this one, from a New York town house, is in the collections of the Metropolitan Museum (unaccessioned).

44
Letter from Robert Bayard to Duncan Campbell, Paris, March 15, 1815. William Bayard Papers, Library, The New-York Historical Society.

45
Letter from Stephen Van Rensselaer IV, Paris, to Stephen Van Rensselaer III, August 24, 1813. Stephen Van Rensselaer Papers, Miscellaneous, Library, The New-York Historical Society.

46
See Bucher and Wheeler, 1993, pp. 304–5, for a reconstructed first-floor plan and a rear view of the house, which was torn down about 1960.

47
Letter from William Bayard, Jr., to William Bayard, Sr., New York, January 30, 1819. BCP Papers, Box 4, NYPL.

48
See note 46, above.

49
Descendants of the Van Rensselaers presented their family papers to the New York State Library in Albany in 1911; however, most of the papers were destroyed in a fire that occurred shortly thereafter.

50
Letter from Bertie Pruyn Hamlin (Mrs. Charles S. Hamlin; 1877–1963) to Ledyard Cogswell, Jr., February 4, 1938 (Archives, Albany Institute of

History & Art): "There are 9 handsome Empire chairs [owned by Elizabeth Van Rensselaer Frazer (Mrs. James Carroll Frazer)]. . . . Mrs. Alden has some of the set & Steve Crosby in Boston has the rest." The Crosby side chairs are those that belonged to Maria Campbell and are now in the Albany Institute of History & Art.

51
Invoice from Platt to Bayard, August 10, 1818, for: "1 Pier glass $60/Box for packing $1.33." Bayard paid Platt on August 13, 1818: Recorded on the back of the invoice is "1818/I.L. Platt/$61.33/Augs.13/Harriet." Bank of America cashier's check to I. L. Platt from William Bayard for $61.33. Invoice to Bayard, July 7, 1819, for one case of freight on the ship Belle for $12.72; noted on the reverse of the invoice is: "Ship Belle freight/of Box Mirrors for/Harriet $12.72." BCP Papers, Box 11, NYPL.

52
See the Mercantile Advertiser of January 5, 1820, and the New-York Gazette & General Advertiser of August 29, 1820.

53
Back of an invoice for Merino wool, September 10, 1817: "23rd of September/Received 2 boxes of china for/Mr. Van Ranselaer [sic]." BCP Papers, Box 10, NYPL.

54
Cargo manifest from Messrs. Villesboisnet [?] & Co. of "Nantz" [Nantes] to LeRoy, Bayard, & McEvers, July 14, 1816. BCP Papers, Box 10, NYPL.

55
A sixty-day note to H. Lannuier for $505.25 from William Bayard, "Value Received," May 29, 1818. A sixty-day note to Honoré Lannuier from William Bayard for $500, $5.25 added at end, May 29, 1818, "on account of my bill rendered." BCP Papers, Box 11, NYPL.

56
Bank of America cashier's check to D. Phyfe from Bayard, March 25, 1819. BCP Papers, Box 11, NYPL.

57
See Bucher and Wheeler, 1993, p. 188.

58
Invoice from Phyfe to Brinckerhoof [sic], October 26, 1816. Robert Troup Papers, Box 3, Folder 4, Manuscripts & Archives Section, Rare Books and Manuscripts Division, The New York Public Library. (Hereafter, this is cited as RT Papers, NYPL.) The bill and surviving furniture are recorded and illustrated in Sloane, 1987, pp. 1106–13.

59
Invoice from Lannuier to "A. Breinkruff [sic]," June 8, 1816. Breinkruff is a misspelling, but the "A" is either an error or else the furniture was a gift to James from his father, Abraham. The Lannuier furniture is also recorded in accounts titled "Household Furniture," July 13, 1816, and September 25, 1816. Invoice from Lannuier to "Mr. Brinckroff [sic]," August 17, 1816. RT Papers, Box 3, Folder 4, NYPL.

60
Invoice from Turcot to "Mr. Brinckerhof [sic]," June 22, 1816. RT Papers, Box 3, Folder 4, NYPL.

61
The upholsterer Joseph Trulock, also on Maiden Lane, supplied a 4-foot-8-inch bed bolster and two pillows ($85), a pair of square pillows and a bolster ($25), and a hair mattress for the bed. Invoice from Trulock to Brinckerhoff, July 22, 1816. RT Papers, Box 3, Folder 4, NYPL.

62
Invoice from Del Vecchio to Brinckerhoff, May 23, 1816. RT Papers, Box 3, Folder 4, NYPL.

63
Invoice from Phyfe to Brinckerhoff, October 26, 1816. RT Papers, Box 3, Folder 4, NYPL.

64
"Copy of Schedule deposited with the Mutual Insurance Co.," December 6, 1816. RT Papers, Box 3, Folder 4, NYPL.

65
Receipt from Wilson to Brinckerhoff, April 10, 1816. RT Papers, Box 3, Folder 4, NYPL. In addition to $450 paid in cash, a pianoforte valued at $150 was given in exchange for a cabinet piano, "which warrants to be a perfect Instrument both as to Tone and Workmanship."

66
Invoice from Turcot to Brinckerhoff, December 20, 1816. RT Papers, Box 3, Folder 4, NYPL. Turcot's newspaper advertisements appeared in The Public Advertiser of January 5, 1807, and the New-York Morning Post of June 7, 1811.

67
See Schaeper, 1995, pp. 25–26, 128–29, 156–61, 295–302. Dr. Schaeper's book gives Chaumont the recognition long due him for his support of American forces during the Revolution. Chaumont mistakenly continued to believe that Congress would redeem its paper dollars at face value.

68
For the "Diary" of Gouverneur Morris, vol. 9, September 25 and 26, 1803, see the microfilm in the

Library of Congress as cited by Pilcher, 1985, pp. 126, 128.

69
A photograph of the French pier table is in the Leray Mansion file at the Jefferson County Historical Society, Watertown, New York, which also contains photographs of some porcelains and metalwork believed to have been owned by James Leray. The secretary, bureau, and other Leray mansion furnishings that descended in the Payen family are in a private collection in upstate New York. A large mahogany bookcase, probably French and said to have been given by James Leray to his gardener, is in the Art Collection of The Roswell P. Flower Memorial Library, Watertown.

70
See Milbert, 1968, p. 154.

71
Ibid.

72
See Pilcher, 1985, p. 226, n. 48, which cites scorched rafters in the attic as evidence that the building survived the fire.

73
See Kennedy, 1989, note p. 37.

74
See Milbert, 1968, pp. 157–58. Vincent, who, earlier, was put in charge of his father's finances, was able to settle all debts, although he was forced to sell the Loire château to a creditor in 1823. The family's imprint in the area today lies in place-names: Leraysville no longer exists, but the town of Chaumont does, and Cape Vincent and Alexandria Bay are named for Leray's two sons and Theresa Falls for his daughter. The Leray family maintained a land office in the area as late as 1910, when their remaining North Country lands were sold.

75
See Samoyault and Samoyault-Verlet, 1992, p. 19.

76
See Samoyault and Samoyault-Verlet, 1992, p. 16. An inventory of Moreau furniture from the Hôtel d'Anjou is in the Musée National du Château de Fontainebleau, France.

77
See Low, 1976, pp. 208–9.

78
See "Sale of Furniture . . . the Household Furniture of the late Gen. Moreau," *Mercantile Advertiser*, March 2, 1814.

79
See Schnapper and Sérullaz, 1989, p. 386. I am grateful to Kenneth Myers at the New Jersey Historical Society, Newark, for this information.

80
See Cooper, 1993, pp. 69, 70.

81
See Bleecker, 1847, p. 11. An earlier auction of paintings and books from Joseph Bonaparte's estate was held on September 17 and 18, 1845.

82
Baltimore County Inventories, Liber 54, Folio 24, State Archives, Annapolis, Maryland. The sofas were not a pair; the yellow sofa was valued at $30, the red one at $40. The values of the chairs were nearly the same: the dozen chairs in the front parlor, $51; the dozen chairs in the upstairs parlor, $50.

83
See Weidman, 1984, nos. 164, 177, 179. For other Bosley furniture see Weidman, 1984, nos. 10, 108.

84
See Agius, 1984, pl. 97, p. 116.

85
See Harvey, 1994, pp. 86–87, 90–92, 96–103, 116–17, 164.

86
For the entry hall of the Owens-Thomas House, Savannah, see Fore, 1991; for the dining room of the Owens-Thomas House see Fore, unpublished notes; for the octagonal room see Shellman, 1982. I am grateful to Olivia Alison at the Telfair Museum of Art, Savannah, for this information.

87
See "Shipping News, Port of Savannah," *Columbian Museum and Savannah Daily Gazette*, November 11, 1818. I am grateful to Lynn Harvey for sharing this information.

88
See Inward Coastwise Manifests, Port of Savannah, October 5, 1819. Record Group 36, Box 13. National Archives, Washington, D.C. See also Talbott, 1995, p. 84, n. 24.

89
See the advertisement for the auction sales by Watts & Joyner in *The Georgian* of October 14, 1819, announcing that, "On Friday the 29th instant [furniture] WILL be sold at the house of A. S. Bulloch, Esq. Reynolds square." Among the items listed were a pair of hair sofas, two card tables, a tea table, a set of dining tables, two dozen chairs, a sideboard, a cellarette, a bedstead with chintz curtains, an easy chair, a bookcase, and so on; as quoted in Harvey, 1994, pp. 168–69.

90
The Georgian of August 6, 1822, announced a "Sheriff's Sale On the first Tuesday in September next, WILL be sold in front of the Court House . . . the following articles of furniture, levied on as the property of A.S. Bulloch"; as quoted in Harvey, 1994, pp. 41–42. Could some of Bulloch's furniture have wound up in Baltimore? It is interesting to note that the southern merchant James Bosley, who owned furniture by Lannuier, married and then moved into a large Baltimore town house in 1822, the year of the Bulloch sale.

91
See *Minutes of the Common Council*, 1917, vol. 6, p. 721, September 30, 1811.

92
See Betts, 1992, n.p.

93
See Blunt, 1817, p. 45.

94
See *Minutes of the Common Council*, 1917, vol. 7, p. 164, June 1, 1812; vol. 7, p. 174, June 15, 1812.

95
See *Minutes of the Common Council*, 1917, vol. 7, p. 199, July 13, 1812. Warrant issued for payment of Lannuier invoice. When this invoice was published in *Antiques* in June 1933, p. 225, it was still preserved in the City Archives. Betts, 1983, p. 42, n. 40, also cites the Lannuier bill. All City Hall invoices from 1812 are now missing.

96
See Blunt, 1817, p. 48, who, in his description of the Common Council Chamber, records that "the chair for the mayor is the same that was used by General Washington when he presided at the first congress, which was held in this city. It is elevated by a few steps on the south side of the room, and surmounted by a canopy."

97
See *Minutes of the Common Council*, 1917, vol. 7, p. 213, July 20, 1812, for the Andrew, Mandeville, Crigier, and Gelston warrants; vol. 7, p. 181, June 22, 1812, for the Malcolm warrant. Stokes, 1918, vol. 3, p. 483, states that the gilded eagle atop the canopy above the mayor's chair was not placed there until 1818.

98
See Stanford, 1814, p. 11. Blunt, 1817, p. 48, also describes the room.

99
An additional matching armchair is owned by Hirschl & Adler Galleries, Inc., New York.

100
See *Minutes of the Common Council*, 1917, vol. 19, pp. 593–94, April 4, 1831. Three hundred dollars was approved for painting the then Court of Sessions to accommodate the additional chamber of the Common Council, and $3,000 for altering the architecture of the room to correspond with that of the Common Council Chamber was set aside for further consideration.

101
See *Minutes of the Common Council*, 1917, vol. 8, p. 84, November 14, 1814. See Betts, 1983, p. 6, for Charles Christian's invoice for furniture for the Governor's Room at City Hall, which reads:

Twenty four mahogany chairs, first quality, stuffed backs and seats @ 21 Doll 504

Two sofas to match the chairs seven feet long each, richly carved, @ 90 Doll 180

A Set of dining tables 4 ft 6 I[nches] long by 11 feet 2 I[nches] best quality mahogany, brass fasteners, all the legs carved 60

Two antique writing tables first quality materials and workmanship each $200 400

One of the "writing tables" (desks) bears the inscription in ink, inside a drawer, "Made by/Charles Christian/New York, June 1814."

102
See Betts, 1983, p. iii.

103
One of the Christian armchairs is also illustrated in an 1827 portrait by John Vanderlyn of Joseph C. Yates, Governor of New York from 1823 to 1825, which presently hangs in the Governor's Room at City Hall.

104
See *Minutes of the Common Council*, 1917, vol. 7, p. 787, June 27, 1814; vol. 8, p. 178, April 3, 1815.

105
"Catalogue of Books on Architecture & C," John McComb, Jr., Papers, Library, The New-York Historical Society. This may have been the London 1793, 1794, or 1803 edition.

106
See Blunt, 1817, pp. 172–73.

107
See Klin[c]kowström, 1952, p. 88.

108
See Duncan, 1823, vol. 1, p. 308.

109
Niles' National Register, vol. 31, December 2, 1826, p. 224. I am grateful to Kenneth Myers at the New Jersey Historical Society, Newark, for sharing his research on Hudson River steamboats with me.

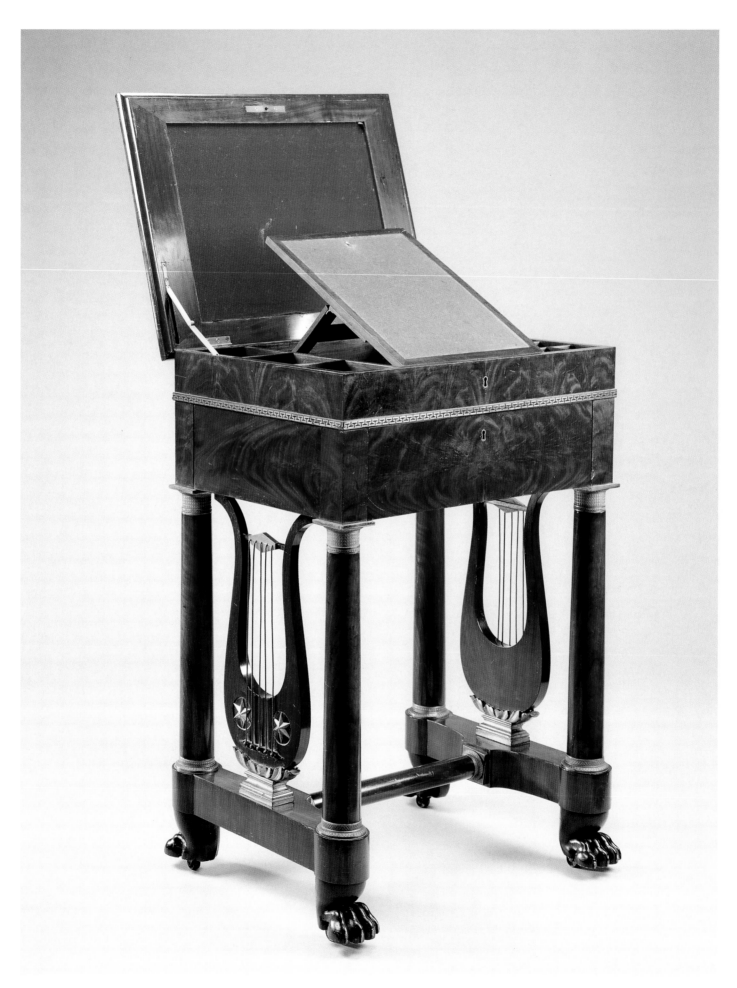

Worktable by Charles-Honoré Lannuier, with its top open, plate 70 (cat. no. 123)

CHAPTER 4   The Essence of Lannuier:
Connoisseurship of His Known Work

According to Charles F. Montgomery, furniture connoisseurs constantly rely on two standards of comparison, "documented pieces—those that can be identified as to maker, time, and place of manufacture—and masterpieces—those that are recognized as the finest in form, ornament, workmanship and materials."[1] Both are rare, and when they appear in volume or in combination by a single maker, as they do with Lannuier, we have the makings of a connoisseur's dream. Lannuier's near-obsessive labeling and stamping of his furniture has proven to be a great boon to furniture scholars, and has allowed him to be identified as a designer and craftsman of the highest caliber, who constantly strove for novelty and innovation in his work. Lannuier's influence was felt in his own lifetime and continued to resonate in the form and ornament of New York classical-style furniture a decade or more after his demise.

LANNUIER'S THREE
LABELS AND FRENCH-
STYLE *ESTAMPILLE*

Why label furniture? Duncan Phyfe felt no great need to, confident in the knowledge that most Americans knew who he was and the quality of the product he had to offer. After all, this was the cabinetmaker about whom Sarah Huger of New York wrote to her relatives in Charleston, relating the difficulties she had in having a furniture order executed in 1816:

> What shall I tell you about Mrs. Lowndes' Furniture? In truth I feel mortified in confessing that it is impossible for me to prophesy when the good lady will receive the card and pier tables. Mr. Phyfe is so much the United States rage, that it is with difficulty now, that one can procure an audience even of a few moments; not a week since I waited in company with a dozen others at least an hour in his cold shop, and after all was obliged to return home, without seeing The *great man*; however a few days since . . . I had the great good fortune to arrive at his house just at the moment he was entering and consequently extorted from him another promise that the furniture should certainly be furnished in three weeks. . . . The Tables from $325 to $350; Phyfe says he cannot tell precisely what will be the price.[2]

Advertising is one answer. Lannuier, given Phyfe's dominant position in the trade, may have felt compelled to keep up a steady stream of advertising, not through newspaper ads, which had a life of only a few days, but through the application of trade labels and his French-style *estampille* (plates 65, 66). Trade labels were also becoming very fashionable among Parisian *ébénistes* in the post-Revolutionary era, when competition increased and the cabinetmaking trade became a free-for-all following the abolition of the guilds.[3] Lannuier shrewdly also

may have calculated on label consciousness among his wealthy New York clientele and the snob appeal that accompanied the acquisition of an original from his French-style manufactory and *magasin de meubles*. Being French was something that Phyfe could never claim, and Lannuier played this to the hilt.

Just how familiar New Yorkers were with the quality that the French *estampille* implied is uncertain. This mark was a holdover from the glory days of cabinetmaking, during the ancien régime, and some Parisian *ébénistes* persisted in its use even after the dissolution of the guilds in 1791, both as visible proof of their rigorous training and as a guarantee that they provided the best in materials and workmanship. On the other hand, the *estampille* may have been Honoré's way of connecting himself to the past—a palpable remembrance of his youth and training in Paris. Honoré's and Nicolas's stamped marks are remarkably similar in their style and typeface (see figs. 1, 2), and it is possible that the stamping iron was given to Honoré as a going-away present by his older brother.

Over the course of his New York career, Lannuier employed three different labels. A chronology for them can be established, but it is based only on the few dated examples of Lannuier furniture and on the style of those pieces whose dates are not known. Had Lannuier changed locations in New York, as many cabinetmakers seemed to do, it would be much easier to set up a precise chronology for the labels and the furniture by tracking his movement over time in the city directory. His earliest label is printed in English (fig. 87), and so far has been found on only two tables: the specimen marble table dated December 26, 1804 (see plate 16), and the delicate satinwood occasional table now in the Winterthur Museum, Delaware (see plate 7). The limited use of this label and its appearance on the dated table indicate that it was Lannuier's first. The second, more elaborate label is bilingual, and has a greater variety of type sizes and typefaces (plate 67). It may be seen on a satinwood pier table (see plate 17) closely related to the 1804 specimen marble table, as well as on some considerably later tables with canted corners (see plate 35, and plate 68), probably made no earlier than 1810 or 1811. A conjectural range in date for this label, therefore, would seem to be between about 1805 and 1812, or perhaps even a couple of years later. Lannuier's third and final label (see plate 13), among the finest cabinetmaker's trade labels known on American furniture, is found on all of his gilded figural furniture with one notable exception—the center table with four figures (see plate 34)—and on many of his later square pier tables and case pieces. It appears on the Duncan Campbell and Maria Bayard furniture (see plates 51,

PLATE 66. Charles-Honoré Lannuier. Square pier table with canted corners. 1815–19 (cat. no. 104). The table bears Lannuier's stamp as well as that of Jacob frères, Paris, the latter perhaps added when the original owner, James Leray, brought the table back to France with him in 1836.

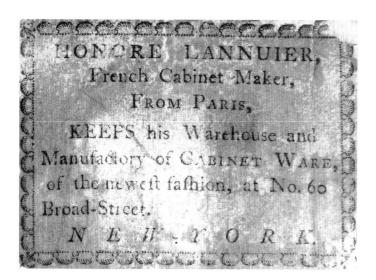

FIGURE 87. Charles-Honoré Lannuier's No. 1 label on the occasional table, plate 7 (cat. no. 119)

PLATE 67. Charles-Honoré Lannuier's No. 2 label on the card table, plate 22 (cat. no. 57)

52), which, from its original invoice, can be dated to 1817, as well as on the now altered pier table (plate 69) that was purchased originally with the Van Rensselaer card table inscribed May 1, 1817 (see plate 53). In an early article about Lannuier in the magazine *Antiques*, Thomas Ormsbee attributed the Lannuier label to Samuel Maverick, based on its similarity to an engraved trade card signed by this New York engraver that was illustrated in the city directory.[4] Close comparison of the two, however, calls Ormsbee's attribution into doubt. The more likely possibility is that the engraving may have been executed by a French engraver in New York or even in Paris, where its phonetic spellings could have slipped by. Lannuier used this label from sometime after 1812 until the end of his life. The appearance of the great seal of the United States on the label, in the tympanum of the pediment of the cheval glass, lends some credence to this dating schema; the use of eagles and other patriotic symbols gained renewed vigor in the United States during and just after America's victory in the War of 1812, when nationalistic fervor was running high. Something else worth noting about the engraved cheval-glass labels is that they were trimmed from sheets in three different ways: in the form of a rectangular shape that left a balanced border around the engraving; in a similar shape except for the top, where the label was cut to the slope of the pitched pediment; and, finally, the entire cheval-glass form was precisely silhouetted (see plate 13). The reasons for these variations are unclear, but perhaps we can surmise that furniture with labels trimmed in the same way were made in fairly close succession. For example, two card tables (see plate 25, and fig. 88), a worktable (plate 70), and a bureau with a dressing glass (see fig. 39) all have the silhouetted label, and all, from a stylistic point of view, could be considered as among Lannuier's later work. No such logic can be applied to Lannuier's sometimes haphazard labeling of other furniture, however. It is not uncommon, for instance, to find two labels on a single piece of furniture and none on others. All of the labels examined by this author appear to be genuine, and there never seems to have been

PLATE 68. Charles-Honoré Lannuier. Stand with marble inset.
1810–15 (cat. no. 118)

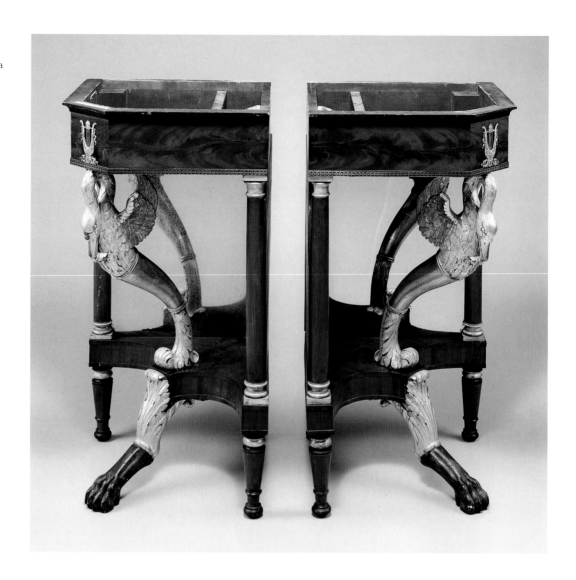

any faking, despite the fact that Lannuier was acknowledged as a major American cabinet-maker as early as the 1930s. Yet, this may not have been the case with the *estampille*, which this author has seen applied to forms—in particular, tables with rounded corners—that have no precedent in Lannuier's documented oeuvre. These tables, all fairly late in date, are only stamped, and never bear the engraved label. In this writer's opinion, a bedstead in the collection of the New York State Museum in Albany, which, based on its style, could not have been made during Lannuier's lifetime, bears one of these apocryphal stamps.

MATERIALS AND
WORKMANSHIP

Woods

During the first two decades of the nineteenth century, the finest materials were available to New York cabinetmakers. Mahogany was king, and the best of it came from Santo Domingo, brought by ships from the Caribbean and auctioned at dockside to the highest bidders. These were either mahogany retailers like J. M. J. Labatut, who sawed it into planks, boards, and veneers, and sold it at their mahogany yards, or master cabinetmakers of sufficient means to purchase logs and send them to mills for custom sawing.[5] East Indian satinwood was also in use, but it was a much rarer wood than Caribbean mahogany, and reached New York via different trade routes as well. Under the influence of English Regency furniture design, Brazilian rosewood veneers gained increasing favor during the 1810s, challenging

FIGURE 88. Charles-Honoré Lannuier. Card table. 1815–19 (cat. no. 65)   PLATE 70. Charles-Honoré Lannuier. Worktable. 1817 (cat. no. 123)

although never completely overtaking richly figured mahogany as the wood of choice for fine furniture. Light-colored burl-elm and figured-maple veneers also became increasingly popular in the 1810s, which suggests a sophisticated knowledge on the part of New Yorkers of the light-colored indigenous and imported woods from which French Empire and Restauration furniture was made. The secondary woods Lannuier employed were of the typical New York variety, rather than the oak and beech of his native France: White pine was used as a veneer substrate; yellow poplar, for drawer linings and the framed backs of case furniture; maple and cherry, for durable hidden framing members like the crossrails between table aprons; and ash, for those places subject to shearing stress, such as the gilded-and-bronzed outstretched legs of card tables (fig. 89). Plate 2 at the back of the 1817 New York price book shows a drawing of a lion's-paw foot with a dotted line indicating the desired grain orientation for maximum strength (fig. 90). Ash was not the easiest wood to carve, but it had the advantage of great strength and flexibility, especially when the long grain was oriented as shown.

Some sense of the quality and volume of the mahogany shipped to New York from Santo Domingo can be gleaned from the newspaper advertisements of the 1810s. In March 1816, the auctioneers Bleecker and Bibby, for instance, offered "the cargo of the brig Fredonia, consisting of 480 logs Mahogany, considered equal or superior to any imported since the peace."[6] Roughly a year and a half later, they advertised a similarly sized cargo, this time "from the ship Greyhound, from St. Domingo, consisting of 471 logs, 250 of which are from

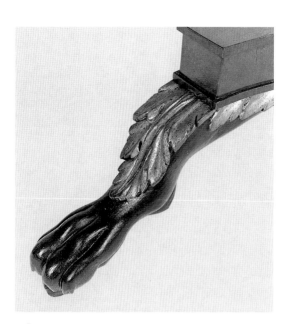

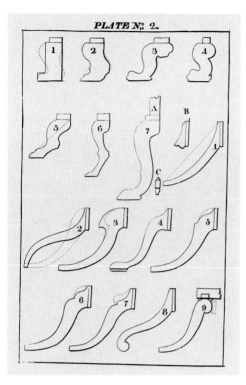

FIGURE 89. Front foot. Detail of the Lannuier card table, figure 102 (cat. no. 68)

FIGURE 90. Plate 2 from *The New-York Book of Prices for Manufacturing Cabinet and Chair Work.* 1817

20 to 30 inches wide, and a great proportion of it mottled wood—the whole being a choice parcel and particularly selected for this market."[7] The fussiness of purchasers and the care that went into the selection of mahogany for the New York market are indicated by an ad addressed to the cabinetmakers of New York in July 1811 by W. F. Pell and Co., who announced the sale of the brig *Alfred*'s cargo of mahogany from Santo Domingo, "confessedly the most valuable cargo of Mahogany ever imported into this city, as a competent judge was sent from this place, and employed six months in the woods of St. Domingo, selecting the most approved sticks."[8]

The most desirable and frequently advertised types of mahogany were "crotch" and "table" wood. The former, cut from the forked trunk or branches of a mahogany tree, was the source of the exquisite flame-like veneers used so effectively by Lannuier, and the latter was an extremely dense, straight-grained wood intended for use as the solid-board tops of Pembroke and dining tables, where it was essential that warping and shrinkage be kept to a minimum. In January 1812, "Mahogany Logs, Boards, Plank, Joist, etc." were offered for sale at the mahogany yard at 255 Cherry Street, as well as "plain, shaded, mottled, and crotch veneers"[9]—the four main types of veneers employed by New York cabinetmakers. Lannuier used plain veneers on the seldom-seen back rails and on the undersides of the lower leaves of his swivel-top card tables. Mottled veneers had cross-grain flashes of color and light, which can be seen in the Egyptian-style term supports on one of Lannuier's early pier tables (see plate 30) and in the aprons of a card table with canted corners (fig. 88). In France, this type of mahogany veneer is called *acajou moiré* because it has a wavy, watery look similar to moiré silk. "Shaded" veneers probably refers to the long ribbon-like grain pattern that produces an effect of light and shade when the wood is viewed from different angles. Shaded veneers were used to great advantage on the inner surfaces of the end panels of the French bedstead Lannuier made for Stephen Van Rensselaer IV, in combination with the book-matched crotch veneer of the scrolled crest (see plate 54). Lannuier and other New

York furniture makers employed undulating shaded veneers to maximum effect on such curved surfaces as the round columns on pier tables or the cylinders of desks to accentuate their rounded shapes and to give them a sense of volume. Crotch-mahogany veneers—a type that, in France, is called *acajou ronceux*—were the most spectacular, and can be seen in all their glory on Lannuier's French sideboard (see plate 23) and French press (see fig. 43). The similarity between the grain patterns favored on New York furniture of the early nineteenth century and on its French counterparts strongly suggests that Lannuier and other French immigrant cabinetmakers, as well as mahogany merchants like Labatut and Deloynes, played major roles as tastemakers in establishing an appreciation for this most characteristic feature of New York classical furniture.

Book-matching crotch-mahogany veneers was a technique employed extensively by Parisian cabinetmakers in the early nineteenth century that was in keeping with the classical architectural principles of symmetry and balance. Lannuier book-matched crotch veneers frequently on his furniture (plate 71), but on his monumental French press (see fig. 43) he

PLATE 72. Front apron . Detail of the Lannuier square pier table
with canted corners, plate 56 (cat. no. 105)

seems to have carried the technique to extremes, for even its pilasters have book-matched veneers. The change in direction of the grain pattern visually diminishes the support function of the pilasters and flies in the face of architectural convention, but Lannuier, in this case, seems to have thrown convention to the wind, choosing instead to celebrate the intense color and optical effects of this wonderfully rich material. Lannuier's interest in the symmetry and balance of book-matching was such that it even led him to reverse the direction of the fancy, die-stamped brass-and-wood borders on some table aprons with book-matched crotch-mahogany veneers (plate 72).

Two additional aspects of veneering that are more apparent in Lannuier's work than in the work of others are the ways in which he matched veneers at the hollow or canted corners of his card tables (plates 73, 74), never breaking the continuous flow of the grain, and his insistence on keeping the friezes of square pier tables crisp and clean at the corners (plate 75), where most New York cabinetmakers tended to apply thin rectangles of mahogany or rosewood (plate 76). Lannuier's approach to veneering provided smooth, unbroken architectural friezes and imparted a crystalline clarity to forms, in keeping with the French design principles underlying *le goût antique*. Such subtleties help us to separate Lannuier's work from that of his many able competitors.

Metalwork

Three main varieties of ornamental metalwork are found on Lannuier furniture: applied brass moldings with wood cores; inlaid brass, either in plain thin strips or in flat bands or borders, and singular ornaments, die-stamped with classical patterns; and applied gilded cast-brass ornaments—or ormolu mounts, as they are often referred to today. Lannuier arguably was the first cabinetmaker in America to have incorporated French-style gilded-brass metalwork in his furniture designs. His inaugural advertisement of July 1803 stated clearly that he had brought with him, for the purpose of making furniture in the "newest and latest French fashion . . . gilt and brass frames [and] borders of ornaments."[10] An example of the "gilt and brass frames" probably is the pierced brass gallery, or frame, that encloses the marble top on his early pier table in *le goût moderne* (see plate 12), while the "borders of ornaments" may signify either the brass inlays like those that outline the scrolled ends of the Lannuier/Cochois French bedstead (plate 77), or possibly the ornaments on the aprons of the

PLATE 73. Attributed to Charles-Honoré Lannuier. Card table. 1815–19 (cat. no. 83)

PLATE 74. Charles-Honoré Lannuier. Card table. 1815–19 (cat. no. 66)

PLATE 75. Front corner. Detail of the Lannuier square pier table, plate 42 (cat. no. 99)

PLATE 76. Front corner. Detail of the pier table by a New York maker, plate 44

Bell family card tables (plate 78). It is also conceivable that the phrase "borders of ornaments" might mean the gilded cast-brass ornaments found on some of Lannuier's earliest square pier tables (plate 79), although this seems less likely.

From the time of his arrival in New York until the end of his career, Lannuier made extensive use of brass moldings, which reflect both *le goût moderne* and his background and training in post-Revolutionary France. These brass moldings came in flat, hollow, quarter-, and half-round profiles. The half-round brass moldings, which the French call *baguettes*, were favorites of Lannuier, who added them to the edges of the tops of his card tables (plate 78) and to the aprons of his early pier tables (see plates 12, 30, and plate 79). In 1813, Lannuier was credited with $1.30 in the account book of New York cabinetmaker David Loring, for having sold him "15 feet 4 in of Brass moulding," although no specific mention is made of its profile.[11]

Production of brass molding with a wooden core seems to have been a fairly complicated process that required a tool or machine capable of shaping the thin sheet brass over a molded wooden core and crisply folding the brass over onto the back; in some instances, the brass was inserted into thin slits cut along the length of the wood. X-ray fluorescence testing on a metal sample taken from the hidden underside of a small quarter-round brass molding on the cross stretchers of the Winterthur Museum's early satinwood-and-mahogany pier table (see plate 17) has revealed the presence of what appears to be an original layer of gold on the surface of the brass, although apparently this was not deposited there by mercury gilding, since no traces of mercury were found. (Mercury gilding is a process in which an amalgam of mercury and gold is applied to brass, which is then heated to evaporate the mercury and leave a film of gold deposited on the metal.) Subsequent scientific testing at the Metropolitan Museum of a piece of original quarter-round brass molding from the plinth

PLATE 77. Detail of the scrolled end of the French bedstead by Charles-Honoré Lannuier and Jean-Charles Cochois, plate 14 (cat. no. 4)

PLATE 78. Front corner. Detail of the Lannuier card table, plate 22 (cat. no. 57)

of the card table shown in plate 80 produced no evidence of gold, which suggests that in
this case the original gilded effect probably came from the application of lacquers.[12] The
rectangles of plain brass at the corners of Lannuier's three known *goût moderne* pier tables
(see plate 12, fig. 11, and cat. no. 90) appear to have been trimmed from a sheet of brass,
which may have been done in his workshop. (On French furniture, such corners frequently
have decorative striations worked into the brass.) Thin brass stringing (figs. 91, 92) also may
have been cut with gauges to various sizes in the shop.

One of the new and advanced decorative techniques employed by Parisian *ébénistes* in
the late eighteenth century, which impressed the wealthy collector, connoisseur, and furniture designer Thomas Hope the most, was the application of ornaments of inlaid brass and
wood that he described thus in his *Household Furniture and Interior Decoration*: "These species of
inlayings in metal, on a ground of ebony or dyed wood, seem peculiarly adapted to the nature of the mahogany furniture so much in use in this country, which they enliven, without
preventing it, by any raised ornaments, from being constantly rubbed, and kept free from
dust and dirt. At Paris they have been carried to a great degree of elegance and perfection.
The metal ornament, and the ground of stained wood in which it is inserted, being there,
stamped together, and cut out, through dint of the same single mechanical process, they are
always sure of fitting each other to the greatest degree of nicety."[13]

The award-winning talents of the Parisian Denis-Michel Frichot in the fabrication of
"inlayings" of this sort, and the previously mentioned later partnership between his son

PLATE 80. Attributed to Charles-Honoré Lannuier. Card table. 1812–15 (cat. no. 62)

FIGURE 91. Attributed to Charles-Honoré Lannuier. Square pier table with canted corners. 1815–19 (cat. no. 108)

FIGURE 92. Attributed to Charles-Honoré Lannuier. Square pier table with canted corners. About 1815–19 (cat. no. 109)

PLATE 81. Front foot. Detail of the Lannuier French bedstead, plate 54 (cat. no. 5)

FIGURE 93. New York maker. Card table. 1815–20. Mahogany veneer, 29³/₈ x 37 x 18¹/₂ in. The Metropolitan Museum of Art, New York. Gift of Mrs. J. Insley Blair, 1947

Pierre-Aurore and Honoré Lannuier in New York cannot be overemphasized, because they establish a direct link between Lannuier's manufactory and the creation of this very special type of French ornament. Aurore Frichot apparently was just as involved as his father in manufacturing precise, intricate inlays, and he founded a factory in Paris that made marquetry for furniture in native woods by means of a mechanical process. After Frichot returned to France, he made furniture inlaid with steel, which he attempted to sell to the Mobilier de la Couronne in about 1829, but it appears that he was rebuffed because his prices were too high. Lightwood furniture with marquetry inlay was extremely popular in France after the restoration of the Bourbon monarchy, and Frichot seems to have been in the thick of this trend. Perhaps if Lannuier had lived, and his collaboration with Frichot had continued, this would have been the next style to overtake New York, too, in the 1820s. Elegant furniture with scroll supports, in the French Restauration style, did not appear in New York until 1830 or later, and usually was of mahogany rather than of light-colored woods.[14]

There can be little doubt that Frichot played a major role in the efflorescence of the Lannuier shop during the last four or five years of its existence, when some truly extraordinary furniture was produced there, much of it with the remarkably precise Parisian-style brass-and-wood borders and ornaments. Questions abound about the Lannuier-Frichot relationship, not the least of which is whether the die-stamped brass was shipped to New York from a Frichot manufactory in Paris, or whether Aurore Frichot may have brought with him a machine capable of producing it in New York. The English Regency cabinetmaker George Bullock's stock-in-trade sale, which was held at his Tenterden Street warehouse

PLATE 83. Brass and wood inlay. Detail of the commode by Bernard Molitor made in Paris about 1787–91, plate 8

PLATE 82. Gilded figure. Detail of the Lannuier card table, plate 53 (cat. no. 72)

and workshops in London in 1819, included great quantities of brass-and-wood borders and ornaments, as well as "a stamping press with iron vice and dies."[15] How large one of these stamping presses was or what it looked like is unknown, as no examples survive, but if Frichot did bring one along with him it might well explain why there are instances of the same patterns of die-stamped brass ornaments and borders on furniture by Lannuier as well as by others. These include the Greek-key patterned borders on the Van Rensselaer bedstead (plate 81) and on a cylinder desk-and-bookcase by an anonymous New York cabinetmaker (see fig. 22), or the inlaid lyre on several Lannuier works (see plate 22, and fig. 92), as well as on the canted corners of a card table by another unknown New York maker (fig. 93). Just as Lannuier had sold brass moldings to David Loring in 1813, Frichot, or the partnership of Lannuier and Frichot, may have supplemented their income by selling die-stamped borders and ornaments to other New York makers. It may be more than just coincidence that Lannuier's partner, Frichot, arrived on the scene in 1816, the year before "fancy brass bands" appeared for the first time in the New York cabinetmakers' price book.

In one instance it can be proven that the same lozenge-patterned border used by Lannuier (plate 82) may be found also on Parisian furniture (plate 83). What is most amazing about this correlation, however, is that the French commode on which the pattern appears was made over twenty-five years earlier—which raises the question of whether Aurore Frichot brought his father's old stamping press with him from Paris. The search for more contemporary French examples with brass-and-wood borders in patterns related to those on Lannuier's furniture has met with minimal success, which may indicate that this style of

FIGURE 94. Griffin. Detail of the card table by a New York maker, figure 52

FIGURE 95. New York maker. Card table. 1815–20. Rosewood veneer, 29½ x 36¼ x 18⅛ in. The Warner Collection of Gulf States Paper Corporation, Tuscaloosa, Alabama

ornament was actually on its way out in Paris by the 1810s. Such was not the case in London or New York, however, where inlaid ornament of this type was by then just coming into fashion, due, in part, to the hearty recommendation it received from Thomas Hope. George Bullock had his own stamping press and was a major proponent of this characteristically French form of decoration, as was the London and Birmingham hardware manufacturer and merchant James Barron, who, in 1814, offered for sale through his catalogue, "Highly polished Brass Ornaments for inlaying in hard wood, either saw pierced or pressed."[16] Barron's catalogue pictures some singular ornaments with a passing resemblance to the types used by Lannuier, but his fancy borders, mainly naturalistic foliate patterns and arabesques, are entirely different. A distinctive Greek-wave border, unrecorded in Lannuier's documented oeuvre but used on figural furniture by some of his competitors (see fig. 54, and fig. 94), appears in a Birmingham trade catalogue possibly issued by the firm of Amphlett and Parrys, which was listed as founders specializing in cabinet brass in Pigot's Birmingham *Directory* of 1816–17. Likewise, simple brass bands with punched lozenge and cruciform designs found on two pairs of New York winged-caryatid card tables in the style of Lannuier (see fig. 51, and fig. 95) are closely related to the borders used on some published English Regency furniture made after the designs of Thomas Hope.[17]

Brass-and-wood ornaments and borders provide just one example of the confusion that exists over the origins of imported metalwork on furniture by Lannuier and his New York colleagues. Luckily, the discovery of the connection between Frichot and Lannuier makes it fairly certain that Paris was the ultimate source of the die-stamped brass inlays Lannuier used—perhaps in the form of a French machine, brought to New York to execute them. The picture is far murkier when it comes to the gilded cast-brass ornaments on furniture by Lannuier and his contemporaries.

Sheraton, in his *Cabinet Dictionary*, provides some useful background information and entertaining period commentary on French gilded-brass ornaments, and he impatiently states, "if our noblemen and gentry would contribute as much to the encouragement of a

PLATE 84. Charles-Honoré Lannuier. Square pier table. 1805–10 (cat. no. 95)

national brass foundry, as they do to some other institutions of less consequence, we might have as elegant brass work for cabinets cast in London, as they have in Paris. It is in this article they excel us and set off cabinet work."[18] Sheraton's comments seem to assure us that, at least throughout the early part of Lannuier's career in New York, the English were neither producing nor marketing gilded cast-brass ornaments in direct competition with the French. Therefore, it would appear safe to assume that the ornaments we find on Lannuier's early work are French. A central ornament of griffins facing an altar and flanked on opposite ends of the apron by classical wreaths was a favorite combination of motifs he used on two of his earliest square pier tables with veneered columns (see plate 28, and cat. no. 96), while a third example bears the same central ornament but substitutes classical grotesques for the wreaths at either side (plate 84). The gilded cast-brass capitals and bases of the columns on all three tables, of the simplest, most chaste design and also probably French, appear to be nearly identical. Overall, the ornaments with which Lannuier decorated his early pier tables tend to be smaller and less ostentatious than on later examples, whose friezes often combine naturalistic elements with those that depict mythical and allegorical subjects (see plate 42, and plate 72).

One might assume that, because Lannuier initially advertised that he had brought hardware with him from France, he had little trouble procuring gilded cast-brass ornaments from Paris throughout his career. This, however, cannot be proven, and it is possible that he was as subject to the vagaries of supply as were other cabinetmakers in the city. If New York newspaper advertisements are any indicator of how readily available these ornaments were,

FIGURE 96. Detail of a caster on the Lannuier card table, plate 35 (cat. no. 61)

then it would appear that they were not always easily found. Only two newspaper ads have been discovered that specifically seem to describe them: One is the Lornier and Bailly ad of December 1815, which offered a variety of articles manufactured in Paris, including, "an assortment of Ornaments for Architecture, Furniture, Looking Glass Frames, & c";[19] the other appeared a little over a year later, and advertised for sale "HARPS, BRONZES etc. JUST received direct from Paris. . . . ALSO, an Invoice of Bronzes or ornaments for Piano Fortes, or Cabinet makers, are offered for sale at No. 138 Broadway, by Charles Del Vecchio."[20] From a different source of advertising, a cabinetmaker's trade label, we learn that, in 1814, the Parisian immigrant *ébéniste* Joseph Brauwers, who worked at 163 William Street, had access to and decorated his furniture "with the Richest Ornaments, just imported from France."[21] (Brauwers's card table with gilded brass ornaments is illustrated in Chapter Two, figure 28.) Lannuier's estate inventory (see Appendix 9) reveals that at the time of his death in 1819 his stock with ornaments was worth $293.59, or roughly one-tenth the total value of his stock of completed furniture. Just how many ornaments this represents is difficult to say, but in the 1825 estate inventory of the Boston cabinetmaker Thomas Emmons, "2 Setts [*sic*] Caps, vases & Bases 2½ inch" and "4 pair Caps & Bases 2/³⁄₈"—all, presumably, of cast brass—were assigned a total value of $15.00.[22] This would seem to suggest that Lannuier's stock of ornaments was adequate but not enormous.

These few advertisements for gilded ornaments coincide with two important world events—the defeat of Napoleon by the allies and the end of the War of 1812—which made possible once again the unimpeded flow of English and French imported goods into the port of New York. The above-mentioned ads clearly included French gilded cast-brass ornaments. No such advertisements exist, however, for English copies of French ornaments, but it is a virtual certainty that these, too, were being marketed in New York.

The chief place of manufacture for these copies was Birmingham, England. During the eighteenth century, a major brass-manufacturing industry developed there to meet the needs of the masses for fireplace equipment, candlesticks, lighting devices, and hardware. As Donald L. Fennimore has pointed out, the genius of English entrepreneurs during the Industrial Revolution was their realization that more money could be made by selling relatively inexpensive items to a vast market than by providing a few expensive ones to a small number of wealthy patrons.[23] By 1816, among the eighty-five brass foundries listed in Pigot's Birmingham *Directory*, eleven specialized solely in casting and stamping hardware for furniture.[24] These ornaments could be copied easily and inexpensively by making patterns from French examples, since no international copyright laws existed. Unfortunately, so little is known about Parisian brass foundries and their products in the early nineteenth century that it is practically impossible to distinguish a French ornament from an English copy when they appear on New York furniture made by Lannuier and his contemporaries. More is known about the Birmingham brass-hardware industry in the early nineteenth century as a result of the published work of Nicholas Goodison, Donald L. Fennimore, and Jillian Ehninger, who have examined and interpreted the important collection of Birmingham metalwork trade catalogues in the Victoria and Albert Museum, London. Despite their efforts, considerable research into this incredibly complex subject still needs to be done in France, England, and the United States.[25]

Lannuier, it seems, was not opposed to using English cabinet hardware. Cast-brass casters of obvious Birmingham manufacture may be seen on several of his card tables, including the standard lion's paw as well as some less common patterns such as square-ended examples with palmettes (cat. no. 63) and blunt-ended ones with acanthus-leaf decoration (fig. 96). An identical match to this last type appears in a Birmingham trade catalogue with a watermark probably of 1814.[26] Lannuier also may have selected some of his cast-brass

ornaments from Birmingham hardware catalogues—a possibility first suggested by Jillian Ehninger, who has investigated the complex subject of imported ornamental hardware on American furniture. Ehninger specifically cites two ornaments found on Lannuier's furniture and in a Birmingham trade catalogue, which is inscribed "R. Smith & Co, Birm, 1822" inside the front cover, in the collection of the Victoria and Albert Museum. One ornament, which depicts Apollo as the God of Truth and Light being pulled across the sky in his chariot by moths (plate 85), decorates the friezes of two documented Lannuier pier tables (see plate 24, and fig. 97) and an attributed looking glass (see plate 64); the other, a personification of Autumn, may be seen on two closely related labeled pier tables with marble columns (see plate 42, and cat. no. 98).[27] Further study of the ornaments used by Lannuier has revealed the presence of three more patterns from the same trade catalogue (fig. 98 a, b), including two winged female figures on either side of a lyre (plate 86); two nymphs, back-to-back, playing the panpipes (cat. nos. 76, 77); and paired cornucopia flanking a wreath (plate 87). Cast on the verso of the ornament composed of winged female figures

FIGURE 98 a–b. Illustrations of cast-brass ornaments, watermarked SE & C/1822 and made in Birmingham, England, from a trade catalogue in the collection of the Victoria and Albert Museum, London

PLATE 86 a–b. Recto (left) and verso (right) of the ornament on the front apron of the Lannuier card table, plate 26 (cat. no. 67)

and a lyre (shown in plate 86) are the initials *CA*. Identical initials have been seen by this author on the reverse sides of three additional ornaments used by Lannuier—a trophy depicting the implements of war (cat. no. 101), a wreath (cat. no. 125), and a spray of flowers (plate 72)—that are not in the trade catalogue but, logically, would seem to have been obtained from the same source. The ornament with the lyre and winged female figures appears at least half-a-dozen times on furniture by New York cabinetmakers other than Lannuier (fig. 94). One other ornament, which enjoyed widespread use and also does not appear in any trade catalogue, is the crossed rose branches flanking a central bowknot. It can be seen on the aprons of the card tables Duncan Phyfe made for James Brinckerhoff in 1816 (see fig. 71), on those Lannuier executed for the Bayard sisters the following year (see plates 51, 53), and in the frieze of a rosewood cylinder desk-and-bookcase by an unknown New York maker (see fig. 22).

The initials *CA* presumably are those of a brass founder. Searches of Birmingham trade directories for a likely name have produced no leads, although it is possible that the *CA* relates to Amphlett, of the firm of Amphlett and Parrys, one of the eleven cabinet brass foundries that appear in Pigot's *Directory* of 1816–17, since a first name or initial is not given in the listing. On the chance that the initials could belong to a French founder whose wares were marketed by the Birmingham firm of R. Smith & Co., the *Almanach du Commerce de Paris* was also consulted, but this research proved fruitless, as Parisian brass founders also are listed only by their surnames. Perhaps the future discovery of invoices or account books will

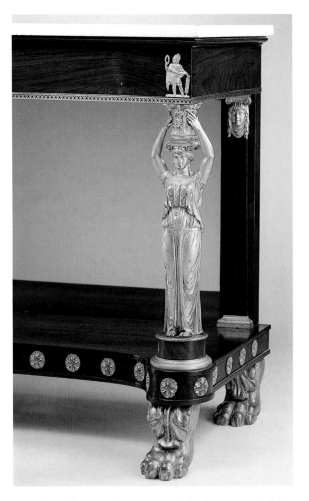

PLATE 87. Gilded figure. Detail of the card table attributed to Lannuier, plate 43 (cat. no. 83)

PLATE 88. Cast-metal caryatid and back pilaster. Detail of the Lannuier square pier table, plate 24 (cat. no. 100)

record a link between New York cabinetmakers and English or French brass founders that will help to identify the mysterious *CA*.[28]

The commonly held assumption that only French gilded cast-brass ornaments were mercury gilded, not merely lacquered to produce a gilt effect, is an untenable one, since we know that the process was carried out in Matthew Boulton's manufactory in Birmingham, where the brass furniture ornaments and mounts treated this way were called "ormolu."[29] Mercury gilding may have been practiced in Birmingham, but the hardware industry there, known for its skills at reducing expenses, also pioneered the technique of dipping brass ornaments into acid to make them bright, then burnishing and lacquering them to create the contrast of mat and shiny surfaces typical of the best mercury-gilded ornaments.[30] This type of *faux* gilding would seem to accord better with the high output of English manufacturers during the Industrial Revolution, in contrast to the mercury-gilding technique that, presumably, was employed by Parisian founders to finish their cast-brass ornaments.[31] The comments of Louis-Auguste-Félix, Baron de Beaujour, in his *Sketch of the United States of North America*, are especially poignant in this regard, as well as on the matter of the English mass marketing of plagiarized French designs. The baron writes: "We [the French] surpass the English in all kinds of choice manufacture. . . . They themselves have acknowledged their inferiority in all articles of magnificence and luxury; and despairing of equalling us in the beautiful, they have imitated us in the common; and they have supplanted us in the trade of all nations, because they have gained them over by their low prices. This is the whole secret of the prosperity of their manufactures. . . . They possess the art of making their goods known and esteemed by patterns, as well as of disguising under English names, the most beautiful works of other countries."[32]

Lannuier sometimes also used gilded cast-composition ornaments on his furniture. These take the form of architectural capitals and bases, borders of rosettes and stars, and mythological masks and heads in profile, such as those seen above the rear pilasters of his richly ornamented square pier table with cast-metal caryatid figures (plate 88), as well as on the plinth of a card table, attributed to Lannuier, at the Brooklyn Museum of Art (plate 80), which features a head of Hera, the wife of Zeus and the protector of marriage, in profile.

These cast-composition ornaments most likely were imported from Europe and sold in looking-glass and frame shops in New York. In a newspaper advertisement in September 1818, Isaac L. Platt, the proprietor of a looking-glass and frame shop at 128 Broadway, included "Gold Borders and Ornaments" at the end of a list of embossed, colored, and gilded paper products offered for sale, which might suggest that these ornaments were of a material other than cast brass.[33] Composition ornaments in classical patterns were illustrated in Ackermann's *Repository*, and they were sold at his emporium, The Repository of the Arts, in the Strand in London. The interior of Ackermann's store was depicted in his serial publication and could have served as a model of sorts for New York looking-glass and frame shops, many of which were located along Broadway, the city's most fashionable shopping district in the early nineteenth century. Newspaper ads reveal the wide variety of high-end merchandise these shops carried. In 1812, for instance, Porri and Rinaldi, at 139 Broadway, offered, among other items, "colored and plain Prints, from the most eminent European Masters, framed or in sheets . . . best English Drawings, Ivory and Gold Paper of all sizes, Drawing Books, Glaziers Diamonds, and a small invoice of Pocket Books."[34] Other shops were stocked with both imports and goods manufactured in New York, ranging from barometers, thermometers, and optical devices to French wallpapers and borders, picture frames, and bed and window cornices custom made to order.

Looking-glass Plates and Marble

Framed looking glasses and looking-glass plates were, of course, among the mainstays of the shops just described. In 1817, Ambrose Crane advertised that he was "now opening a large assortment of Looking Glass Plates from the Royal Manufactory at Paris . . . And a large assortment of German Looking Glass Plates, wholesale and retail."[35] Ads like this inform us of at least two of the principal sources of the exports that supplied the looking-glass plates that Lannuier and other New York cabinetmakers incorporated into their furniture, but London also was mentioned frequently in these ads. However, in the absence of bills and receipts, there is no way to determine whether Lannuier preferred French looking-glass plates above all others.

According to Sheraton, looking-glass plates came in standard sizes "manufactured for particular purposes." He listed these in *The Cabinet Dictionary*, noting that the smallest were generally of German and the largest of English glass. The standard sizes for English looking-glass plates ranged from 24 × 38 to 30 × 50 inches.[36] In 1817, a New York wholesaler named O'Connor offered for sale a general assortment of looking-glass plates from the royal manufactory in Paris that were larger than any described by Sheraton, and which ranged from 50 × 35 to 87 × 23 inches.[37] These enormous plates probably were meant for the piers between windows that by now had become the main focus in the decoration of New York homes. Ensembles of marble-topped tables with looking glasses above, and elaborate window-curtain treatments like those illustrated by Ackermann and La Mésangère (see plate 20), helped to popularize that quintessential French form, the square pier table, and,

consequently, looking-glass plate retailers, cabinetmakers, and upholsterers benefited from this fashion trend. The cost of looking-glass plates in the early nineteenth century is difficult to assess, since neither wholesale nor retail prices were given in the ads. However, they must have been expensive, due to the complicated and labor-intensive manufacturing process involved in producing them and the added expenses of packing and shipping them overseas.[38]

In France, after the Restauration, there was considerable interest in exploiting the medium of glass for furniture, beyond its use as reflective plates in doors or on the backs of pier tables. In 1819, an entire suite of cut-glass furniture was executed, including a dressing table and chair, and then exhibited at the Louvre. This French fascination with glass furniture seems to have extended to New York as well, during Lannuier's lifetime. In 1817, the English traveler Henry Bradshaw Fearon had remarked, "I have seen some [furniture] with cut glass, instead of brass ornaments, which had a beautiful effect." No Lannuier furniture with cut-glass ornaments has come to light as yet, but at least one New York card table of about 1820 is known that has round corners and columnar supports at the back and cut-glass capitals and bases.[39]

The sumptuousness of the materials introduced into New York furniture by Lannuier was both dazzling and revolutionary. Slabs and columns of imported marble underscored the impression of fashionable luxury of his classical designs, while adding a sense of architectural permanence and monumentality. Lannuier and his customers seem to have been particularly enamored of the expensive and luxurious pure and veined white marble—the kind found in all his known work that incorporates this material, except for some small tables or stands (see plate 16, and plates 68, 89). Not only were a variety of colored marbles used in France in the 1790s and early 1800s, but New York newspaper ads as well record the availability of other colors before 1820, so that the nearly exclusive use of white by Lannuier and many of his competitors is somewhat difficult to explain. It may be that white was most popular with Lannuier's elite patrons because it was considered the quintessential marble of antiquity, and carried with it associations of ancient Greek and Roman statuary and classical ruins, which some of them had experienced firsthand on the Grand Tour.

Marble, both domestic and imported, came from a number of sources, and was sold principally at marble yards, where slabs were cut and polished for use as chimney facings,

a.

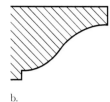

b.

c.

d.

FIGURE 99 a–d. Full-size profiles of applied moldings on Lannuier furniture (cat. nos. 52 [a], 112 [b], 100 [c], 72 [d])

mantel shelves, and the tops of pier tables, or else elaborately carved and turned for architectural chimneypieces. Lannuier's favorite white marble probably came from Italy and, in the period, was known as Italian statuary when it was pure white and Italian veined when it was white streaked with varying amounts of gray or golden brown. A charming 1822 newspaper advertisement in the form of a rhyme extolling the virtues of the merchandise sold at the marble warehouse of W. and J. Frazee at 425 Broadway helps to identify the sources of some of the colored marble imported into New York:

> And constant as the Sun rolls on his way,
> The marble here is wrought from day to day;
> The hard and massive blocks are cut in twain
> Of Irish Black and Egypt's golden vein,
> Italian statuary, pure and white,
> In which the sculptor works with much delight:
> These with all other kinds, quite rich and fine,
> With cheerful labour here are made to shine.
> Some highly finished work we have on hand,
> Made of these marbles from the foreign land.[40]

The white marble with gray veins typically found on New York pier tables and sideboards often has been described as Tuckahoe marble from Westchester County, New York. Imported Italian marble was advertised far more heavily than New York marble during Lannuier's career in New York, but the domestic variety was also available. As early as 1805, P. McGrath placed an ad for "N[ew] York State real Block Marble, beautifully variegated with shells, fossils, & c," and announced the "Valuable discovery of [the] kings-bridge white Marble quarry, answering the full and extensive purposes of Monuments, Tombs, Gravestones, etc."[41] In 1808, the partnership of Douglass and Fotheringame advertised marble from a quarry in Mount Pleasant, which was said to be "on the margin of the North river, and only 35 miles from this city."[42] Unlike wood, marble presently cannot be scientifically analyzed to determine if it is of American or European origin, so the question of whether Lannuier ever utilized New York marble remains moot. The suspicion is that American white marble was not of the same quality as Italian, something that certainly would have been taken into account by Lannuier and his elite clientele.

Cabinetmakers had become such steady customers at New York marble yards by the 1810s that increasingly they were targeted with advertisements like the one in 1816 that offered "Pier and Sideboard tops of pure statuary white," or imported "ANTIQUE AND MODERN MARBLE TABLE PLATES."[43] By 1820, the French-style square pier table, with marble top and columns, had become so popular that ads like the following one began to appear: "TO CABINET MAKERS / ANTHONY GIRARD, No. 14 Fulton-slip, offers for sale one case of Marble Columns, suitable for Pier Tables, or other pieces of elegant Furniture."[44] There are no records of whom Lannuier patronized for his marble, but an intriguing newspaper ad of 1807, in which the firm of Benjamin Seixas and Son announced its intention to sell "on Monday next . . . a large and elegant assortment of chimney ornaments, made of Derbyshire, spar and Marble" may offer a clue, if, in fact, either of these men can be linked with the Moyse Seixas who served as one of the witnesses to the Lannuiers' 1814 *acte de mariage*.[45]

Moldings

Lannuier employed a fairly limited range of moldings, which, for greatest architectural effect, he tended to concentrate in the frieze areas of his case furniture and various table

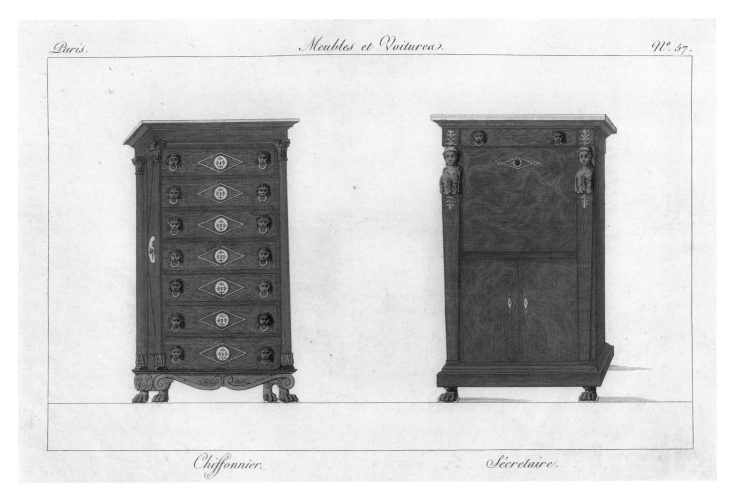

Chiffonnier.   *Sécretaire.*

PLATE 90. Pierre de La Mésangère. Designs for a chiffonier and a *secrétaire à abattant* (Plate 57 from *Collection de Meubles et Objets de Goût*). 1803. Colored engraving, 7¾ x 12¼ in. The Metropolitan Museum of Art, New York. Harris Brisbane Dick Fund, 1930

forms. The limited use of applied moldings was in keeping with the French antique taste, which emphasized clean, cubic volumes and smooth expanses of the richest mahogany veneers. Two of Lannuier's three main molding profiles—a deep cavetto and an elegant cyma recta (fig. 99 a, b)—can, in fact, be recognized easily on the friezes of Consulat furniture forms illustrated in La Mésangère (see plate 5, and plate 90). The cavetto profile Lannuier used, with a curve representing slightly more than ninety degrees of a circle (plate 78), occurs in several sizes, scaled to specific applications. The same is true for what is perhaps Lannuier's most beautiful molding profile, the cyma recta, which seems to have been utilized by him alone in New York, and thus provides one of the keys to identifying undocumented work from his manufactory. What is surprising about the cyma-recta molding is that it is not found on Lannuier's furniture until the 1810s. This may indicate that Lannuier, himself, did not bring a set of molding planes with this profile from France, but his one-time partner, Frichot, or Jean Gruez could have done just that. The most frequently used size of cyma-recta molding appears on Lannuier's gilded figural pier tables with canted corners (plate 91); larger such moldings are found at the tops of the posts that support the canopy of the French bedstead made for Isaac Bell (see plate 49) and on the cornices of the looking glass made—possibly in 1816—for the steamboat *Chancellor Livingston* (see plate 64), as well as on a French press attributed to Lannuier (cat. no. 51).[46]

By way of contrast, some of Lannuier's earliest pier tables have rather soft looking quarter-round moldings under the tops (see plate 18), which, in their somewhat elongated, flattened profiles, foreshadow his later use of the Grecian ovolo molding that is based on the curves of an ellipse (fig. 99 c). These Grecian ovolo moldings probably did not become popular in New York until the 1810s, as suggested by their appearance for the first time in a

PLATE 91. Dovetail joint and cyma-recta molding. Detail of the rear apron of the Lannuier square pier table with canted corners, plate 56 (cat. no. 105)

plate of molding profiles at the back of the 1817 New York cabinetmakers' book of prices. Lannuier most appropriately selected this profile for use on his square pier tables with the strongest classical Greek overtones. For example, he used the molding under the edge of the marble top of a rosewood table with pure white statuary marble columns and Corinthian order gilded cast-brass capitals (see plate 42), and again on his most overtly Grecian pier table, the magnificent rosewood example (see plate 24) with gilded cast-metal caryatids designed after the carved marble figures of the Erechtheum on the Acropolis in Athens. Lannuier's Grecian ovolo profile differs from many of those used on other New York square pier tables with columns, which tend to be smaller, flatter, and more elongated, with a sharper arris, or edge (plates 75, 76). A second Grecian ovolo profile Lannuier developed especially for the edges of the lower leaves of his signature series of gilded figural card tables is blunter still (fig. 99 d), as it had to equal in thickness the lower table leaf, and was flattened to keep it from protruding beyond the plane of the upper leaf, which it served architecturally as a sort of abbreviated entablature (plate 82).

Construction Details

Unfortunately, Lannuier's large body of documented work provides few construction features or details that could be described as unique to him, and that might help to identify the products of his manufactory among the enormous amount of anonymous New York furniture that survives from the period. From the start, Lannuier seems to have conformed to the New York cabinetmaking trade's emphasis on sturdy framing and consistent but minimalist construction techniques suited to the local climate and designed to keep labor costs down. These local preferences and cabinetmaking techniques are all documented in the several journeymen cabinetmakers' lists and books of prices issued over the course of Lannuier's career in New York. The very existence of these books indicates the high degree of uniformity in the trade—one of the key problems in looking for simple, straightforward signs of the work produced by Lannuier's shop.

PLATE 92. Back of the Lannuier square pier table, plate 24 (cat. no.100)

PLATE 93. Back of a pier table by a New York maker, plate 44

The square pier tables provide an example of one of Lannuier's decided construction preferences, but not one that can be considered distinctive or unique. Tables of this type made before the War of 1812 characteristically have thick rear posts more like square columns than pilasters (plate 84), which Lannuier, over time, reduced in size and to which he applied highly ornamented tapered pilasters of rich, figured veneers or marble, and gilded composition capitals and bases (plate 88). As luxurious and impressive looking as these

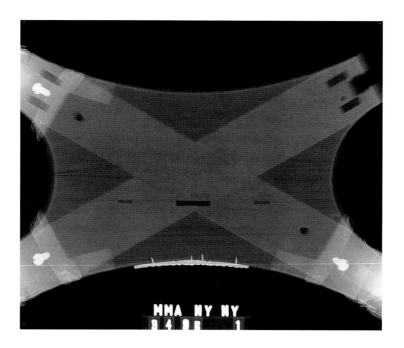

tables were, from a cabinetmaking perspective they were totally formulaic, their upper and lower box-like structures connected by means of columns at the front and posts at the back. Their lateral stability was provided by thin backboards either screwed on flush with the upper and lower back rails and the two back posts, or tacked into rabbets—as Lannuier seemed most often to prefer. He consistently chose to connect the back posts to the rear rails of the upper frame and the veneered plinth below with mortise-and-tenon joints (plate 92), as opposed to large dovetail joints with screws (plate 93). In the pre-1815 list of additional prices, only the former method of attachment is described as standard. By 1817, however, in the newly published revised price book, "plain turned columns in front, framed with pins prepared by the turner, square pillars at back, framed with tenons or dovetailed" are included as standard features of the square pier-table form.[47] This evidence provides a cautionary note against the wholesale attribution to Lannuier of square pier tables with back posts connected by mortise-and-tenon joints, for, as the price books clearly indicate, this was a standard type of joint.

Lannuier's splendid square pier tables with canted corners and gilded figural supports display especially noteworthy workmanship and construction. The fit and finish of the dovetail joints in the aprons (plate 91) are as close to perfection as is humanly possible, with no evidence of hurried or sloppy work, such as saw kerfs that extend below the base of the joint. Similar care is seen in the precisely trimmed and chamfered mahogany blocks—or stumps, as they are called in the price books—on the inside corners of the aprons (plate 65).

Card tables from the Lannuier shop vary somewhat in their construction depending on when they were made. In two of his finest and most exquisitely proportioned examples, of about 1810, Lannuier resorted to a typically French method of construction in which the two back legs slide out on a frame to support the opened top (plate 94). In all other known examples, Lannuier relied on a swivel-top construction, which became standard in New York by about 1812. Although swivel tops did not appear in a London cabinetmakers' price book until 1811, they are known from French post-Revolutionary card tables in *le goût moderne*, which therefore makes Lannuier's employment of them almost exclusively in his work not at all surprising.

For his swivel-topped card tables with tight, block-like octagonal plinths (see plates 22, 35), Lannuier favored a method of construction described in the pre-1815 list of additional

revised prices as "glueing up the block long and cross way, each joint,"[48] which involved stacking and gluing several boards on top of one another with the direction of the grain at right angles in each succeeding layer to help reduce the overall shrinkage of the core. An optional but more expensive method, listed next in the price list, necessitated forming the core of X-shaped pieces of wood "lapp'd and the corners filled in."[49] While New York makers, other than Lannuier, used this technique on some tables with block-like plinths, it was employed almost exclusively on examples with broad, flat ones—which is how Lannuier fashioned the plinths on nearly all of his figural card tables (fig. 100). On the figural pier tables with canted corners, he modified this type of core construction with strut-like pieces that angle out from a lateral rail at the back of the plinth. Once again, however, it is important to emphasize that these are standard New York features recorded in the price books, and reveal Lannuier's preferences rather than his unique approach to construction.[50]

The swivel-topped card tables that bear Lannuier's earlier printed bilingual label display some distinct differences in the manner in which the bottoms are fitted into the aprons. Sometimes, as in the Bell family's card tables (see plate 22), the bottoms are full, chamfered on all sides, and fitted into grooves, while the tables with the sliding-back frames (see plate 94) have full bottoms composed of thin boards nailed into rabbets. The card tables with

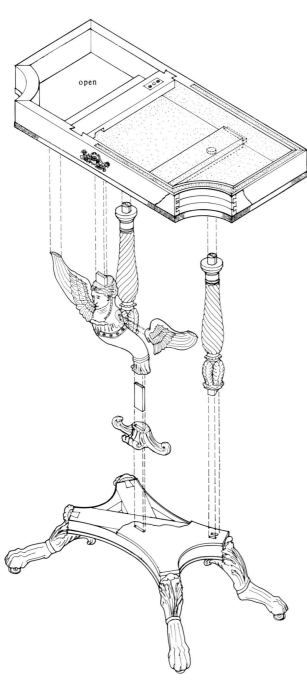

FIGURE 101. Exploded view of the card table attributed to Lannuier, plate 43 (cat. no. 83). Drawing by Robert S. Burton

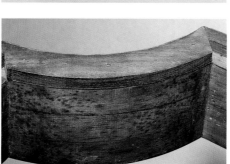

PLATE 95 a–b. Detail of the underside (left, top) and of a triple-laminated front corner (left, below) of the Lannuier card table, plate 53 (cat. no. 72)

PLATE 96. Detail of the underside of the card table by a New York maker, plate 45, showing the use of glue blocks rather than nails to secure the bottom boards to the frame

Lannuier's latest engraved bilingual label are characterized by a far greater uniformity and a precision with regard to the fit and finish similar to that of the figural pier tables. The gilded figural card tables, Lannuier's flagship models, were extremely well planned and expertly made (fig. 101). The bottom boards of the well, which take up roughly two-thirds of a table's width, are nailed into rabbets formed by mahogany strips that were applied to the bottom edges of the aprons and also provide surfaces on the outside for glue to hold the fancy die-stamped brass borders in place (plate 95 a). The curved, front sections of the tables with hollow corners are made up of three laminated strips of white pine joined by dovetails to the front and side aprons. A carefully planned and superbly executed detail, which is evident at the bottoms of the triple-laminated corners (plate 95 b), is the thin slips of exotic hardwood—possibly ebony—sandwiched between the bottom edges of the pine aprons and the mahogany strips, and designed to project through to the front and overhang the die-stamped brass borders. There are no such projecting slips of hardwood at the bottom of the fancy borders—an intentional deletion that gives the borders a crisp, precise look (plates 82, 87). Lannuier sometimes varied this technique, cutting rabbets in the outside lower edges of the aprons of his card tables and pier tables into which he would glue overhanging slips of the exotic hardwood at the top and the decorative brass bands backed with a secondary wood (plate 101). This exacting method seems to have been Lannuier's alone, for, while other cabinetmakers favored setting the fancy bands into strips of exotic hardwood with equal-sized fillets on either side (fig. 94)—which protected the lower edges of the thin metal bands from catching on pant legs or dustcloths—it did not provide the bottom edges of the aprons with the same crispness and clarity.

Lannuier seems to have been one of the few New York furniture makers, who produced card tables by the thousands in the Federal period, concerned with disguising card-table hinges. On tables with the French-style brass-baguette moldings along the edges of the tops, he simply hid the hinges underneath, as he also did on his later figural tables with die-stamped borders set into their upper leaves. The Grecian ovolo moldings of the lower leaves required some fussier work, which entailed removing sections of wood near the top and

FIGURE 102. Charles-Honoré Lannuier. Card table. 1815–19 (cat. no. 68)

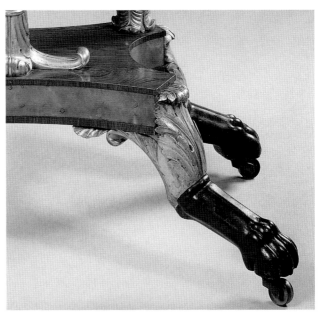

FIGURE 103. Detail of the front foot of the card table attributed to Lannuier, plate 43 (cat. no. 83)

then patching over the hinges with the utmost care so as to be barely perceptible. A few card tables have crossbanded square edges in which the hinges were left exposed (see plates 25, 35, and fig. 88).

A superb and possibly distinctive type of joint was discovered when, as part of a recent conservation treatment, a figural card table and a pier table by Lannuier were taken apart and the joints reglued. This kind of joint, which employs a tapered, dovetailed key to affix the distinctive bent, hock legs to the canted corners of the plinth (figs. 101, 103), is particularly well suited to this application, because it keeps the male part of the joint from pushing through the veneered plinth cap. In addition, it was always kept tight by the sheer weight of the table itself. Whether or not these tapered, dovetailed keys are unique to furniture from Lannuier's manufactory is unknown, but they certainly accord well with the superb planning, construction, and workmanship underlying all his figural furniture.

Carving, Gilding, and Bronzing

Among the most extraordinary—and ephemeral—aspects of Lannuier's furniture are the carved, gilded, and bronzed sculptural supports and animal-paw feet typical of French Consulat and Empire design. On furniture made before the War of 1812, Lannuier's use of these elements is more restrained than on his richly ornamented productions of the teens, which were made to satisfy the tastes of a wealthy American elite enthralled by the opulence and luxury of the French Imperial style. In the plates published by La Mésangère we see this pattern as well. Early designs from 1802 show a balanced mix of gilded and bronzed ornamental details on mahogany, and carved sculptural supports that are either solely bronzed or are bronzed with gilt highlights (see plates 5, 48, and plate 97). Increasingly after 1806, however, fully gilded antique monopodes (see plate 47) and gilded cast-brass ornaments predominate. Lannuier, in keeping with this stylistic evolution in general, nonetheless seems to have experienced a style lag of as much as half-a-dozen years or more in the introduction of gilded figural supports into his work. It is possible that this can be ascribed to a period of quiescence at the Lannuier manufactory before the arrival of Frichot and Gruez—cabinetmakers who probably had considerably more experience with the luxurious, gilded French Empire style.

Lannuier's use of typical New York water-leaf carving on ogee baluster turnings and on pillar-and-claw table legs has already been discussed in Chapter Two. The carving on the balusters is naturalistically rendered and robust, and sometimes there is a tendency for the carving at the top to fold over backward in exaggerated fashion, like the everted lip of a vase (plate 68). The water-leaf carving on table legs also tends to be full-bodied and deeply cut, but it would be hard to characterize it (or the water-leaves on the balusters for that matter) as so distinctly different from all other New York work that it alone could be relied upon as the basis for a Lannuier attribution.[51]

The heavy lion's-paw feet on Lannuier's square pier tables, case furniture, and French bedsteads show considerable variation in their design and carving, which probably should be expected, since they occur on works made throughout his career in New York and almost certainly were executed by several different carvers. The feet on an early French bureau (see plate 9) are unique among those on Lannuier's known work and in character and stance are closely related to the feet on a commode that appeared in La Mésangère's publication in 1802 (plate 97). This relationship serves as a reminder that Lannuier was one of the first, if not the first cabinetmaker in America, whose furniture incorporated bronzed lion's-paw feet of this type. It was not until five years after Lannuier's arrival in New York, in 1808, that George Smith published *A Collection of Designs for Household Furniture and Interior Decoration*, a pattern book whose color engravings served to popularize anglicized versions of bronzed

PLATE 97.   Pierre de La Mésangère. Design for a *commode antique* (Plate 49 from *Collection de Meubles et Objets de Goût*). 1802. Colored engraving, 7³⁄₄ x 12¹⁄₄ in. The Metropolitan Museum of Art, New York. Harris Brisbane Dick Fund, 1930

lion's-paw feet, modeled after French prototypes. Thus, for a brief period in the early 1800s, Lannuier's competitors in the use of this stylish new motif probably were limited to other immigrant French cabinetmakers working in New York City.

The majority of Lannuier's seven square pier tables with terms or columns that bear his second printed trade label have plinths with square front corners, and sit flat on the floor (see plate 28, and plate 79), as do many French examples from the late 1790s and early 1800s. One has gilded bun feet (plate 84) while two others, probably the latest examples in this group, are raised up on heavy lion's paws (cat. nos. 97, 98). Heavy paw feet are found more often on Lannuier's later square pier tables, all of which have plinths with rounded rather than square front corners—apparently a later feature (see plates 24, 42). A distinctive detail but not necessarily one exclusive to Lannuier is the claws, or nails, carved into the sides of the outside toes of these feet, instead of into the fronts. This same predilection for placing the claws on the side is seen on all Lannuier card tables with heavier outstretched lion's paws (figs. 89, 102). Feet like these appear on seven figural card tables, all of which have canted corners and partially bronzed winged caryatids (cat. nos. 66–69, 80–82), and on a single example with water-leaf-carved ogee balusters as well as canted corners (fig. 88). Comparison of these lion's-paw feet with the ones on the card table made by Duncan Phyfe for James Brinckerhoff in 1816 (see fig. 71) shows Lannuier's version to be slightly more outstretched, with a more prominent knob, or hock, at the back. In Phyfe's interpretation of the foot, claws are carved into the front of the outside toes instead of at the sides and pronounced channels or grooves are visible. Seldom are these heavy, outstretched lion's-paw feet as

FIGURE 104. Duncan Phyfe. Card table. Label dated August 1820. Mahogany veneer. Private collection

FIGURE 105. Detail of the front foot of the Duncan Phyfe card table, figure 104

successful as on a pair of card tables Lannuier made for George Harrison of Philadelphia (plate 74) on which he lightened and enlivened them by adding acanthus returns that scroll inward under the plinth to lend an airy openness to the composition.

Even feet as successful as these seem heavy and languid when compared with the second model foot Lannuier employed on pier tables and card tables with canted corners. This type of foot (fig. 103) bends naturally at the hock and envelops the corner of the plinth in lush naturalistic acanthus carving similar to the kind of elaborate, leafy decoration seen in the published designs of Percier and Fontaine. Carved either in ash with small laminations of mahogany on the toes or in solid mahogany, most of these feet originally were oil gilded and bronzed, although on a few tables they were only varnished. (The heavy outstretched lion's paws are generally ash with pine laminations on the toes.) Other makers, in imitation of Lannuier, developed a similar foot (see plate 45, and fig. 51), but none of these comes off as well. A Duncan Phyfe card table (figs. 104, 105) bearing his label, dated August 1820, provides another opportunity to compare the feet on documented examples by these two masters.[52]

In addition to lion's-paw feet, Lannuier used dolphin feet on his richly ornamented furniture of the 1810s. These playful-looking dolphins, with their wonderfully rounded, bulbous heads (fig. 106), are like those on French Empire furniture, and may be seen on three pier tables, one center table, and a pair of card tables, as well as on the magnificent Van Rensselaer bedstead. On the card tables (cat. nos. 76, 77), the dolphin feet are slightly overpowering in relation to the tables' otherwise compact designs. (They also look like they want to swim off in four different directions.) There is something slightly awkward about the dolphins on two of the pier tables, as well, where they seem to be lunging forward, away from the plinth (figs. 92, 97).[53] The dolphins on another pier table (now in the Brooklyn Museum of Art; fig. 91) and on the Van Rensselaer bedstead (see plate 54), however, are integrated much more successfully into the overall design of the piece. The large, curving fins of the

FIGURE 106. Detail of the front foot of the Lannuier pier table, figure 97 (cat. no. 112)

PLATE 98. Gilded swan. Detail of the Lannuier pier table, plate 52 (cat. no. 113)

dolphins endow them with added vigor, and lend visual support at the corners of the plinth. Among Lannuier's various dolphins, those on the bedstead (plate 81) reveal the highest level of artistic expression: the openings created where the tails fold over accentuate the sculptural quality of the forms, and the way in which the fins are rendered as acanthus leaves and stylized partial anthemions is both fantastic and brilliant. Dolphin feet appear on the work of some of Lannuier's contemporaries, but on these examples they tend to be much smaller in scale and far less sophisticated.[54]

The most dynamic and complicated carving on Lannuier's furniture is found on the three-dimensional sculptural figures that grace the richly ornamented tables produced at his manufactory during roughly the last half-dozen years of his life. Lannuier seems to have specialized in French-style winged caryatids, inspired by ancient Greek and Egyptian design sources (plates 82, 87), as well as in swans, which he used occasionally as supports on his pier tables (plate 98). The full-bodied griffins and the eagles with scrolled tails that were employed as table supports by some of his competitors (see figs. 52, 53), and which were shown in a plate at the back of the 1817 price book (see fig. 50), apparently held little interest for Lannuier, as no surviving tables with these motifs can be ascribed to his hand. Future discoveries, however, may prove this statement incorrect.

Winged caryatids appear on a total of twenty-eight surviving tables from the Lannuier shop, as well as on a rare suite of seating furniture, where they are used as arm supports. Noticeable differences exist among the figures, but these are difficult to explain without shop records to document who was involved in their production or when certain models were introduced or phased out. In eighteenth-century France, the carving and gilding of sculptural figures involved the collaboration of several different crafts, and this was very likely the case at Lannuier's manufactory as well, which probably included a special workroom in which this sensitive work was carried out.

Carving and gilding in the French manner involved three distinct phases of production.

a.

b.

c.

First, a foot or figure would be roughly shaped by a *menuisier* (joiner); then, it would be sent to a *sculpteur* (carver), who executed the fine carving of the wood; and finally, it was passed along to a *peintre-doreur* (painter-gilder), who applied the gesso and did the recutting, to accentuate the details the carver had already outlined in the wood. These three steps can be discerned consistently in Lannuier's work, and it seems fairly certain that the craftsmen he employed to create the caryatid figures were accomplished in this eighteenth-century French technique of carving and gilding. That at least the first step of this process was standard practice in New York can be inferred from the following proviso in the preface to the 1817 price book: "When paw feet, eagle heads, & c. for carving, are filed up, [they are] to be paid for according to time," as well as from a chart at the back of the book, which listed the charges for making table supports like those shown in plate No. 5 (see fig. 50) and included the statement that "Standards marked B and D [are] to be made of pine, and not filed up."[55]

There seems to be more consistency among the figures on Lannuier's pier tables and one known center table (fig. 107 a–f) than on the card tables. All have double reeds at the bases of their serpentine bodies; turbaned heads, with pleasant, round faces; and, in all but one example, six-pointed stars on the bands that come up high under the wings like the raised waist of a French Empire gown. The feathers of the inner parts of the wings are nearly flat, with perfectly rounded ends, and change direction part way up each wing. (This directional change is evident in the distinct V shape in the outermost row of feathers.) While it has not been possible to determine the type of wood used in every one of these figures due to their overall surface coatings, mahogany was identified as the carver's wood of choice in several examples (fig. 107 a, d, e).[56] (As mahogany was extremely expensive in France in the early nineteenth century, its use there would have been uncommon, and it would have been polished and waxed to show it off to best advantage. However, as it is an excellent carving wood, economics made it an appropriate choice in New York.) The pier-table figures are superbly carved, with delicate, cupped sculpturesque wings that curve upward to the aprons in

d.   e.   f.

a very life-like way, and were given only a light coating of gesso and subjected to a modest amount of recutting. This same style of carving and gilding also characterizes the figures on the suite of Lannuier seating furniture (see plates 59, 60).

The winged caryatids on the card tables are a far more diverse group, and comprise three distinct varieties. The first type, which appears on a total of five examples (cat. nos. 78–82), relates to the preceding figures in the presence of the six-pointed stars on the bands partway up their bodies, the tight upward curve of the lotus leaves at the bases, and the rounded ends of the inner-wing feathers, but the overall effect is clearly different. Figures of this type occur on a pair of card tables (fig. 108) that originally was purchased along with the suite of seating furniture, which raises questions about whether Lannuier's carver and gilder were versatile enough to work in two different styles at once, or whether he employed multiple carvers and gilders. The second figure type, which is found on only one pair of tables (plates 87, 100), is more believably the work of the carver and gilder responsible for the figures on the pier tables, center tables, and seating furniture. Similarities include the wood (mahogany), the double reeds at the base of each figure's body, the use of six-pointed stars, a directional change in the inner-wing feathers, and a light recutting of the gesso. These figures are exceptional for their look of serene classical beauty and graceful repose. The third type of caryatid (see plate 26, and plate 82) is the most common, and may be seen on twelve card tables (cat. nos. 66–77). It is bold and forthright in design, compared to the second type, which can be appreciated for its delicacy and finesse, and is meant to attract attention from across a room. The figures' shoulders are at right angles to their necks, and the wings spread wide and terminate in gilded and burnished volutes instead of being clipped off where they engage the upper frame. The inner-wing feathers are stylized to produce a strong Egyptianizing effect clearly meant to refer to the winged orb of ancient Egypt, the symbol of the rising sun. One of the figures was microanalyzed and discovered to be made of basswood, a cheap, light wood that was easy to carve. The gesso layers of these figures

FIGURE 108. Charles-Honoré Lannuier. Card table. 1815–19 (cat. no. 78)

underwent the most extensive recutting, which may indicate the presence of an expert Parisian recutter at the Lannuier manufactory in 1817—the precise date of manufacture of four of the card tables (cat. nos. 70–73) that have figures of this type.

The original gilding techniques used on several of these winged caryatid figures were carefully studied during recent conservation projects undertaken at The Metropolitan Museum of Art in preparation for this publication and the accompanying exhibition of Lannuier's work. One of the figures (plate 82), an example of "type three," from a card table, revealed that a combination of water gilding and oil gilding was applied to the wings in order to achieve the subtle effect of mat, softly burnished, and brightly burnished gold. Under the gold leaf, a reddish-brown bole the color of dried blood was used, but only in the areas that were meant to be brightly burnished: the top shoulder feathers, the volutes on the wing tips and the fillets that extend back from these to the inner-wing feathers, the fillets and the stars of the mid-band and the inverted V above it, the smooth lower body, the fillets and rosettes in the lower band, and the lotus leaves at the bottom. The rest of the oil and water gilding was done directly on the gesso. The "type two" card-table figures (plate 87) were completely water gilded and were coated with the same reddish-brown bole, but it had been used throughout. Burnishing was brightest on the uppermost shoulder feathers, on all the fillets, and on the stars, reeds, and lotus leaves. The color of the gold varies noticeably between the "type two" and "type three" figures: The former have a warm red tone and the latter more of a greenish cast. One of the more remarkable discoveries was the survival of the original water gilding on the twisted back columns of the tables with the "type two" figures (plates 99, 100). Their hard, bright appearance had been achieved through the use of a charcoal-black bole, which gives them a much cooler aspect than that of the winged caryatids, and was meant to resemble gilded-metal architectural balusters. The ornaments below the balusters are oil gilded, as are those on the back of the card table with the "type three" figure (see plate 26). Oil gilding was Lannuier's favored technique for the acanthus leaves on the lion's-paw feet, and probably was chosen as much for its acknowledged durability as for aesthetic reasons. The gilding employed on one of the pier tables (see plate 46)

PLATE 99. Attributed to Charles-Honoré Lannuier. Card table, with
original green wool cloth on the playing surface. 1815–19 (cat. no. 84)

PLATE 100. Gilded figure and back columns. Detail of the card table attributed to Lannuier, plate 99 (cat. no. 84)

also was studied and was found to be practically identical in technique to that used on the "type two" card-table figures. The same reddish-brown bole was discovered under several restoration layers, including the later bronzing of the smooth parts of the figures' bodies.[57]

Bronzing, or the *faux*-painting technique that makes wood or gesso look like excavated antique bronze, went hand in glove with gilding in the creation of furniture in the French antique taste. As it seems to have been a French invention of the late 1790s, Lannuier undoubtedly had to be among the first in America to employ the technique. Robert Mussey, in a soon to be published paper on the subject of the bronzing of American furniture, translates the following passage from an 1837 guidebook for French craftsmen on the chemical patination of cuprous metals and the *faux*-bronze painting of metal, plaster, and wood: "Bronzing, which forms today one of the bronze manufacturing branches, has only existed as a speciality for 40 years, and was not as widespread then as it is today. . . . Up until 1825 only one tint of bronzing was known, which was *vert antique* or *vert à l'eau* [sea green], which . . . sought to imitate bronze as closely as possible which was exposed to corrosion of the weather."[58] Sea green is the color used consistently on furniture depicted in La Mésangère's *Collection de Meubles* (see plate 5, and plate 97), and it was perhaps the original color that Lannuier intended for such early pieces as the Egyptian-term pier table (see plate 30). Unfortunately, *faux*-bronze painted surfaces deteriorate badly over time, and, today, very few survive in good condition or resemble their appearance when they left the shop. Most of this degradation stems from "inherent vice," or the unstable nature of the paints, varnishes, and metals used to create this effect.[59] The uppermost semi-transparent glazing and varnish layers—in which, initially, a smattering of bronze particles was sometimes embedded for a worn gilded effect—darkened over time to look almost black. Many restorers have assumed that these dark upper layers were the painter's original intent, so they applied additional black paints and tinted varnishes that give the feet an ebonized rather than a *faux*-bronze appearance. The dolphin feet on the Van Rensselaer bedstead (plate 81) present just one example of this type of deteriorated blackened surface—an irony, given the bedstead's lavish beauty and the sophistication of the feet themselves, which suggests that their original bronzed surfaces must have been extraordinary. Lannuier seems to have been experimenting with a *faux*-bronze finish with golden brown highlights on some of the card tables with winged caryatids, so we cannot be sure that these dolphin feet, which are now nearly black, were intended originally to have the sea-green hue.

Determining actual original colors and tonal effects can be extremely difficult. On a surprising number of card tables, the rear columns with fluted shafts, modeled after antique bronze candelabra, survive with what appears to be their original and rather flat green surface layers (see plate 26). A similar shade of green also seems to have been used as the original base color on some of the lion's-paw feet, although these initially had more complicated layerings of glazes and bronze powders than the back columns, which were either left unvarnished or given only a light, dulling coat. Analyses of both the surface layers and the pigments used on the feet of Lannuier's furniture were conducted in the departments of Objects Conservation and Paintings Conservation at the Metropolitan Museum in order to uncover more evidence on the materials and techniques Lannuier's painters used to achieve these *faux*-bronze effects. The surface layers (exclusive of obvious later restorations) on the carved mahogany feet of a pair of card tables (cat. nos. 83, 84) were shown to be identical to those on the center-table dolphins (cat. no. 115), and included, working outward from the wood: (1) a gesso layer; (2) a thick, coarsely pigmented blue-green paint layer; (3) a thin, pigmented glaze; and (4) one or two layers of varnish, with those on the card table containing metal particles. The feet on a pair of pier tables (cat. nos. 104, 105) revealed the same layering system, but in the second layer the pigments were finer, and two coats of paint seem to have been applied. The feet of another card table (cat. no. 72), which were carved of ash as opposed to mahogany, had the following layers: (1) gesso; (2) a dense, pigmented layer more blue or black than the ones described above; (3) a green-pigmented glaze or natural-resin varnish; and (4) an oil-base polish or finish. The surface of one of the heavy, ash, outstretched lion's paws from a card table (cat. no. 81) was also sampled and found to have the following layers: (1) gesso; (2) a very blue, finely pigmented layer; (3) a transparent greenish glaze; and (4) a natural-resin varnish. The pigments used to produce the blue-green base color over the gesso on the five sampled feet vary, but Prussian blue was found consistently mixed either with chrome yellow (cat. nos. 81, 104) or earth pigments, possibly Indian yellow (cat. no. 115) or yellow ocher and sienna (cat. no. 72). In addition, two of the samples (cat. nos. 72, 81) revealed an interlayer of gesso that had been tinted gray—perhaps with carbon

black—beneath the blue-green base color. In one instance (cat. no. 84), over the blue-green base color, composed of Prussian blue and an unidentified earth pigment, there appears to be a thin layer of glaze, which contains an earth pigment—possibly terre verte—and a copper pigment such as malachite. A small amount of lead was also discovered in this layer—probably white lead. A thin layer over this one (perhaps a later restoration coating) contains chrome yellow and Prussian blue, as well as some barium sulfate—a paint filler or extender common in the nineteenth century. (Barium sulfate was not detected in any of the four other samples.) Later restorations, and the degradation of the substances used in the upper layers of glaze, make it extremely difficult to determine the original appearance of the materials employed to create the *faux*-bronze surfaces of many of the surviving examples of Lannuier's furniture.[60]

This litany of layers and pigments is so far from complete in relation to all the known Lannuier *faux*-bronzed furniture, and subject to such a broad range of interpretations, that it would be inappropriate to draw too many conclusions about a distinctive Lannuier bronzing style or styles based on these alone. The analyses are useful, however, in that a pattern emerges, from the samples tested, of similar surface layering on the mahogany feet of the center table, card tables, and pier tables, which also have related carved-and-gilded winged caryatids of the same wood. Also, it is interesting that the ash feet of the table that has the carved basswood figure with the bold, broad wingspan and extensive recutting in the gesso, which varies so greatly in technique and artistic intent from the carved mahogany figures, should display different surface layers as well.

In many instances, collectors and connoisseurs would be more than satisfied if, with complete confidence, they could assign a date range of sixteen years to a given piece of furniture. Any examples by Lannuier, who worked in New York from the spring of 1803 until his death in October 1819, can be dated broadly in this fashion, but there is still an understandable human urge to order his work chronologically. Throughout this book some assumptions have been made regarding the ordering of the furniture. The first and most important supposition was that the labels Lannuier used were applied consecutively, and the second one was that his work evolved stylistically over the course of his career. Only Lannuier's specimen marble table, initialed and dated the day after Christmas in 1804 (see plate 16), and the suites of furniture he made for the Van Rensselaers and the Campbells in 1817 (see plates 51, 52, 53, and plates 69, 70), can be dated with precision. Thus, the dates assigned to the objects in the catalogue section are at best educated guesses.

Attributions, when all is said and done, are also guesses. They have not been dispensed lightly, and every effort has been made to base them on the stamped and labeled work. More attention was paid to small details and habits of workmanship than to broad construction methods, such as the way a carcass was framed, or a drawer was constructed. Molding profiles, in some instances, have proven to be reliable indicators of work from the Lannuier manufactory. Always, before an attribution was made, more than one reliable index had to be provided by a work. For instance, on a large framed looking glass (see plate 64) at Clermont, the Livingston family homestead near Germantown, New York, we find the distinctive French cyma-recta molding profile in the cornice, the bellflower-patterned die-stamped brass-and-wood border in the plinth below the pilasters that has a fillet of hardwood just at the top, and the Apollo ornament in the frieze, which so far only is found on Lannuier's work. A second example is a pier table with burl-elm veneers and painted tôle columns (see plate 21), attributed to Lannuier, that displays the identical Greek-key pattern and die-stamped borders as on the labeled Van Rensselaer bedstead, in addition to the distinctive cyma-recta molding below the marble top, and also reveals that the same method was used to set the die-stamped border into the apron (plate 101) as on the labeled pier tables. The attribution to Lannuier of a card table long in the possession of the Brooklyn Museum of Art (plate 80) was made on the basis of five important characteristics: the way in which the bottom boards are fitted into the aprons in an identical fashion to that employed on the labeled examples with winged caryatids; the book-matched veneers, which mate perfectly at the canted corners; the bellflower-patterned die-stamped borders, which reverse direction at the center of the apron, as on other, labeled tables; the cavetto molding under the top, as well as the brass baguette moldings on its edges; and the saber legs, which have the same crotch-mahogany panels on their top surfaces and the blunt-nosed casters as do the legs of a labeled card table (see plate 35, and fig. 96). However, the major challenges in establishing attributions to Lannuier lie ahead. There are several French forms that one would have expected him to have made, but which, to date, have not surfaced, such as square and cylindrical pedestal nightstands, or *tables de nuit*; fall-front secretaries, or *secrétaires à abattant*; and seating furniture, for instance, of which there is an incredible dearth: Not a single sofa has been discovered as yet that confidently can be ascribed to his hand. Nevertheless, it is hoped that some of the peculiarities of Lannuier's working methods, which have been highlighted in these pages, will be of assistance to future scholars and connoisseurs interested in the work of this brilliant Franco-American master, and in the wonderfully complex and engrossing subject of New York classical furniture of the Late Federal period.

Peter M. Kenny

1

See Montgomery, 1966, p. 48.

2

Letter from Sarah Elliot Huger to Harriott Pinckney Horry, October 21, 1815. Mrs. Julien Ravenel Family Papers, South Carolina Historical Society, Columbia. As cited in McInnis and Leath, 1996, p. 147.

3

Numerous examples of trade labels used by Parisian *ébénistes* are illustrated in Ledoux-Lebard, 1951.

4

See Ormsbee, 1933 b, pp. 224–26.

5

See the account book of John Hewitt, for April 4 and May 7, 1812. New Jersey Historical Society, Newark. Photocopy in the Scholarship Files, Department of American Decorative Arts, The Metropolitan Museum of Art. On these dates Hewitt records in his account book that he sent a total of twenty-two mahogany logs, including crotches, to Mr. Dean's mill in Springfield—presumably, New Jersey—with custom orders for sawing the wood into boards, joists, planks, bedposts (four inches square), and "Top Stuff" (³/₈ inch for use on sideboards).

6

See the *New-York Courier* of March 15, 1816.

7

See the *New-York Evening Post* of October 17, 1818.

8

See the *Mercantile Advertiser* of July 31, 1811.

9

See the *Mercantile Advertiser* of January 14, 1812.

10

See the *New-York Evening Post* of July 15, 1803, as quoted in Gottesman, 1965, p. 148.

11

See Sikes, 1976, p. 147.

12

I would like to thank Michael Podmaniczky and John Courtney at the Winterthur Museum, Delaware, for pursuing the testing of the brass molding there and providing information on the results. Mark Wypyski, of the Department of Objects Conservation, The Metropolitan Museum of Art, conducted all testing on metal and paint samples for this project, for which he deserves special thanks.

13

See Hope, 1971, pp. 66–67.

14

For information about Pierre-Aurore Frichot see Ledoux-Lebard, 1984, p. 211. I would like to thank Ulrich

Leben for this reference. See also Chapter One, note 63.

15

See M. Levy, 1989, p. 153.

16

See Barron, 1814. I would like to thank Wendy A. Cooper, curator at the Winterthur Museum, Delaware, for providing photocopies of plates from Barron's publication that are relevant to the die-stamped brass inlays on Lannuier furniture.

17

The Greek-wave patterned border may be seen in a trade catalogue at the Victoria and Albert Museum, London (acc. no. M6oD). I would like to thank Jillian Ehninger for bringing this to my attention in the course of searching for die-stamped brass inlays among the Victoria and Albert Museum's collection of trade catalogues. I would also like to thank Mary Ann Apicella for conducting similar research at the Victoria and Albert, the Birmingham Public Library, and the Public Record Office, London, for patents related to machinery for producing die-stamped brass inlays. For information about the Birmingham brass founders, as well as a discussion of the above-mentioned trade catalogue (acc. no. M6oD) see Goodison, 1975, pp. 8, 20–21. For related English examples see Joy, 1977, pp. 58, 76. For another figural card table in the style of Lannuier, with die-stamped brass bands in a lozenge pattern, see McInnis and Leath, 1996, p. 150.

18

See Sheraton, 1970, vol. 1, p. 117.

19

See the *New-York Gazette & General Advertiser* of December 7, 1815.

20

See the *New-York Courier* of June 3, 1816.

21

See Montgomery, 1966, pp. 475, 479.

22

See Ehninger, 1993, p. 60.

23

See Fennimore, 1996, p. 36.

24

See Goodison, 1975, p. 8.

25

I am grateful to Donald L. Fennimore for his continued help and his interest in my ongoing research into the ornamental metalwork on Lannuier furniture.

26

See Goodison, 1975, p. 18, ill. 55.

27

See Ehninger, 1993, pp. 75–78.

28

Once again, I would like to thank Mary Ann Apicella for searching the

Birmingham trade directories, and Robert Parker for checking the Paris trade almanacs.

29

See Goodison, 1974, p. 23, as cited in Ehninger, 1993, pp. 56–58.

30

Maria Bayard Campbell of New York described the Birmingham brass foundry that she toured in 1814 as follows: "Casting of Brass in furniture ornaments . . . is done by a heavy machine . . . [which] makes the stamp. . . . They then give it colour by first dipping it in a preperration [*sic*], then in aquafortus [*sic*] & the change is instantaneous, some are made by pourring [*sic*] the Liquid Brass in moulds afterwards they are polished with an agate." Maria Bayard, "Diary," 1814–15, n.p. Bayard-Campbell-Pearsall Papers, Manuscripts & Archives Section, Rare Books and Manuscripts Division, The New York Public Library.

31

In the interest of future scholarship, and in order to gain more quantifiable evidence regarding the materials that comprised the ornaments used by Lannuier and that appear in the Birmingham trade catalogues, three ornaments—the Apollo (cat. no. 100), the lyre and winged female figures (cat. no. 67), and the paired cornucopia flanking a wreath (cat. no. 83)—were subjected to elemental analysis by Mark Wypyski in the conservation laboratories at the Metropolitan Museum. Analyses revealed that all three ornaments contained traces of mercury and gold, indications of the original mercury gilding.

32

See Beaujour, 1814, pp. 196–97.

33

See the *New-York Daily Advertiser* of September 30, 1818.

34

See the *New-York Gazette & General Advertiser* of May 2, 1812.

35

See the *New-York Evening Post* of September 29, 1817.

36

See Sheraton, 1970, p. 235.

37

See the *New-York Gazette & General Advertiser* of April 26, 1817.

38

See Hadsund, 1993. I would like to thank Steve Pine, conservator at the Museum of Fine Arts, Houston, and Wendy A. Cooper, curator at the Winterthur Museum, Delaware, for bringing this article to my attention.

39

See Fearon, 1818, p. 24. The table,

which is in The White House, is illustrated in Pearce, 1962 b, p. 95, fig. 2.

40
See the *New-York Daily Advertiser* of February 22, 1822.

41
See *The Daily Advertiser* of August 19 and 22, 1805.

42
See the *Republican Watch Tower* of March 1, 1808.

43
See the *New-York Gazette & General Advertiser* of July 3, 1816. The partnership of Norris and Kain similarly offered in this same newspaper on June 15, 1812, "Pier and Sideboard tops of pure statuary white." In this same ad they claimed to make "the most fashionable MARBLE CHIMNEY PIECES that have been executed in this city. . . . Two complete specimens of the latter may be seen in the Council Chamber of the New City Hall."

44
See the *Mercantile Advertiser* of May 2, 1820.

45
See *The Public Advertiser* of December 29, 1807.

46
I would like to thank Thomas Gordon Smith for bringing this French press (cat. no. 51) to my attention.

47
See *The New-York Book of Prices*, 1817, pp. 38–39.

48
See the pre-1815 *Additional Revised Prices*, n.d., p. 4, See Chapter Two, note 93.

49
Ibid.

50
I would like to thank Mark Minor, as well as Marinus Manuels and Mechthild Baumeister of the Department of Objects Conservation at The Metropolitan Museum of Art, for helping to determine this construction technique through X-rays.

51
Edward V. Jones, in E. Jones, 1977, p. 10, was the first to describe this style of carving, seen on documented Lannuier furniture as, "softer and more fluid."

52
I would like to thank Robert Leath for bringing this table to my attention, as well as its owners, for allowing it to be photographed.

53
The dolphin feet on both of these

pier tables have circular hollows under the extra pieces added below the jaws, which, possibly, were intended originally to house casters. The feet, therefore, initially may have been made for a furniture form other than a pier table that was designed to be moved.

54
A card table with griffins and with these small dolphin feet, which has a Livingston family provenance, is in the Mills Mansion in Staatsburg, N.Y.

55
Information on French eighteenth-century carving and gilding techniques comes from Considine, 1991, p. 87. See *The New-York Book of Prices*, 1817, pp. 6, 46. I would like to thank Giovanni Bucchi for pointing out the sophisticated French-style recutting of the gesso of Lannuier's gilded figures.

56
Conservator Mark Minor identified by eye the wood of figure 107 a and d, and that of 107 e by means of microanalysis. I would like to thank John Driggers of Robert Mussey Associates for information on the woods in figure 107 e.

57
Mark Minor, independent conservator, and Pascale Patris of the Department of Objects Conservation at The Metropolitan Museum of Art, carried out the conservation of the gilded figures on this pier table in May and June 1996. The treatment report on the table by Mark Minor states: "The body sections of both caryatids had been stripped of their gold at some unknown date, and were long considered to possess an original scheme of *bronzine* underneath an uncharacteristic recent synthetic gloss-black paint layer. Subsequent investigations found remnants of two separate gold layers (an original, and apparently a restoration layer) underneath the older verdigris layer. The presence of a second layer strongly suggests an exposure history of the earliest layer, and not the possibility of a shop or design change on the part of the maker from a gilded to a bronze appearance." I would like to thank Peter Terian, the owner of the table, and Mark Minor for sharing this treatment report with me.

58
See Debonliez and Malepeyre, 1837, as cited in Mussey, forthcoming. I would like to thank Robert Mussey for sending me a draft copy of his article, which originally was presented at the "Painted Wood: History and Conservation" symposium held in Williamsburg, Va., November 11–14, 1994.

59
See Mussey, forthcoming.

60
The surface-layer analyses are contained in reports by Mark Minor and Marinus Manuels submitted to Peter M. Kenny and retained in the Lannuier exhibition research files in the Department of American Decorative Arts at The Metropolitan Museum of Art. Pigment identifications were made by Christopher McGlinchey of the Department of Paintings Conservation, and Mark Wypyski of the Department of Objects Conservation, at The Metropolitan Museum of Art. The samples first were analyzed by McGlinchey, using polarized light microscopy (PLM) and X-ray defraction (XRD), and then by Wypyski, using energy-dispersive X-ray spectrometry (EDS). The results of the analyses are also in the Lannuier exhibition research files in the Department of American Decorative Arts.

CATALOGUE

1 *(see plate 49)*

French Bedstead with Crown 1812–19

Engraved No. 3 label inside the front rail, proper left

Mahogany veneer, gilded brass, gilded composition, gilded gesso and *vert antique;* secondary woods: mahogany, yellow poplar, white pine; iron

125³/₈ x 80¹/₄ x 67¹/₂ in. (318.5 x 203.8 x 171.5 cm)

Bartow-Pell Mansion Museum, Bronx, New York. Gift of Henry S. Peltz and Mrs. Mary Nevius, 1985 (85.06)

NOTES: The bedstead retains its original large French casters, but a second original set of smaller casters under the feet is missing. Gilded cast-brass eyes survive under the rails, indicating the original presence of a rod for a low fabric valance. There are unexplained empty mortises behind the gilded finials at the top of the front columns. The bedstead originally had a separate frame bottom (now missing) supported on loose, stub-like tenons inserted in the rails. The canopy is veneered on a white pine substrate of stacked or brick-like laminate construction. The back uprights that support the canopy arms are of solid mahogany with mahogany veneer. The bed hangings were fabricated by Nancy C. Britton in the Department of Objects Conservation at The Metropolitan Museum of Art in 1996–97, and were based upon the *lit ordinaire* shown in Plate 3 of Pierre de La Mésangère's *Collection de Meubles et Objets de Goût.*

PROVENANCE: By tradition, acquired by Isaac Bell (1768–1860) and Mary Ellis (1791–1871) at the time of their marriage in 1810; in their town house at 14 Greenwich Street, New York, 1818–60; their son, Edward Rogers Bell, and his first wife, Caroline Farnum (1830–1860); their daughter Edith Bell (1857–1946) (Mrs. Leonard Opdycke), who lived with her grandmother Mary Ellis Bell in New York at 41 West 21st Street, 1860–71, and later at 117 East 79th Street; her daughter Mary Ellis Opdycke (Mrs. John De Witt Peltz), at 136 East 79th Street; placed on loan to the Bartow-Pell Mansion Museum by Mrs. Peltz, 1949; her children, Henry S. Peltz and Mary Peltz Nevius, the donors.

REFERENCES: Downs, 1943 a, fig. 4; Downs, 1949, ill. p. 277; Ralston, 1950, fig. 4; Waxman, 1958, no. 3, pl. XI; Bartlett and Huber, 1979, pl. VII; Cooper, 1993, pp. 129–30, no. 90.

2

French Bedstead with (missing) Crown about 1810

Stamped four times, twice on the upper surface of each front and rear rail: H. LANNUIER/NEW-YORK

Mahogany veneer, gilded brass; secondary wood: mahogany; iron

43¹/₄ x 81¹/₈ x 60¹/₄ in. (109.9 x 206.1 x 153 cm)

Collection Richard and Gloria Manney

NOTES: Like catalogue number 1, this bedstead initially had taller back posts with arms to support a crown. The casters currently under the posts are replacements for the original ones, most likely of the same design. The ornament on the front rail appears to be original, but at some point it was broken, slightly reduced in length, and reattached. The rails now have wooden laths that support a mattress, but originally the bottom consisted of a wood frame, with attached sacking, as evidenced by the presence of stub tenons in the rails. The back rail of the bedstead is unornamented.

PROVENANCE: The dealers Richard and Eileen Dubrow, Bayside, New York; Berry Tracy Incorporated, Goshen, New York, about 1984.

3 *(see plate 40)*

French Bedstead 1805–15

Stamped four times, twice on the upper surface of each front and rear rail: H. LANNUIER/NEW-YORK

Mahogany, mahogany veneer, gilded gesso and *vert antique*, gilded brass; secondary wood: white pine; iron

52⁷/₈ x 89¹/₈ x 55⁷/₈ in. (134.3 x 226.4 x 141.9 cm)

Private collection

NOTES: This bed (or an identical one) appears in a photograph from the 1910s inscribed "Interior chamber showing Napoleon bed, Indian Hill House, Newburyport, Mass." (Scholarship Files, Department of American Decorative Arts, The Metropolitan Museum of Art). The bottom of the bedstead originally was of sacking, suspended by cords from turned pegs in the rails; the pegs are now cut flush with the rails. The bedstead is finished on all four sides.

PROVENANCE: Edward V. Jones, Albany, Georgia; placed on loan to The Metropolitan Museum of Art by Mrs. Jones, 1971–88, and by her daughter Jeanette Jones Balling, 1988; Hirschl & Adler Galleries, Inc., New York, 1990.

REFERENCES: E. Jones, 1977, fig. 22 (detail of post), fig. 23 (stamp); Sotheby's, New York, 5968 (January 24–27, 1990), lot 1087; Feld and Garrett, 1991, no. 1.

2

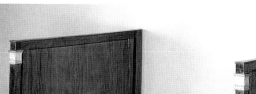

4 (*see plate 14*)

French Bedstead 1805–8

Two printed No. 2 labels, one inside the headrail and one inside the footrail

Stamped four times, once on each corner block, inside the frame: H. LANNUIER/NEW-YORK; J. B. COCHOIS

Mahogany veneer, gilded brass, gilded gesso, die-stamped brass inlays, steel; secondary woods: yellow poplar, ash

42¼ x 92½ x 58 in. (107.3 x 235 x 147.3 cm)

Collection Richard and Gloria Manney

NOTES: The eagles' heads and lion's-paw feet have been regilded. Microscopic analysis of the surface layers of the eagles' heads and lion's-paw feet revealed no traces of earlier original gilded or *vert-antique* layers under the restoration gilding. The bedstead retains its original large French casters, but initially it also had smaller casters (now missing) under the lion's-paw feet. An unusual construction feature is the rails, which are not connected by bed bolts and do not come apart. The back rail is unornamented. For a discussion of Cochois see Chapters One and Two.

PROVENANCE: By tradition, this bedstead is said to have belonged to Alfred Seton (1793–1859), who married Frances Barnewall in 1819 (his journal, *Astorian Adventure: The Journal of Alfred Seton 1811–1815* [Robert F. Jones, ed., Fordham University Press, New York, 1993], records the five years he spent on a Columbia River trading expedition with John Jacob Astor's Pacific Fur Company, and was a source for Washington Irving's *Astoria, or, Anecdotes of an Enterprise Beyond the Rocky Mountains* [1836]); Mrs. George Sommaripa, New York, until 1978; Trump & Co., Flourtown, Pennsylvania, 1978–84.

REFERENCES: Sotheby Parke Bernet Inc., New York, 4180 (November 16–18, 1978), lot 1004; Fitzgerald, 1982, fig. VI-38; Sotheby's, New York, 5142 (January 26 and 28, 1984), lot 812.

5 (*see plate 54*)

French Bedstead 1817–19

Two engraved No. 3 labels, one inside the headrail and one inside the footrail

Mahogany [burl elm, by microanalysis] and rosewood veneers, gilded brass, die-stamped brass borders, gilded gesso and *vert antique;* secondary woods: [maple, white pine, ash, cherry, by microanalysis]; iron

45½ x 85½ x 60 in. (115.6 x 217.2 x 152.4 cm)

Albany Institute of History & Art, New York. Gift of Mrs. William Dexter (Constance Van Rensselaer Thayer), 1951 (1951.61)

NOTES: The dolphin feet, of ash, are fastened to the rails with iron bolts, which thread into a nut embedded inside. In an 1868 stereoscopic view of the interior of the Van Rensselaer Manor House, the bedstead is shown with lace curtains suspended above it, although no method of attachment to the ceiling is visible. It is pictured again, with curtains and crown, in 1885, in a drawing in *The American Architect and Building News.* See also Chapter Three: The Bayard-Van Rensselaer-Campbell Commissions.

PROVENANCE: The bed was made for Stephen Van Rensselaer IV (1789–1868) and Harriet Bayard (1799–1875), who married on January 2, 1817 (it originally stood in their Albany town house, of about 1817—attributed to the architect Philip Hooker—on North Market [now Broadway] and North Ferry Streets, until about 1840, when it was moved to the Van Rensselaer Manor House); their daughter Cornelia Paterson Van Rensselaer (1823–1897) (Mrs. Nathaniel Thayer); her son Bayard Thayer (b. 1862), who married Ruth Simpkins (b. 1864); their daughter Constance Van Rensselaer Thayer (b. 1900) (Mrs. William Dexter), great-granddaughter of Stephen Van Rensselaer IV.

REFERENCES: Stereoscopic interior view of the Van Rensselaer Manor House, Albany, 1868 (now in the Department of Photographs, The Metropolitan Museum of Art); *The American Architect and Building News*, November 7, 1885, ill. p. 219 (drawing); Bjerkoe, 1957, pp. 141–42, pl. XXXI; Waxman, 1958, no. 5, pl. XIII; Rice, 1962, pp. 12–13, ills. pp. 34, 35 (mounts), 36 (mount and label); Comstock, 1962, nos. 410 A, B (label); Pearce, 1964, fig. 3; Otto, 1965, no. 104; Tracy and Johnson, 1970, no. 39; Reese, 1983, ill. p. 138; Cooper, 1993, pp. 128–29, no. 89.

6 (*see figure 48*)

Bedstead 1803–12

Stamped: H. LANNUIER/NEW-YORK

Mahogany; secondary woods: unknown

Dimensions not available

Location unknown

NOTES: This bedstead may have had iron tester rods attached to the tops of the four posts that rose toward the center to support a crown or canopy smaller than the bedstead frame. A closely related bedstead with pineapple finials atop the four posts is illustrated in a gallery publication of Bernard & S. Dean Levy, Inc., 1984, p. 87. This bedstead—or catalogue number 7—is stamped twice, on the inside of the front rail: H. LANNUIER/NEW-YORK, as noted in Parke-Bernet, New York, 1946.

PROVENANCE: Ginsburg & Levy, Inc., New York, 1933; private collection, New Jersey, 1933–46 (or cat. no. 7).

REFERENCES: Ormsbee, 1933 b, fig. 4; Parke-Bernet Galleries Inc., New York, 723 (January 10–11, 1946), lot 151 (or cat. no. 7); Waxman, 1958, no. 2, pl. X.

7

Bedstead 1803–12

Stamped: H. LANNUIER/NEW-YORK

Mahogany; secondary woods: unknown

Dimensions not available

Location unknown

NOTES: This bedstead is virtually identical to catalogue number 6. Similarly, it, too, may be lacking an iron tester.

PROVENANCE: The dealer W. S. Holmes, Freehold, New Jersey, 1933; private collection, New Jersey, 1933–46 (or cat. no. 6).

REFERENCES: *Antiques*, July 1933, p. 31 (advertised by W. S. Holmes, The Christopher House, Freehold, New Jersey); Parke-Bernet Galleries Inc., New York, 723 (January 10–11, 1946), lot 151 (or cat. no. 6).

8

High-post Bedstead 1815–19

Stamped twice on the upper surface of one side rail: H. LANNUIER/NEW-YORK

Mahogany, mahogany veneer, gilded gesso and *vert antique;* secondary woods: none; iron

98 x 82³⁄₄ x 68 in. (248.9 x 210.2 x 172.7 cm)

Collection Richard and Gloria Manney

NOTE: The bedstead's side rails, which are paneled similarly on the front faces of all four sides, retain evidence of regularly spaced ornaments that are now missing, and may have looked like those on catalogue number 9.

PROVENANCE: The dealer Clifford Buisch, Union Springs, New York, 1978.

REFERENCES: *Antiques*, October 1978, p. 751 (advertised by Samuel T. Freeman & Co., Philadelphia); Samuel T. Freeman & Co., Philadelphia (October 30–31, November 1, 1978), lot 371.

9

High-post Bedstead 1815–19

Stamped twice on the upper surface of one side rail: H. LANNUIER/NEW-YORK

Mahogany, mahogany veneer, gilded gesso and *vert antique;* secondary woods: unknown; iron

100¹⁄₂ x 80¹⁄₂ x 65 in. (255.3 x 204.5 x 165.1 cm)

Location unknown

NOTE: This bedstead appears to be identical to catalogue number 8, but it retains its applied wood guilloche and gilded rosette ornaments on the rails.

REFERENCE: Sotheby's, New York, 4942 (October 23, 1982), lot 172.

8

9

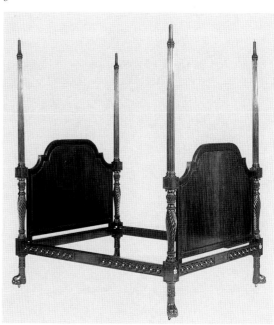

10

High-post Bedstead 1812–19

Attributed

Inscribed in black paint on the inside surface of one side rail: G R Hallam New York; in chalk: [illegible]

Mahogany, mahogany veneer, gilded brass, gilded gesso and *vert antique;* secondary woods: white pine, cherry; iron

98¹/₂ x 80³/₄ x 59¹/₂ in. (250.2 x 205.1 x 151.1 cm)

Winterthur Museum, Delaware. Gift of Henry Francis du Pont (55.789)

NOTES: The tester, which may be the work of an anonymous carver and gilder, and was purchased separately from the bedstead, appears to be original, and bears remnants of an old and possibly original orange-and-black wallpaper border around the perimeter of the surface facing the bed. The bedstead retains its large French casters. The bottom initially may have been of a separate frame type, which rested on the transverse iron bars that connect the French casters to the bedstead. There are no stub tenons inside the rails. The ornaments on the tester are of brass, probably originally lacquer gilded. The central ornament is like some seen on New York fancy chairs of the 1810s.

REFERENCES: Downs and Ralston, 1934, no. 152; Waxman, 1958, no. 1, pl. IX; Montgomery, 1966, no. 5.

11–33 (*see plate 62*)

Twenty-three Armchairs 1812

Mahogany, mahogany veneer, die-stamped brass inlays; secondary woods: cherry, white pine

17 chairs, each: 36³/₈ x 23³/₈ x 22¹/₂ in. (92.4 x 59.4 x 57.2 cm);

6 chairs, each: 36³/₈ x 25 x 23¹/₄ in. (92.4 x 63.5 x 59.1 cm)

[11–32] Collection City of New York, City Hall (twenty-two chairs)

[33] Hirschl & Adler Galleries, Inc., New York (1 chair)

NOTES: All twenty-three armchairs appear to be from the first period, which makes their dimensional differences difficult to explain. In addition, there are two armchairs at City Hall that seem to have been made somewhat later to fill out the set; these have nineteen-inch-wide crest rails like the group of six armchairs above. Another later copy was illustrated in the catalogue to the exhibition "Neo-Classicism in America: Inspiration and Innovation, 1810–1840," Hirschl & Adler Galleries, Inc., New York, 1991. The original heights are unknown, as the feet of all twenty-three armchairs were cut down over time. The feet of eight of the armchairs were replaced below the swelled and reeded legs during conservation by Olaf Unsoeld at The Metropolitan Museum of Art in spring 1997. The foot pattern was derived from similar New York seating furniture with swelled and reeded legs. The armchairs are depicted in an 1831 watercolor by Charles Burton of the Common Council Chamber. For the invoice for twenty-four armchairs for the Common Council Chamber see Appendix 2; see also Chapter Three: Public Commissions.

PROVENANCE: Made for the Common Council Chamber, City Hall, New York; moved to the Governor's Room, City Hall, 1847; [33] removed from City Hall, date unknown.

REFERENCES: *Minutes of the Common Council,* 1917, vol. 7, p. 199, July 13, 1812; Ormsbee, 1933 b, p. 225 (records invoice); Williamson, 1938, p. 252; Keyes, 1938, fig. 10; Craigmyle, 1970, figs. 1, 2; Betts, 1983, pp. iii, 8.

34–35 (*see plate 59*)

Pair of Armchairs 1815–19

Attributed

Inscribed in chalk on the inside of the back seat rail of chair (xx.1.1e): Mrs. B[osley]

Mahogany, mahogany veneer, gilded gesso, gilded brass, die-stamped brass borders; secondary wood: maple

35¹/₂ x 22 x 20¹/₂ in. (90.2 x 55.9 x 52.1 cm)

Maryland Historical Society, Baltimore. Bequest of J. B. Noel Wyatt (xx.1.1e, f)

NOTE: See Chapter Three: Southern Clients.

PROVENANCE: These armchairs were part of a suite of seating furniture and a pair of card tables (cat. nos. 36–41, 42–43, 78–79) owned by James Bosley (1779–1843), who married Elizabeth Noel (1797–1851) in 1822; among the furnishings of their Fayette Street, Baltimore, town house, which they moved into at the time of their marriage; Mrs. Bosley's sister, Margaret Noel Wyatt (1812–1897), who was married in the house in 1843; her son James Bosley Noel Wyatt (1847–1926), the Baltimore architect.

REFERENCES: Waxman, 1958, no. 6, pl. XIV; Pearce, 1960, fig. 5; Tracy, 1963, no. 5; Davidson, 1968, no. 131; Tracy and Johnson, 1970, no. 43; Bishop, 1972, no. 462; Somerville, 1976, plates I, III; Cooper, 1980 a, no. 288; Weidman, 1984, pl. XIV, no. 61; Cooper, 1993, no. 126.

10

36–41 *(see plate 36)*

Six Side Chairs 1815–19

Attributed

[36–39] Inscribed in chalk on the seat rails of four chairs: Mrs. Bosley

[41] Inscribed in chalk on the inside of the front seat rail: Mrs. Bosley

Printed label on the back seat rail of [38] and [41] C. F. MEISLAHN & CO./19 Clay St. BALTIMORE MD./FINE FURNITURE, MANTELS & ARTISTIC DECORATIONS; written in ink on the label of [38]: 7400 J.B.N.W./Repairing & refinishing/1 side chair; on the label of [41]: 7686, JBNW/1 chair

Mahogany, mahogany veneer, gilded gesso, gilded brass, die-stamped brass borders; secondary wood: maple

$33^1/2$ x 18 x $19^1/4$ in. (85.1 x 45.7 x 48.9 cm)

[36–40] Maryland Historical Society, Baltimore. Bequest of J. B. Noel Wyatt (xx.1.1a-d) and Gift of Mrs. Gerald Hoare-Smith (59.10.1)

[41] The Metropolitan Museum of Art, New York. Purchase, The Sylmaris Collection, Gift of George Coe Graves, by exchange; and Bequest of Flora E. Whiting, Gift of Mr. and Mrs. William A. Moore, and Gift of Mrs. Russell Sage, by exchange, 1996 (1996.366)

NOTES: See Chapter Three: Southern Clients. The Metropolitan Museum's chair, catalogue number 41, retains its original upholstery foundation on the slip seat.

PROVENANCE: For all Maryland Historical Society chairs but one (59.10.1) see catalogue numbers 34–35. [40] Presented by J. B. Noel Wyatt to his business associate William G. Nolting, whose daughter gave the chair to the Society. [41] Recently in a private collection, Cape Cod, Massachusetts; the dealer Margaret Caldwell, New York, 1996.

REFERENCES: [36–40] Waxman, 1958, no. 7, pl. XV; Pearce, 1960, fig. 6; Tracy, 1963, no. 6; Somerville, 1976, pl. I; Weidman, 1984, no. 62.

42–43 *(see plate 60)*

Pair of Benches or **Ottomans** 1815–19

Attributed

Printed label on the bottom of the back rail of [43]: C. F. MEISLAHN & CO./19 Clay St. BALTIMORE MD./FINE FURNITURE, MANTELS & ARTISTIC DECORATIONS; written in ink on the label: 7 3.99 J. B. N. W./Repairing & refinishing /1 mahogany sofa

Mahogany veneer, gilded gesso and *vert antique*, gilded brass; secondary woods: mahogany, cherry, ash

$31^1/4$ x $58^1/2$ x 21 in. (79.4 x 148.6 x 53.3 cm)

Maryland Historical Society, Baltimore. Bequest of J. B. Noel Wyatt (xx.1.1i,j)

NOTES: One of the benches still has its original upholstery foundation of canvas sacking and girt-web straps, and both retain their original horsehair squabs, or mattresses. Additionally, all four bolsters survive in their original linen cases, under subsequent layers of padding and show covers. See Chapter Three: Southern Clients.

PROVENANCE: See catalogue numbers 34–35.

REFERENCES: Waxman, 1958, no. 12, pl. XX; Pearce, 1960, fig. 4; Tracy, 1963, no. 9; Tracy and Johnson, 1970, no. 40; Bishop, 1972, no. 460; Somerville, 1976, plates I, IV; Weidman, 1984, no. 178.

44 *(see plate 9)*

French Bureau 1805–15

Two partial printed No. 2 labels, one inside the top drawer and one on a back panel

Mahogany, mahogany veneer, gilded brass, *vert antique*, marble; secondary woods: yellow poplar, ash

38 x 48 x 23 in. (96.5 x 121.9 x 58.4 cm)

Private collection

NOTES: According to Stuart P. Feld of Hirschl & Adler Galleries, Inc., New York, who sold the bureau to its current owner, the large cast-brass ornament is thought to be original, except for the proper left portion, which is a replacement, as are one escutcheon and one drawer pull. When illustrated in a Parke-Bernet sales catalogue in 1950, the bureau had an escutcheon only on the middle drawer, but the same stamped brass lion's-mask drawer pulls. The sides of the bureau are of solid mahogany, with a thin mahogany board glued horizontally to the top to resemble a structural top rail. Both the front and back feet are joined to the case with mortise-and-tenon joints.

PROVENANCE: William Richmond, of William's Antique Shop, Old Greenwich, Connecticut, states in a later dated November 20, 1957, that he purchased the bureau from Miss Moulton of Stamford, Connecticut, who owned a matching wardrobe and washstand, both labeled. Richmond presumed the pieces were made for Miss Moulton's family (Waxman, 1958, p. 140). Richmond sold the bureau through Parke-Bernet Galleries, New York, in 1950; location unknown, 1950–92; Hirschl & Adler Galleries, Inc., New York, 1993.

REFERENCES: Parke-Bernet Galleries Inc., New York, 1157 (April 29, 1950), lot 137; Hinckley, 1953, no. 158; Waxman, 1958, no. 8, pl. XVI; Gaines, 1959, p. 145; *Antiques*, May 1993, p. 653, ill. (also label) (advertised by Hirschl & Adler Galleries, Inc., New York).

45

French Bureau 1805–15

Stamped four times on the case under the marble top: H. LANNUIER/NEW-YORK

Mahogany, mahogany veneer, gilded brass, marble; secondary woods: unknown

40 x 49 x 24½ in. (101.6 x 124.5 x 62.2 cm)

Location unknown

REFERENCE: Sotheby's, New York, 5376 (October 26, 1985), lot 39.

46

French Bureau with Doors 1805–15

Stamped four times on the case under the marble top, at each corner: H. LANNUIER/NEW-YORK

Mahogany, mahogany veneer, gilded brass, gilded gesso and *vert antique*, marble; secondary woods: mahogany, poplar, maple, white pine

39¼ x 47¾ x 24 in. (99.7 x 121.3 x 61 cm)

The Warner Collection of Gulf States Paper Corporation, Tuscaloosa, Alabama

NOTE: Like catalogue number 44, this bureau also has a framed panel under the marble top and a paneled dust board under the top drawer.

PROVENANCE: By tradition, as related in the 1994 Christie's, New York, sales catalogue, the bureau descended in the family of Rufus (1755–1827) and Mary Alsop King, and may have been intended for their third son, James Gore King (1791–1853), and Sarah Rogers Gracie on the occasion of their marriage in 1813; to Edward and Isabella Cochrane King; their daughter Elizabeth Gracie King (b. 1872) (Mrs. John Keyes); her daughter Gracie King Keyes, from whom it was purchased by Berry B. Tracy; Ronald S. Kane, until 1994.

REFERENCE: Christie's, New York, 7822 (January 22, 1994), lot 395.

47 *(see figure 39)*

French Bureau with Dressing Glass 1815–19

Engraved No. 3 label in the proper left drawer of the top section; outline of a possible missing label in the center drawer of the top section

Mahogany, mahogany veneer, gilded brass, looking-glass plate; secondary woods: mahogany, white pine, yellow poplar

66⅜ x 35¾ x 20½ in. (168.6 x 90.8 x 52.1 cm)

Diplomatic Reception Rooms, U.S. Department of State, Washington, D.C. Funds donated by the J. S. Johnson and Barbara P. Johnson Fund (80.103)

NOTE: The stamped brass drawer pulls are original.

PROVENANCE: Mr. and Mrs. Norvin H. Green, until 1957; Mr. and Mrs. John McCracken, after 1957; Edward V. Jones, Albany, Georgia, who acquired the bureau at a New York auction house, possibly William Doyle Galleries, in the 1970s.

REFERENCES: Parke-Bernet Galleries Inc., New York, 1740 (March 9, 1957), lot 345 (not attributed to Lannuier); Waxman, 1958, no. 9, pl. XVII; Conger and Rollins, 1991, no. 148, ill. (also label).

45

46

French Bureau with Dressing Glass
1815–19

Attributed

Mahogany, mahogany veneer, gilded brass, looking-glass plate; secondary woods: mahogany, white pine, yellow poplar

66 x 36 x 20½ in. (167.6 x 91.4 x 52.1 cm)

Hirschl & Adler Galleries, Inc., New York

NOTES: When this bureau was examined it was found to be identical to catalogue number 47, and the fact that the twisted reeding on the mirror supports here is in the opposite direction suggests that the two may have been a pair, meant to stand, as pendants, against a bedroom wall. The brass drawer pulls are replacements.

French Press 1812–19

Inscribed in script in the plaster on the bottom of the bust: H. Lannuier/New York

Mahogany, mahogany veneer, remnants of original die-stamped brass border, gilded composition, gilded brass, plaster; secondary woods: yellow poplar, white pine

101¾ x 63 x 25¾ in. (258.5 x 160 x 65.4 cm)

The New-York Historical Society. Gift of Mrs. William Hyde Wheeler (1943.368)

NOTE: The remnants of a die-stamped brass border on the proper right side of the top molding of the plinth that holds the bust reveal the same egg-and-dart pattern as the border on the apron of catalogue numbers 72–73.

PROVENANCE: By tradition, owned by Garret Byvanck Abeel (1768–1829), a New York iron and hardware merchant, and his wife, Catherine Manchalk (d. 1832), who were married in 1794; their son John Howard Abeel (1815–1896), who married Catherine Emeline Strobell and was the grandfather of the donor, Mrs. William Hyde Wheeler.

REFERENCES: Tracy, 1963, no. 1, ill. (also signature); Gaines, 1964 b, p. 442, ill. (also signature); Gaines, 1965, ill. p. 100; E. Jones, 1977, fig. 1.

French Press 1812–19

Attributed

Mahogany, mahogany veneer, gilded composition, gilded brass; secondary woods: mahogany, poplar, white pine

98⅛ x 62⅞ x 25¾ in. (250.2 x 159.7 x 65.4 cm)

Collection Mr. and Mrs. Peter G. Terian

NOTES: This press is nearly identical to The New-York Historical Society's example, catalogue number 49, except that the bust here is a modern copy of the one on the latter example, whose carved-and-gilded capitals and book-matched veneers on the pilasters it also lacks. The gilded-composition rosettes probably are not original.

PROVENANCE: Mrs. George Sommaripa, New York, until 1978; Edward V. Jones, Albany, Georgia; Berry Tracy Incorporated, Goshen, New York.

REFERENCE: Sotheby Parke Bernet Inc., New York, 4180 (November 16–18, 1978), lot 1005.

48

50

51

French Press 1815–19

Attributed

Inscribed in chalk or crayon on the outside of the back: E. Turner/McMurran/Melrose/Mary Louisa Turner/Mary Macrery Britton Conner/Woodlands/Clovernook

Mahogany, mahogany veneer, die-stamped brass, gilded brass

Dimensions unavailable

Private collection

NOTES: This French press, which is known through photographs sent to Peter M. Kenny by Thomas Gordon Smith in March 1997, has a single, long panel on each door, veneered with crotch mahogany. There appear to be applied brass-covered moldings on the inside edges of the doorframes that surround the panels. The stiles and rails of the doors have mitered rather than right-angle joints. On the molding that separates the doors is a long strip of die-stamped brass, with ebonized fillets on either side extending the full length. The die-stamped brass strip is decorated with a bellflower pattern identical to that on the apron of the pier table shown in plate 72. Square columns, with gilded-brass capitals and bases like those on the bedstead in catalogue number 2, flank the two doors. Below a cornice that employs Lannuier's typical large cyma-recta molding, which is similar in scale to the one on the looking glass shown in plate 64, is a prominent frieze with crossbanded crotch-mahogany veneers. The feet—gilded-and-bronzed lion's paws—have long, thin claws that approximate those on some of Lannuier's card tables. The two gilded cast-brass escutcheons on the doors that feature paired dolphins surmounted by flower-filled vases with pendant bellflower swags appear to be original.

PROVENANCE: According to information provided by Mimi Miller of the Historic Natchez Foundation, Mississippi, the press was originally owned by Edward Turner, a wealthy Natchez cotton planter and Chancellor of the State of Mississippi, and was in Holly Hedges, his home in Natchez, possibly in 1817; his daughter Maria Louisa Turner McMurran (d. 1891); her sister, Frances Turner Conner; her son Lemuel Conner, Jr.; purchased from Edward Turner's descendants by Mrs. Hubert Barnum, 1930s, and taken to Arlington, the house in Natchez where it now stands.

52 (see plate 23)

French Sideboard 1812–19

Engraved No. 3 label in the proper right top drawer

Mahogany, mahogany veneer, gilded brass, *vert antique;* secondary woods: yellow poplar, mahogany, white pine, ash

57 x 76³⁄₈ x 27³⁄₄ in. (144.8 x 194 x 70.5 cm)

The Metropolitan Museum of Art, New York. Gift of Fenton L. B. Brown, 1972 (1972.235.1)

NOTES: The unusually high backsplash has a wide shallow center pedestal possibly designed for a specific type of decorative object or porcelain. In addition, a serving board slides out from the proper left end. The lion's-paw feet were completely repainted before the sideboard was given to the Museum. Surface analysis has revealed the presence of an original layer of *faux*-bronze paint under the restoration coat, and no original gilding on the acanthus leaves.

PROVENANCE: The donor reported that he acquired the sideboard from the Treadwell family of New York.

REFERENCE: Tracy, 1975, ill. p. 27.

53 (see plate 94)

Card Table 1805–12

Printed No. 2 label inside the well

Stamped on the bottom edge of the front rail: H. LANNUIER/NEW YORK

Paper label on the underside of the frame of the sliding rear-leg assembly: Sypher & Co./Successors to D. Marley/Antiques & Articles of Vertue/739 & 741.Broadway.N.York

Mahogany, mahogany veneer, gilded brass; secondary woods: mahogany, white pine

29⁷⁄₈ x 35¹⁄₄ x 17⁵⁄₈ in. (75.9 x 89.5 x 44.8 cm)

The Metropolitan Museum of Art, New York. Rogers Fund, 1946 (46.24)

PROVENANCE: The table was acquired by W. Colston Leigh, from Benjamin Flayderman of Boston, according to Parke-Bernet, 1946.

REFERENCES: Parke-Bernet Galleries Inc., New York, 736 (February 9, 1946), lot 159; "Almanac," 1946, p. 312; "American History," 1946, no. 17; Downs, 1946, p. 13; Hinckley, 1953, no. 134; Waxman, 1958, no. 14, pl. XXII; Otto, 1965, no. 88; Tracy, 1967, ills. nos. 8 (label), 9.

54 *(see plate 31)*

Card Table 1805–12

Printed No. 2 label on the underside of the bottom board

Stamped twice, once on top of each rear leg: H. LANNUIER/NEW-YORK

Mahogany, mahogany veneer, gilded brass; secondary woods: mahogany, white pine

30 x 35¹/₄ x 17¹/₂ in. (76.2 x 89.5 x 44.5 cm)

Winterthur Museum, Delaware. Gift of Henry Francis du Pont (54.44)

NOTE: As the veneer pattern on this table's top does not match that of the Metropolitan Museum's card table (cat. no. 53), the tables, although identical in other respects, may not originally have been a pair.

PROVENANCE: By tradition, the table was owned by Dolly Madison, and was part of the White House furnishings; probably her niece Annie Payne (Mrs. James H. Causten, Jr.); her daughter Mary Causten Kunkel, who sold her Madison effects at auction, 1899: this may be the table listed in the auction catalogue of Dolly Madison's furnishings as "Mahogany Antique Folding-top Card Table, fluted legs"; Judge Hiram G. Bond; his daughter-in-law Mrs. Louis W. Bond, Rossford, Ohio.

REFERENCES: Possibly auction catalogue of the Kunkel collection, Philadelphia, May 9, 1899, lot 185; Waxman, 1957, ill. p. 143; Waxman, 1958, no. 13, pl. XXI; Pearce, 1960, fig. 1; Pearce, 1962 b, fig. 1; Montgomery, 1966, no. 305, ills. p. 476 (stamp and label); Hunt, 1971, pp. 144, 145, 251; Blackburn, 1981, figs. 17, 17 a (stamp).

55–56 *(see plate 25)*

Pair of Card Tables 1815–19

Engraved No. 3 label inside the well on each

Mahogany, mahogany veneer, brass; secondary woods: white pine, yellow poplar, cherry; iron

29³/₄ x 36 x 17³/₄ in. (75.6 x 91.4 x 45.1 cm)

Winterthur Museum, Delaware. Gift of Henry Francis du Pont (57.707.1,2)

NOTES: The well of each table is lined with a yellowish laid paper precisely trimmed and glued, even to the corner glue blocks. The engraved cheval-glass labels are silhouetted and glued on the laid paper (see plate 13). When it was illustrated in Ormsbee (see References, below), the table lacked its casters.

PROVENANCE: The tables were acquired from the James House, Norwalk, Connecticut, by the dealer Charles Woolsey Lyon, who believed that they had descended in the James family.

REFERENCES: Ormsbee, 1933 b, figs. 2, 3, 10 (label); McClelland, 1939, pl. 172 (label); Waxman, 1958, no. 15, pl. XXIII; Montgomery, 1966, no. 306, ill. p. 476 (label); Hewitt, Kane, and Ward, 1982, no. 41, ill. (also label).

57–58 *(see plate 22)*

Pair of Card Tables 1810–12

Printed No. 2 label in the center of the well on each

[58] Inscribed in pencil in the well, next to the label: partner of Duncan Phyfe/Mary Peltz has twin

Mahogany, mahogany veneer, gilded brass, die-stamped brass inlays; secondary wood: mahogany; iron

29¹/₂ x 36¹/₄ x 18¹/₈ in. (74.9 x 92.1 x 46 cm)

[57] Private collection

[58] The White House, Washington, D.C. Gift of The White House Historical Association (992.1704.1)

NOTE: [58] There is a large veneer patch at the center of the apron.

PROVENANCE: [57] See catalogue number 1; from Mrs. John De Witt Peltz to the present owner. [58] as [57], except at some point the table descended laterally to Dr. Edward Bell Krumbhaar, Chestnut Hill, Pennsylvania; the Pennsylvania dealer Robert Trump, by 1973; Edward V. Jones, Albany, Georgia, who placed the table on loan to The White House, 1973, where it remained until acquired from his daughter Jeanette Jones Balling, 1992.

REFERENCES: [57] Downs and Ralston, 1934, no. 213; Miller, 1956, no. 124; R. Smith, 1957, fig. 4; Waxman, 1958, no. 17, pl. XXVI. [58] *Antiques*, March 1974, p. 621 (advertised by Trump & Co., Flourtown, Pennsylvania); E. Jones, 1977, figs. 18, 19 (label).

59–60 *(see plate 58)*

Pair of Card Tables 1810–15

Attributed

Mahogany, mahogany veneer, gilded brass, die-stamped brass inlays; secondary woods: white pine, yellow poplar; iron

30³/₈ x 36¹/₂ x 18¹/₄ in. (77.2 x 92.7 x 46.4 cm)

[59] The Metropolitan Museum of Art, New York. Anonymous loan in memory of Margaret Stearns

[60] The White House, Washington, D.C. (974.1074.1)

NOTE: See also Chapter Three: French Clients in the United States.

PROVENANCE: A note by Mary Swartzlander (notarized January 9, 1967) found in The White House table states that the pair of tables was purchased at the 1847 sale of the estate of Joseph Bonaparte by John Stokes Bryan (1812–1863) and General William T. Rogers (1799–1866), respectively, of Doylestown, Pennsylvania; Bryan's table descended to his daughter Susan (Mrs. Frank Swartzlander); her son Dr. Joseph Rankin Swartzlander; his sister Sue Bryan Swartzlander. The Rogers table was acquired from that family by Mrs. James Monroe Shellenberger; her son George Shellenberger, who sold it to another son of Susan Swartzlander, Dr. Frank Bryan Swartzlander, about 1920; his three children. Both tables were acquired by the Pennsylvania dealer Robert Trump, 1967. Then [59] Margaret Stearns, 1967–89; to the present owners. [60] Berry B. Tracy, 1967–74.

REFERENCES: Possibly Bleecker, 1847, lot 91; *Antiques*, May 1967, p. 599 (advertised by R. T. Trump & Co., Philadelphia). [60] Tracy and Johnson, 1970, no. 26; Conger, 1979, pl. VI.

61 *(see plate 35)*

Card Table 1810–15

Printed No. 2 label on the bottom of the front-to-back rail

Inscribed in pencil on the bottom of the lower leaf: Hosack; in pencil on the front-to-back rail under the top: D. J. Pevick-Interiors//11 Union St.//Camden, Me//5/29/1988

Mahogany, mahogany veneer, gilded brass; secondary woods: white pine, yellow poplar, maple; iron

29⁵/₈ x 36¹/₈ x 17⁷/₈ in. (75.2 x 91.8 x 45.4 cm)

Collection Bernard & S. Dean Levy, Inc., New York

NOTE: There is an outline drawing, in chalk, of a scrolled end for a bedstead or sofa on the underside of the well that appears to date to the time of the table's manufacture.

PROVENANCE: Possibly made for Dr. David Hosack (1769–1835); Bernard & S. Dean Levy, Inc., New York, 1988; private collection, 1988–92; Bernard & S. Dean Levy, Inc., New York, from 1992.

REFERENCE: B. Levy, 1996, p. 63.

62 *(see plate 80)*

Card Table 1812–15

Attributed

Mahogany, mahogany veneer, gilded gesso, gilded composition, gilded brass, die-stamped brass borders; secondary woods: mahogany, white pine, yellow poplar, maple; iron

30¹/₄ x 36³/₄ x 18¹/₄ in. (76.8 x 93.3 x 46.4 cm)

Brooklyn Museum of Art, New York. Henry L. Batterman Fund (16.517)

NOTES: The profile of Hera on the plinth is a gilded-composition ornament, as are the rosette terminals of the lyres. Conservation conducted on the table by Olaf Unsoeld in July 1996 revealed that the nest of acanthus leaves at the base of the crossed lyres originally was water-gilded. All gilding is restored, and what remained of the original water-gilding was preserved underneath and left exposed on the back side. The ebony keys on the lyres are modern replacements. The playing surface is covered with the original green wool cloth. A very closely related card table with a crossed-lyre base was illustrated in *Antiques* in August 1997 (p. 132). Templates taken of a leg and of the lyre of that example do not match the Lannuier-attributed card table—nor does the construction of the bottom of the well, which in this instance is held in place with glue blocks, instead of being nailed into rabbets.

PROVENANCE: Purchased by Luke Vincent Lockwood for the Brooklyn Museum of Art, 1916.

63

Card Table 1812–15

Wood unknown (probably mahogany), die-stamped brass border

Dimensions not available

Location unknown

NOTES: This table is known from a photograph in the Scholarship Files of the Department of American Decorative Arts at The Metropolitan Museum of Art. The table is identical to catalogue number 62, except for the ornament missing from the plinth where, on the former, Hera appears, and the different pattern in the die-stamped brass border and casters.

64

Card Table 1815–19

Attributed

Mahogany, mahogany veneer, gilded brass; secondary woods: unknown; iron

30 x 35⁷⁄₈ x 17⁷⁄₈ in. (76.2 x 91.1 x 45.4 cm)

Location unknown

REFERENCE: Sotheby's, New York, 6350 (October 25, 1992), lot 462 (includes a reference that a possible mate to this table is in a New York private collection).

65 *(see figure 88)*

Card Table 1815–19

Engraved No. 3 label inside the well

Mahogany, mahogany veneer, gilded gesso and *vert antique*, gilded brass; secondary woods: yellow poplar, white pine, maple, mahogany; iron

30⁵⁄₈ x 36 x 17⁷⁄₈ in. (77.8 x 91.4 x 45.4 cm)

Private collection

NOTES: The carved-and-turned columns and lion's-paw feet, of mahogany, were gilded and bronzed when the table was restored by Hirschl & Adler Galleries, Inc., New York. The original marbleized paper remains inside the well. The label is silhouetted like those on the card tables in catalogue numbers 55–56 and on the worktable in catalogue number 123.

PROVENANCE: Hirschl & Adler Galleries, Inc., New York, 1995–96.

63

64

66–67   (*see plates 26 and 74*)

Pair of Card Tables 1815–19

Two engraved (badly deteriorated) No. 3 labels on the underside of the well on each

Rosewood and mahogany veneers, gilded gesso and *vert antique*, gilded composition, gilded brass, die-stamped brass borders; secondary woods: white pine, yellow poplar, mahogany, maple, probably basswood, ash; iron

30 x 36 x 18 in. (76.2 x 91.4 x 45.7 cm)

Private collection

NOTES: Catalogue number 67 has clearly defined lines in the shape of the plinth scribed into the undersides of the bottom boards of the well. The die-stamped brass borders on the bottom edges of the aprons, which were in a pattern identical to that of the borders of catalogue numbers 68–69, are missing from both tables. Catalogue number 67 is also missing its original eagle ornaments on the canted corners that, originally, faced in the same direction, opposite that of the pair of eagles on catalogue number 66. Having the eagle ornaments face each other in this fashion indicates that the tables were meant to be placed against the same wall. Paired girandole mirrors from this period, with gilded eagle finials that face each other, also are known.

PROVENANCE: By tradition, originally owned by George Harrison (1762–1845), a Philadelphia merchant and naval agent, and his wife, Sophia; in their house at 156 Chestnut Street; her nephew Joshua Francis Fisher (1807–1873) and his wife, Eliza Middleton; their daughter Maria Middleton Fisher (Mrs. Brinton Coxe). [66] A granddaughter, Anna Gerhard (Mrs. Winslow Ames), until 1997. [67] A daughter, Eliza Middletown Coxe (Mrs. Charles Morris Young); her son Arthur Young, until 1996.

REFERENCES: Downs and Ralston, 1934, nos. 214 (ill.), 215 (the tables are reversed in the catalogue: no. 214 was lent by Mr. and Mrs. Winslow Ames, not Mrs. Charles Morris Young; no. 215 was lent by Mrs. Young). [66] "Editor's Attic," 1936, fig. 6; Waxman, 1958, no. 19, pl. XXVIII; *Antiques*, May 1997, p. 679 (advertised by Christie's, New York); Christie's, New York, 8696 (June 17, 1997), lot 428, fig. 1 (center mount). [67] Sotheby's, New York, 6800 (January 19–21, 1996), lot 1627.

68–69   (*see figure 102*)

Pair of Card Tables 1815–19

Engraved No. 3 label on the underside of the well on each

Rosewood, mahogany, and satinwood veneers, gilded gesso and *vert antique*, gilded brass, die-stamped brass borders; secondary woods: white pine, yellow poplar, maple, ash; iron

$29^{7}/_{8}$ x $36^{1}/_{8}$ x $18^{1}/_{4}$ in. (75.9 x 91.8 x 46.4 cm)

Valentine Museum, Richmond, Virginia. Bequest of Captain Williams Carter Wickham (V.85.46.1,2)

NOTES: These are the only known figural card tables by Lannuier with a gilded Grecian ovolo molding on the edge of the lower top leaf. Scribed lines similar to those on catalogue number 67 are visible on the bottom boards of the well.

PROVENANCE: Made for John Wickham (1763–1839), a Richmond lawyer originally from Southhold, New York; in his Richmond town house, designed by the architect Alexander Parris, 1811–12. The interiors of the house were completed by 1815, and are notable for the elaborate painted wall decorations of classical designs. The card tables are thought to be those valued at $50 in "drawing room A" of the 1839 inventory of Wickham's estate (Cooper, 1993, p. 171). They descended in the Wickham family to Captain Williams Carter Wickham, who left the tables to the museum.

REFERENCES: Cooper, 1993, pp. 169–71, no. 127; Deschamps, 1994, ill. p. 222; Christie's, New York, 8696 (June 17, 1997), lot 428, fig. 4.

70–71   (*see plate 51*)

Pair of Card Tables 1817

Engraved No. 3 label on the underside of the well on each

Mahogany veneer, gilded gesso and *vert antique*, gilded brass, die-stamped brass borders; secondary woods: mahogany, ash [yellow poplar, white pine, cherry, basswood, by microanalysis]; iron

$31^{1}/_{8}$ x 36 x $17^{7}/_{8}$ in. (79.1 x 91.4 x 45.4 cm)

Albany Institute of History & Art, New York. Gift of Stephen Van Rensselaer Crosby (1957.70.8.1,2)

NOTES: Probably the pair of card tables listed in a June 19, 1817, invoice to William Bayard with delivery to "P. D. Campell [*sic*]" (see Appendix 5). The casters are modern replacements copied from the originals on catalogue number 72. See also Chapter Three: The Bayard-Van Rensselaer-Campbell Commissions.

PROVENANCE: Purchased by William Bayard (1761–1826) of New York, 1817, either for his daughter Harriet, who married Stephen Van Rensselaer IV on January 2, 1817 (see cat. no. 5), or more likely his daughter Maria (1789–1875), who married Duncan Pearsall Campbell (1781–1861) on June 16, 1817. Campbell ownership is made credible by a letter at the Albany Institute of History & Art from the donor's wife, which states that the Empire furniture owned by her husband came from the Campbells and not the Van Rensselaers. Probably to the Campbells' daughter Maria Louisa Campbell (d. 1911); possibly acquired by her nephew Stephen Van Rensselaer Crosby (1868–after 1957), a grandson of Harriet and Stephen Van Rensselaer, in a private sale of Maria Campbell's estate to family members, 1912.

REFERENCES: Waxman, 1958, no. 21, pl. XXX; Pearce, 1960, fig. 2; Comstock, 1962, no. 560; Rice, 1962, ill. p. 32; Pearce, 1964, figs. 1, 2; Christie's, New York, 8696 (June 17, 1997), lot 426, fig. 1.

72–73 *(see plate 53)*

Pair of Card Tables 1817

One table [72] inscribed in ink on the back-to-front brace below the top: Fait a New-York/Le I May 1817/HL; in ink on the top of the figure's head: 1817/May/HL

Mahogany veneer, gilded gesso and *vert antique*, gilded brass, die-stamped brass borders; secondary woods: yellow poplar, white pine, mahogany [ash; basswood (72), by microanalysis]; iron

31¹⁄₈ x 36 x 17³⁄₄ in. (79.1 x 91.4 x 45.1 cm)

The Metropolitan Museum of Art, New York. Gift of Justine VR Milliken, 1995 (1995.377.1,2)

NOTES: The proper-right bottom flipper of the gilded figure on [72] is a modern replacement, as are all of the die-stamped brass borders on [73]. See also Chapter Three: The Bayard-Van Rensselaer-Campbell Commissions.

PROVENANCE: Purchased by William Bayard of New York, 1817, probably for his daughter Harriet, who married Stephen Van Rensselaer IV on January 2, 1817 (see cat. no. 5); their daughter Justine Van Rensselaer (1828–1912) (Mrs. Howard Townsend); her daughter Harriet Bayard Townsend (1864–after 1910) (Mrs. Thomas Hunt Barber), who kept the tables in her late-19th-century summer house in Southampton, Long Island, an adaptation of the Van Rensselaer Manor House in Albany; her daughter Justine Van Rensselaer Barber (Mrs. Roger F. Hooper); her daughter Justine Van Rensselaer Hooper Milliken, the great-great-granddaughter of the original owners.

REFERENCE: Kenny, 1997, p. 62, ill.

74

Card Table 1815–19

Engraved No. 3 label on the underside of the well

Rosewood and mahogany veneers, gilded gesso and *vert antique*, gilded composition, gilded brass; secondary woods: mahogany, white pine, yellow poplar, ash, maple; iron

30⁵⁄₈ x 35⁷⁄₈ x 17³⁄₄ in. (77.8 x 91.1 x 45.1 cm)

The Art Institute of Chicago. Restricted gift of Jamee J. and Marshall Field; Pauline Armstrong Endowment (1994.712)

NOTES: Conservation was undertaken by Robert Mussey Associates, Boston, in June and July 1996. The casters are replacements copied from those on catalogue number 72. The brass of the original die-stamped brass-and-wood border on the apron is missing; its lozenge-and-dot pattern is unique among Lannuier's known work.

PROVENANCE: Acquired by Rosemary Crane Hastings for her New York apartment and taken to Rainthorpe Hall, her home in Norfolk, England, late 1920s; her son George Frederick Hastings, until 1994.

REFERENCES: Sotheby's, New York, 6613 (October 23, 1994), lot 373, ill. (also label); "Art Institute of Chicago," 1995, pp. 86–89, ill. p. 89; Gustafson, 1995, ill. p. 656; Christie's, New York, 8696 (June 17, 1997), lot 428, fig. 3.

75

Card Table 1815–19

Engraved No. 3 label on the underside of the well

Paper label on the underside of the well: Schmidt Bros.//35¹⁄₄ x 35³⁄₄ x 29³⁄₄//2/5 /09//HEH

Inscribed in chalk on the underside of the well: 25=/1695

Mahogany and rosewood veneers, gilded gesso, die-stamped brass inlays; secondary woods: mahogany, white pine, yellow poplar, maple, ash; iron

29³⁄₈ x 35³⁄₄ x 17³⁄₄ in. (74.6 x 90.8 x 45.1 cm)

The Huntington Library, Art Collections, Botanical Gardens, San Marino, California (14.21)

NOTES: The tabletop is veneered in four book-matched quarters of crotch mahogany and crossbanded in rosewood; the rails are crossbanded in mahogany—the only Lannuier card table known with this veneer pattern. When the table is open, the pattern in the veneer of each leaf matches that of the closed top, but there is no rosewood crossbanding. The figure, back columns, and legs all appear to have been regilded, before which the volutes on the tips of the wings seem to have been clipped off and the ends of the wings reshaped. The die-stamped brass border is missing at the bottom edge of the apron. There is no evidence of an original ornament on the front apron. The casters are modern replacements.

PROVENANCE: It is believed that Henry Edwards Huntington (1850–1927) purchased the table—which is called an "Antique Adam card table" on a schedule of purchases signed by his wife, Arabella Duval Huntington—from Schmidt Bros., 343 Madison Avenue, New York, about 1909.

REFERENCES: Waxman, 1958, no. 20, pl. XXIX; *Huntington Art Collections*, 1986, p. 174, ill. p. 175.

74

75

76–77

Pair of Card Tables 1815–19

Attributed

Rosewood and mahogany veneers, gilded gesso and *vert antique,* gilded brass, die-stamped brass inlays; secondary woods: mahogany, white pine, yellow poplar, maple, cherry; iron

30¼ x 36⅛ x 17⅞ in. (76.8 x 91.8 x 45.4 cm)

Collection Richard and Gloria Manney

NOTES: The ornaments currently on the tables at the center of the aprons are replacements for earlier ones identical in design to the one that depicts nymphs playing panpipes shown in figure 98. (For an illustration of the tables with these ornaments see the 1981 Sotheby's, New York, catalogue.) The die-stamped brass borders on the lower edges of the rails are missing. An extra board has been added underneath each table, thus fully enclosing the bottom.

PROVENANCE: Marchese Giuseppe Paterno, Castello di San Giuliano, until 1981.

REFERENCES: *Antiques,* April 1981, p. 733 (advertised by Sotheby's, New York); Sotheby's, New York, 4590Y (April 29–May 1, 1981), lot 1068.

78–79 *(see figure 108)*

Pair of Card Tables 1815–19

Each table has the outline of a label on the underside of the plinth

Inscribed twice in chalk, on the underside of the well of each table: Bosley

Mahogany veneer, gilded gesso and *vert antique,* gilded brass, die-stamped brass borders; secondary woods: yellow poplar, maple, white pine; iron

30½ x 36 x 18 in. (77.5 x 91.4 x 45.7 cm)

Maryland Historical Society, Baltimore. Bequest of J. B. Noel Wyatt (xx.1.1g,h)

NOTES: The die-stamped brass border is missing from the bottom edge of the apron of each table. See Chapter Three: Southern Clients.

PROVENANCE: See catalogue numbers 34–35.

REFERENCES: Waxman, 1958, no. 22, pl. XXXI (erroneously listed as pl. XXI); Pearce, 1960, fig. 3; Tracy, 1963, no. 8; Butler, 1965, p. 247, no. 948; Somerville, 1976, plates I, II; Weidman, 1984, pl. XVIII, no. 160.

80

Card Table 1815–19

Engraved No. 3 label on the bottom of the plinth

Mahogany veneer, gilded gesso and *vert antique,* gilded brass; secondary woods: white pine, yellow poplar, mahogany, cherry; iron

30 x 36½ x 18½ in. (76.2 x 92.7 x 47 cm)

High Museum of Art, Atlanta. Purchase with funds from the Decorative Arts Endowment (1988.27)

NOTES: The missing brass border on the aprons most likely was die-stamped with a laurel-leaf pattern identical to that on the Harrison and Wickham card tables (cat. nos. 66–69). The molding on the edge of the upper leaf replaces an original die-stamped brass-and-wood band probably similar to those on catalogue numbers 66 and 67. The style and construction of the plinth are unique among Lannuier's known card tables: Its core is formed from three boards joined at the edges and set at an angle to the front. Conservation of the gilded and bronzed surfaces of this table was executed by Fodera Fine Arts, Ltd., New York, 1991.

PROVENANCE: By tradition, the table descended for two generations in a Baton Rouge, Louisiana, family before its purchase by the High Museum, 1988.

REFERENCES: *High [Museum] Newsletter,* 1994, pp. 5 (ill.), 6; *Highlights from the Collection,* 1994, ill. p. 36.

76

80

81–82

Pair of Card Tables 1815–19

Engraved No. 3 label on the underside of the well on each

Rosewood veneer, gilded gesso and *vert antique;* secondary woods: mahogany, yellow poplar, white pine, ash; iron

30 x 36 x 18 in. (76.2 x 91.4 x 45.7 cm)

Private collection

NOTES: Each table is missing its original ornaments at the center of the apron and on the canted corners, as well as its original die-stamped brass border on the lower edge of the apron. The winged caryatids are carved in a style nearly identical to that of the caryatid on the High Museum's card table (cat. no. 80), but the plinths are square on the edge, rather than coved. The back columnar supports, also nearly identical to those on catalogue number 80, are unusual in that the column sections are smooth instead of fluted. The feet, as on the High Museum example, are in the form of heavy outstretched lion's paws, but on this pair of tables there are returns under the plinth similar to those on the Wickham tables (cat. nos. 68–69).

PROVENANCE: Descended in the family of Richard Varick, Mayor of New York, 1789–1801.

83–84 *(see plates 43 and 99)*

Pair of Card Tables 1815–19

Attributed

Inscribed in chalk on the underside of the well on each table: MS | RS/each; 1363

Rosewood, curly and bird's-eye maple [satinwood, by microanalysis] veneers, gilded gesso and *vert antique,* gilded brass, die-stamped brass borders; secondary woods: [83] [mahogany, yellow poplar, maple, by microanalysis], white pine

31 x 35³⁄₄ x 17³⁄₄ in. (78.7 x 90.8 x 45.1 cm)

[83] The Metropolitan Museum of Art, New York. Funds from various donors, 1966 (66.170)

[84] Collection Mr. and Mrs. Peter G. Terian

NOTES: Catalogue number 84 appears to retain its original green wool playing surface, although all of the die-stamped brass border on the lower edge of the apron is a modern replacement, as are all of the die-stamped brass anthemions on the top edge. On catalogue number 83, all of the die-stamped brass border except the front strip has been replaced, and only one die-stamped brass anthemion is original.

PROVENANCE: [83] According to Tracy, 1967, the table was purchased by Senator George Peabody Wetmore (1846–1921), of Chateau-sur-Mer, Newport, Rhode Island, and New York, in the late 19th century; his daughter Edith Wetmore (1870–1966); her estate. Miss Wetmore may have furnished the information that the table originally had been owned by Philip Hone (1780–1851), the New York businessman and diarist and friend of her grandfather William Shepard Wetmore (1801–1862), the shipping merchant, although proof has yet to be found that supports this published and now well-known attribution. [84] By tradition, believed to have been owned by Judge Barlow of Gramercy Park, New York, in the early 20th century; Mrs. August Lewis, New York; a Connecticut family, until 1993.

REFERENCES: [83] McClelland, 1939, p. 191; Waxman, 1958, pp. 169, 203; Parke-Bernet Galleries Inc., New York, 2466 (October 22, 1966), lot 135; Tracy, 1967, pp. 283–91, nos. 4, 6 (detail), frontispiece ill.; Tracy and Johnson, 1970, no. 44; *Guide to the Metropolitan,* 1972, p. 36, no. 16, ill.; Bordes, 1975, ill. p. 27; Cooper, 1980a, no. 286; Davidson and Stillinger, 1985, fig. 90; Deschamps, 1994, ill. p. 223; Peck, 1996, pp. 220–23, color ills. pp. 220, 221, 223; Christie's, New York, 8696 (June 17, 1997), lot 428, fig. 2. [84] Sotheby's, New York, 6483 (October 24, 1993), lot 358.

85

Card Table 1815–19

Attributed

Mahogany, mahogany veneer, gilded gesso and *vert antique,* gilded brass, die-stamped brass border; secondary woods: mahogany, yellow poplar, white pine, cherry or maple; iron

31 x 36 x 17⁷⁄₈ in. (78.7 x 91.4 x 45.4 cm)

Private collection

NOTES: Traces of the original gilding and *vert-antique* decoration on the feet remain. The wood inlay on the lower edge of the apron is probably not original, and the brass strings of the lyre may have replaced a solid-wood lyre like the one on catalogue number 86.

PROVENANCE: Mr. and Mrs. H. Yerbury Hooper, before 1963–about 1983; a New Jersey auction house; Berry Tracy Incorporated, Goshen, New York, 1983; private collection, until 1997.

REFERENCES: Tracy, 1963, no. 7; Christie's, New York, 8696 (June 17, 1997), lot 426.

85

86

Card Table 1815–19

Attributed

Mahogany, mahogany veneer, gilded gesso and *vert antique*, gilded brass; secondary woods: unknown

Dimensions not available

Location unknown

REFERENCE: Hinckley, 1953, no. 157.

87

Card Table 1815–19

Attributed

Mahogany, mahogany veneer, gilded gesso and *vert antique*, gilded brass, die-stamped brass borders; secondary woods: white pine, oak or ash

30½ x 36 x 18 in. (77.5 x 91.4 x 45.7 cm)

Governor's Mansion, Austin, Texas

NOTE: This table was not examined by Peter M. Kenny.

PROVENANCE: Bernard & S. Dean Levy, Inc., New York.

REFERENCES: *Antiques*, November 1977, p. 795 (advertised by Bernard & S. Dean Levy, Inc., New York); B. Levy, 1977, p. 42.

88 *(see plate 12)*

Pier Table 1803–10

Stamped twice on the top edge of the drawer front: H. LANNUIER/NEW-YORK

Mahogany, mahogany veneer, gilded brass, marble; secondary woods: yellow poplar, white pine

36½ x 37 x 14¾ in. (92.7 x 94 x 37.5 cm)

Winterthur Museum, Delaware. Gift of Henry Francis du Pont (61.1693)

NOTES: The drawer pulls are old but not original, and as several different sets have been used in the drawer over time, it is difficult to assess what form the originals may have had. Possibly the key alone functioned as the original drawer pull, although the recent discovery of a closely related table (cat. no. 90) that retains its original stamped-brass drawer pulls may indicate otherwise.

PROVENANCE: The Paulding family believed that the table had been given to James Kirke Paulding (1778–1860), in partial payment of a debt, by Citizen Genêt, French minister to the United States in 1793, who later married a daughter of New York governor George Clinton. Paulding, Commissioner of the Navy under President Madison and later Secretary of the Navy, and his wife, Gertrude Kemble, owned a house on Whitehall Street in New York as well as one on Pennsylvania Avenue in Washington, D.C., where the table is thought to have stood; his granddaughter, the mother of Marion Paulding Aigner, who inherited the table.

REFERENCES: Pearce, 1964, fig. 7; R. Smith, 1965, no. 739; Montgomery, 1966, no. 346; Fennimore, 1981, fig. 1; Reese, 1983, ill. p. 138.

86

87

89 *(see figure 11)*

Pier Table 1805–10

Printed No. 2 label (upper, or English, half only) on the inside surface of the bottom of the drawer

Stamped four times, once on top of each front leg, and once on the top surface of each back corner block: H. LANNUIER/NEW-YORK

Mahogany, mahogany veneer, gilded brass, marble; secondary wood: mahogany

33¼ x 31 x 14⅛ in. (84.5 x 78.7 x 35.9 cm)

Private collection

NOTES: The marble top and marble shelf at the bottom are replacements. X-rays taken at the Metropolitan Museum revealed original mortise holes in the front and back legs, for the low rails at the sides only, as in catalogue number 88. The low shelf on this example, therefore, probably looked like the one on catalogue numbers 88 and 90, and originally may have had a similar top as well, with a brass frame or gallery. The current stamped-brass drawer pulls are old and possibly original; the ends are threaded and pointed to screw into the wood. The lock and keyhole escutcheon are also original.

PROVENANCE: Israel Sack, Inc., New York, about 1959–63.

REFERENCE: Sack, 1981, vol. 1, no. 227.

90

Pier Table 1805–10

Printed No. 2 label (upper, or English, half only) on the outside surface of the bottom of the drawer

Stamped twice, once on the rear surface of the block of each back leg: H. LANNUIER/NEW-YORK

Mahogany, mahogany veneer, ebony stringing, gilded brass, marble; secondary woods: mahogany and yellow poplar

34¾ x 30½ x 14½ in. (88.3 x 77.5 x 36.8 cm)

Collection John Kean, on long-term loan to the Liberty Hall Foundation, Union, New Jersey

NOTES: This small pier table, or "dressing table with marble top"—as it seems to have been called in the inventory of the estate of Susan Livingston Kean Niemcewicz, taken at her home, Ursino, in 1834—is practically identical in every detail to catalogue number 89, and has survived in remarkable condition. Recently brought to the attention of the present authors by Ulysses Grant Dietz, curator of Decorative Arts at the Newark Museum, the table helps to explain and confirm the suspected losses and alterations to catalogue number 89. The top of the table is composed of a thin slab of white marble with gray veins over a thin sub top of yellow poplar, framed by a gilded-brass gallery pierced in a diamond pattern. The side rails and front drawer are identical to those of catalogue number 89, and, in addition, the present example originally had the same smooth sheet-brass inserts on the corners, surrounded by thin slips of ebony; the ebony remains, but the brass is missing from all but one back corner. The table has gilded-brass baguette moldings with wooden cores along the lower edges of the aprons and its legs are identical to those of catalogue number 89. Its low shelf consists of a thin board of "plum-pudding," or speckled, mahogany—a rare type greatly prized in post-Revolutionary France, where it was called *acajou moucheté*. The table's tapered feet have brass caps at their tops, which are suspended in position by means of a series of (original) iron brads nailed directly into them; the feet also retain their original gilded-brass tips, fitted like ferrules onto the ends. Such brass tips also once may have adorned the feet of catalogue number 89, and could explain why the latter is an inch and a half shorter than this example. The table has old but replaced stamped-brass drawer pulls, which have finely beaded circular backplates and are decorated with a circular pattern; a basket-weave pattern is embossed on their convex centers. The pulls display much of their original gilded finish,

which probably was accomplished with lacquers instead of by mercury gilding. All of the table's gilded-brass surfaces likewise retain a large part of their original coating. The drawer lock and keyhole escutcheon are original.

Important differences between this table, catalogue number 89, and catalogue number 88, the only other known pier table in *le goût moderne*, include the use of mahogany for the sides and bottoms of the drawers of the first two tables, as opposed to yellow poplar as the secondary wood of the last example. Catalogue number 88 also employs a standard reeded leg instead of the fluted column with sheet-brass inserts in the flutes—the type more commonly associated with the "modern taste," as interpreted by Parisian *ébénistes* of the 1790s.

PROVENANCE: By tradition, the table originally was owned by Susan Livingston Kean Niemcewicz (d. 1833), who married the Polish count, writer, and patriot Julian Ursin Niemcewicz (1757–1841) in 1800, four years after the death of her first husband, John Kean, in 1796. Niemcewicz returned to Poland, to his estate near Warsaw, in 1807, and his wife, Susan, in 1811, purchased Liberty Hall, the manor house in Elizabeth, New Jersey, that formerly had belonged to her uncle Governor William Livingston (d. 1790), renaming it "Ursino," after her husband's Polish estate. Through Susan's son Peter Kean (1788–1828), the table descended to successive generations of the Kean family, and it remains at Liberty Hall (the house reacquired its original name). Less likely is the possibility that the table originally belonged to Peter Kean, who married in 1813.

91 *(see plate 17)*

Pier Table 1805–10

Printed No. 2 label on the outer surface of the back rail

Mahogany, and mahogany, satinwood, and rosewood veneers; secondary woods: mahogany, white pine

37 x 49 x 24½ in. (94 x 124.5 x 62.2 cm)

Winterthur Museum, Delaware. Gift of Henry Francis du Pont (57.685)

NOTES: The drawer pulls are replacements for an earlier set, of approximately this size, with circular backplates. As on catalogue number 89, the ends of these earlier pulls appear to have been threaded and pointed so that they could be screwed into the wood.

PROVENANCE: Louis Guerineau Myers; to Henry Francis du Pont.

REFERENCES: Girl Scouts Loan Exhibition, 1929, no. 709; Downs and Ralston 1934, no. 147; McClelland, 1939, pl. 176; Waxman, 1957, ill. p. 143; Waxman, 1958, no. 27, plates XXXVII, XXXVIII (label); Montgomery, 1966, no. 347, ill. p. 361.

92 *(see plate 30)*

Square Pier Table 1805–10

Ghost of printed No. 2 label on the inside surface of the back rail of the upper section

Stamped five times, four times on the inside surface of the back rail of the upper section, and once on the bottom of the base, inside the proper right figure: H. LANNUIER/NEW-YORK

Mahogany veneer, gilded gesso and *vert antique*, gilded brass, marble, looking-glass plate; secondary woods: white pine, mahogany

36½ x 51¾ x 16½ in. (92.7 x 131.4 x 41.9 cm)

Private collection

NOTE: The back boards are replacements, as may be the marble top and the gilded molding beneath it.

PROVENANCE: By tradition, descended in the Ogden and Schuyler families until 1990; George Subkoff Antiques, Inc., Wilton, Connecticut, 1990; Bernard & S. Dean Levy, Inc., New York, 1991.

REFERENCES: Sotheby's Arcade Auctions, New York, 1334 (September 18, 1990), lot 512; *Antiques*, April 1991, p. 625 (advertised by Bernard & S. Dean Levy, Inc.).

93 *(see plate 79)*

Square Pier Table 1805–10

Two printed No. 2 labels, one on the underside of the plinth, and one on the inside surface of the back rail of the upper section (illegible)

Mahogany veneer, gilded gesso, gilded composition, gilded brass, marble, looking-glass plate; secondary woods: yellow poplar, white pine

36⅞ x 40 x 18¼ in. (93.7 x 101.6 x 46.4 cm)

Collection Jeanette Jones Balling, on loan to The White House, Washington, D.C. (L.80.141.1)

NOTES: The entire top of the plinth has been reveneered. The marble top is probably not original.

PROVENANCE: George Subkoff Antiques, Inc., New York, acquired the table from the William Doyle Galleries, New York, mid-1970s; Edward V. Jones, Albany, Georgia, before 1977, who placed the table on loan to The White House, 1980.

REFERENCES: E. Jones, 1977, figs. 4, 5 (label); Cortesi and Harrell, 1982, p. 21, ill. p. 20.

94 *(see plate 28)*

Square Pier Table 1805–10

Printed No. 2 label inside the back rail of the upper section

Mahogany veneer, gilded brass, marble, looking-glass plate; secondary woods: mahogany, white pine, yellow poplar

35 x 41^1/$_2$ x 19 in. (88.9 x 105.4 x 48.3 cm)

The White House, Washington, D.C. Gift of Robert Knox (961.168.1)

NOTES: This table was on loan to the Museum of the City of New York, from 1942 to 1946. A photograph in the museum's archives of an interior in Mrs. Henry Wilmerding Payne's home at 14 West 36th Street, New York, shows the pier table adjacent to a chimneypiece, and with the curule seating furniture attributed to Duncan Phyfe now in the collections of The Metropolitan Museum of Art and the Museum of the City of New York.

PROVENANCE: By tradition, the table originally was owned by Thomas Cornell Pearsall (1768–1820) and his wife, Frances Buchanan (b. 1779), who married in 1799. A 1946 Parke-Bernet catalogue traces the ownership to the Pearsalls' daughter Phoebe (1813–1895), who lived at 3 Waverly Place and later at 175 Madison Avenue, New York; her niece Frances Pearsall Bradhurst (1834–1907) (Mrs. Augustus Field); her daughter Mary Field (1860–1942) (Mrs. Henry Wilmerding Payne); her nieces Frances Field Walker (Mrs. Samuel S. Walker) and Mary Field Hoving (Mrs. Osgood F. Hoving), until 1946; Robert Knox, 1946–61.

REFERENCES: Parke-Bernet Galleries Inc., New York, 805 (November 9, 1946), lot 137; Waxman, 1958, no. 28, pl. XXXIX; Gaines, 1959, ill. p. 145; Pearce, 1962 a, figs. 4, 5 (label); Pearce, 1962 c, ill. p. 67; Gaines, 1965, ill. p. 100; Cortesi and Harrell, 1982, ills. pp. 12, 13.

95 *(see plate 84)*

Square Pier Table 1805–10

Two printed No. 2 labels, one on the inside of the rear upper rail and one on the backboard (fragmentary)

Mahogany veneer, gilded brass, gilded gesso, marble, looking-glass plate; secondary woods: white pine, yellow poplar

34^5/$_8$ x 37^1/$_2$ x 18^1/$_2$ in. (87.9 x 95.3 x 47 cm)

Private collection

NOTES: The table, altered by the addition of a drawer, the front of which was formed by the original apron, was sold at Sotheby's, New York, in this condition in 1993, but subsequently was restored by Hirschl & Adler Galleries, Inc., New York. The gilded bun feet are original, although the gilding has been restored. The current marble top replaces the one with a molded edge seen in the photograph in the 1993 Sotheby's sales catalogue.

PROVENANCE: Mrs. A. B. DeGaris, Millbrook, New York, until 1993; Hirschl & Adler Galleries, Inc., New York, 1993.

REFERENCE: Sotheby's, New York, 6392 (January 28–31, 1993), lot 1185.

96

Square Pier Table 1803–10

Attributed

Mahogany veneer, gilded brass, marble, looking-glass plate; secondary woods: unknown

35^1/$_2$ x 41 x 18^1/$_2$ in. (90.2 x 104.1 x 47 cm)

Location unknown

NOTE: This table appears to be nearly identical to catalogue number 94.

PROVENANCE: The table was owned by Byam Kerby Stevens and his wife, Frances Gallatin, who were married in 1830. Frances, the only daughter of Albert Gallatin (1761–1849) and his wife, Hannah Nicholson (who married in 1793), may have inherited the table from her parents or from her grandmother Frances Witter Nicholson (d. 1832), Hannah Gallatin's mother. Or Byam Kerby Stevens might have been given the table by his parents, Major General Ebenezer S. Stevens and his wife, Lucretia Ledyard. The table stood in the Stevens family summer house, The Mount, in Astoria, Long Island—which had been purchased by Ebenezer S. Stevens about 1814—in the late 19th century.

REFERENCE: K. Jones, 1978, p. 1140, ill. p. 1148.

96

97

Square Pier Table 1810–15

Printed No. 2 label on the inside surface of the back rail of the upper section

Mahogany veneer, gilded gesso and *vert antique*, gilded brass, marble, looking-glass plate; secondary woods: white pine, yellow poplar

41¼ x 48 x 24 in. (104.8 x 121.9 x 61 cm)

Private collection

NOTES: The capitals and bases of the columns are of gilded cast brass, as are those of the back pilasters. The stiles of the back frame are joined to the rear rail with mortise-and-tenon joints.

PROVENANCE: Ginsburg & Levy, New York, 1930s.

REFERENCES: Ormsbee, 1933 b, figs. 1, 9 (label); McClelland, 1939, plates 177, 178 (label); Waxman, 1958, no. 29, pl. XL.

98

Square Pier Table 1812–15

Printed No. 2 label on the inside surface of the back rail

Stamped three times, on the top of the frame at each front corner and at the center of the inside surface of the front rail: H. LANNUIER/NEW-YORK

Rosewood veneer, gilded gesso and *vert antique*, gilded composition, gilded brass, die-stamped brass borders, marble, looking-glass plate; secondary woods: white pine, yellow poplar, ash

37⅝ x 54 x 22 in. (95.6 x 137.2 x 55.9 cm)

The White House, Washington, D.C. Gift of Mrs. Lammot du Pont Copeland (983.1532.1)

NOTES: The lion's-paw feet are modern restorations; when the table was sold at Sotheby's, New York, in 1980, only the upper part of the feet remained. The composition rosettes on the plinth also were restored. The marble top appears to be old but probably not original. The table is nearly identical to catalogue number 99, but unlike the latter it has a different patterned die-stamped brass border on its apron.

PROVENANCE: The table was owned by an Atlanta, Georgia, family, from the turn of the century until 1980; Berry Tracy Incorporated, Goshen, New York, 1980–83.

REFERENCE: Sotheby Parke Bernet Inc., New York, 4478Y (November 19–22, 1980), lot 1354.

99 *(see plate 42)*

Square Pier Table about 1815–19

Engraved No. 3 label on the inside surface of the back rail

Inscribed in pencil at the top of the proper left brace: Chesterman

Rosewood veneer, gilded gesso and *vert antique*, gilded composition, gilded brass, die-stamped brass borders, marble, looking-glass plate; secondary woods: white pine, yellow poplar, ash

37 x 54 x 22½ in. (94 x 137.2 x 57.2 cm)

Collection Mrs. W. Scott Cluett, on extended loan to Historic Deerfield, Inc., Deerfield, Massachusetts

NOTES: When this table underwent conservation at the Williamstown Regional Art Conservation Center, Massachusetts, in 1989, surface analysis of the *vert-antique* and gilded feet revealed the presence of three different blue-green pigmented paint layers. The original layer, on a gesso ground, was described in the conservator's report as being a dark blue green, with a resin-varnish coating. When the cast-brass ornaments on the front of the plinth were removed for cleaning, one was discovered to have the initials PEG on the reverse: the mark of P. E. Guerin, a New York brass foundry that has been in operation in New York since 1857. It is uncertain if these ornaments replaced earlier composition rosettes, similar to those on catalogue number 100. The looking-glass plate is a modern replacement.

PROVENANCE: The table has a history of having been found in New Orleans; George A. Cluett; to his heirs.

REFERENCES: Ralston, 1945, fig. 6; Comstock, 1954, ill. p. 382; Waxman, 1958, no. 31, pl. XLIV; *Historic Deerfield Annual Report*, 1989, ill. p. 29.

97

98

100 *(see plate 24)*

Square Pier Table 1815–19

Engraved No. 3 label on the inside surface of the back rail of the upper section

Stamped four times, twice at each front corner, on the top of the rail: H. LANNUIER/NEW-YORK

Rosewood veneer, cast and gilded lead or white metal, gilded gesso, gilded composition, gilded brass, die-stamped brass borders, marble, looking-glass plate; secondary woods: white pine, mahogany, ash, yellow poplar; iron

36 x 50¼ x 22½ in. (91.4 x 127.6 x 57.2 cm)

The Metropolitan Museum of Art, New York. Rogers Fund, 1953 (53.181)

NOTES: Surface analysis of this table, conducted by Mark Minor in the conservation laboratory at the Metropolitan Museum, revealed the presence of an original *vert-antique* layer under the gold leaf currently on the feet. The table is shown in the drawing room of Augustus Stuyvesant's home, to the right of the mantel-piece, in a photograph by Bernard F. Folts (The New-York Historical Society, Print Department), taken in November 1953 at the time of the auction of the furnishings of the house.

PROVENANCE: The table, which is believed to have descended in the Stuyvesant family, may have been made for Nicholas William Stuyvesant (1769–1833), who married Catherine L. Reade, 1795; probably Gerard Stuyvesant (1805–1859), who married Susan Rivington Van Horne, 1836; Augustus Van Horne Stuyvesant (1838–1918), who married Harriet LeRoy Steward, 1864; Augustus Van Horne Stuyvesant, Jr. (1870–1953), of 2 East 79th Street, New York; purchased at auction, directly from his house, by the dealers Ginsburg & Levy, 1953.

REFERENCES: Powel, 1954, ill. p. 211; Waxman, 1958, no. 30, plates XLI, XLIII (stamp); Comstock, 1962, no. 586; Pearce, 1964, figs. 4, 5 (stamp); Otto, 1965, no. 196; Tracy, 1967, p. 290, nos. 10, 11 (label), 12 (mount); Bishop, 1972, no. 461 (label); Conger, 1979, pl. V; Davidson and Stillinger, 1985, fig. 224 (detail of foot); Cooper, 1993, no. 122.

101

Square Pier Table about 1815–19

Two engraved No. 3 labels, one on the inside surface of the back rail of the upper section and the other (partial) on the backboard

Stamped four times, twice on the top surface of the front molding and once on top of each rear corner block: H. LANNUIER/NEW-YORK

Mahogany veneer, gilded gesso and *vert antique*, gilded brass, marble, looking-glass plate; secondary woods: white pine, yellow poplar, mahogany, ash

37½ x 48⅛ x 21 in. (95.3 x 122.2 x 53.3 cm)

Collection Mr. and Mrs. Peter G. Terian

NOTES: The gilding on the acanthus leaves and the *vert antique* of the lion's-paw feet have been restored, and the table is missing its original die-stamped brass borders on the aprons. The center mount has the incuse mark *CA* cast into the back.

REFERENCE: F. O. Bailey Antiquarians, Portland, Maine (July 10, 1986), lot 56.

101

102 *(see plate 21)*

Square Pier Table about 1815–19

Attributed

Burl elm, painted tôle (front columns), gilded gesso and *vert antique*, gilded composition, gilded brass, die-stamped brass borders, marble, looking-glass plate; secondary woods: white pine, yellow poplar, mahogany

35⅞ x 42 x 18⅞ in. (91.1 x 106.7 x 47.9 cm)

Collection Mr. and Mrs. Stuart P. Feld

PROVENANCE: The dealer Valdemar Jacobsen, Cold Spring Harbor, New York, 1971.

103

Square Pier Table about 1815–19

Engraved No. 3 label inside the back rail of the upper section

Mahogany and rosewood veneers, mahogany, tôle, gilded brass; secondary woods: maple, yellow poplar, white pine

36¹/₂ x 46 x 20 in. (92.7 x 116.8 x 50.8 cm)

Private collection

NOTES: The back pilasters are veneered in rosewood, while the aprons and lower shelf are veneered in mahogany. The lion's-paw feet are solid mahogany and may never have been gilded or painted *vert antique*. When the painted-tôle front columns were subjected to surface analysis in the Department of Objects Conservation at The Metropolitan Museum of Art by Marinus Manuels, they were discovered to have an original green-toned base color, which may have been intended as an imitation of bronze. The elaborate cast capitals and bases of the front columns are identical to those on catalogue number 102. At the time that this pier table was shown to Peter M. Kenny by its former owner, in 1996, it was missing its marble top, backboards, looking-glass plate, gilded-brass center ornament, and die-stamped brass border on the aprons.

104–105 *(see plates 66 and 56)*

Pair of Square Pier Tables with Canted Corners 1815–19

[104] Engraved No. 3 label on the inside surface of the back rail of the upper section

Stamped twice, once on the top of each of the stumps or blocks inside the front corners: H. LANNUIER/NEW-YORK; with a separate stamp in the same location: JACOB

[105] Stamped twice, once on the top of each of the stumps or blocks inside the front corners: H. LANNUIER/NEW-YORK

[105] Inscribed on the back side of the marble top, which is dressed: *Connelly*

Mahogany veneer, gilded gesso and *vert antique*, gilded brass, die-stamped brass borders, marble, looking-glass plate; secondary woods: white pine, yellow poplar, mahogany, maple

35¹/₄ x 48¹/₂ x 20 in. (89.5 x 123.2 x 50.8 cm)

[104] Collection Mr. and Mrs. Stuart P. Feld

[105] Collection Mr. and Mrs. Peter G. Terian

NOTES: One of the pair [104] has winged caryatids with greenish-bronze-toned bodies and the other [105] gilded ones—the result of two different approaches toward conservation. Both tables originally had a first layer of water-gilding on the smooth parts of the bodies of the winged caryatids. See Chapter Three: French Clients in the United States; for more on the conservation of these tables see Chapter Four: Carving, Gilding, and Bronzing.

PROVENANCE: By tradition, both tables originally were owned by James Leray de Chaumont (1760–1840), and were in his mansion in Jefferson County, near Watertown, New York. Leray is thought to have brought the tables with him to France when he returned there in the 1830s. Their subsequent history is related in a letter of 1992—since destroyed in a 1997 fire in the records facility of Sotheby's, New York—to Leslie Keno, of Sotheby's, from the French owner (now deceased) of table [104] (and of cat. nos. 106–107). According to the letter, Leray left his Lannuier furniture—including the pair of pier tables seen here in catalogue numbers 106–107—to his French mistress, the young actress Eugénie de Bouchart, after which the furniture descended in her family. The inventory of James Leray's estate, dated January 19, 1841 (Archives Nationales de Paris, ET/XXVI/1091), reveals that, at the time of his death, he was living with his son Vincent in Paris in an apartment in the rue de Varenne, and that his sole possessions were a wardrobe and its

contents. Leray is thought by some historians to have declared bankruptcy, but no records were located in France, nor was his will. At some point, the present pair of tables was separated. Their later history is as follows: [104] a French family, until 1988. [105] a French gentleman, a lateral descendant, until 1991.

REFERENCES: [104] Sotheby's, New York, 5755 (October 22, 1988), lot 421 (with a Mme Eugénie de la Bouceardie provenance—a possible misspelling of Bouchart); Feld and Garrett, 1991, no. 16, ill. (also details of a figure and of mounts). [105] Christie's, New York, 7214 (January 26, 1991), lot 310 (with an Armand de Balbi provenance, now thought to be incorrect); "Auction News from Christie's," January/ February 1991, ill. p. 4; Cooper, 1993, no. 125.

106–107 *(see plate 57)*

Pair of Square Pier Tables with Canted Corners 1815–19

Stamped twice, once on the top of each of the stumps or blocks inside the front corners: H. LANNUIER/NEW-YORK

Mahogany veneer, gilded gesso and *vert antique*, gilded brass, die-stamped brass borders, marble, looking-glass plate; secondary woods: mahogany, white pine [the figure of one table mahogany, by microanalysis]

$35^5/_8$ x $52^1/_8$ x $19^1/_2$ in. (90.5 x 132.4 x 49.5 cm)

Private collection

NOTES: This pair of tables underwent significant restoration before being brought to New York for sale at Sotheby's in 1992. Subsequent investigation and conservation of the tables by Robert Mussey Associates, Boston, revealed that no original gilding or *vert antique* survived on the winged figures or the feet. Regilding and rebronzing were based on the conservators' interpretation of the surface layers and materials of catalogue numbers 104–105. See Chapter Three: French Clients in the United States.

PROVENANCE: See catalogue number 104; a French family, until 1995.

REFERENCES: Sotheby's, New York, 6350 (October 25, 1992), lots 454, 455; Sotheby's, New York, 6660 (January 24, 26, 27, and 30, 1995), lots 2206, 2207.

108 *(see figure 91)*

Square Pier Table with Canted Corners 1815–19

Attributed

Rosewood veneer, gilded gesso, gilded brass, marble, looking-glass plate; secondary woods: mahogany, yellow poplar, white pine

$35^3/_4$ x $55^7/_8$ x $21^1/_2$ in. (90.8 x 141.9 x 54.6 cm)

Brooklyn Museum of Art, New York. Gift of the Pierrepont Family, 1941 (41.1)

NOTE: The unusual extensions on the back of the table, unique in Lannuier's oeuvre, suggest that it was made for a specific architectural setting.

PROVENANCE: The table probably was made for Hezekiah Beers Pierrepont (1768–1838), a merchant, landowner, and the proprietor of a large distillery in Brooklyn Heights, New York, who married Anna Constable (1783–1859), a daughter of the New York land speculator William Constable, 1802; believed to have descended in the Pierrepont (also spelled Pierpont) family.

REFERENCES: Downs, 1943 a, fig. 3; Downs, 1943 b, no. 49; Ralston, 1950, fig. 6; Waxman, 1958, no. 33, pl. XLVI; Comstock, 1962, no. 587; Tracy, 1963, no. 10; Otto, 1965, no. 194; Peirce, 1979, pl. VIII.

109 *(see figure 92)*

Square Pier Table with Canted Corners about 1815–19

Attributed

Rosewood veneer, gilded gesso and *vert antique*, gilded composition, die-stamped brass inlays, marble, looking-glass plate; secondary woods: mahogany, white pine

$34^1/_8$ x $42^1/_2$ x $20^1/_8$ in. (86.7 x 108 x 51.1 cm)

The Detroit Institute of Arts. Founders Society Purchase, Robert H. Tannahill Foundation Fund (1989.1)

NOTES: Extra pieces of wood originally were attached to the underside of the dolphins' jaws, as on catalogue number 112. This table is shown with these pieces of wood still intact in *Antiques*, September 1985. Subsequent restoration by the dealer who sold the table to The Detroit Institute of Arts, Peter Hill, resulted in the removal of the lower jaw of the dolphins and the bases of the plinths under the back columns.

PROVENANCE: Doris M. Uppercue, Washington, D.C., who is thought to have acquired the table from Elsie Cobb Wilson of Washington, in the 1920s; Doris M. Uppercue estate, until 1985; the dealer Peter Hill, East Lempster, New Hampshire, until 1987.

REFERENCES: *Antiques*, September 1985, p. 333 (advertised by C. G. Sloan & Co., Inc.); C. G. Sloan & Co., Washington, D.C., 779 (October 25–27, 1985), lot 1860; *Bulletin of the Detroit Institute of Arts*, no. 2/3 (1989), p. 7, fig. 4.

110–111

Pair of Square Pier Tables about 1815–19

Attributed

Mahogany veneer, gilded gesso, gilded brass, die-stamped brass borders, marble, looking-glass plate; secondary woods: maple, mahogany, yellow poplar, ash

38¹/₈ x 53³/₄ x 16⁷/₈ in. (96.8 x 136.5 x 42.9 cm)

Museum of the City of New York. Gift of Mrs. Edmund W. Peaslee (54.207.1,2ab)

NOTES: Examination of these tables revealed that at some point they were reduced in length and their central arches possibly were added. Clear evidence that the tables were cut down also exists on the undersides of the original marble tops, where staining and oxidation marks are evident from the originally wider braces, set front to back on the upper frame, as are signs of recutting and of the later dressing of the ends.

PROVENANCE: By tradition, made for Nathaniel Prime (1768–1840), the New York merchant, who resided at 1 Broadway, 1810–31, and is also believed to be the original owner of a suite of curule seating furniture attributed to Duncan Phyfe, now at the Boscobel Restoration, Garrison-on-Hudson, New York; descended in the Prime family to the donor.

REFERENCES: "Special Events," 1954; Miller, 1956, no. 126; Waxman, 1958, no. 34, pl. XLVII; Otto, 1965, no. 196.

112 (see plate 38 and figure 97)

Square Pier Table with Canted Corners
about 1815–19

Three engraved No. 3 labels, one on the underside of the plinth and (remnants) on the inner and the outer surface of the back rail of the upper section

Rosewood veneer, gilded gesso and *vert antique*, gilded composition, gilded brass, die-stamped brass borders, marble, looking-glass plate; secondary woods: white pine, maple, yellow poplar, ash [basswood (the breasts of the swans), mahogany (the bases of the swans, lower jaw of the dolphin, and the scrolls beneath the plinth), beech (the dolphins), by microanalysis]

35 x 48 x 20 in. (88.9 x 121.9 x 50.8 cm)

The Metropolitan Museum of Art, New York. Friends of the American Wing Fund, 1968 (68.43)

NOTE: Possibly originally *en suite* with catalogue numbers 83–84.

PROVENANCE: See catalogue number 83. Edith Wetmore; her estate; Ginsburg & Levy, New York, 1967.

REFERENCES: Coleman Auction Galleries, Inc., New York (March 22–23, 1967), lot 376; "Bicentennial Treasury," 1975–76, no. 41; Davidson, 1980, fig. 104; Reese, 1983, ill. p. 138; Davidson and Stillinger, 1985, figs. 88, 222 (swan support); Peck, 1996, pp. 219, 222, colorpl. p. 218.

113 (see plate 52)

Square Pier Table with Canted Corners
1817

Engraved No. 3 label on the inside surface of the back rail of the upper section

Mahogany veneer, gilded gesso and *vert antique*, gilded composition, gilded brass, die-stamped brass borders, marble, looking-glass plate; secondary woods: white pine, mahogany, maple [yellow poplar, by microanalysis]

35⁵/₈ x 40³/₄ x 19¹/₈ in. (90.5 x 103.5 x 48.6 cm)

Albany Institute of History & Art, New York. Gift of Stephen Van Rensselaer Crosby (1957.70.9)

NOTES: Probably the pier table listed in a June 19, 1817, invoice to William Bayard with delivery to "P. D. Campell [*sic*]" (see Appendix 5). See Chapter Three: The Bayard-Van Rensselaer-Campbell Commissions.

PROVENANCE: See catalogue numbers 70–71, 123.

REFERENCES: Waxman, 1958, no. 32, pl. XLV; Comstock, 1962, no. 585; Rice, 1962, ill. p. 33 (also detail of mount); Pearce, 1964, ill. p. 712 (mount), fig. 8.

110

114 (*see plate 69*)

Square Pier Table with Canted Corners
1817 (reconfigured into a pair of encoignures
probably after 1840)

Engraved No. 3 label on the inner surface of a
rear rail of encoignure (1960.17.2)

Mahogany veneer, mahogany, gilded gesso and
vert antique, gilded brass, die-stamped brass
borders, marble, looking-glass plate; secondary
woods: [mahogany, white pine, yellow poplar,
maple, by microanalysis]

35^5/$_8$ x 19^7/$_8$ x 19^7/$_8$ in. (90.5 x 50.5 x 50.5 cm)

Albany Institute of History & Art, New York.
Gift of Mrs. Roger F. Hooper (Justine Van
Rensselaer Barber) (1960.17.1,2)

NOTES: This pier table was reconfigured into a
pair of encoignures probably after 1840, when
Stephen and Harriet Van Rensselaer moved
into the Van Rensselaer Manor House (the
encoignures are shown positioned as a pier table
in plate 69); the central ornament was removed
and the table was cut through the middle. Holes
from the spikes that secured the central
ornament to the front apron are still visible,
and the front foot of each encoignure has
unbalanced returns under the plinth that match
those on the feet of the pier table in catalogue
number 113. The plinths are replacements, and
the three back columns and tapered, turned feet
are additions. The original back rail was cut and
reused for the same purpose on the encoignures:
Each retains one piece. The original marble top,
however, apparently was discarded. Overall, the
reconfiguration was sensitively done, probably by
an Albany cabinetmaker. Further research may
reveal documented Albany classical furniture
with similarly turned feet and columns. See
Chapter Three: The Bayard-Van Rensselaer-
Campbell Commissions.

PROVENANCE: See catalogue numbers 72–73;
Justine Van Rensselaer Barber Hooper, a great-
granddaughter of Stephen Van Rensselaer IV.

REFERENCES: Rice, 1962, ill. p. 34; Pearce,
1964, fig. 9; Cooper, 1980 a, no. 305.

115 (*see plate 34*)

Center Table (Gueridon) 1812–15

Outline and fragment of printed No. 2 label on
the inside of the rail

Mahogany veneer, gilded gesso and *vert antique*,
gilded brass, die-stamped brass borders, marble;
secondary woods: mahogany, white pine; iron

Height, 29^1/$_2$ in. (74.9 cm); diameter, 45^3/$_8$ in.
(115.3 cm)

Collection Mr. and Mrs. Stuart P. Feld

NOTES: Surface analysis of the winged caryatids
revealed the presence of multiple layers of
restoration gilding over the original water-gilding
and Lannuier's characteristic brownish red bole.
All later gilding was removed, the first gilding
stabilized, and ingilding and regilding applied
to match the original decorative scheme of mat
and burnished surfaces. The surfaces of the
vasiform central shaft and the dolphin feet also
were analyzed and discovered to have been
bronzed in parts before they were gilded.
Analysis of the gilding and bronzing was
conducted by Mark Minor, independent
conservator, and by Marinus Manuels of the
Department of Objects Conservation at The
Metropolitan Museum of Art; gilding
conservation was carried out by Pascale Patris,
also of the Metropolitan Museum's Department
of Objects Conservation, in the summer and fall
of 1997.

PROVENANCE: Jacob Dana, Hillsborough,
California, until 1975.

REFERENCES: Cooper, 1980 a, pl. 48; Cooper,
1980 b, pl. XII.

116 (*see plate 10*)

Small Center Table (Gueridon)
about 1810

Printed No. 2 label on the underside of the
sub top

Mahogany, and mahogany, rosewood,
satinwood, and possibly sycamore veneers, *vert
antique*, gilded brass, marble; secondary woods:
yellow poplar, white pine, mahogany

Height, 29^3/$_4$ in (75.6 cm); diameter, 26 in.
(66 cm)

The White House, Washington, D.C. Gift of Mr.
and Mrs. C. Douglas Dillon (961.33.2)

NOTES: When the bronze busts at the top of the
legs were conserved by Robert Mussey
Associates, Boston, the original gilding was
discovered on the necklaces. The table originally
had casters.

PROVENANCE: The table may have descended
in the Livingston family. John Robert Livingston
(1754–1851), the possible first owner of the table,
married Eliza McEvers in 1789 and built the
Hudson River mansion Massena in Barrytown,
New York, in 1797; their son Robert Mont-
gomery Livingston (1790–1838), who also could
have been the table's first owner, married Sarah
Barclay Bache; possibly their son Charles
Octavius Livingston (1831–1914), who married
Sarah E. Ramsey (b. 1847); their son Charles
Victor Livingston (1873–1954), who married
Nellie K. Hasbrouck (d. 1961); purchased from
the estate of Mrs. Charles Victor Livingston,
Ulster Township, New York, by the Kingston,
New York, dealer Eugene Brossard, 1961.

REFERENCES: Pearce, 1962, p. 96, ills.
frontispiece, p. 3 (detail of marble top); Pearce,
1962 a, ill. p. 519; Tracy, 1976, p. 12, ill. p. 13;
Conger, 1976, pp. 6, 7, ill.; Conger, 1979, plates
XXXIV, XXXV; Cortesi and Harrell, 1982, ill. p.
52; Sack, 1986, vol. 8, ill. p. 2316.

117 *(see plate 16)*

Table 1804

Printed No. 1 label on the outer surface of the board that seals the bottom of the upper frame

Inscribed in chalk on the inner surface of the same bottom board: HL/fait a New-York/le 26 Decembre/1804

Inscribed in ink on the inner surface of the same bottom board: [illegible]/1884./Lofft

Mahogany, brass, marble, light-wood inlays; secondary wood: yellow poplar

29¼ x 28½ x 28½ in. (74.3 x 72.4 x 72.4 cm)

Morristown National Historical Park, New Jersey, on loan to the Brooklyn Museum of Art, New York (L82.58.1a)

PROVENANCE: By tradition, originally made for Commodore Richard Valentine Morris (1768–1815), who married Anne Walton in 1797; from 1802–3, commander of a United States naval squadron in the southern Mediterranean, where and when he may have collected the marble specimens set into the tabletop (Waxman, 1958, p. 177); the dealer Charles W. Lyon, New York, 1940; location unknown, 1940–52; given by Mrs. Constance M. Bainbridge and Mrs. V. G. Garverick to the Morristown National Historical Park, 1952.

REFERENCES: *American Collector*, April 1940, p. 1 (advertised by C. W. Lyon, Inc., New York); Waxman, 1958, no. 26, plates XXXV, XXXVI (label); Gaines, 1959, ill. p. 145.

118 *(see plate 68)*

Stand with Marble Inset 1810–15

Printed No. 2 label on the underside of the sub top

Mahogany, mahogany veneer, marble; secondary woods: white pine, yellow poplar, mahogany, maple

28¼ x 23¾ x 16¼ in. (71.8 x 60.3 x 41.3 cm)

The White House, Washington, D.C. Gift of the White House Historical Association (973.965.1)

NOTE: The present casters appear to be replacements.

PROVENANCE: By tradition, the table descended in the family of Rufus King (1755–1827), a statesman, diplomat, and, in 1816, the last Federalist presidential candidate; see catalogue number 46 for the line of descent; Berry B. Tracy.

REFERENCES: Conger, 1979, pl. II; Cooper, 1980 a, fig. 304.

119 *(see plate 7)*

Occasional Table 1803–5

Printed No. 1 label on the outer surface of the bottom board of the top section

Satinwood and exotic hardwood veneers, possibly holly inlays; secondary woods: white pine, yellow poplar, mahogany

31⅛ x 17⅝ x 12⅝ in. (79.1 x 44.8 x 32.1 cm)

Winterthur Museum, Delaware. Gift of Henry Francis du Pont (53.67)

REFERENCES: Waxman, 1957, ill. p. 143; Waxman, 1958, no. 25, pl. XXXIV; Montgomery, 1966, no. 394, ill. p. 476 (label).

120 *(see plate 11)*

Gaming Table (Trictrac Table) 1804–10

Printed No. 2 label on the inside surface of the bottom of one drawer

Stamped on the top front edge of the drawer that bears the label: H. LANNUIER/NEW-YORK

Inscribed in script on the inside of the apron of a table end: E F Hagen 213 East 26 st./New York/June 15, 1922

Mahogany, mahogany veneer, natural and dyed light-wood veneers (possibly holly), ivory (peg holders in the top edge of the rails surrounding the backgammon well); secondary woods: yellow poplar, white pine

29³/₈ x 42¹/₄ x 21⁷/₈ in. (74.6 x 107.3 x 55.6 cm)

Museum of the City of New York. Gift of Mrs. Harry Horton Benkard (34.400.1ab)

NOTES: The table has a separate top of solid mahogany with an old and probably original padded green wool covering on one surface. The sliding, combination chessboard and checkerboard is inlaid on both surfaces. The drawer pulls are replacements.

PROVENANCE: Believed to have descended in the Benkard family; Mrs. Harry Horton Benkard.

REFERENCES: Cornelius, 1922, pl. XXI (attributed to Phyfe); Ormsbee, 1935, ill. p. 8; McClelland, 1939, pl. 173; Waxman, 1958, no. 23, pl. XXXII; Pearce, 1964, fig. 10; E. Jones, 1977, fig. 2.

121 *(see plate 32)*

Pembroke Table 1805–10

Printed No. 2 label, with nearly all writing obliterated, in the center of the drawer bottom

Mahogany, mahogany veneer, brass; secondary woods: yellow poplar, white pine, cherry

28¹/₂ x 37 x 24 in. (72.4 x 94 x 61 cm) [with leaves dropped]

Private collection

NOTES: The stamped-brass lion's-mask pulls on the drawer and on the *faux* drawer at the opposite end are replacements for a pull that originally had a fairly large, circular backplate and a single threaded shaft. The pendant drops at the corners of the frame are integral to the rectangular blocks above. The board to which the carved and turned columns are connected, at the upper frame, has been rasped and filed to create softly rounded contours along its edges, and all four of its corners are cut out in a circular, hollow shape.

PROVENANCE: Edward V. Jones, Albany, Georgia.

REFERENCE: E. Jones, 1977, fig. 12.

122 *(see figure 20)*

Dining Table 1815–19

Stamped four times on the upper surfaces of the lopers: H. LANNUIER/NEW-YORK

Mahogany, mahogany veneer; secondary woods: white pine, ash

29¹/₂ x 59 x 59³/₄ in. (74.9 x 149.9 x 151.8 cm) [without leaves]

Winterthur Museum, Delaware (71.6)

NOTES: The table retains two leaves, but only the wider one is thought to be original. The double beading on the edge of the apron may be a replacement or the core for a brass molding.

PROVENANCE: By tradition, the table belonged to John MacPherson Berrien (1781–1856), the distinguished Savannah attorney, who also served as United States Senator and as Attorney General during President Andrew Jackson's administration; descended in Berrien's family to Mrs. Helen W. Littledale, Webster Groves, Missouri.

REFERENCE: J. Smith and Hummel, 1978, ill. p. 1300, p. 1301.

123 *(see plate 70)*

Worktable 1817

Engraved No. 3 label on the inside surface of the bottom of the drawer

Mahogany, maple and rosewood veneers, gilded gesso, gilded brass, die-stamped brass borders; secondary woods: mahogany, white pine, yellow poplar

30⅝ x 22 x 17⅛ in. (77.8 x 55.9 x 43.5 cm)

Winterthur Museum, Delaware. Gift of Henry Francis du Pont (60.6)

NOTES: Probably the worktable listed in a June 19, 1817, invoice to William Bayard with delivery to "P. D. Campell [*sic*]" (see Appendix 5). The label in the drawer has been cut to a precise silhouette, as on the pair of card tables in catalogue numbers 55–56 and on the single card table in catalogue number 65. Originally, there may have been a looking-glass plate under the top. The table is missing its original casters. A nearly identical worktable in the furniture collection of the Winterthur Museum appears to be an authentic period copy of this Lannuier design. See Chapter Three: Bayard-Van Rensselaer-Campbell Commissions.

PROVENANCE: See catalogue numbers 70–71, 113; estate of Mrs. Stephen Van Rensselaer Crosby; Ginsburg & Levy, New York, by 1958–60.

REFERENCES: Waxman, 1958, no. 37, pl. L; Pearce, 1964, fig. 11; Kaye, 1987, pp. 182–83, fig. 205 (Kaye pronounces the worktable a fake, but subsequent examination has proven it to be authentic).

124 *(see plate 71)*

Worktable 1815–19

Attributed

Inscribed in pencil on the inside surface of the lid: M OConnell / Canal Street / New York / [illegible]

Mahogany, mahogany veneer, gilded brass; secondary woods: mahogany, white pine, yellow poplar

32¼ x 23¾ x 17⅝ in. (81.9 x 60.3 x 44.8 cm)

Private collection

NOTES: There are traces of silvering from a looking-glass plate, visible on the wood under the lift lid, which would have been used when dressing and also as a source of reflected light. On the inside of the table is an adjustable writing surface. When the table underwent conservation by Olaf Unsoeld in 1996, it was discovered that neither the gilded-brass corner ornaments nor the pulls were original (see Christie's, New York, 8238, October 21, 1995); as evidence of the original pulls had been obliterated, the decision was made to forgo them altogether, as on catalogue number 123. The keyhole escutcheon and the lock are original, however, and the key may have been the only means by which the drawer was pulled out. The central ornament also appears to be original; its surface was tested in the Metropolitan Museum's Department of Objects Conservation and was found to contain both gold and traces of mercury, evidence of the original mercury gilding.

PROVENANCE: Richard and Gloria Manney, 1984–95.

REFERENCES: Sotheby's, New York, 5142 (January 26 and 28, 1984), lot 765; Sotheby's, New York, 6613 (October 23, 1994), lot 381, ill. (also detail of lyre); Christie's, New York, 8238 (October 21, 1995), lot 229.

125 *(see plate 64)*

Looking Glass 1816–19

Attributed

Mahogany, gilded composition, gilded brass, die-stamped brass borders; secondary woods: white pine, yellow poplar

49¾ x 73⅞ x 6¼ in. (126.4 x 187.6 x 15.9 cm)

New York State Office of Parks, Recreation and Historic Preservation, Clermont State Historic Site, Germantown, New York (CL.1974.14)

NOTES: The incuse mark *CA* is cast into the back of one of the gilded cast-brass wreaths on the frieze. A section of wood was removed from the back of the top of the frame, perhaps so that the looking glass could be fitted to a particular location. For more on the history of this looking glass see Chapter Three: Public Commissions.

PROVENANCE: The history of the looking glass is related in a letter dated September 21, 1981 (in the files at Clermont, the Livingston family home), which states that it came from a steamboat that belonged to the North River Steamboat Company, a partnership of Robert Fulton and Robert Livingston; was acquired by the Red Hook Hotel, Red Hook, New York; and subsequently was owned by the Livingston family.

P.M.K. and F.F.B.

APPENDIX, BIBLIOGRAPHY,
INDEX, AND PHOTOGRAPH CREDITS

New york Febuary 23 — 1805

Mr. Wᵐ Bayard

Dr to h. Lannuier French Cabinet Maker Broad St Nᵒ 60

For one Mahogany Bed sted _ _ _ _ $ 30 _

Recived Payements in full
honoré
Lannuier

H. Lannuier, Mahogany chairs etc. for Common Council room approved by chairm. of Committee $409, July 6, 1812.

The Honor —

April 15, 1812

To 24 mahogany arm chairs $14 —

" a mahogany for ——

" six Windsor chairs

Repairing

and 17

John H. Sickles   The above account

is correct

Nich Fish

Chairman

Committee

Common Council

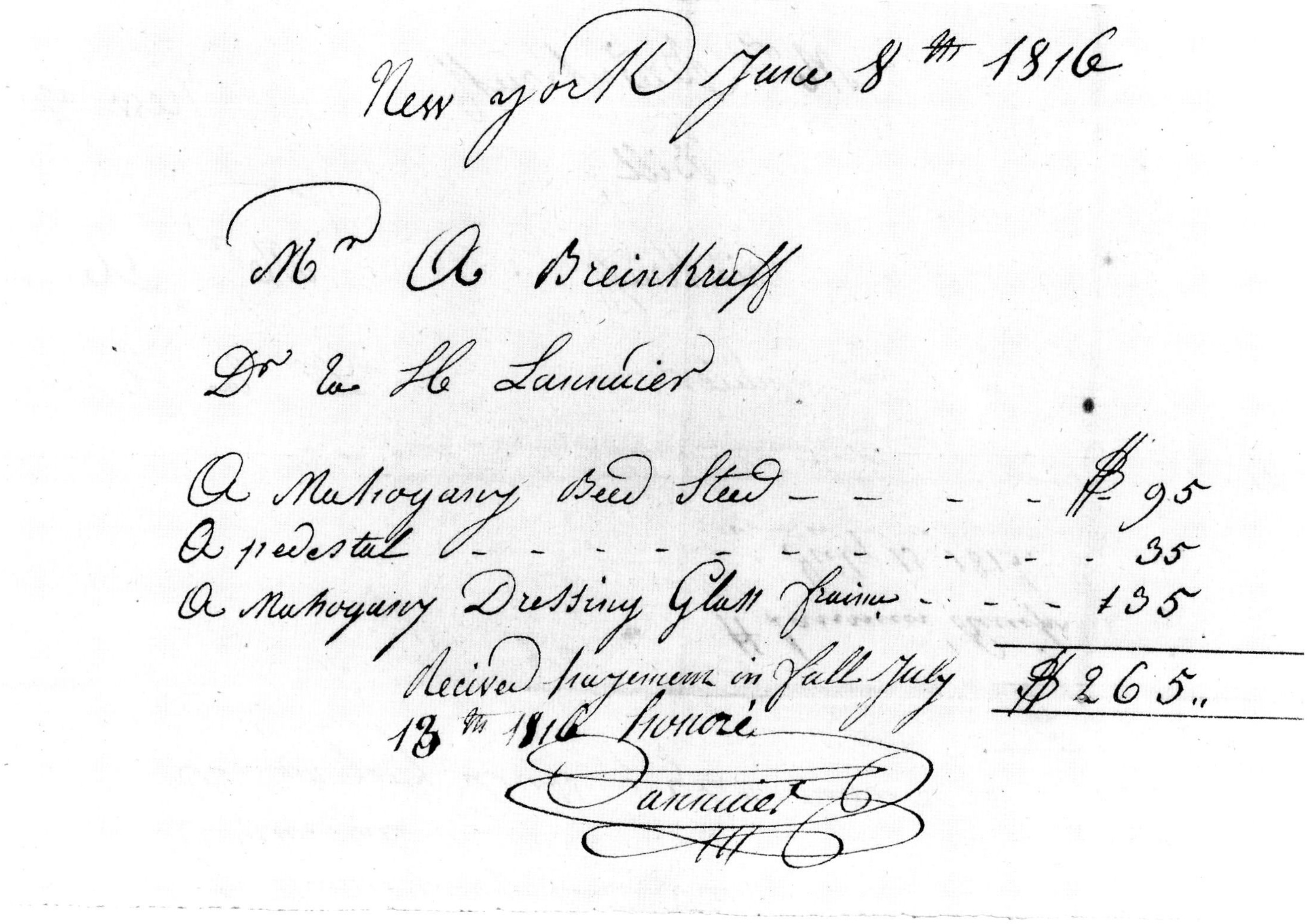

New York June 8th 1816

Mr A Breinkruff

Dr to H Lannuier

A Mahogany Bed Stead — — — — —	$ 95
A pedestal — — — — — — —	35
A Mahogany Dressing Glass frame — — —	135
Recived payement in full July	$265.

13th 1816 honoré

Lannuier

New york August 17th 1816

Mr Brinckhoff

Dr to H Lannuier

A Mahogany Crebe . — — — — — — $42

Recived frayement in full
September 25th 1816 honoré

Lannuier

New York June 19th 1817.

W. Bayard Esqr

Dr to H. Lannuier, for fournitures Delivered
to Mr P. D. Campbell, Broad Way.

A Mahogany pier table _ _ _ _ _ _ $ 300

A Pair of Carn table _ _ _ _ _ _ _ 250

A York table _ _ _ _ _ _ _ _ _ 85

Repairing a pier table Gilt figure and
ornement in the frame _ _ _ _ _ _ _ 15

$ 650 „ o

Red Sept 25 On Acd of the Above
Six Hundred Dollars _____ honoré
Lannuier

THIS INDENTURE

WITNESSETH, That *François Chailleau aged fifteen years*

Hath put himself, and by these Presents, with the consent and approbation of two of the Aldermen of the City of New-York, and of the Commissioners of the Alms-House of the said City, doth voluntarily, and of his own free will and accord, put himself Apprentice to *Honore Lannuier* to learn the Art, Trade and Mystery of *a Cabinet maker* and after the manner of an Apprentice to serve from the day of the date hereof, for and during, the full end and term of *Six years* next ensuing: During all which time, the said Apprentice his Master faithfully shall serve, his secrets keep, his lawful commands every where readily obey: He shall do no damage to his said Master, nor see it done by others, without letting or giving notice thereof to his said Master: He shall not waste his said Master's goods, nor lend them unlawfully to any: He shall not commit fornication, nor contract matrimony within the said term: at cards, dice, or any other unlawful game he shall not play, whereby his said Master may have damage: with his own goods, nor the goods of others, without licence from his said Master, he shall neither buy nor sell: He shall not absent himself day nor night from his said Master's service, without his leave; nor haunt ale-houses, taverns, nor play-houses; but in all things behave himself as a faithful Apprentice ought to do, during the said term. And the said Master shall use the utmost of his endeavour to teach, or cause to be taught or instructed, the said Apprentice, in the Trade or Mystery of *a Cabinet maker* And procure and provide for him sufficient meat, drink, apparel, lodging, and washing, fitting for an apprentice, during the said term of *Six years teach him to read write and cypher to the Rule of Three, give him a suit of new cloathes and a new Bible at the expiration of the Term*

AND for the true performance of all and singular the Covenants and Agreements aforesaid, the said parties bind themselves each unto the other firmly by these Presents. IN WITNESS whereof, the said parties have interchangably set their hands and seals hereunto. Dated the *Twenty sixth* day of *July* in the *Thirty fourth* year of the Independence of the United States of America, and in the year of our Lord One Thousand Eight Hundred and *nine*.

Sealed and Delivered
in the Presence of

John H. Sickels

Jno. J. Westervelt

Honoré Lannuier

Consulat Général de france à New-york

Du Douze Octobre Mil huit Cent quatorze

Acte de Mariage de Sieur Charles honoré <u>Lannuier</u>,—Ebéniste demeurant en Cette Ville de New-york Broad Street N.º 60 natif du Canton de Chantilly, Département de Loise le Vingt Sept Juin Mil Sept Cent Soixante dix neuf, fils légitime de Sieur Michel Serille Lannuier et de Marie Genevieve Malice Lannuier Ses Pere et Mere tous deux décédés; D'une Part:

Et de D.^{lle} Thereze <u>Baptist</u> née à New-york le Cinq Mai Mil Sept Cent quatre vingt Sept, fille de M.ʳ Jean, Baptist, et Suzanne Piquet, Ses pere et Mere, tous deux décédés; la dite Demoiselle demeurante en Cette Ville Broad Street-N.º 60; D'autre part. _____

Les actes préliminaires Extraits du Registre des actes de la chancellerie du Consulat Général et Coté **I**; sont l'acte de promesse de mariage des futurs Epoux et le Certificat du Chancelier en marge de lad. promesse de mariage; le quel Certificat en datte de Ce Jour atteste que le Susdit acte a eté par lui affiché dans le lieu le plus apparent de la chancellerie et par Extrait, pour Servir de publication dudit mariage et qu'il n'est Survenû aucune Opposition à la prononciation d'icelui.

Des quels actes en bonne forme il a été donné Lecture aux termes de la loi ainsi que des articles du Chapitre **VI** du Code Civil des français Concernant les droits et les devoirs respectifs des Epoux par M. Jean Baptiste Anne Marie Lombart chancelier du Consulat Général.

Les dits futurs Epoux ont déclaré prendre en mariage, l'un;

D.^{lle} Thereze Baptist et Celle ci;

S.ʳ Charles honoré Lannuier;

En la présence de Messieurs Moyse Seixas Pere; francois Caille, Joseph Lopèz Dias; Et Jean Juhel

_____

Tous quatre majeurs demeurants chacun séparement en Cette dite Ville de New-york.

Sur quoi Nom Baron Lescallier, l'un des Commandants de la Légion d'honneur, Consul Général de France aux Etats-Unis d'Amérique, remplissant à New-york les fonctions attribuées à l'officier de l'Etat Civil des français et assisté du d. Sieur Lombart notre Chancelier; avons prononcé au nom de la Loi que les dits Sieur Charles honoré Lannuier et la D.^{lle} Therèze Baptist, sont unis en Mariage.

Et à l'instant les dits Epoux nous ont déclaré que le huit May Mil huit Cent Cinq, ils Se Sont unis en Mariage par devant un Ministre du Culte catholique Romain en Cette dite Ville de New-york, parcequ'ils ignoraient alors que les Consuls de France, avaient dans les paÿs Etrangers, le pouvoir de remplir les fonctions attribuées à l'officier chaÌrgé de Constater l'Etat Civil des français, ainsi qu'ils en ont été informés depuis peu detems: que C,'est pour cette Cause qu'ils s'empressent d'obeir à la Loi a cet egard. _____

Déclarent encore les dits Epoux que de leur Mariage sus relaté sont issus les trois enfans nés en Cette dite Ville de New-york et Ci après nommés, savoir: _____

Moyse Stanislas, Garçon né le Vingt huit Juillet Mil huit Cent Six: _____

Sophie, fille, née le Sept Mars Mil huit Cent Dix:

Et Louis Theophilus, autre Garçon né le Vingt Cinq Avril Mil huit Cent treize: _____

Lesquels trois Enfants, les dits Epoux nous ont présentés et nous ont dit qu'ils les reconnaissent pour être leurs propres enfants, les appellants Comme tels á leurs futures Successions.

Desquelles Declaration et Reconnaissance d'Enfants, les dits Epoux nous ont requis acte que nous leur avons Octroyé; Dont acte: Et ont les dits Epoux, les quatre temoins susnommés et le dit Sieur Lombart Signé avec nous Consul Général susdit Ces présenter.

honoré Lannuier, Therese Lannuie*r*, Moses Seixas, John Juhel, J.^h Lopes Dias, f.ʳ Caille, Lombart, Lescallier

Je, Soussigne Charles Honoré Lannuier, fils legitimé de Michel Cerille Lannuier & de Genevieve Mulice, mes Pere & Mere; né à Chantilly, Canton de Senlis, Departement de Loyse, en France, residant actuellement à New York dans les Etats unis d'Amerique; jouissant de mon entiere liberte & de tout l'usage de ma raison et desirant de disposer des biens qu'il a plu a Dieu de me donner & qu'il lui plaira encore de me donner avant mon décès, fais aujourd'hui mon Testament comme suit, savoir <u>J</u>e donne et legue à mon Epouse Therese Baptist actuellement à New York, tous les meubles Linge, argenterie, livres & tous autres objets portatifs que je laisserai a mon deces & qui forment entierement mon menage & ameublement de plus je donne et legue à ma dite Epouse apres mon décès & jusqu a sa mort naturelle la jouissance de tous les biens immeubles que je pourrai laisser, de même que le Produit de tout ce qui formera alors mon actif net, indepéndamment des effets formant mon menage & ameublement à elle légués en toute proprieté, comme il est deja dit et attendu que J'ai dernierement vendu divers objets fesant partie de mon ameublement, Je veux et j'ordonne que ma dite Epouse ait le droit de remplacer les dits objets en fesant son choix parmi ceux qui se trouveront invendues dans mon magasin. Les legs mentionnés ci dessus sont fait aux Conditions. 1° que ma dite Epouse pourvoira à l'education, nourriture & entretien de nos enfans selon les moyens que je lui laisserai apres mon décès jusqu'a l'age ou chacun d'eux aura atteint respectivement sa majorité d'apres les loix de l'etat de New York 2° Que dans le cas ou elle convolerait en secondes noces, elle ne pourra avoir et retirer de ma succession qu'une part d'Enfant, c'est à dire qu'elle partagera par egale portion avec nos enfans & que cette part ou portion lui sera alors acquise en toute proprieté avec droit d'en jouir et disposer selon sa volonté, bien entendu que cette condition ne deroge en rien au droit de mon Epouse sur la donnation que Je lui ai faite des meubles & de tous autres effets de mon menage & ameublement comme il est dit plus haut. 3° Qu'elle ne pourra en aucun cas aliener les sus dits immeubles & net produit de mon actif ou aucune portion quelconque d'i' ceux. 4° Que le dit Produit net de mon actif sera par elle employé en l'achat d'un immeuble ou immeubles dans l'année qui suivra mon décès ou plutôt si cela se peut. 5° Que mon Epouse ne sera tenue de fournir à l'education nourriture & entretien de notre fille que j'usques a l'epoque ou celle ci se marriera, si son marriage avait lieu avant qu'elle ne fut parvenue à sa majorité, et dans le cas ou notre dite fille ne se marrierait pas apres avoir acquis le dit age, J'entends & veux que mon Epouse continue de pourvoir à sa nourriture & entretien tout comme elle serait tenue de la faire si notre dite fille etait encore non majeure. Si nos enfans decedaient avant ma dite Epouse, leur mère, Je veux & J'entends qu'au décès de celle ci tous les biens immeubles laisses par elle et dont elle aurait eu la Jouissance aux termes du present testament, aillent par droit d'heritier & par portions egales à ma demi Soeur, issue du second marriage de mon père & à mes <u>neveux</u> & nieces dont les noms suivent, savoir, 1° a Sophie Lannuier fille legitime de Nicholas Lannuier, mon frere; 2° a Jean & Auguste, tous deux fils legitimes de Maximilian Cerille Auguste Lannuier mon frere; 3° aux enfans de Victor Lannuier mon frere demeurant à Gand; 4° a Elisa Veincent fille de Jaine Baptist, Soeur de mon Epouse; 5° à Francis Veincent; 6° à Pierre Veincent, tous trois enfans legitimes de Peter Veincent & de Jaine Baptist leurs Père & Mère; 7° à Mark Year fils de Robert Year & de Jaine Baptist remarriée en secondes noces qui en jouiront en toute proprieté & en qualité de mes legitimes legalaires. Au cas ou ma dite Epouse decederait avant nos Enfans, J'entends & J'ordonne que tous les biens immeubles par moi laissés & dont elle aura eu la Jouissance, ainsi qu'il est déjà dit deviendront et seront la proprieté de nos enfans ou de ceux d'entre eux qui seraient alors vivants & dans cette hypothese, Je veux & ordonne de plus que si nos dits enfans etaient alors au dessous de leur majorite, il leur soit donné deux tuteurs de confiance qui administreront les dits biens immeubles au profit de nos dits enfans jusqu'à l'age ou ils auront atteint leur majorite, & qu'il leur soit donné à chacun d'eux aussi tôt qu'ils seront majeurs respectivement ce qui leur reviendra pour leur part à ma succession Et pour l'execution du present testament, Je nomme Messieurs John M J Labatut & Joseph Lopes Dias tous deux residants en cette ville, & Thérèse Baptist mon epouse; si l'un deux venait à déceder les deux survivants en nommeraient de concert un autre, leur recommandant de la manière la plus particuliére de vouloir bien faire tout ce qui sera en leur pouvoir pour exécuter & faire exécuter toutes les clauses & conditions du present Testament. telles sont mes volontés: fait a New York ce treize d'Octobre de l'an de notre Seigneur mille huit cent dix neuf.

Signé, Scellé & publié par le Testateur pour etre son dernier Testament en presence de nous, qui à sa requisition, avons mis notre signature en sa presence & en celle de chacun de nous. New York, le jour, mois & an que dessus.

Honoré Lannuier

Temoins Gruez. Wm H. Walsh. Thos H. Powell.

I the undersigned Charles Honore Lannuier legitimate son of Michael Cerille Lannuier and Genevieve Mulice my father and Mother born at Chantilly Canton of Senlis Department of the Oise, in France now residing at New York in the United States of America enjoying perfect freedom and the full use of my reason, and <u>desiring to</u> dispose of the property which it has pleased God to give me and which it may also please him to give me before my decease do make this day my last Will as follows to wit I give and bequeath to my wife Therese Baptist now at New York all the furniture linen plate books and all other portable articles which I shall leave at my decease and which compose the whole of my household Goods and furniture. I also give and bequeath to my said wife after my decease and until her natural death the possession or enjoyment of all the real estate that I may leave, and likewise the product of every thing that shall then compose my net Capital independently of the articles composing my household goods and furniture bequeathed to her in full property as aforesaid and considering that I have recently sold sundry articles making part of my furniture I will and direct that my said wife have the right of replacing the said Articles by making her choice among those that shall be unsold in my warehouse the legacies above mentioned are made on Condition 1st That my said wife shall provide for the education nurture and maintenance of our children according to the means that I shall leave to her from the time of my decease until each of them shall have respectively attained full age according to the laws of the State of New York 2^d That in case she shall marry again she shall have and take from my estate only a Childs part that is to say that she shall share equally with our Children and that that part or share shall then belong to her in full property with right to enjoy and dispose of it at her pleasure provided however that this Condition is in no wise to effect the rights of my wife in respect to the gift that I have made to her of the furniture and of all the other articles of housekeeping as above mentioned 3^d that she can in no case alienate the above mentioned real estate and net product of my Capital or any part whatsoever of the same. 4th that the said Net product of my Capital shall be by her employed in the purchase of a real estate or estates within the year next ensuing my decease or sooner if practicable. 5th that my wife shall be obliged to provide for the education nurture and maintenance of our daughter <u>only</u> until the time of her marriage, if she shall marry before she arrives at full age and in case our said daughter shall not marry after having attained that age I will and direct that my wife continue to provide for her support and maintenance in the same manner as she would be bound to do if our said daughter were still underage. If our Children should die before my said wife their mother I will and direct that on her decease all the real estate left by her and of which she shall have had the possession agreeably to this Will shall go by right of inheritance and in equal shares to my half sister, issue of the second marriage of my father and to my nephews and nieces whose names are as follows to wit. 1st to Sophie Lannuier legitimate daughter of Nicholas Lannuier my brother. 2^d to Jean and Auguste both legitimate sons of Maximilien Cerille Auguste Lannuier my brother. 3^d to the Children of Victor Lannuier my brother residing at Ghent. 4th to Eliza Veincent daughter of Jaine Baptist my wifes sister. 5th to Francis Veincent 6th to Pierre

Veincent all three legitimate children of Peter Veincent and Jaine Baptist their father and Mother. 7th to Mark Year son of Robert Year and Jaine Baptist by her second marriage who shall enjoy the same in full property and as my lawful legatees. In case my said wife shall die before our Children I will and direct that all the real estate left by me and of which she shall have had the possession as before mentioned shall become and be the property of our Children or of such of them as shall be then living and in that event I also will and direct that if our said Children shall then be underage two trusty Guardians shall be given to them who shall administer the said Real Estate for the benefit of our said Children, until they shall have attained their full age and that their shares of my estate shall be given to each of them as soon as they shall respectively become of age. and for the execution of the present will I appoint Messieurs John M. J. Labatut and Joseph Lopes Dias both residing in this City and Therese Baptist my wife If one of them should die, the two survivors shall jointly appoint another. recommending to them in the most particular manner to do everything in their power to execute and cause to be executed all the clauses and conditions of this testament such is my will. Done at New York the thirteenth of October in the year of our Lord one thousand and eight hundred and nineteen. Signed Sealed and published by the testator as his last Will and Testament in the presence of us who at his request have subscribed our names in his presence and in that of each other. New York the day month and year above written. Honoré Lannuier

Witnesses Gruez Wm H. Walsh. Thos A. Powell. City and County of New York S.S. Andrew S. Garr of said City Esquire being duly sworn saith that the preceding is a true and correct translation of the original thereof purporting to be the will of Charles Honoré Lannuier deceased from the french into the English Language. Andrew S. Garr----Sworn the 22nd day of October 1819. Silvanus Miller. Surrogate. City and County of New York S.S.; Be it remembered that on the twenty second day of October in the year of our Lord one thousand eight hundred and nineteen personally came and appeared before Silvanus Miller Surrogate of said County John Gruez and Thomas A. Powell both of the City of New York Cabinet Makers [illegible] being duly sworn on their oaths declared that they saw Charles H Lannuier sign and seal an Instrument in writing purporting to be the will of the said Charles H. Lannuier bearing date the thirteenth day of October in the year last aforesaid (the preceding whereof is a true copy) and heard him publish and declare the same as and for his last Will and Testament that at the time thereof he the said Charles H. Lannuier was of sound disposing mind and memory to the best of the Knowledge and belief of these deponents, that their names subscribed as witnesses to the said Will are of their own proper hand writing respectively which they subscribed as witnesses thereto in the presence of the Testator and that they saw William H. Walsh the other witness to the said Will subscribe his name as a witness thereto in the presence of the Testator. Silvanus Miller. The People of the State of New York by the grace of God, free and Independent [illegible] to whom these presents shall come or may concern Send Greeting Know Ye that as the City and County of New York on the day of the date hereof before Silvanus Miller Esquire Surrogate of our said County the last Will and Testament of Charles H. Lannuier deceased (A copy whereof in the french language and also a translation is hereunto annexed) was proved and is now approved and allowed by us and the said deceased Lannuier whilst he lived and at the time of his death Goods Chattels or Credits with this State by means where of the proving and registering of the said Will and the granting Administration of all and singular the said Goods Chattels and Credits and also the auditing all owing and final discharging the account thereof doth belong unto us the administration of all and singular the Goods Chattels and Credits of the said deceased and any way concerning his will is granted unto Therese B. Lannuier the Executrix John M. J. Labatout. and Joseph Lopes Diaz the Executors in the said Will named they being first duly sworn well and faithfully administer the same and to make and exhibit a true and perfect Inventory of all and singular the said Goods Chattels and Credits and also to render a just and true account thereof when thereunto required. In Testimony where of we have caused the seal of office of our said Surrogate to be hereunto affixed. Witness Silvanus Miller Esquire Surrogate of the said County at the City of New York the twenty second day of October in the year of our [Lord one] thousand eight hundred and nineteen and of our Independence the forty fourth. Silvanus Miller

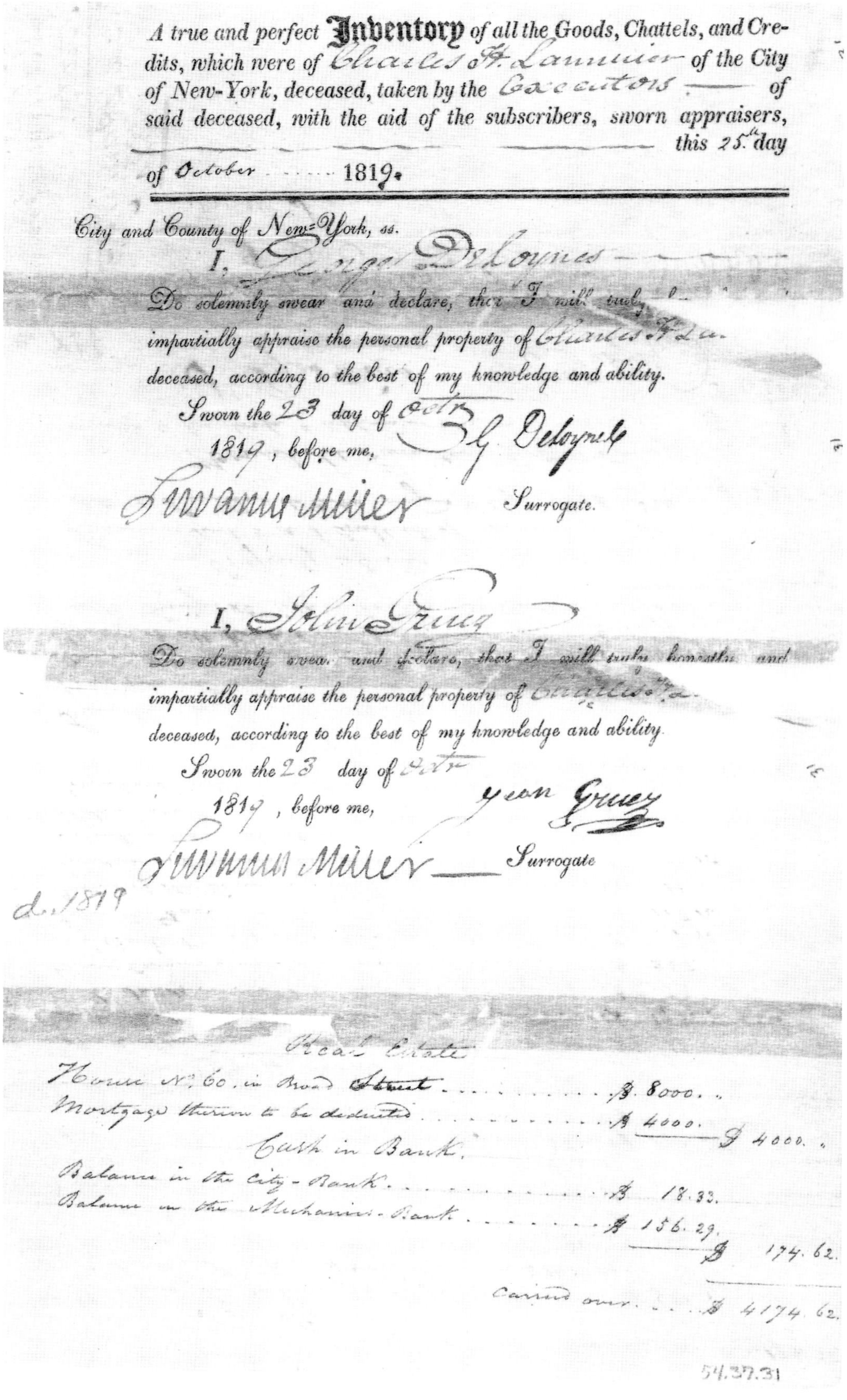

A true and perfect **Inventory** of all the Goods, Chattels, and Credits, which were of *Charles H. Lannuier* of the City of New-York, deceased, taken by the *Executors* ——— of said deceased, with the aid of the subscribers, sworn appraisers, ——— this 25. day of October ...... 1819.

City and County of New-York, ss.

I, *George Deloynes*

Do solemnly swear and declare, that I will truly & impartially appraise the personal property of *Charles H. La.* deceased, according to the best of my knowledge and ability.

Sworn the 23 day of *Octr* 1819, before me,   *G. Deloynes*

Suwann Miller   Surrogate.

I, *John Gruez*

Do solemnly swear and declare, that I will truly honestly and impartially appraise the personal property of *Charles H. La.* deceased, according to the best of my knowledge and ability.

Sworn the 23 day of *Octr* 1819, before me,   *Jean Gruez*

Suwann Miller   Surrogate

d. 1819

Real Estate

House N°. 60. in Broad Street	$ 8000..	
Mortgage thereon to be deducted	$ 4000.	$ 4000..
Cash in Bank.		
Balance in the City - Bank	$ 18.33.	
Balance in the Mechanics-Bank	$ 156.29.	
		$ 174.62.
carried over		$ 4174.62.

54.27.31

Notes & Drafts due him

E. Malibran's Two notes. of $ 475. 50/100. each	$ 951. .	
D. A. Smith's Three notes of $ 470. 53/100. each $ 1411. 59.		
D. A. Smith's Draft on W.m Goodwin	91.	$ 1502. 59
James Reid's note for Balance	$ 18. .	
Brunhard's note for dit.o	$ 7. .	
Alfred S. Pell's note for	$ 425. .	
Idem for	366. 43	$ 791. 43.
Gautier's note	$ 50.	$ 3320. 02

Sums due him by

John E. Glover	$ 66. .	
H. H. B.	$ 175. .	
A. E. Sands	$ 78 .	
Henry Cary	$ 225. .	
Van Boskirk	$ 7. 93.	
John B. Dash	$ 118. 12.	
Justice of the Peace	$ 18. .	
Sundries as p Memorandum found in his Papers	$ 269. 15.	
Mark Mills, about	$ 80. .	
Welsh, about	$ 100. .	
Brunhard's rights in France on an annuity, about	$ 300. .	$ 1437. 20.

Stock in Furniture &c.o

Furniture in Store	$ 2739. .	
Hardware in dit.o	$ 105 .	
Ornaments in dit.o	$ 293. 59.	
Woods of all Kinds & Benches	$ 1096. .	
Silks, Fringes &c.o left on hand by D. A. Smith	$ 900. .	$ 5134. 49.

Property abroad.

Furniture sent to A. S. Bulloch of Savanah	$ 2401. 25.	
dit.o to Trinidad de Cuba, consigned to Capt.n Roy	$ 534. .	$ 2935. 25.

Household Furniture & other Things

divided to his wife & appraised at	$ 748. .	
		$ 17,749. 58

J.t Lopes Diaz   G. Delognet

1819

J. B. J. Thibault

Fairasse Lonnuier

Selected Bibliography

Ackermann, 1816
Ackermann, Rudolph. *The Repository of Arts, Literature, Commerce, Manufactures, Fashions, and Politics.* 2 vols. London, 1816.

Additional Prices, 1815
Additional Prices Agreed Upon by the New-York Society of Journeyman Cabinet Makers. New York, 1815.

Additional Revised Prices, n.d.
Additional Revised Prices. [New York], n.d.

Agius, 1984
Agius, Pauline. *Ackermann's Regency Furniture & Interiors.* Wiltshire, England, 1984.

Albion, 1970
Albion, Robert Greenhalgh. *The Rise of New York Port, 1815–1860.* New York, 1970.

Alexander, 1989
Alexander, Forsyth M. "Cabinet Warehousing in the Southern Atlantic Ports, 1783–1820." *Journal of Early Southern Decorative Arts* 15, no. 2 (November 1989), pp. 1–42.

"Almanac," 1946
"The Almanac: Accessions to the American Wing." *Antiques* 49, no. 5 (May 1946), pp. 312–14.

"American History," 1946
"American History and American Crafts." *Antiques* 50, no. 4 (October 1946), pp. 245–59.

"Ameublement–Möbelverzierung durch Leistenwerk," 1803
"Ameublement–Möbelverzierung durch Leistenwerk." *Zeitung für die elegante Welt.* June 7, 1803.

"Art Institute of Chicago," 1995
"The Art Institute of Chicago, Newly Installed Galleries & Recent Acquisitions." *American Art Review* 7, no. 2 (April–May 1995), pp. 86–89.

Augarde, 1985
Augarde, Dominique. "Historique et signification de l'estampille des meubles." *L'Estampille,* no. 182 (1985), pp. 52–57.

Barron, 1814
Barron, James. *Modern & Elegant Designs of Cabinet & Upholstery Furniture.* London, 1814.

Bartlett and Huber, 1979
Bartlett, Jean Smith, and Mary Means Huber. "History in Houses: The Bartow-Pell Mansion in New York City." *Antiques* 115, no. 5 (May 1979), pp. 1032–41.

de Beaujour, 1814
de Beaujour, Félix. *Sketch of the United States of North America, at the Commencement of the Nineteenth Century, from 1800 to 1810.* Translated by William Walton. London, 1814.

de Bellaigue, 1974
de Bellaigue, Geoffrey. *Furniture, Clocks and Gilt Bronzes: The James A. de Rothschild Collection at Waddesdon Manor.* 2 vols. London and Fribourg, 1974.

Betts, 1983
Betts, Mary Beth. "The Governor's Room, City Hall, New York." Typescript. Art Commission of the City of New York, 1983.

Betts, 1992
[Betts, Mary Beth]. *Building City Hall: Competition, Construction, and Context* (exhib. brochure), The New-York Historical Society. New York, 1992.

"Bicentennial Treasury," 1975–76
"A Bicentennial Treasury: American Masterpieces from the Metropolitan." *The Metropolitan Museum of Art Bulletin* 33, no. 4 (Winter 1975– 1976). New York, 1976, pp. 168–244.

Bishop, 1972
Bishop, Robert. *Centuries and Styles of the American Chair 1640–1970.* New York, 1972.

Bjerkoe, 1957
Bjerkoe, Ethel Hall. *The Cabinetmakers of America.* Garden City, N.Y., 1957.

Blackburn, 1981
Blackburn, Roderic H. "Branded and Stamped New York Furniture." *Antiques* 119, no. 5 (May 1981), pp. 1130–45.

Bleecker, 1847
Bleecker, Anthony J. *Catalogue of Rare, Original Paintings . . . Valuable Engravings, Elegant Sculpture, Household Furniture . . . Belonging to the Estate of the Late Joseph Napoleon Bonaparte . . . to be sold . . . on Friday, June 25, 1847.* New York, 1847.

Blunt, 1817
[Blunt, Edmund March]. *Blunt's Stranger's Guide to the City of New-York.* New York, 1817.

Bordes, 1975
Bordes, Marilyn Johnson. "Charles-Honoré Lannuier: *Card table.*" *The Metropolitan Museum of Art: Notable Acquisitions 1965–1975.* New York, 1975, p. 27.

Brayer, 1805
[Brayer de Beauregard, Jean-Baptiste-Louis]. *Panorama de Paris et de ses environs.* 2 vols. Paris, 1805.

Brown, 1978
Brown, Michael Kevin. "Duncan Phyfe." Master's thesis, University of Delaware, 1978.

Bucher and Wheeler, 1993
Bucher, Douglas G., and W[alter]. Richard Wheeler. *A Neat Plain Modern Stile: Philip Hooker and His Contemporaries, 1796–1836* (exhib. cat.), Clinton, N.Y., Emerson Gallery, Hamilton College. Amherst, Mass., 1993.

Butler, 1965
Butler, Joseph T. "America 1815–1918." In *World Furniture,* edited by Helena Hayward, pp. 247–56. New York, 1965.

Cabourdin, 1980
Cabourdin, Guy. *Quand Stanislas régnait en Lorraine.* Paris, 1980.

Clarke, 1941
Clarke, T. Wood. *Émigrés in the Wilderness.* New York, 1941.

Comstock, 1954
Comstock, Helen. "Living with Antiques: The Summer Residence of George A. Cluett, Williamstown, Massachusetts." *Antiques* 66, no. 5 (November 1954), pp. 382–86.

Comstock, 1962
Comstock, Helen. *American Furniture: Seventeenth, Eighteenth, and Nineteenth Century Styles.* New York, 1962.

Conger, 1976
Conger, Clement E. "The White House." *The Connoisseur* 192, no. 771 (May 1976), pp. 3–10.

Conger, 1979
Conger, Clement E. "Decorative Arts at the White House." *Antiques* 116, no. 1 (July 1979), pp. 112–34.

Conger and Monkman, 1976
Conger, Clement E., and Betty C. Monkman. "President Monroe's Acquisitions." *The Connoisseur* 192, no. 771 (May 1976), pp. 56–63.

Conger and Rollins, 1991
Conger, Clement E., and Alexandra W. Rollins. *Treasures of State: Fine and Decorative Arts in the Diplomatic Reception Rooms of the U.S. Department of State.* New York, 1991.

Considine, 1991
Considine, Brian B. "The Gilders Art in Eighteenth-Century France." In *Gilded Wood, Conservation and History*, edited by Deborah Bigelow, pp. 87–98. Madison, Conn., 1991.

Cooper, 1980 a
Cooper, Wendy A. *In Praise of America: American Decorative Arts, 1650–1830, Fifty Years of Discovery Since the 1929 Girl Scouts Loan Exhibition* (exhib. cat.), National Gallery of Art, Washington, D.C. New York, 1980.

Cooper, 1980 b
Cooper, Wendy A. "In Praise of America, 1650–1830: An Exhibition at the National Gallery of Art." *Antiques* 117, no. 3 (March 1980), pp. 602–13.

Cooper, 1993
Cooper, Wendy A. *Classical Taste in America, 1800–1840* (exhib. cat.), The Baltimore Museum of Art. New York, 1993.

Cornelius, 1922
Cornelius, Charles Over. *Furniture Masterpieces of Duncan Phyfe* (exhib. cat.), The Metropolitan Museum of Art. Garden City, N.Y., 1922.

Cornu, 1914
Cornu, Paul. *Meubles et objets de goût, 1796–1830: 678 documents tirés des Journaux de Modes et de la "Collection" de La Mésangère.* Paris [1914].

Cortesi and Harrell, 1982
Cortesi, Wendy, and Mary Ann Harrell. *The White House: An Historic Guide.* Washington, D.C., 1982.

Craigmyle, 1970
Craigmyle, Mary Martin. "Chairs by Lannuier at New York's City Hall." *Antiques* 97, no. 2 (February 1970), pp. 258–59.

Craven, 1968
Craven, Wayne. *Sculpture in America.* New York, 1968.

Davidson, 1968
Davidson, Marshall B. *Three Centuries of American Antiques.* Vol. 2: *The American Heritage History of American Antiques from the Revolution to the Civil War.* New York, 1968.

Davidson, 1980
Davidson, Marshall B. *The American Wing, A Guide.* New York, 1980.

Davidson and Stillinger, 1985
Davidson, Marshall B., and Elizabeth Stillinger.

The American Wing at The Metropolitan Museum of Art. New York, 1985.

Debonliez and Malepeyre, 1837
Debonliez, G., and F. Malepeyre. *Nouveau manuel complet du bronzage des métaux et du plâtre . . . suivi de la peinture et du vernissage des métaux et du bois . . . d'après M. le Dr E. Winckler et autres patriciens.* Paris, 1837.

Deschamps, 1994
Deschamps, Madeleine. *Empire.* New York, 1994.

de Diesbach, 1984
de Diesbach, Ghislain. *Histoire de l'émigration, 1789–1814.* Rev. ed. Paris, 1984.

Downs, 1943 a
Downs, Joseph. "The Greek Revival in the United States." *Antiques* 44, no. 5 (November 1943), pp. 218–20.

Downs, 1943 b
Downs, Joseph. *The Greek Revival in the United States: A Special Loan Exhibition* (exhib. cat.), The Metropolitan Museum of Art. New York, 1943.

Downs, 1946
Downs, Joseph. "On Collecting American Furniture." *American Collector* 15, no. 3 (April 1946), pp. 12–14, 22.

Downs, 1949
Downs, Joseph. "History in Houses: Bartow Mansion." *Antiques* 55, no. 4 (April 1949), pp. 274–77.

Downs and Ralston, 1934
Downs, Joseph, and Ruth Ralston. *A Loan Exhibition of New York State Furniture with Contemporary Accessories* (exhib. cat.), The Metropolitan Museum of Art. New York, 1934.

Duncan, 1823
Duncan, John M. *Travels Through Part of the United States and Canada in 1818 and 1819.* 2 vols. New York, 1823.

Dunlap, 1834
Dunlap, William. *History of the Rise and Progress of the Arts of Design in the United States.* 2 vols. New York, 1834.

Dwight, 1969
Dwight, Timothy. *Travels in New England and New York.* 4 vols. New Haven, Conn., 1821. Reprint, edited by Barbara Miller Solomon. Cambridge, Mass., 1969.

"Editor's Attic," 1936
"The Editor's Attic: Two New York Tables." *Antiques* 29, no. 5 (May 1936), p. 191.

Ehninger, 1993
Ehninger, Jillian. " 'With the Richest Ornaments Just Imported from France': Ornamental Hardware on Boston, New York, and Philadelphia Furniture, 1800–1840." Master's thesis, University of Delaware, 1993.

Exposition des produits, 1806
Exposition des produits de l'industrie française. Rapport du jury sur les produits de l'industrie française présenté à S.E.M. de Champagny, Ministre de l'Intérieur, précédé du procès-verbal des opérations de jury. Paris, 1806.

Fearon, 1818
Fearon, Henry Bradshaw. *Sketches of America: A Narrative of a Journey of Five Thousand Miles Through the Eastern and Western States of America. . . .* 2nd ed. London, 1818.

Feld and Garrett, 1991
Feld, Stuart P., and Wendell Garrett. *Neo-Classicism in America: Inspiration and Innovation, 1810–1840* (exhib. cat.), Hirschl & Adler Galleries, Inc. New York, 1991.

Fennimore, 1981
Fennimore, Donald L. "American Neoclassical Furniture and Its European Antecedents." *The American Art Journal* 8, no. 4 (Autumn 1981), pp. 49–65.

Fennimore, 1990
Fennimore, Donald L. "Egyptian Influence in Early Nineteenth-Century American Furniture." *Antiques* 137, no. 5 (May 1990), pp. 1190–1201.

Fennimore, 1996
Fennimore, Donald L. *Metalwork in Early America: Copper and Its Alloys from the Winterthur Collection.* Winterthur, Del., 1996.

Fitzgerald, 1982
Fitzgerald, Oscar P. *Three Centuries of American Furniture.* Englewood Cliffs, N.J., 1982.

Flores, 1990
Flores, Jan. "Archibald Stobo Bulloch." Unpublished ms., Armstrong State College, Savannah, 1990.

Fore, 1991
Fore, George T., & Associates. *The Owens-Thomas House, Savannah, Georgia, Conservation Studies, Finishes Analysis.* Raleigh, N.C., 1991.

de Forest, 1909
de Forest, Emily Johnston. *John Johnston of New York, Merchant.* New York, 1909.

Fowble, 1974
Fowble, E. McSherry. "Without a Blush: The Movement toward Acceptance of the Nude as an Art Form in America, 1800–1825." *Winterthur Portfolio* 9 (1974), pp. 103–21.

Gaines, 1959
Gaines, Edith. "Collectors' Notes: Lannuier Pieces in Hiding." *Antiques* 76, no. 2 (August 1959), p. 145.

Gaines, 1964 a
Gaines, Edith, ed. "Collectors' Notes: Meeks Footnote." *Antiques* 85, no. 5 (May 1964), p. 579.

Gaines, 1964 b
Gaines, Edith, ed. "Collectors' Notes: The Case of the Plaster Bust." *Antiques* 85, no. 4 (April 1964), p. 442.

Gaines, 1965
Gaines, Edith, ed. "Collectors' Notes: Double Take." *Antiques* 88, no. 1 (July 1965), p. 100.

Girl Scouts Loan Exhibition, 1929
[National Council of Girl Scouts]. *Loan Exhibition of Eighteenth and Early Nineteenth Century Furniture & Glass . . . for the Benefit of the National Council of Girl Scouts, Inc.* (exhib. cat.), American Art Galleries. New York, 1929.

Goodison, 1974
Goodison, Nicholas. *Ormolu: The Work of Matthew Boulton*. London, 1974.

Goodison, 1975
Goodison, Nicholas. "The Victoria and Albert Museum's Collection of Metal-work Pattern Books." *Furniture History* 11 (1975), pp. 1–30.

Gottesman, 1965
Gottesman, Rita Susswein. *The Arts and Crafts in New York, 1800–1804: Advertisements and News Items from New York City Newspapers*. New York, 1965.

Gross, 1967
Gross, Katharine Wood. "The Sources of Furniture Sold in Savannah, 1789–1815." Master's thesis, University of Delaware, 1967.

Guide to the Metropolitan, 1972
Guide to The Metropolitan Museum of Art. New York, 1972.

Gustafson, 1995
Gustafson, Eleanor H. "Museum Accessions." *Antiques* 147, no. 5 (May 1995), pp. 656–60.

Hadsund, 1993
Hadsund, Per. "The Tin-Mercury Mirror: Its Manufacturing Technique and Deterioration Process." *Studies in Conservation* 38, no. 1 (February 1993), pp. 3–16.

Harvey, 1994
Harvey, Lynn. "William Jay: A Conjectural Reconstruction of the Archibald Stobo Bulloch House, Savannah, Georgia." Typescript. Chicago, 1994.

Haswell, 1897
Haswell, Charles H. *Reminiscences of an Octogenarian of the City of New York (1816 to 1860)*. New York, 1897.

Hawkins, 1992
Hawkins, Glenn. *The LeRay Family in the North Country* (U.S. Army, Fort Drum, New York, Pamphlet, No. 200–2). New York, 1992.

Hewitt, Kane, and Ward, 1982
Hewitt, Benjamin A., Patricia E. Kane, and Gerald W. R. Ward. *The Work of Many Hands: Card Tables in Federal America 1790–1820* (exhib. cat.), Yale University Art Gallery. New Haven, Conn., 1982.

Highlights from the Collection, 1994
Highlights from the Collection: Selected Paintings, Sculpture, Photographs & Decorative Art, High Museum of Art, Atlanta. Atlanta, 1994.

High [Museum] Newsletter, 1994
"Card Table and Grecian Couch Grace Classical Gallery." *High Friends of the Decorative Arts Newsletter* 16, no. 1 (Fall 1994), pp. 5–6.

Hinckley, 1953
Hinckley, F. Lewis. *A Directory of Antique Furniture*. New York, 1953.

Hope, 1971
Hope, Thomas. *Household Furniture and Interior Decoration, Classic Style Book of the Regency Period, Thomas Hope*. 1807. Reprint, introduction by David Watkin. New York, 1971.

Hornor, 1930
Hornor, Jr., W. M. "A New Estimation of Duncan Phyfe." *The Antiquarian* 14, no. 3 (March 1930), pp. 36–40, 96.

Hungerford, 1928
Hungerford, Edward. "An Old French House Built by James and Vincent LeRay at Cape Vincent, New York." *House Beautiful* 64, no. 1 (July 1928), pp. 38–39, 79–81.

Hunt, 1971
Hunt, Katharine Conover. "The White House Furnishings of the Madison Administration 1809–1817." Master's thesis, University of Delaware, 1971.

Huntington Art Collections, 1986
The Huntington Art Collections: A Handbook. San Marino, Calif., 1986.

Johnson, 1968
Johnson, Marilynn A. "John Hewitt, Cabinetmaker." *Winterthur Portfolio* 4 (1968), pp. 185–205.

E. Jones, 1977
Jones, Edward V. "Charles-Honoré Lannuier and Duncan Phyfe, Two Creative Geniuses of Federal New York." *The American Art Journal* 9, no. 1 (May 1977), pp. 4–14.

K. Jones, 1978
Jones, Karen M. "Collectors' Notes: Albert Gallatin's Pier Table?" *Antiques* 113, no. 5 (May 1978), pp. 1140, 1148.

Jones, Newman, and Ewbank, 1848
Jones, Newman, and J. S. Ewbank. *The Illuminated Pictorial Directory of New York*. No. 1. New York, 1848.

Journal des dames, 1805
Journal des dames et des modes. Paris, 1805.

Joy, 1977
Joy, Edward T. *English Furniture, 1800–1851*. London, 1977.

Kaye, 1987
Kaye, Myrna. *Fake, Fraud, or Genuine?: Identifying Authentic American Antique Furniture*. Boston, 1987.

Kennedy, 1985
Kennedy, Roger G. *Architecture, Men, Women and Money in America 1600–1860*. New York, 1985.

Kennedy, 1989
Kennedy, Roger G. *Orders from France: The Americans and the French in a Revolutionary World, 1780–1820*. New York, 1989.

Kenny, 1997
Kenny, Peter M. "One of a Pair of Card Tables." *Recent Acquisitions: A Selection, 1996–1997, The Metropolitan Museum of Art Bulletin* 55, no. 2 (Fall 1997), p. 62.

Keyes, 1938
Keyes, Homer Eaton. "The Stylistic Aspects of Furniture Credited to Federal Hall, An Editorial Postscript." *Antiques* 33, no. 5 (May 1938), pp. 253–56.

Kjellberg, 1989
Kjellberg, Pierre. *Le Mobilier français du XVIIIe siècle: Dictionnaire des ébénistes et des menuisiers*. Paris, 1989.

Klin[c]kowström, 1952
Klin[c]kowström, Axel Leonhard. *Baron Klinkowström's America, 1818–1820*. 1824. Translated and edited by Franklin D. Scott. Evanston, Ill., 1952.

Lambert, 1813
Lambert, John. *Travels through Canada and the United States of North America in the Years 1806, 1807, & 1808*. 2nd ed. 2 vols. London, 1813.

de La Mésangère, 1802–35
de La Mésangère, Pierre. *Collection de Meubles et Objets de Goût*. Paris, 1802–35.

Leben, 1992
Leben, Ulrich. *Molitor, ébéniste from the Ancien Régime to the Bourbon Restoration*. Translated by William Wheeler. London, 1992.

Ledoux-Lebard, 1951
Ledoux-Lebard, Denise. *Les Ébénistes Parisiens (1795–1830): Leur Oeuvres et leur marques*. Paris, 1951.

Ledoux-Lebard, 1984
Ledoux-Lebard, Denise. *Les Ébénistes du XIXe siècle (1795–1889): Leurs Oeuvres et leurs marques*. Paris, 1984.

Lerski, 1983
Lerski, Hanna Hryniewiecka. *William Jay, Itinerant English Architect 1792–1837*. Lanham, Md., 1983.

B. Levy, 1977
Levy, Bernard, and S. Dean Levy. *Distinguished American and English Antiques, Fine Paintings* (gallery cat.). New York, 1977.

B. Levy, 1984
Bernard and S. Dean Levy Inc. (gallery cat. 4). New York, 1984.

B. Levy, 1996
Levy, Bernard, S. Dean Levy, and Frank M. Levy. *In Search of Excellence* (gallery cat. 8). New York [1996].

M. Levy, 1989
Levy, Martin. "George Bullock's Partnership with Charles Fraser, 1813–1818, and the Stock-in-Trade Sale, 1819." *Furniture History* 25 (1989), pp. 145–213.

The London Cabinet-Makers' Union Book of Prices, 1811
The London Cabinet-Makers' Union Book of Prices. London, 1811.

Longworth's *Directory*
Longworth, David. *Longworth's American Almanack, New-York Register, and City Directory*. New York, 1796–1842.

Low, 1976
Low, Betty-Bright P. "The Youth of 1812: More Excerpts from the Letters of Josephine du Pont and Margaret Manigault." *Winterthur Portfolio* 11 (1976), pp. 173–212.

Marshall, 1915
Marshall, James Collier. "Duncan Phyfe, American Cabinet Maker." *Country Life in America* 27 (April 1915), pp. 48–50.

McClelland, 1939
McClelland, Nancy. *Duncan Phyfe and the English Regency 1795–1830*. New York, 1939.

McInnis and Leath, 1996
McInnis, Maurie D., and Robert A. Leath. "Beautiful Specimens, Elegant Patterns: New York Furniture for the Charleston Market, 1810–1840." *American Furniture* (1996), pp. 137–74.

Milbert, 1968
Milbert, J[acques-Gérard]. *Picturesque Itinerary of the Hudson River and the Peripheral Parts of North America. 1828–29*. Translated and annotated by Constance D. Sherman. Ridgewood, N.J., 1968.

Miller, 1956
Miller, V. Isabelle. *Furniture by New York Cabinetmakers, 1650 to 1860* (exhib. cat.), Museum of the City of New York. New York, 1956.

Minutes of the Common Council, 1917
Minutes of the Common Council of the City of New York, 1784–1831. Vols. 6–9. New York, 1917.

Monkhouse, 1983
Monkhouse, Christopher P. "Department of Decorative Arts: French Mantelpiece, ca. 1817." *Rhode Island School of Design Museum Notes* 70, no. 2 (October 1983), p. 20.

Montgomery, 1966
Montgomery, Charles F. *American Furniture: The Federal Period in the Henry Francis du Pont Winterthur Museum*. New York, 1966.

Morley, 1993
Morley, John. *Regency Design 1790–1840: Gardens, Buildings, Interiors, Furniture*. London, 1993.

Mussey, forthcoming
Mussey, Jr., Robert D. "Verte Antique Decoration on American Furniture: History, Materials, Techniques, Technical Investigations." In *Painted Wood: History and Conservation. Proceedings of a Symposium, Williamsburg, Virginia, November 1994*. Edited by Valery Dorge and F. Carey Howlett. By permission of the publisher, The Getty Conservation Institute. Los Angeles, forthcoming.

The New-York Book of Prices, 1817
The New-York Book of Prices for Manufacturing Cabinet and Chair Work. New York, 1817.

The New-York Revised Prices, 1810
The New-York Revised Prices for Manufacturing Cabinet and Chair Work. New York, 1810.

Nicolay, 1956
Nicolay, Jean. *L'Art et la manière des maîtres ébénistes français au XVIIIe siècle*. Vol. 1. Paris, 1956.

Nicolay, 1976
Nicolay, Jean. *L'Art et la manière des maîtres ébénistes français au XVIIIe siècle*. Vol. 1. Paris, 1976.

d'Oberkirch, 1970
d'Oberkirch, Baronne. *Mémoires de la Baronne d'Oberkirch sur la cour de Louis XVI et la société française avant 1789* (Le Temps retrouvé, 21). Edited by Suzanne Burkard. Paris, 1970.

Ormsbee, 1933 a
Ormsbee, Thomas Hamilton. "A Franco-American Cabinetmaker, Charles Honoré Lannuier." *Antiques* 23, no. 5 (May 1933), pp. 166–67.

Ormsbee, 1933 b
Ormsbee, Thomas Hamilton. "The Furniture of Lannuier and His Successor." *Antiques* 23, no. 6 (June 1933), pp. 224–26.

Ormsbee, 1935
Ormsbee, Thomas Hamilton. "Phyfe's Able Competitors." *American Collector* 4, no. 1 (June 27, 1935), pp. 8–9, 13.

Otto, 1961
Otto, Celia Jackson. "French Furniture for American Patriots." *Antiques* 79, no. 4 (April 1961), pp. 370–73.

Otto, 1965
Otto, Celia Jackson. *American Furniture of the Nineteenth Century*. New York, 1965.

Pallot, 1995
Pallot, Bill G. B. "Les différents types de lits et les créations des ornemanistes." *Dossier de l'art* 22 (February–March 1995), pp. 16–19.

Pearce, 1960
Pearce, Lorraine Waxman. "The Work of Charles-Honoré Lannuier, French Cabinetmaker in New York." *Maryland Historical Magazine* 55, no. 1 (March 1960), pp. 14–29.

Pearce, 1962 a
Pearce, Lorraine Waxman. "American Empire Furniture in the White House." *Antiques* 81, no. 5 (May 1962), pp. 515–19.

Pearce, 1962 b
Pearce, Lorraine Waxman. "Lannuier in the President's House." *Antiques* 81, no. 1 (January 1962), pp. 94–96.

Pearce, 1962 c
Pearce, Lorraine Waxman. *The White House: An Historical Guide*. Washington, D.C., 1962.

Pearce, 1964
Pearce, Lorraine Waxman. "The Distinctive Character of the Work of Lannuier." *Antiques* 86, no. 6 (December 1964), pp. 712–17.

Peck, 1996
Peck, Amelia, et al. *Period Rooms in The Metropolitan Museum of Art*. New York, 1996.

Peirce, 1979
Peirce, Donald C. "New York Furniture at the Brooklyn Museum." *Antiques* 115, no. 5 (May 1979), pp. 994–1003.

Percier, 1812
Percier, C[harles]., and P[ierre]. F[rançois]. L[éonard]. Fontaine. *Recueil de décorations intérieures comprenant tout ce qui a rapport à l'ameublement, comme vases, . . .* Paris, 1812.

Pictorial Dictionary, 1989
Pictorial Dictionary of British 19th Century Furniture Design. Woodbridge, Suffolk, England, 1989.

Pilcher, 1985
Pilcher, Edith. *Castorland: French Refugees in the Western Adirondacks, 1793–1814*. Harrison, N.Y., 1985.

Powel, 1954
Powel, Lydia B. "The American Wing." *The Metropolitan Museum of Art Bulletin* 12, no. 7 (March 1954), pp. 194–216.

Pradère, 1989
Pradère, Alexandre. *French Furniture Makers: The Art of the Ébéniste from Louis XIV to the Revolution*. Translated by Perran Wood. London, 1989.

Ralston, 1945
Ralston, Ruth. "The Style Antique in Furniture: II. Its American Manifestations and their Prototypes." *Antiques* 48, no. 4 (October 1945), pp. 206–9, 220–23.

Ralston, 1950
Ralston, Ruth. "The 'Style Antique' in American Furniture." In *The Antiques Book*, edited by Alice Winchester, pp. 123–34. New York, 1950.

Reese, 1983
Reese, Richard Dana. "Phyfe and Lannuier: New York Cabinetmakers." In *Early American Furniture From Settlement to City: Aspects of Form, Style and Regional Design from 1620 to 1830*, edited by Mary Jean Madigan and Susan Colgan, pp. 132–39. New York, 1983.

Rice, 1962
Rice, Norman S. *New York Furniture Before 1840 in the Collection of the Albany Institute of History and Art*. Albany, N.Y., 1962.

Royall, 1826
Royall, Anne. *Sketches of History, Life, and Manners in the United States. By a Traveller*. New Haven, Conn., 1826.

Sack, 1981–
[Sack, Israel]. *American Antiques from Israel Sack Collection*. Washington, D.C. and Alexandria, Va., 1981– .

de Salverte, 1962
de Salverte, François. *Les Ébénistes du XVIIIe siècle: Leurs Oeuvres et leurs marques*. 5th ed., rev. Paris, 1962.

Samoyault and Samoyault-Verlet, 1992
Samoyault, Jean-Pierre, and Colombe Samoyault-Verlet. *Un Ameublement à la mode en 1802: Le Mobilier du Général Moreau* (exhib. cat.), Musée National du Château de Fontainebleau. Paris, 1992.

Sargentson, 1996
Sargentson, Carolyn. *Merchants and Luxury Markets: The Marchands Merciers of Eighteenth-Century Paris*. London, 1996.

Schaeper, 1995
Schaeper, Thomas J. *France and America in the Revolutionary Era: The Life of Jacques-Donatien Leray de Chaumont, 1725–1803*. Providence, R.I., and Oxford, England, 1995.

Scherer, 1984
Scherer, John L. *New York Furniture at the New York State Museum*. Alexandria, Va. [1984].

Schnapper and Sérullaz, 1989
Schnapper, Antoine, and Arlette Sérullaz. *Jacques-Louis David, 1748–1825* (exhib. cat.), Musée du Louvre. Paris, 1989.

Scott, 1988
Scott, Kenneth. *New York City Court Records, 1801–1804: Genealogical Data from the Court of General Sessions* (National Genealogical Society Special Publication, No. 57). Arlington, Va., 1988.

Shellman, 1982
Shellman, Feay. *The Octagon Room*. Savannah, 1982.

Sheraton, 1802
Sheraton, Thomas. *The Cabinet-Maker and Upholsterer's Drawing-Book*. 3rd ed., rev. London, 1802.

Sheraton, 1970
Sheraton, Thomas. *Thomas Sheraton's Cabinet Dictionary*. 1803. 2 vols. Reprint, edited by Wilford P. Cole and Charles F. Montgomery. New York, 1970.

Sikes, 1976
Sikes, Jane E. *The Furniture Makers of Cincinnati, 1790 to 1849*. Cincinnati, 1976.

Sloane, 1987
Sloane, Jeanne Vibert. "A Duncan Phyfe Bill and the Furniture It Documents." *Antiques* 131, no. 5 (May 1987), pp. 1106–13.

J. Smith and Hummel, 1978
Smith, James Morton, and Charles F. Hummel. "The Henry Francis du Pont Winterthur Museum." *Antiques* 113, no. 6 (June 1978), pp. 1268–1306.

R. Smith, 1957
Smith, Robert C. "Key Pieces of Federal Furniture." *Antiques* 72, no. 3 (September 1957), pp. 240–43.

R. Smith, 1965
Smith, Robert C. "America." In *World Furniture*, edited by Helena Hayward, pp. 182–200. New York, 1965.

Somerville, 1976
Somerville, Romaine S. "Furniture at the Maryland Historical Society." *Antiques* 109, no. 5 (May 1976), pp. 970–89.

"Special Events," 1954
"Special Events: The Federal Period in New York." *Antiques* 66, no. 5 (November 1954), p. 404.

Stanford, 1814
[Stanford, Thomas N.]. *A Concise Description of the City of New York*. New York, 1814.

Still, 1994
Still, Bayrd. *Mirror for Gotham: New York as Seen by Contemporaries from Dutch Days to the Present*. New York, 1994.

Stillman, 1956
Stillman, Samuel Damie. "Artistry and Skill in the Architecture of John McComb, Jr." Master's thesis, University of Delaware, 1956.

Stokes, 1915–28
Stokes, I. N. Phelps. *The Iconography of Manhattan Island, 1498–1909*. 6 vols. New York, 1915–28.

Talbott, 1995
Talbott, Page. *Classical Savannah: Fine & Decorative Arts 1800–1840* (exhib. cat.), Telfair Museum of Art. Savannah, 1995.

Tracy, 1963
Tracy, Berry B., and William H. Gerdts. *Classical America 1815–1845* (exhib. cat.), The Newark Museum. Newark, 1963.

Tracy, 1967
Tracy, Berry B. "For 'One of the Most Genteel Residences in the City.'" *The Metropolitan Museum of Art Bulletin* 25, no. 8 (April 1967), pp. 282–91.

Tracy, 1975
Tracy, Berry B. "Charles-Honoré Lannuier: Sideboard." *The Metropolitan Museum of Art: Notable Acquisitions 1965–1975*. New York, 1975, p. 27.

Tracy, 1976
Tracy, Berry B. "Federal Period Furniture." *The Connoisseur* 192, no. 771 (May 1976), pp. 11–15.

Tracy and Johnson, 1970
Tracy, Berry B., Marilynn Johnson, Marvin D. Schwartz, and Suzanne Boorsch. *19th-Century America: Furniture and Other Decorative Arts* (exhib. cat.), The Metropolitan Museum of Art. New York, 1970.

Verlet, 1991
Verlet, Pierre. *French Furniture of the Eighteenth Century*. Translated by Penelope Hunter-Stiebel. Charlottesville, Va., 1991.

Watson, 1976
Watson, Sir Francis. "Americans and French Eighteenth-Century Furniture in the Age of Jefferson." In *Jefferson and the Arts: An Extended View*, edited by William Howard Adams, pp. 274–93. Washington, D.C., 1976.

Waxman, 1957
Waxman, Lorraine. "The Lannuier Brothers, Cabinetmakers." *Antiques* 72, no. 2 (August 1957), pp. 141–43.

Waxman, 1958
Waxman, Lorraine. "French Influence on American Decorative Arts of the Early Nineteenth Century: The Work of Charles-Honoré Lannuier." Master's thesis, University of Delaware, 1958.

Weber, 1994
Weber, Bruce. *American Paintings VII, 1994* (gallery brochure), Berry-Hill Galleries, Inc. New York, 1994.

Weidman, 1984
Weidman, Gregory R. *Furniture in Maryland 1740–1940: The Collection of the Maryland Historical Society*. Baltimore, 1984.

Williamson, 1938
Williamson, Scott Graham. "Extant Furniture Ascribed to New York's Federal Hall." *Antiques* 33, no. 5 (May 1938), pp. 250–53.

Winchester, 1962
Winchester, Alice. "Antiques." *Antiques* 81, no. 1 (January 1962), pp. 84–85.

Wolfe, 1963
Wolfe, Richard J. "Early New York Naturalization Records in the Emmet Collection, with a List of Aliens Naturalized in New York 1802–1814." *Bulletin of The New York Public Library* 67, no. 4 (April 1963), pp. 211–17.

Woodside, 1986
Woodside, Joan. "French Influence on American Furniture as Seen through the Engraved Designs of Pierre de la Mésangère's *Collection des Meubles et Objets de Goût* Published from 1802 to 1835." 2 vols. Ph.D. diss., University of Chicago, 1986.

MANUSCRIPT COLLECTIONS

Albany Institute of History & Art.

American Trader. Rhode Island Historical Society, Providence.

Archives de Condé, Château de Chantilly.

Archives Départementales de l'Oise, Beauvais.

Archives Nationales de Paris.

Assessed Valuation of Real Estate. New York Municipal Archives.

Baltimore County Inventories. Liber 54, Folio 24. State Archives, Annapolis, Md.

William Bayard. Papers. Library, The New-York Historical Society.

Bayard-Campbell-Pearsall Papers. Manuscripts & Archives Section, Rare Books and Manuscripts Division, The New York Public Library.

Centre des Archives Diplomatiques de Nantes.

Constable-Pierrepont Papers. Manuscripts & Archives Section, Rare Books and Manuscripts Division, The New York Public Library.

John Hewitt. Account Book. New Jersey Historical Society, Newark.

Inward Coastwise Manifests, Port of Savannah. National Archives, Washington, D.C.

Jefferson County Historical Society, Watertown, N.Y.

Fenwick Lyell. Account Book. Monmouth County Historical Association, Freehold, N.J.

John McComb, Jr. Papers. Library, The New-York Historical Society.

Minutier Central des Notaires Parisiens. Archives Nationales de Paris.

Mrs. Julien Ravenel. Family papers. South Carolina Historical Society, Columbia.

Register of Deeds. City Register's Office, Surrogate's Court, New York.

Register of Mortgages. City Register's Office, Surrogate's Court, New York.

Berry B. Tracy. Archives. Department of American Decorative Arts, The Metropolitan Museum of Art, New York.

Robert Troup. Papers. Manuscripts & Archives Section, Rare Books and Manuscripts Division, The New York Public Library.

Stephen Van Rensselaer. Papers. Library, The New-York Historical Society.

Wills. Surrogate's Court, New York.

Index

Photograph Credits